W9-BOA-662

DISCARD

New Perspectives in German Political Studies

General Editors: **William Paterson OBE** is Honorary Professor in German and European Politics at the University of Aston and Chairman of the German British Forum.

Charlie Jeffery is Professor of Politics at the University of Edinburgh.

Germany remains a pivotal country in Europe. It is Europe's biggest economy, continues to play a central role in the European Union, and has a growing significance in international security politics based on its strategic location at the centre of Europe and its evolving role as a provider of security in Europe and beyond. All this is nuanced by the legacies of a turbulent recent history: the two World Wars, the Holocaust, Germany's division after World War Two and its unification in 1990.

New Perspectives in German Political Studies has been designed as a platform for debate and scholarship on contemporary Germany. It welcomes contributions from political science, international relations, political economy and contemporary history. It follows on from the success of the earlier series on New Perspectives in German Studies, co-edited by William Paterson and the late Professor Michael Butler.

Titles include:

Wilhelm Hennis
POLITICS AS A PRACTICAL SCIENCE

Alister Miskimmon, William E. Paterson and James Sloam (*editors*)
GERMANY'S GATHERING CRISIS
The 2005 Federal Election and the Grand Coalition

Y. Michal Bodemann (*editor*)
THE NEW GERMAN JEWRY AND THE EUROPEAN CONTEXT
The Return of the European Jewish Diaspora

Anne Fuchs
PHANTOMS OF WAR IN CONTEMPORARY GERMAN LITERATURE,
FILMS AND DISCOURSE
The Politics of Memory

Caroline Pearce
CONTEMPORARY GERMANY AND THE NAZI LEGACY
Remembrance, Politics and the Dialectic of Normality

Axel Goodbody
NATURE, TECHNOLOGY AND CULTURAL CHANGE IN TWENTIETH-CENTURY
GERMAN LITERATURE
The Challenge of Ecocriticism

Beverly Crawford
POWER AND GERMAN FOREIGN POLICY
Embedded Hegemony in Europe

Dan Hough, Michael Koß and Jonathan Olsen
THE LEFT PARTY IN CONTEMPORARY GERMAN POLITICS

Roger Woods
GERMANY'S NEW RIGHT AS CULTURE AND POLITICS

Christian Schweiger
BRITAIN, GERMANY AND THE FUTURE OF THE EUROPEAN UNION

Karl Christian Führer and Corey Ross (*editors*)
MASS MEDIA, CULTURE AND SOCIETY IN TWENTIETH-CENTURY GERMANY

Matthew M. C. Allen
THE VARIETIES OF CAPITALISM PARADIGM
Explaining Germany's Comparative Advantage?

Gunther Hellmann (*editor*)
GERMANY'S EU POLICY IN ASYLUM AND DEFENCE
De-Europeanization by Default?

Charles Lees
PARTY POLITICS IN GERMANY
A Comparative Politics Approach

Ronald Speirs and John Breuilly (*editors*)
GERMANY'S TWO UNIFICATIONS
Anticipations, Experiences, Responses

James Sloam
THE EUROPEAN POLICY OF THE GERMAN SOCIAL DEMOCRATS
Interpreting a Changing World

Margarete Kohlenbach
WALTER BENJAMIN
Self-Reference and Religiosity

Henning Tewes
GERMANY, CIVILIAN POWER AND THE NEW EUROPE
Enlarging NATO and the European Union

Wolf-Dieter Eberwein and Karl Kaiser (*editors*)
GERMANY'S NEW FOREIGN POLICY
Decision-Making in an Interdependent World

Gerard Braunthal
RIGHT-WING EXTREMISM IN CONTEMPORARY GERMANY

New Perspectives in German Political Studies
Series Standing Order ISBN 978–0–333–92430–3 hardcover
Series Standing Order ISBN 978–0–333–92434–1 paperback
(*outside North America only*)

You can receive future titles in this series as they are published by placing a standing order. Please contact your bookseller or, in case of difficulty, write to us at the address below with your name and address, the title of the series and one of the ISBNs quoted above.

Customer Services Department, Macmillan Distribution Ltd, Houndmills, Basingstoke, Hampshire RG21 6XS, England

Right-Wing Extremism in Contemporary Germany

Gerard Braunthal
Professor Emeritus of Political Science
University of Massachusetts Amherst, USA

palgrave
macmillan

© Gerard Braunthal 2009
Foreword © Peter H. Merkl 2009

All rights reserved. No reproduction, copy or transmission of this
publication may be made without written permission.

No portion of this publication may be reproduced, copied or transmitted
save with written permission or in accordance with the provisions of the
Copyright, Designs and Patents Act 1988, or under the terms of any licence
permitting limited copying issued by the Copyright Licensing Agency,
Saffron House, 6–10 Kirby Street, London EC1N 8TS.

Any person who does any unauthorized act in relation to this publication
may be liable to criminal prosecution and civil claims for damages.

The author has asserted his right to be identified as the author of this work
in accordance with the Copyright, Designs and Patents Act 1988.

First published 2009 by
PALGRAVE MACMILLAN

Palgrave Macmillan in the UK is an imprint of Macmillan Publishers Limited,
registered in England, company number 785998, of Houndmills, Basingstoke,
Hampshire RG21 6XS.

Palgrave Macmillan in the US is a division of St Martin's Press LLC,
175 Fifth Avenue, New York, NY 10010.

Palgrave Macmillan is the global academic imprint of the above companies
and has companies and representatives throughout the world.

Palgrave® and Macmillan® are registered trademarks in the United States,
the United Kingdom, Europe and other countries.

ISBN 978–0–230–23639–4   hardback

This book is printed on paper suitable for recycling and made from fully
managed and sustained forest sources. Logging, pulping and manufacturing
processes are expected to conform to the environmental regulations of the
country of origin.

A catalogue record for this book is available from the British Library.

A catalog record for this book is available from the Library of Congress.

10 9 8 7 6 5 4 3 2 1
18 17 16 15 14 13 12 11 10 09

Printed and bound in Great Britain by
CPI Antony Rowe, Chippenham and Eastbourne

Contents

Foreword   vii
Acknowledgements   xi
List of Acronyms   xii

Introduction   1

1 The Setting   4
Scholarly analyses   5
Further scholarly analyses   6
Racism and nationalism   8
Xenophobia   9
Anti-Semitism   13
Gender issues   14
Public support for right-wing extremism   16

2 The German Right-Extremist Scene, 1945–1990   19
The Federal Republic   21
The German Democratic Republic   34
Conclusion   41

3 Right-Extremist Parties   43
The Republikaner   43
German People's Union   51
National Democratic Party of Germany   57
Conclusion   75

4 Neo-Nazi Groups, Skinheads, and Violence   77
A splintered movement   77
Free Comradeship Groups   86
National liberated zones   89
Skinheads   91
Eastern Germany: prelude to violence   96
Violence in western Germany   103
Anti-Semitic acts   110
Government actions   114
Conclusion   114

5 Tools of Propaganda and Recruitment   117
Newspapers   117
Journals   118

Publishing houses   119
Cultural organizations   121
The visual media   122
The electronic network   124
Electronic games   128
Music as a propaganda tool   130
Fanzines and youth   135
Conclusion   136

6 **The New Right**   **137**
Birth of a movement   138
Ideological components   139
A plethora of authors and journals   142
The Heidelberg Manifesto and the Thule Seminar   149
Historians' dispute   151
Frankfurter Allgemeine Zeitung advertisements   152
New Right links to ultra-conservatives   153
Coming to terms with the past   159
The Martin Walser controversy   160
National pride and *Leitkultur*   163
An appraisal   167

7 **Responses: Public and Private**   **169**
The law and the courts   169
The police   173
The federal, Länder, and local governments   178
Grassroots actions   185
An array of local and regional projects   187
Schools and students   190
Youth and social workers   194
The exit strategy   196
Summation   199

Conclusion   **201**
Right-wing extremism   201
A challenge to democracy   203
Immigration: source for controversy   205
Weimar and the Berlin Republic compared   206
Links abroad   209
The present and future   211

Notes   214
Bibliography   239
Index   252

Foreword

This book presents a well-balanced analysis of the past, present, and future of the German radical right by one of the foremost scholars on the history of contemporary Germany. Gerard Braunthal's reputation rests particularly on his investigations of post-World War Two German Social Democracy (SPD) and civil rights in the Bonn and Berlin republics. His present work focuses directly and implicitly on the contrast between the contemporary German radical right and its predecessor under the ill-fated Weimar Republic (1918–1933), which gave birth to the Third Reich and the atrocities and power politics associated with it. The comparison takes into account the international environment and the domestic shape of the German extreme right.

The rise of German National Socialism and of kindred movements after the Great War took place under the shadow of the catastrophic German defeat by the Western Allies, of the painful losses of German territory and colonies, and of the traumatic collapse of two mighty empires and imperial dynasties, Hohenzollern and Hapsburg. Many German patriots felt humiliated by the Treaty of Versailles, which required the admission of German responsibility for the war and the surrender of the German emperor for trial (this was never carried out), of the imperial navy and air force, and the imposition of size limits on the armed forces. Many were haunted by paranoid fantasies of having been "stabbed in the back" by their own successor government – especially the centrist and left-wing politicians in it – who signed the Versailles Treaty of Peace. They thought of revenge, against both the Western victors and their alleged domestic collaborators some of whom were assassinated by military conspirators. There were unsuccessful right-wing coup attempts against the national government and against at least one state government – Bavaria – where a Workers and Soldiers Council had seized power in imitation of Bolshevik takeovers in St. Petersburg, Budapest, and Vienna. There was also an underground border war along some of the new frontiers, for example with Poland and, after the Franco-Belgian invasion of 1923, with the occupation of the Ruhr area. We must acknowledge all these factors in the minds of the rising Nazis in the midst of many extreme right-wing organizations at that time; however, nothing similar was in the minds of the defeated Germans after World War Two. The defeat of 1945 was actually far more devastating and, this time, the Germans really admitted total defeat. The Allies had insisted on "unconditional surrender" and imposed years of military occupation, denazification, and democratic reeducation on the Germans, which also involved the suppression of any Nazi revivals.

Another important aspect of the Weimar situation that enabled Adolf Hitler and his movement to rise to power in 1933 was that Germany in many ways had not matured enough to support a thriving democracy. Two telling images come to my mind, which show the particular weaknesses of Germany's first attempt at democracy: one is of a session of the Reichstag (Parliament) in 1932, which features a large section of its membership in Nazi storm-trooper uniforms. It was a sign of the Nazis' contempt for parliamentary democracy and heralded the coming of dictatorship with the help of a combined popular majority of Nazis and communists in imminent elections as well as the battles of the militant armies of both in the streets. The second image emerges from an interview with Fritz Schäffer, the conservative (CSU) finance minister who had been in the thick of Weimar politicking with the equally conservative Bavarian People's Party (BVP). Mr. Schäffer described to me the incredibly hectic and violent election campaigns at all levels, as he raced from one rally to the next, constantly threatened by extremist street violence from the right and the left. There was simply no room for a moderate politics of democratic discussion. At the same time, so many basic structures of German society were coming undone, as the German historian Karl D. Bracher and others have explained: relations between capital and labor, farming, capitalism, civil-military relations, the civil service, the greatly reduced army amidst militant veterans'organizations, the federal system; everything was in tenuous transition or outright crisis. Even the prewar political parties were splitting up, particularly on the moderate right and left where new radical mass movements such as the communists and Nazis experienced explosive growth and threatened to take over the unloved republic.

The democratic post-World War Two fathers (and mothers) of the West German Federal Republic were determined to base their democratic politics on strong, resilient institutions and a constitution, the Basic Law, that the major parties vowed to defend "militantly" against all extremists of the right and left (*streitbare Demokratie*), unlike their Weimar predecessors who had never defended Weimar's constitutional democracy. Never again, they resolved, should German democracy be left to the tender mercies of the sworn enemies of democracy. Among other steps, such as the electoral barriers to splinter parties described in this book and the special anti-extremist powers of the Federal Constitutional Court, the Bonn government created a *Verfassungsschutzdienst* (constitutional protection service) which played an important role investigating subversion and, in the 1970s, the terrorist conspiracies of the Red Army Faction (RAF). It publishes annual surveys of political extremism, including the radical right The surveillance and intrusion of this secret service into German civil liberties, for example by tapping telephones, has also attracted much criticism from German civil libertarians and representatives of the political left, as Braunthal has described in his book on the subject.

A major challenge to West German stability before 1990 was posed by the East German Stasi, the communist secret service of the self-styled German Democratic Republic (GDR) which, among other things, sent out and embedded spies in the highest West German offices, such as in the Foreign Office and in Chancellor Willy Brandt's staff. The Stasi also compiled voluminous secret files on many prominent West Germans for potential blackmail purposes, and to embarrass them before the Western public and abroad. German unification in 1990 posed new major challenges including that of integrating the public services of the communist east into the democratic state and society, especially the schools and universities. This process of systematic cleansing was not always fair and even-handed, and was often accompanied by dire warnings that the elimination of communist rule would inevitably lead to a revival of Nazism. The old state Communist Party, the SED, transformed itself into a strong extreme left successor, the PDS (now part of the Left Party), even as its remnants in the public services of the east were spotted and removed. The Stasi archives were now firmly in Western hands.

Because the rehabilitation and development of the formerly communist economy of the GDR by West German leaders fell far short of the "blossoming" promised by the unification chancellor, Helmut Kohl, the unification left behind a legacy of failures and resentments which have been reflected in East German voting: after initially following West German political patterns, East Germans soon began to distinguish themselves not only by voting for a large successor party to the communist SED (now PDS), but in recent elections also in great numbers for the neo-Nazi NPD and DVU; however, in all these elections no extreme right party has been able – except for a few stealth candidates in the 1950s – to elect a neo-Nazi to the Bundestag. East Germany remains a major trouble spot in the control of the extreme right in the Berlin Republic.

In the early decades of the Bonn Republic, perhaps as late as 1970, public opinion polls clearly revealed the spell of Nazi opinions over the public, for example on such nationalistic issues as acceptance of the Oder–Neisse line as the German–Polish border or German responsibility for World War Two, as the work of Anna and Richard Merritt, among others, has shown. After the end of Allied occupation, successive waves of neo-Nazi parties under names like the Socialist Reich Party (SRP) or the National Democrats (NPD) scored minor regional victories in spite of the hostility of democratic governments. Their activists and voters were mostly diminishing numbers of old Nazis and their families and offspring. As long as these parties were small and could be kept under control by local and state-level measures of harassment, the first West German chancellors, and especially Adenauer, avoided direct confrontation – for example by attempts to outlaw or suppress them. The democratic leaders were probably afraid to provoke these elements into forming a Fronde, a "national opposition" that would have obstructed democratization as had happened in the Weimar Republic. Or perhaps they too still held some partial

Nazi views that inclined them to tolerate old Nazis and Nazified groups and to spare them rigorous judgement – cases such as Hans Globke and others seem to suggest this. As new generations of democratic young Germans with strong anti-Nazi views grew to voting age and their political activities began to dominate German opinion, the neo-Nazi parties found that they could no longer expect a ready reception for their views. They began to shift towards issues like German unification and opposition to the progressive policies, foreign and domestic, of the Willy Brandt and Helmut Schmidt administrations.

In the meantime and especially since German unification, youthful new groups have emerged that in their own ways vie for the mantle of Hitler and his movement, often with little or no knowledge of the old ideology. Many of them are extremely violent skinheads operating in small groups and their lethal hostility is directed mostly at foreign migrants and refugee hostels, which they have attacked and set on fire. They are motivated as much by alcohol and the psychological stimuli of youth gang activity as by a general ideology of racism. There is a difference between a personal reaction against people of color and an elaborate ideology. To the extent that they rationalize their anti-foreigner hatred, it translates into a kind of "welfare chauvinism": a mistaken belief that these migrants and refugees receive public benefits above and beyond what the frequently unemployed and down-and-out right-wing skinheads get. In east German urban ghettos and small towns they also feud with young socialists who like to wear their hair in dreadlocks as a kind of uniform. In some east German locations, extreme right coordination is so dominant it creates a terror regime for leftists and people of color. Even the DVU and NPD are not sure how they can integrate the unruly skinheads into their political activities. But the youth gang-like street violence of today's Germany – not unlike the vicious urban warfare of the Bloods and Crips, two large African-American gangs in Los Angeles – is different to the political marching, proselytizing and fighting of the storm troopers of another day. By contrast, the young neo-Nazis of today make the old Nazis of the 1920s and 1930s look almost rational.

Peter H. Merkl, Professor Emeritus, Political Science
University of California, Santa Barbara

Acknowledgements

I am grateful to the many specialists whom I interviewed at length over a period of years. These included various German party officials, including three Republikaner in Bonn and Munich; academics who have studied the subject from different perspectives; members of anti-fascist organizations; and several government officials. The latter included the National Commissioner for Foreigners, two staff members of the Federal and Berlin Offices for the Protection of the Constitution, and a specialist in the Federal Office for Political Education. I am also indebted to Peter Munkelt, head of the SPD archive in Berlin; the Goethe-Institut Inter Nationes staff members; and the University of Massachusetts librarians who were most helpful in their support of this project. Carolyn Gillette provided invaluable research assistance in the preparation of the manuscript.

I thank Klaus Dammann, Manfred Holler, Roger Karapin, David Patton, Klaus-Henning Rosen, and Joel Wolfe for reading all or sections of the manuscript with great care. Their constructive comments were most helpful in shaping the final draft of this volume. I am also most appreciative of the invaluable support of Professors Willie Paterson and Charlie Jeffery, General Editors of the series *New Perspectives in German Studies*, in which this study appears. At Palgrave Macmillan, Alison Howson, Gemma d'Arcy Hughes and Liz Blackmore have provided invaluable editorial assistance. I also thank Jo North for her copyediting work on the book. As always, I would like to thank my wife, Sabina Braunthal, for her patience during the long gestation of this project, and my sons Peter and Stephen for technical computer support.

List of Acronyms

ANR	Aktion Neue Rechte (Action of the New Right)
ANS/NA	Aktionsfront Nationaler Sozialisten/Nationale Aktivisten (Action Front of National Socialists/National Activists)
BfV	Bundesamt für Verfassungsschutz (Federal Office for the Protection of the Constitution)
BHE	Bund der Heimatvertriebenen und Entrechteten (League of Expellees and Dispossessed)
BMI	Bundesministerium des Innern (Federal Ministry of the Interior)
CDU/CSU	Christlich-Demokratische Union/Christlich-Soziale Union (Christian Democratic Union/Christian Social Union)
DA	Deutsche Alternative (German Alternative)
DA/VR	Deutsche Allianz – Vereinigte Rechte (German Alliance – United Right)
DGB	Deutscher Gewerkschaftsbund (German Trade Union Federation)
DKP-DRP	Deutsche Konservative Partei-Deutsche Rechtspartei (German Conservative Party-German Right Party)
DL	Deutsche Liga für Volk und Heimat (League for a German People and Homeland)
DNVP	Deutsche National Volkspartei (German National People's Party)
DRP	Deutsche Reichspartei (German Reich Party)
DVP	Deutsche Volkspartei (German People's Party)
DVU	Deutsche Volksunion (German People's Union)
EU	European Union
FAP	Freiheitliche Deutsche Arbeiterpartei (Free German Workers Party)
FDP	Freie Demokratische Partei (Free Democratic Party)
FPÖ	Freiheitliche Partei Österreichs (The Freedom Party of Austria)
FRG	Federal Republic of Germany
GDR	German Democratic Republic
JN	Junge Nationaldemokraten (Young National Democrats)
MAD	Militärischen Abwehrdienst (Military Counter-Intelligence Corps)
NATO	North Atlantic Treaty Organization
NDPD	National-Demokratische Partei Deutschlands (National Democratic Party of Germany [GDR])

NF	Nationalistische Front (Nationalist Front)
NPD	Nationaldemokratische Partei Deutschlands (National Democratic Party of Germany)
NRAO	Nationalrevolutionäre Aufbauorganisation (National Revolutionary Building Organization)
NSDAP	Nationalsozialistische Deutsche Arbeiterpartei (National Socialist German Workers' Party)
NSDAP/AO	Nationalsozialistische Deutsche Arbeiterpartei/Auslands-Organisation (National Socialist German Workers' Party/Foreign Organization)
NZ	National-Zeitung/Deutsche-Wochenzeitung
PdA/DS	Partei der Arbeit/Deutsche Sozialisten (Party of Work/German Socialists)
PDS	Partei des Demokratischen Sozialismus (Party of Democratic Socialism)
SA	Sturmabteilung (Storm troopers)
SED	Sozialistische Einheitspartei Deutschlands (Socialist Unity Party of Germany)
SPD	Sozialdemokratische Partei Deutschlands (Social Democratic Party of Germany)
SRP	Sozialistische Reichspartei (Socialist Reich Party)
SS	Schutzstaffel (Elite guards)
Stasi	Ministerium für Staatssicherheit (Ministry for State Security)
WAV	Wirtschaftliche Aufbau-Vereinigung (Economic Reconstruction Association)

Introduction

This study focuses primarily on the activities of German right-wing extremist parties, groups, and individuals since the Berlin Wall's fall in 1989 and the unification of the two Germanys one year later. German scholars, journalists, and government officials have written much on the topic in German, but much less has been published in English. Thus this volume seeks to make a contribution to the literature on a subject matter that remains topical and, no pun intended, explosive. To understand German history since 1990, which has been marked by the end of the Cold War, increasing social inequalities and pockets of poverty, and the pressures of immigration and inter-ethnic tensions, a look back in history, especially to post-1945 divided Germany, is necessary. This post-1945 period was strongly influenced by the policy-makers rejecting the Nazi past but, as will be seen, not by the fledgling right-wing extremist movement, especially in West Germany, that accepted aspects of the Nazi past.

In classifying German rightist parties and groups on a political chart, one must note that they dare not accept the totalitarian features of the Nazi dictatorship. Yet their positions on domestic and foreign policies hardly resemble those that the democratic governments in Bonn and Berlin have espoused. In such a classificatory scheme, the German right-wing extremist movement represents a more virulent form of right populism, which is a political movement that appeals to the common man but that has hardly been successful in post-unification Germany.[1] This extremism has always been of concern for the country's policy-makers and to many of its citizens – and also to foreign observers. In light of the disastrous Third Reich era (1933–45), such individuals worry about a comparatively small but shrill right-extremist movement that has not fully rejected the Nazi past and that does not believe in a pluralist society, democracy, and individual human rights. Such a movement, whose policies are backed on occasion by centrist politicians, has increasingly shed its political inhibitions and has espoused a nationalist position, not unlike that of some of its European neighbors or even, to a lesser extent, Germany's democratic parties.

1

From 1949 on, four years after the Nazi state collapse, new right-extremist parties and groups operated openly to challenge the programs and policies of the newly formed mainstream parties of the Federal Republic of Germany (FRG). In the postwar German Democratic Republic (GDR) small rightist groups, alienated by a communist system that did not respond to their concerns, also formed. Since the two Germanys' unification in 1990 the small right-extremist parties have not fared well in most national and Länder (state) elections, and neo-Nazi groups and skinheads have increasingly taken the non-party political route. They intermittently assault, injure, and kill those individuals seen as "other," who are primarily the permanently settled foreigners and political asylum-seekers coming from the Third World or from the less developed Eastern European countries, but who may also be German leftists, the handicapped, the homeless, and the Gypsies. The anti-Semitic neo-Nazis and skinheads also desecrate synagogues and Jewish cemeteries.

Some observers fear that in the future the country's democratic political system, especially in eastern Germany, may face increasing rightist challenges or that governmental policy-makers may incorporate even more of the rightist planks, such as a tightening of immigration, into the democratic parties' political agenda. These observers also worry that a charismatic leader heading a right populist movement might arise some day to challenge the country's democratic system, with unknown consequences. This might happen if the major parties remain clustered in the middle of the political spectrum and provide, as the New Social Movement theorists call it, a "political opportunity space" to the right populists. The latter's incendiary populist messages may one day get a positive response from dissatisfied citizens who are already opting out as members of the democratic parties, and who feel that these parties are not offering meaningful policy alternatives to pressing economic and social problems, which have been exacerbated by the major worldwide recession engulfing most states in 2008 and 2009.[2] If Germany's economic situation fails to improve and tumbles into a serious depression, will right-extremist parties and groups reap dividends from a surge in protest and anger among those negatively affected? Could this mean that there will be a repetition of Weimar when the government could not cope with mass unemployment and major social dislocations, resulting in the rise of Nazism?

I address in this volume the question of the German democratic system's strengths and weaknesses, and its ability to appreciably reduce the potential sectarian threat from the right of the political spectrum. What strategies should the government, the public and private sectors, and citizens adopt to minimize the threat? If there is a congruence of views between mainstream and right-extremist Germans, how much support for rightist views exists among the centrist elite and the ordinary Germans? Do the rightist views originate in the middle of the political spectrum and spread to the right-extremist scene or vice-versa? Are there significant differences, especially in the number of violent acts, between western and eastern Germany?

Is German right extremism more dangerous to the survival of the German democratic state than rightist forces in other European democracies? Does the post-1990 violence in Germany parallel the Nazi violence leading up to the Weimar Republic's demise in 1933? Does the current violence represent a transitory phenomenon or is it a consequence of embedded structures in society? Are there parallels between the electoral support received by rightist parties in the Weimar era and in the Federal Republic, which could endanger the present democratic system in Germany? Or, on the contrary, is the Bonn Republic and its successor the Berlin Republic not comparable to Weimar, as the path-breaking book by Fritz René Allemann suggested in 1956?[3]

In order to answer these questions in terms of the post-1990 unified Federal Republic, which is the focus of this volume, Chapter 1 defines right extremism, assesses its causes, and examines the impact it has on German society and politics. Chapter 2 looks briefly at the pre-1945 historical antecedents of right-wing extremist parties and groups, and then examines their development in West and East Germany from 1945 to 1990. The chapters that follow deal more extensively with rightist developments in united Germany from 1990 to the present. Chapter 3 covers the numerous right-extremist parties that have not been able to coalesce. Some of them grew and declined in power, others have maintained longevity. Chapter 4 assesses the strength of neo-Nazi groups and xenophobic skinheads, chronicles the rightist public demonstrations, and examines the periodic violence against foreigners, leftists, the homeless, and other groups. Chapter 5 surveys the tactics of rightist parties and groups in recruiting more members and followers. The parties and groups have developed their own media, a publishing industry, and internet websites. They have also staged rock concerts. Chapter 6 considers the controversial writings of New Right academics and journalists who, especially in the 1990s, have put new accents on the legacy of Germany's past but who distance themselves from right extremism. Chapter 7 assesses the responses to the rightist threat by the courts, the police, the government, democratic political parties, trade unions, churches, and the public. The concluding chapter provides an overview and assessment of the German right-extremist scene in the past, present, and, speculatively, the future. It will seek to answer the question of whether Germany can maintain its democratic system in the face of a major recession that began in 2008 and that could slide into another Great Depression. If the answer is yes, the central thesis of this book that the Berlin Republic is not Weimar can be answered satisfactorily.

1
The Setting

A historical review of the array of political and social movements in numerous countries indicates that the extreme right is not a recent phenomenon. The left–right political spectrum originated in revolutionary France's Assembly, in which the right stood for the *ancien régime* and the left for radical change. At that time, the right, made up of the privileged classes, defended the overthrown monarchy, the Catholic Church, and the feudal economy. The left, constituting the working classes, stood for equal and universal voting rights, a free economy, and an end to the old religious and cultural privileges. Since then, the concepts have changed significantly. Presently the right in various countries does not constitute a monolithic bloc but may have subgroups ranging from moderate conservative to radical to extreme. In most cases, the extremist right has opposed socialist and communist movements on the left that emerged during the nineteenth and early twentieth centuries.

A study of Germany's contemporary right extremism, whose roots go back primarily to fascism and Nazism, must begin with a search for a definition. The movement encompasses a fixed ideology, a pattern of behavior, a set of political activities, and individual attitudes. Hence it is a sociological, psychological, and political mixture that shapes the movement, which is made up primarily of right-extremist parties and neo-Nazi and skinhead groups. Most individuals belonging to these parties and groups have deep prejudices and hatred against persons who they do not include as part of the "superior" German society. The rightists' prejudices and hatred are manifested in a palette of racism, nationalism, xenophobia, homophobia, and religious intolerance, which are then also directed against the "weak" parliamentarian-pluralist democratic government and democracy in general.[1] The effect is that, according to Leonard Weinberg, right-extremist individuals and groups "do not abide by the rules of the game." They oppose open debate and discussion among competing points of view. They have no inhibitions against using "dirty tricks," subversion, and violence, unlike most of those who uphold democratic politics.[2]

Scholarly analyses

The deep political divergences found in democratic societies reflect the sharp economic and social divisions in the population. In the late 1950s, American sociologists, such as Seymour M. Lipset, noted that in studying mass movements comparatively, each country showed evidence of democratic as well as left- and/or right-wing extremist tendencies. To him fascism was "basically a middle class movement representing a protest against both capitalism and socialism, big business and big unions."[3]

Some German scholars and the Federal Office for the Protection of the Constitution (*Bundesamt für Verfassungsschutz*), the latter in 1974, made a terminological shift that had political consequences. They dropped the term "right radicalism," which connoted a lukewarm acceptance of the democratic state, in favor of "right extremism." This made it easier for the *Bundesverfassungsschutz* to classify right-wing extremist parties and groups as subversive and anti-democratic. Such organizations were considered as a threat to the free and democratic basic order and therefore, under Article 21 of the Basic Law (*Grundgesetz*), subject to prohibition if the Federal Constitutional Court (*Bundesverfassungsgericht*) in Karlsruhe so ruled.[4]

Despite this shift in terminology, many sociologists and political scientists contend that the earlier classificatory term – right radicalism – was not passé. Rather it should be used as a catch-all term to include all political parties and groups to the right of the established conservative parties, but to exclude "right-wing extremist" organizations. Such right-radical parties, imbued with nationalistic and ethnocentric sentiments, should commit themselves to uphold the democratic order.[5]

There are other rightist movements, such as rightist populism, that have surfaced in Germany and in numerous other countries. Rightist populism is less a new ideological movement than an agitation technique in which populist leaders foment or draw on the dissatisfaction of citizens with the establishment parties. The populist leaders claim that these parties have not solved pressing political, economic, or social problems. There have been few right-populist parties in Germany, but many in other countries, such as France, the Netherlands, Austria, and Eastern Europe. The New Right in Germany (see Chapter 6), consisting of ultra-conservative and rightist intellectuals and politicians, is also part of the right fringe scene. Another movement, national conservatism, with its roots in the Empire era (1871–1918), has faded in importance.

During the Cold War some conservative German political scientists, such as Uwe Backes and Eckhard Jesse, espoused the concepts "left extremism" and "right extremism" as building blocks in their theory of the totalitarian state. Hence to these scholars the democratic constitutional state needed to be defended against its aggressive enemies located on the left and right sides of the political spectrum. The scholars considered these enemies as a threat to the state and its constitution.[6]

In the 1980s, some liberal German political scientists, such as Peter Dudek, Hans-Gerd Jaschke, and Richard Stöss, also used the concept of "right extremism," but others, such as Claus Leggewie, avoided it because they did not want to equate left and right extremism. All, however, criticized the conservative writers who took too narrow an approach when studying right-wing extremism. These writers focused on law-and-order issues handled by the *Verfassungsschutz*, the ministries of the interior, the courts, and the police. According to the liberal political scientists, the conservatives who supported a tough law-and-order position did not deal with the root causes of right-wing extremism and the rise of right-wing movements. These causes included historical and societal factors, which resulted in a low level of conflict tolerance, social inequalities, economic issues, and deep-seated historical prejudices. Such causes might then explain the magnetic attractions that many young people from one generation to the next feel toward right-extremist groups.[7]

The theoretical model of the German liberal political scientists was based on one that Theodor W. Adorno had developed. He contended that the residue of National Socialism within the population posed more of a potential internal threat to the democratic system than any external agitation against such a system. Adorno also emphasized the need to study the right-extremist individuals' personality and behavioral profiles. These included intolerance, rigidity in thought, and authoritarianism. Building on Adorno's model, the liberal political scientists concentrated on the links between right-wing extremism and conservatism, and on the society's reactions to the rise of right-wing organizations.[8]

Further scholarly analyses

Scholars have advanced three conflicting socio-psychological and cultural explanations for the rise of right-wing extremism in Germany. Professor Wilhelm Heitmeyer of the Bielefeld Institute for the Interdisciplinary Study of Conflict and Force and his research team have put forward the first explanation. According to them, right-wing extremism is not a problem originating in rightist marginal groups but has emerged from the fulcrum of society. Youth with "normal" biographies have become the victims of society's modernization or postmaterialist process. Many have become marginalized, partly as a result of the erosion or anatomization of local communities, political parties, social groups, cohesive families, and neighborhoods. The erosion is visible in the increasing number of broken homes, single mothers, and divorce rates. As Hannah Arendt indicates in her study of totalitarianism, isolated and aggressive youth, who have little or no support in the family and society, join right-wing extremist groups because they cannot fall back on their traditional anchors. Instead, they may belong to a group setting that has a collective identity and represents strength and support. Without such groups, many individuals would become pathologically disoriented and further alienated from society, even though most of them are employed.[9]

Scholars defending the second explanation refute the Heitmeyer thesis. They assert that the modernization process also has taken place in countries where youth has not formed right-wing extremist groups or, as in Germany, where not all individuals in a modernizing society become pathological. These scholars insist that violence-prone youth, whether of the right or the left, stem from all kinds of families and homes. However, the youth are more likely to come from authoritarian than liberal families. The scholars cite the psychoanalytic and neo-Marxist studies of Erich Fromm and Theodor Adorno about the authoritarian personality, which they see as relevant to this explanation.[10] The scholars contend that individuals with a weak ego and inclined toward authoritarianism are conciliatory toward the more powerful establishment elites but aggressive toward society's weak members. Such individuals' views of the world are narrow, fixed, and pessimistic. These individuals support an absolute authority – the state – but are intolerant toward those who think differently than they do. The rightists' ideas stem from childhood years growing up in a repressive father-dominated family structure. Once they grow up, such individuals are influenced only slightly by the society's modernization. But some scholars insist that such a world will have at least a minimum influence on these individuals.[11]

A Tubingen study of youth in western and eastern Germany in the mid-1990s confirms the authoritarian position. According to the study, 80 percent of respondents holding nationalist and racist views asserted that their political views were similar to those of their parents.[12] In further interviews with youth, some scholars have concluded that if these young people feel that their attitudes correspond to the population's dominant and conventional views then they will have an easier time integrating into society rather than joining right-wing extremist groups. But if some democratic political parties and the media take the initiative and openly support the exclusion of foreigners, as has happened, such youth will have fewer inhibitions joining right-wing extremist groups. These groups, with their nationalistic overtones, will challenge the often dominant liberal views and tendencies in Germany.[13]

In the third academic explanation of the rise of right extremism, other scholars advance psychological and economic factors. They view the disadvantaged individuals' loss of status, deprivation, and frustration when growing up as key factors. Disappointment and dissatisfaction result from not being able to fulfill certain life expectations, especially that of acquiring material goods in a mass society.[14] But once these individuals have such goods, they do not want to lose them to those who do not have them. The rightists, many of whom are not poor, adopt or identify with Western values, such as competition, achievement, and career. They view the nation's relative economic success as proof of its superiority; hence they do not want foreigners to share in the welfare benefits. Many of these right-extremist youth are convinced that eventually they will become the victors in the competitive society because they will receive the support of most citizens. To them force and violence is a drug against fear.

Ted Gurr, in his study *Why Men Rebel*, develops the "relative depriva-tion" theory. This theory "is a psychological state in which individuals have become dissatisfied, or frustrated, with the ability of the political system to meet economic, political, and social expectations."[15] There are other plausi-ble explanations for the rise of right-wing movements that cut across national boundaries. Herbert Kitschelt, in a comparative country study, posits the the-sis that the right's appeal rests on profound socio-structural changes taking place in advanced capitalist societies. As individual initiative and responsi-bility become more important in postindustrial economies, those persons, many of them blue-collar workers, who are the "losers" in an economic modernization process, cannot cope with the swift changes taking place and become attracted to right-extremist parties.[16]

Erwin Scheuch and Hans-Dieter Klingemann similarly claim that the potential for right-extremist movements is prevalent in all modernizing soci-eties. According to them, many individuals find it difficult to cope with economic and social pressures. As a reaction they become rigid and join right-wing groups that offer them the hope of a simpler and better society.[17] Their grievances become politicized; their targets are the politicians who are assumed to be responsible for the inequalities. Dale Tuttle contends that scarce economic goods and services lead to unemployment and poverty, and exacerbate social problems. Right-wing extremists take advantage of these problems to gain support from the general population and to recruit new members. Thus economic hardships become politicized, producing on occasion violent conflicts between groups.[18]

Edward E. Azar posits the theory of the protracted social conflict between various groups, especially in underdeveloped societies. Such a conflict can only be remedied if the groups' needs for security, identity, and social recog-nition are met in a multicultural society. Germany does not fall into the underdeveloped category, yet the analysis may still be relevant, as this study will show.[19] Other authors note that the convergence of mainstream parties on major issues leads to frustration among rightists, who will then support parties or movements that reflect their views.

Racism and nationalism

Regardless of the differences in the above theoretical analyses, German spe-cialists are agreed that right-wing extremists, but not exclusively, are imbued with a palette of deeply held prejudices. Such extremists see racism, which already surfaced during the nineteenth century in Germany, as the natural difference between groups of people, with some deemed superior to others.

Hence, the individual's ethnic membership in a nation or race is the crucial variable. People and state amalgamate into a natural order, producing an ideology of a "people's community" (*Volksgemeinschaft*). In such an order, which reflects a fear and hate of the unknown, there is no space for a pluralistic and multiethnic democratic society. The weaker groups, such as immigrants, will be discriminated against. These racist attitudes, though they may not be openly expressed, stem from an array of sources, such as the individuals themselves, the family, the schools, the media, and the political establishment. Racism in German history peaked during the Holocaust when the Nazis eliminated most of the "inferior" Jews, Roma, and Sinti. But a residue of racism, with its Nazi overtone and its view that the Germans have unique superior racial characteristics, continues to persist among a segment of the population.

Contemporary German right-wing extremist parties adhere to an aggressive nationalist position, which in the long run could lead to the establishment of an authoritarian state that is antithetical to a constitutional democratic basic order and that opposes immigration of non-Germans. Such extremist parties do not necessarily want a return to National Socialism. But, in this study, those groups are labeled as neo-Nazi if their members exhibit strong anti-democratic attitudes and overtly or covertly support a return to National Socialism.[20]

The rightist German parties and neo-Nazi and skinhead groups have espoused a chauvinistic and aggressive nationalism, akin to that propagated by New Right intellectuals. According to many rightists, such nationalism must be based on an authoritarian state. It means in theory that only people belonging to a specific nationality have a right to live within that group's country. In practice, as noted above, such exclusivity is hard to achieve.[21] Nationalist sentiments also have a *Heimat* (homeland, native country) component, which is especially evident among the approximately 12 million Germans and displaced persons who were expelled from their homes in Eastern Europe after 1945. Right-wing extremists support the cause of these displaced Germans, who have requested, unsuccessfully, that the German governments demand that Poland and the Czech Republic return their former territory to Germany. Prior to German unification in 1990, the right-wing extremists also demanded a German unified country based on pre-World War Two borders. Unification to them meant creating a strong German state that would uphold law and order.

Xenophobia

Among the many sentiments held by right-extremist adherents, xenophobia ranks high. It is the fear and hatred of, and hostility toward, foreigners, whom rightists relegate to an inferior position. Thus xenophobia is closely linked to racism, with its perverted view that some people, depending on skin color, are superior to others. In Germany, as in other countries, xenophobia encompasses a historic pattern of prejudices and hatred toward strangers and minorities and all that is foreign in developed societies. This *Weltanschauung* pervades the rightist scene and, to a lesser extent, much of the population.[22] Such views, honed to an extreme by the Nazi ideologists, have deep-seated roots in the unconscious. The psychoanalyst Werner Bohleber writes: "The Nazi past which has been denied and passed over in silence, but which will not go away, constantly generates a deep-seated memory blockage."[23] The blockage is especially evident in the refusal of many Germans to empathize with the fate of asylum seekers and refugees, whom they have depersonalized and made into abstractions. Thus these Germans fail to identify with the persecuted, not to speak of the weak and the sick. The victims become the miscreants.[24]

According to Erwin Scheuch, Hans-Dieter Klingemann, and Michael Minkenberg, this pattern of prejudice is caused by a loss of ties to traditional communities, a changing social and cultural milieu, and a passing way of life. It is also caused by a lack of orientation, perspective, and resistance to the relentless modernization process that is changing society in Germany and other industrial or postindustrial societies.[25] Young right-wing extremists see their status, lifestyles, and values threatened because they feel left out of a highly competitive "elbow" society, are doing poorly in school, hold insecure jobs, and are often not trained for well-paying ones. They must compete with other low-income groups. As a consequence, they find it difficult to cope with economic and social pressures, and become rigid or closed-minded. They join right-extremist groups that offer them the vision of a simpler and better society. These individuals, reflecting a pathological condition, thereupon rebel against society and the established parties. They become marginalized in a "two-thirds" well-to-do society. They join the ranks of millions of poor Germans who constitute the bottom one-third of society. As a consequence they reject traditional politics and the established parties, and they lash out violently at scapegoats, who are the dark-skinned foreigners, leftists, gays, and the homeless, rather than the upper well-off strata of society.

The right-wing extremists hate these foreigners and other scapegoat groups, who often are no better off than they are, for psychological or political reasons. The groups, such as the Gypsy Sinti and Roma, have a different lifestyle that threatens the established German lifestyle of order and cleanliness. Right-wing German youth, who have grown up believing in that lifestyle, become aggressive toward the Sinti and the Roma and the "others" who allegedly compete with them to obtain jobs, low-rent apartments, and welfare payments. Michi Ebata notes that "hatred is far more than just an expressed sentiment; it is a source of action dedicated to expelling the offending outsider from society in order to remake society into its 'purer historical' form."[26]

Such a symbolic expulsion in its extreme form can lead to the murder of the outsider. Foreigners, in this instance Turks and other South or

Eastern Europeans, Arabs, Asians, and Africans living in Germany, provide the rightist activists with a sense of superiority, "thus giving meaning and purpose to their lives."[27] This aggressive xenophobic group spirit becomes addictive as it does not solve the right-wing extremists' social or personal problems. As a consequence, according to Adorno and colleagues, the extremists perceive themselves in a paranoid way as "persecuted persecutors" who are frustrated with the political system's failure to meet their expectations. Such individuals can be characterized as suffering from relative deprivation, in which they lash out violently against foreigners in a society that finds it difficult to integrate and assimilate foreigners, even though such a society is already ethnically diverse.[28] In a 2006 regional Thuringia study 50–60 percent of respondents acknowledged that they opposed foreigners in their midst and espoused nationalism. Nearly 10 percent supported a right-wing philosophy, and of this group 17 percent were ready to achieve their goals through force.[29]

It must be noted parenthetically that Germans are not the only ones holding anti-immigration views; such views are expressed by nationals of many countries. It must also be noted that in Germany some foreign youth have formed gangs to defend themselves. Such gangs, whose members may also be rightists, on occasion attack German youth, precipitating a melée between them and contributing toward hate of foreigners. Such attacks reinforce anti-foreigner views held by many mainstream German citizens who blame foreigners for Germany's problems ranging from high unemployment and crime to housing shortages.

In 2005, the total number of persons with a foreign passport stood at 7.3 million or nearly 9 percent out of a total population of 82.6 million. This total does not include another 7.7 million naturalized immigrants.[30] In 2002 and 2004 surveys, Wilhelm Heitmeyer of Bielefeld University found that 59 percent of respondents contended that there were too many foreigners in Germany. The 2004 study indicated that women were more xenophobic and racist than men, primarily because women in eastern Germany have been hit hard by unemployment. Their consequent resentment of foreigners has contributed to a significantly higher degree of xenophobia in eastern Germany (56 percent) than in western Germany (36 percent).[31]

The hostility toward foreigners arose because from the 1950s on West Germany became once again an immigrant country, as in earlier periods of German history. At the time, immigrants, many from Italy and later Turkey, came as "guest workers" because of labor shortages in factories; others came to do the menial jobs that at the time were plentiful. The immigrants' descendants, numbering more than 40 percent of all immigrants, have lived in Germany for decades. In many cases they have not been able or in other cases have not desired to get German citizenship. After the Soviet Union's fall, the German government encouraged 5 million ethnic Germans (*Aussiedler*) to immigrate into Germany from Eastern Europe and Russia where their ancestors had settled a century or more ago. Upon their arrival in Germany they received German citizenship almost immediately. They were considered German on the basis of their blood relations (*jus sanguinis*), on which citizenship was based, even though they hardly knew the German language or the country's customs. As many Germans consider them foreigners, there is discrimination against them, which in turn leads Russians to form gangs. The German government also permitted Jews from Russia to immigrate freely, producing adjustment problems, including relations to German Jews. Finally, there are large groups of asylum seekers, especially from the Balkans and the Middle East. They come from countries where war has broken out or political oppression exists and where their personal safety is at stake.

For decades the fiery immigration issue has loomed large in German political discourse. The conservative Christian Democratic Union/Christian Social Union (CDU/CSU) especially took a tough position on immigration in the 1980s, a position that was hardly less xenophobic than that of the right-wing extremists. It claimed that "Germany is no immigration country," which was only partly true. In 1993, after years of discussion and pressures by right-extremist parties, the CDU/CSU-led government, backed by a more reluctant left-centrist Social Democratic Party (SPD), toughened the law on granting political asylum to foreigners. The government's anti-asylum position was accompanied by increasing rightist violence against foreigners. However, in 1994 the CDU/CSU-led government changed course and backed a bill allowing third-generation children born in Germany of foreign parents to opt for German citizenship at the age of eighteen. Within the SPD the sentiment for liberalizing citizenship laws for young foreigners and integrating migrant workers into German society also grew during that period.

Right-wing extremists feared an encroaching multicultural world. They denounced the new SPD-Greens government's liberalization of immigration laws after it assumed power in 1998. As of January 2000, a new law took effect that German nationality was acquired at birth by children born in Germany of foreign parents, of whom at least one has had to live in Germany for eight years or more. The children must choose between German nationality and the nationality of their parents before they turn twenty-three years of age. Thus, the law diluted the principle of *jus sanguinis* that had been in effect since 1913 in German jurisprudence.[32]

In January 2005, a law came into effect that allowed highly qualified persons to enter Germany as immigrants. Such persons have to take language instruction and courses on the country's history and culture prior to settling in Germany. But the law also facilitated the expulsion of foreigners deemed dangerous to the country's security. Rightist individuals are in the forefront of the battle to stop Germany from becoming even more of a multicultural state in which foreigners can easily assimilate into German society. Whether they can persuade the majority population to join them in their intolerant stance is of great importance in the national dialogue on immigration.

Politicians must choose whether to use xenophobia as a tool to gain more popular support or to reject it for its dangerous implications.

Anti-Semitism

Despite the Nazis' murder of millions of European Jews in the Holocaust, right-wing extremists in postwar Germany have not shied away from holding anti-Semitic views or participating in anti-Semitic actions. Such actions, normally in the form of cemetery desecration and vandalism, are discussed in Chapter 4. They reflect the individuals' deep prejudice against Jews who represent the "other," the foreign. This prejudice is nourished by the view that there is an insidious cabal of Jews, manipulated by Zionists and Israeli leaders, who control governments, finance, business, and the media throughout the world. According to the anti-Semites, this cabal was responsible for the high German government reparations payments made in the 1950s and 1960s to Israel. Even though most rightists have never met a Jew, the rightists' latent hostility toward the Jews and Israel has not dissipated. There are perhaps 200,000 Jews who are currently living in Germany, of whom the great majority have emigrated from the former Soviet Union since 1989. Of these immigrants, about 83,000 became members of a Jewish congregation.[33]

To the fanatic rightists, the Jews in Germany, who are the fastest growing group of Jews anywhere in the world in recent years, constitute a minority group that hardly differs from the non-Jewish foreigners in Germany. Both are seen as the outsiders who are inferior to Germans. However, as rightists can normally identify a non-white foreigner, it is the foreigner and not the unrecognizable Jew who becomes the target of violence. The conspiracy theory has also nourished the view that the Holocaust never took place, but constitutes a Zionist lie. The theory has been used effectively as a recruiting and mobilizing tool for rightists, who claim that the Germans were the real war victims.

Until German unification in 1990, the degree of expressed anti-Semitism was lower in the GDR than in the FRG, partly because during the communist era GDR leaders lauded the nation's anti-fascist struggle, which did not include anti-Semitism. The leaders sought to eradicate any residue of the Nazi propagated anti-Jewish sentiment in the GDR population.[34] They insisted that anti-Semitism and right-wing extremism were not compatible with socialism. Yet the leaders were not eager to extend diplomatic ties to Israel. Since unification in 1990 there has been a growth in anti-Semitic stereotypes among eastern Germans, especially among the youth. One 1993 poll indicates that in Land Brandenburg, for example, the 14–18-year-old cohort had become more anti-Semitic and xenophobic than other age groups. In another poll students were asked whether they agreed with the Nazi slogan that "Jews are our misfortune." Of the respondents 9 percent agreed completely and an additional 15 percent partly.[35]

A 1991 survey of a representative sample of the population in the FRG indicates that 15 percent of the respondents were clearly anti-Semitic and another 40 percent somewhat anti-Semitic.[36] The 15 percentage figure of committed anti-Semites corresponds to the degree of anti-Semitism in Austria and Poland, but surpasses that of Sweden and England in the early 1990s.[37] While, according to one survey in 2003, the degree of anti-Semitism among Germans was as high as 23 percent, latent anti-Semitism was even higher, ranging between 30 and 40 percent of the general population.[38] However, a 2006 poll taken by the University of Leipzig indicated that only 8.4 percent of respondents held anti-Semitic views.[39] Although the results of these surveys vary over time and do not correspond to one another because of methodological differences, survey data agree on the relative degree of anti-Semitism among major occupations. Negative stereotypes of Jews are more frequently encountered among farmers in rural areas than among residents in urban areas. In the latter, unskilled workers are more inclined toward anti-Semitism than higher civil servants, salaried employees, and professionals.

In general most Germans know little about, or are indifferent to, Jews, whom many consider as just another group of immigrants. Undoubtedly, the fact that Jews in Germany have a somewhat privileged status based on collective guilt produces resentment among right-wing extremists but also among many citizens. For instance, Germans are hesitant to publicly criticize Israel's foreign policies, especially those involving the Palestinians. Under the façade of indifference among these Germans lies the guilt and burden of the past. As a result, as shown in a 2003 poll, 61 percent of respondents said that it was time to forget the Holocaust.[40] As will be noted in Chapter 6, the New Rightists, among others, have focused their attention on this topic.

Gender issues

In Germany, the gender factor is crucial to an understanding of which individuals support right-extremist movements. Young males are especially attracted to rightist groups, even though they may not be racists when they join. But once they are group members they adopt its prevailing racist and machismo views. Many male extremists, who would never as individuals think of using violence, engage in it because they feel that Germany should not allow immigrants to settle in the country. These men commit 95.5 percent of criminal acts; women account for the rest. In the political sphere, two-thirds of voters casting their ballots for right-wing parties are men and one-third women. This ratio is also prevalent in other European states.[41]

A chief reason why more young women do not back right-wing parties and groups is the organizations' lack of support for feminist causes, ranging from the right to work to family planning, which transcend ideological differences. However, the gender differences disappear when it is a matter of discriminating against foreigners and excluding them from society, partly because unemployed women often blame foreigners for their failure to obtain jobs. Rightist women also project their fears of dark-skinned foreigners by visualizing themselves as victims of rape or other crime. In other instances of discrimination, some rightist females refuse to take care of black foreign or black German children. Rightist women are also spreading nationalist propaganda and recruiting new members. Thus, it is not surprising that, according to one study, 38 percent of women and 30 percent of men hold anti-foreigner views.[42] Although poll results differ, a North-Rhine Westphalia study in 2001 indicated that the rate of increase of xenophobic views among young women, not necessarily neo-Nazis or skinheads, had more than doubled in eight years to 13 percent while that of young men had remained almost steady at 14 percent.[43] Whether this change will affect the women's vote for right-wing parties remains to be seen.

Both working-class young men and women often lack a feeling of self-worth, have no career plans, and see themselves in a negative light in a consumer-oriented materialistic society. These feelings surface especially in eastern Germany where around 68 out of 100 unemployed persons are women.[44] Thus, many youth join rightist parties or groups, first, for the emotional support provided by them, which the young people may not have received at home when growing up, and second, for projecting their self-hate on to foreigners. Yet surveys have also shown that rightist male youth shy away from having a woman friend for a long-term relationship. If they do have a woman friend and differences of views arise between them, often the males break up the relationship immediately.[45]

According to a 1995 North-Rhine Westphalia study of more than 1,000 women and men between the ages of seventeen and nineteen, half of the women said that a woman needs a strong man at her side.[46] These tradition-oriented women have internalized the norms of a male-dominated culture. Thus they project feelings of power and fantasies of force on to the strong men. They let themselves be dominated by such men, who in turn give them protection and let them share in the symbolic feeling of power. Such women, unlike feminists, put emphasis on the traditional roles of being married and becoming mothers, partly because career opportunities in politics and the economy are still limited for them. In the male-dominated rightist groups, these women act as the escorts and supporters of the men. In a few cases, they fight alongside the men for "law and order."[47] The parallels to the subservient role of women in Nazi Germany are striking – and disturbing. Finally, there is a paradoxical issue in which well-educated women, especially in demanding positions, are hostile to foreigners because the women expect the foreign males to be less supportive of women's rights. Such a situation produces a reverse xenophobia where one would not have expected it.

Public support for right-wing extremism

The rightist extremists have always had support among those Germans who from the postwar years until the present have had nostalgic feelings for Adolf Hitler and the Nazi regime. Obviously, as this older generation of Nazis – the Old Right – dies out the support for a neo-Nazi regime can develop only if young Germans opt for such a political alternative. Polls indicate that a sizable degree of support for certain ideological components of National Socialism has not disappeared. Perhaps not surprisingly, in the period following Nazi Germany's collapse, many unreconstructed Nazis and their supporters among the public agreed with the question in public opinion polls whether Hitler would have been one of the greatest German statesmen had it not been for the war. In a 1955 poll 48 percent of respondents said "yes" while only 36 percent said "no." In 1978, 31 percent still replied in the affirmative to a similar question, while 55 percent replied in the negative. Other questions revealed that only 26 percent of respondents disapproved of the worst excesses of the Nazi regime. Stöss estimates that as late as the 1970s and 1980s the Germans' potential for approval of the Nazi regime varied between 20 and 40 percent.[48]

In 1979–1980, the Federal Chancellery commissioned a public opinion institute to survey a representative sample of 7,000 West Germans concerning their views on right-wing extremism. The results indicated that 13 percent of those polled, corresponding to 5 million adult Germans eighteen years or older, had right-wing views. About half of these individuals supported acts of violence. The survey also showed that an additional 37 percent of respondents, who had voted primarily for democratic political parties, had authoritarian but not extremist views, which meant that they could be potential "bridges to the right" in a crisis situation. Older respondents were more favorably inclined toward right-wing extremism than younger cohorts. Similarly, farmers, the self-employed, persons who could not get into an apprenticeship program, as well as those who felt social discrimination, were more prone toward right extremism than other occupational groups.[49] In a 1996 survey of university students in Land Hesse 15 percent showed right-wing views, even though most of them were not members of a right-extremist party. Among all polled students, those majoring in business, law, and engineering were more likely to be rightists than those majoring in the social sciences and humanities, which is also the pattern in other countries.[50]

In 1998, Stöss estimated that 13 percent of the respondents (12 percent western Germans; 17 percent eastern Germans) fell into the right-extremist potential category. This total nearly corresponded to the above-cited polls. Stöss arrived at this total by polling individuals on their views of authoritarianism, nationalism, xenophobia, welfare state chauvinism, pro-Nazism, and anti-Semitism.[51] In a socio-structural analysis, he compared those individuals holding right-wing views with the population as a whole. He noted that younger people, especially in western Germany, were not as susceptible to such views as middle-aged and older people. Members of the SPD, the liberal Free Democratic Party (FDP), and the trade unions were somewhat more resistant to extremist views. Yet there were no significant gender, educational attainment, and religious differences among the groups. In all of Germany, the right extremists clustered more in Hesse and Bavaria than in other Länder, and more in large villages, small towns, and suburbs than in major cities. Stöss concluded that 80 percent of potential rightist supporters had voted for one of the large democratic parties. However, in a crisis situation, such as the 2008–2009 major global recession, many might switch their vote to a right-extremist party.[52]

In a 2000 poll, 26 percent of eastern Germans and 21 percent of western Germans expressed support for a "strong leadership" in the Federal Government to maintain law and order.[53] In a 2002 poll, 69 percent of respondents were angry that they were still being confronted in Germany and abroad by references to the Nazi crimes. Most of these respondents came from the political middle and even the left, who probably felt that there were more pressing issues on the political agenda. In a 2009 Lower Saxony government poll of 15-year-old students, 5 percent of the male respondents were involved in right-extremist groups as compared to less than 2 percent who were active in mainstream politics. More than 14 percent of the youth considered the Holocaust as not being "awful," and believed that the Jews, through their behavior, were not entirely blameless for their persecution.[54] In short, right-wing views as expressed in the numerous polls were not restricted to those supporting right-extremist parties or to those who were right-extremist group members. Rather, numerous supporters of democratic parties might in a major crisis situation opt for a right-populist leader, a phenomenon that is not restricted to Germany.

There is a danger in making sweeping generalizations about individuals who might support right-extremist parties and groups. But, according to Hans-Gerd Jaschke, psychological explanations indicate that most of these individuals show "illiberality, intolerance, crude simplification, unquestioned acceptance of fixed rules and regulations, steadfastness and the rejection of strangers ('people of a different nature')."[55] Perhaps not surprisingly, many of these individuals back the mainstream democratic parties.

This chapter has surveyed the works of numerous scholars who have analyzed the motivations of why a number of individuals support the right-extremist parties and why a number of them join neo-Nazi and skinhead groups. Although the scholars are not in accord in their assessments, they agree on the reasons why a significant number of citizens are more likely to be racist and nationalist, xenophobic, and anti-Semitic. A brief assessment of gender issues indicates accord and differences among males and females as to why they join right-extremist groups. Finally, the chapter looked at the degree of public support for right-wing ideas and concludes that it is significant, especially concerning the immigration question, among those who normally cast their ballots for democratic parties.

In the chapters to follow the focus will be on the right-extremist parties, the neo-Nazi groups, and the skinheads. Are these organizations and individuals strong enough to produce an implosion of the present democratic system, comparable to the Weimar era?

2
The German Right-Extremist Scene, 1945–1990

In order to understand German right extremism in a country that has been unified only since 1990, it is necessary to look back at its antecedents. This chapter will deal primarily with the rightist political parties and neo-Nazi and skinhead groups that made up the right-wing extremist side of the West German political landscape from 1945 to 1990. We must ask why some of the groups arose so soon after the Nazi regime collapsed in 1945 and why former Nazis in leadership positions found a political home in some of the newly established democratic parties. What led to the right-wing extremist parties' and groups' rapid cyclical rise and fall? Did they constitute a danger to the fledgling new democratic order? Did the democratic parties take a stand on the issues raised by the rightist parties and groups? This chapter will also deal with rightist groups in the German Democratic Republic prior to its demise in 1990. Why did the groups play a lesser role than similar ones in West Germany? Did they ever constitute a threat to the GDR regime?

To provide answers to these questions, it will be helpful to briefly survey the antecedent organizations of the two rival states' right-wing parties. During the German Empire era (1871–1918), but especially in the 1880s, racist and national populist groups were formed, such as the Agrarian League, the Pan-German League, and the anti-Semitic *Deutschbund* (German League). In addition, the ruling bourgeois elite founded conservative premodern parties. One was the National Liberals, whose conservative wing harbored extreme nationalists; the other was the Conservatives, who espoused a powerful state backed by the military, upheld Christian ideals, and advocated keeping Jews out of the army, the bureaucracy, and the universities. Toward the end of World War One, leftist groups in the Social Democratic Party (SPD) and the newly formed Independent Social Democratic Party (USPD) staged massive strikes protesting the government's failure to make democratic reforms. By November 1918, leftist strikes and military defeats led to the imperial government's downfall. The SPD and USPD formed a transitional government, which was almost toppled by radical left-wing councils. The government called on the conservative Reichswehr and an anti-republican Free Corps to crush the councils, which meant that after 1918 these groups laid the foundation for the rise of a fascist movement. They were supported by the newly formed German National People's Party (DNVP), a successor to the Conservatives, and the German People's Party (DVP), a successor to the National Liberals.

In 1920, in Munich, Adolf Hitler founded the National Socialist German Workers' Party (NSDAP), the successor to the short-lived German Workers' Party. In November 1923 he carried out an unsuccessful putsch against the government. A court sentenced him to five years in jail. He served only nine months, which was a testimonial to the conservative judiciary's leniency with right-wing extremists. While in jail, he wrote *Mein Kampf* (My Struggle), which became the movement's official bible. The party's roots can be traced to the conservative Empire groups and parties. Its appeal built on the popular outcry over the country's military defeat in World War One, the Versailles Treaty's imposition of high reparations on the country, and the catastrophic inflation of the early 1920s. Popular support for the Nazis was evident among numerous marginalized citizens, including unskilled workers and discharged soldiers. The NSDAP and the ultra-conservative parties, which had parliamentary representation, contributed to the Weimar Republic's inability to create confidence in the democratic system and to maintain law and order until its downfall in 1933. Although NSDAP leaders denounced the capitalist system in their attempts to recruit workers who had little food, they emphasized anti-communism and conservatism, thus speaking to other population segments. These included farmers and other groups who were hit hard by the Great Depression. The economic catastrophe led to the party's swift growth in the November 1932 election, the parliamentary system's collapse, and President Paul von Hindenburg's appointment of Hitler on January 30, 1933 as chancellor.

During Hitler's twelve-year totalitarian rule from 1933 to 1945, the Nazi Party recruited 10 million members. In February 1933, Hitler dissolved the Reichstag and issued a set of emergency decrees, approved by Hindenburg, which laid the foundations for total power. In the following months, the Nazis, despite their inability to gain a parliamentary majority in the last "free" election in March 1933, banned all democratic institutions. The state, including President von Hindenburg, became a tool of the Nazis. The NSDAP, led by Hitler in his capacity as Führer, had its tentacles in all institutions to ensure utmost conformity. The party had an authoritarian semi-military structure in which the rank and file could not challenge policy decisions made at the top. The Gestapo and the paramilitary groups *Sturmabteilung* (SA, the Storm Troopers) and *Schutzstaffel* (SS, the elite guards) played a key role in crushing dissent among the regime's opponents, many of whom were sent to concentration camps. In addition, the Nazi doctrine's racist and anti-Semitic ideological components assumed an increasingly dangerous role in Germany's propaganda campaign. As a consequence, Jews and other persecuted minority groups were forced to emigrate or were murdered in the Holocaust.

The Federal Republic

Right-wing parties

Once the Nazi system collapsed as a result of Germany's wartime defeat in 1945, the United States, British, French, and Soviet occupying authorities prohibited the revival of Nazi parties, the use of Nazi symbols, and the utterance of racist statements. As part of the Allied denazification efforts, the top Nazi leaders were tried at Nuremberg and most of them were sentenced to death or life imprisonment. Less prominent individual Nazis were removed from office and positions of responsibility. Since overt Nazi groups could not organize, a number of German conservative revolutionary and national racist groups surfaced. Many of these small groups had belonged to the rightist scene prior to 1933.

The initial denazification efforts failed. By 1949 Western Allied authorities and the new West German government could not accomplish their mission, partly because of their diverse policies and partly because the denazification program had been ineffective in rooting out all hard-core Nazis. The Western Allies halted war crimes trials, granted amnesty to numerous former Nazi officials, and, as a result of the Cold War, encouraged the formation of a new German army. American officials also hired ex-Nazi scientists to work on projects in the United States, while West German intelligence agencies hired former Nazi intelligence agents to wage the Cold War more effectively against the Soviet Union and the GDR. Protestant and Catholic church leaders, most of whom failed to resist the Hitler regime, did not properly confront the Third Reich legacy. Heading key social institutions in the post-1945 era, many church leaders did not warn their parishioners about the danger of right-wing extremism. Rather they joined the United States-sponsored anti-communist crusade and warned about the danger of an expansionist Soviet Union. In the United States zone, the governing authorities allowed numerous ex-Nazis to become active in politics. These persons promptly reestablished right-wing connections, distributed newsletters to sympathetic individuals, and held meetings during the 1950s and 1960s. They still tried to propagate the totalitarian Third Reich's tenets, its leadership elitism, and its racist ideology.

Despite these disturbing developments an anti-totalitarian spirit gradually evolved in West Germany based on the 1949 approval of state (Länder) parliaments of a democratic constitution and political system. Most people became democrats, through opportunism or conviction, but primarily because of lingering war weariness, the memory of Nazi atrocities, and the crushing military defeat. Many had been democrats during the Weimar period, and some of them had taken part in the resistance against Hitler from 1933 to 1945. The CDU/CSU and the SPD became the major democratic parties. The conservative CDU/CSU, which did not want to see a neo-Nazi party on its right flank, attempted to integrate the former Nazis into its organization, with varying degrees of success.

On the political spectrum's right side, numerous German citizens did not view the Allies as their country's liberators from Nazi tyranny but rather as occupiers of a shrunken German territory who during the war had waged massive aerial campaigns against civilian targets in the major German cities, causing untold number of deaths and destruction. According to public opinion surveys conducted from 1945 to 1949, 15–18 percent of respondents, including many who held leading positions, such as civil servants, judges, doctors, teachers, and employers, remained unreconstructed Nazis.[1] During the Hitler era, the Nazis' indoctrination had been so strong that two years after the war, in a 1947 poll in the US zone of occupation, between 47 and 55 percent of Germans believed that National Socialism had been a good idea badly carried out. From 55 to 65 percent of the respondents answered the question whether "some races (were) more fit to rule than others" in the affirmative. Yet most of these citizens voted for one of the two major democratic parties. Even though many of them had become nominal democrats, they had difficulty confronting their past as enthusiastic supporters of Hitler and his policies. As a result, many sought to minimize or deny the evil aspects of Nazism.[2]

In the following decades, according to poll results, the number of convinced Nazis gradually declined. Those who remained Nazis provided the nucleus for new radical nationalist right-wing organizations. They were pitted against conservative nationalist leaders who had been active during Weimar and who during the late 1940s had received permission from the Allied and German government leaders to form new conservative organizations.[3]

The revival of neo-Nazism in West Germany produced a scholarly debate. Some foreign historians, such as Edmond Vermeil, saw in the revival a continuity in German history going back to the Holy Roman Empire's Germanization. They contended that Germans have a penchant for authoritarian rule and values, anti-Semitism, militarism, and imperialism. These were manifest in Prussia's dominance of German territories, Bismarck's authoritarian state and its colonial expansion, World War One, and Hitler's striving for world domination during World War Two.[4]

On the opposite side of this academic battle, other historians, such as Gerhard Ritter, insisted that there was no continuity of authoritarianism in German history. Hitler's supporters throughout the 1920s were loud but weak in numbers in a liberal democratic system. In 1933 their rise to power was an aberration in the country's development over centuries. On this view the roots of National Socialism do not go back further than November 1918 when World War One ended. Moreover, the NSDAP's ideology mirrored that of other European rightist parties at the time and did not constitute a peculiar German ideological trait.[5]

First cycle: the Socialist Reich Party and the League of Expellees and Dispossessed

Right-extremist parties mushroomed briefly, but they were short on a popular leader or an appealing platform. The Western Allies were wary of allowing former Nazis who had been in various NSDAP groups to organize politically. However, they soon relented and, in a spirit of democracy, permitted parties of all political colorations to form first at the local, then regional, then zonal level. Thus, in December 1945, the US military government allowed the rightist Economic Reconstruction Association (*Wirtschaftliche Aufbau-Vereinigung*, WAV) to form in the Munich area. Three months later the party received permission to organize in all of Bavaria. In 1949, the WAV and other parties were allowed to form nationwide organizations. WAV received enough votes in the first Bundestag (Lower House) election to have twelve out of 402 deputies. But once a Bavarian party of expellees was formed, it absorbed a sizable number of WAV supporters. Alfred Loritz, the WAV founder, who had been a Conservative Party member during the Weimar era, attempted in vain to form ties with rightist parties. By 1953, the leadership declared the party dissolved.[6]

In March 1946, British occupation authorities permitted the German Conservative Party-German Rightist Party (*Deutsche Konservative Partei-Deutsche Rechtspartei* [DKP-DRP]) to form in their zone.[7] The DKP-DRP was an amalgamation of several smaller right-populist parties. It gained strength among erstwhile Nazis, especially in Lower Saxony, which had long been a stronghold of the Nazis. In addition the DKP-DRP harbored German national, conservative-revolutionary, and monarchist members. In the 1949 federal election, the party received enough votes to send five deputies to the Bundestag, including Adolf von Thadden, a prominent leader active in right-wing circles during the Federal Republic's first twenty years.

In October 1949, the DKP-DRP's nationalist majority expelled former Nazis, who had gained strength within the organization. Thereupon the ousted Nazis founded the Socialist Reich Party (SRP), which was to become a rallying point for right-wing groups, especially in Protestant northern Germany. The SRP chairman Fritz Dorls had been a loyal NSDAP member since 1929.

In 1951 the SRP mustered 11 percent of the Landtag (state parliament) vote in Lower Saxony. Among many of its 10,000 members were expellees and refugees from Eastern Europe. Although many joined the SRP, most supported the newly formed *Bund der Heimatlosen und Entrechteten* (BHE, League of Expellees and Dispossessed) as a way to publicize their irredentist demands. Eventually the CDU/CSU espoused their cause, thus reducing a BHE electoral threat. Chancellor Konrad Adenauer even appointed former BHE leaders, who had been NSDAP members and who had joined the CDU/CSU, to his cabinet. Former NSDAP members also held posts in numerous ministries because of a shortage of qualified civil servants.[8]

The SRP gained backing from ultra-nationalists and anti-Semites who dreamt of a reconstituted powerful Germany. As a result the Bonn government called on the Länder governments to limit the party's activities and to ban its youth division and paramilitary units. In 1952, when the SRP continued its activities, the Bonn government, worried about the reactions abroad and a repetition of Weimar's instability, requested the Federal Constitutional Court to declare the party unconstitutional. In October 1952, in a landmark ruling, the Court charged that the SRP had not supported the country's free and democratic order, was anti-Semitic, had an authoritarian party structure, and a program resembling that of the NSDAP. Therefore, under Article 21 of the Basic Law the Court had the right to ban a party if it violated democratic principles and was hostile to Germany's basic constitutional order.[9]

Once the party was banned, many of its former supporters joined the *Deutsche Reichspartei* (German Reich Party), which von Thadden and others had formed two years earlier. It won seats in the Lower Saxony legislature. The SRP ban also led to the demise of numerous neo-Nazi groups. One explanation was the CDU/CSU's policy to integrate former Nazis into its ranks and the willingness of industry and the civil service to hire them. Such moves lessened the hostility of former Nazis to the democratic renewal.

Second cycle: the National Democratic Party and the Free German Workers' Party

In the second cycle of right-extremist parties, two right-wing parties emerged. In November 1964, a sharp economic downturn in a country that had not seen any unemployment for a decade was the rationale for right-extremist leaders to found the National Democratic Party of Germany (NPD). It absorbed the weakened German Reich Party and other small rightist regional parties. The conservative Friedrich Thielen became chairman, but in 1967 the more radical Adolf von Thadden replaced him. Of the party's eighteen-member executive committee, twelve were believed to have been active Nazis during the Hitler era. The NPD, one year after its founding, had less than 14,000 members, many of whom were older middle-class members living in areas that had supported the Nazis during the Great Depression. The NPD mustered 600,000 votes or 2 percent of the total vote in the 1965 federal election. However, in the 1969 federal election, the NPD gained 1.4 million votes, or 4.3 percent of the total vote, a sizable increase in strength since 1965. In addition, between 1966 and 1969, the NPD received more than the minimum 5 percent of the total vote needed to qualify for seats in seven out of eleven state elections. Its best performance was in the 1968 Baden-Wuerttemberg Land election in which it received 9.8 percent of the vote.

This significant support in Länder elections came primarily from voters who lived in structurally weak regions with a low income level. They were worried about the 1966 recession leading to another depression. Among them was the generation of discharged front soldiers; disgruntled workers, especially in the ailing coal and steel industries; the self-employed; and farmers who switched to the NPD. The party also picked up votes from law-and-order conservatives and neo-Nazis who were dissatisfied with the government's rapprochement with the communist bloc. These voters disliked the CDU/CSU-SPD grand coalition and were outraged by the 1968 student revolt.[10]

Although the NPD's electoral support was alarming to domestic and foreign observers, who drew parallels to Nazi strength in Weimar elections, neither the NPD nor any other right-extremist party ever received a single seat in the Bundestag from the 1960s to the present. In addition, after 1969, once the recession ended, the NPD vote plummeted and the party lost all representation in the state parliaments.

The party's decline was also caused by the CDU/CSU taking up issues that the NPD had espoused. This led to a fast plummeting NPD membership from 28,000 in 1969 to 6,000 in 1982. Moreover, the NPD's electoral support for federal elections in the 1980s shrank to less than 1 percent. The NPD criticized the establishment parties, the modernizing sectors of society, the dominance of US and Soviet influences on the two Germanys, and the charge that the Germans were collectively guilty for Hitler and World War Two. But in all these pronouncements the party maintained a democratic façade to prevent it being declared unconstitutional.[11]

The NPD organization, saddled by internal quarrels and programmatic difficulties, nearly collapsed. One quarrel concerned younger members who were not given leadership posts. They left the party and joined neo-Nazi groups such as the Free German Workers' Party (*Freiheitliche Deutsche Arbeiterpartei*, FAP), founded in March 1979 by Martin Pape, a former Hitler Youth leader. Of all the rightist parties, this one reflected most closely the Nazi philosophy. The FAP fielded candidates for elections; its members put up posters and distributed flyers, with mottoes such as "German Jobs for German Workers." In April 1989, the title page of its information bulletin "FAP-Intern" had the number "100" and the words "The Birthday" on its cover page, thus commemorating Adolf Hitler's 100th birthday. Many members took part in violent acts against foreigners and other political enemies. The FAP split apart over the question as to whether members could be homosexuals. By 1987 most FAP members had left the party.[12]

Third cycle: the Republikaner and the German People's Union

In 1983, in the third cycle of right-wing politics, two new strong rival parties emerged. Franz Schönhuber, a former Waffen-SS sergeant during the war and a Bavarian Christian Social Union (CSU) member, and two other CSU dissidents, founded the Republikaner party (popularly known as the REPs). The three rebels criticized the CSU's lack of internal democracy and the generous credit of DM 1 billion ($412 million) that Bavarian CSU Minister-President Franz-Josef Strauss had offered the East German communist government.

After the war Schönhuber had become a newspaper editor in Munich. In 1975, he was appointed host of a popular Bavarian television political talk show. Seven years later he was fired from his position because of his autobiography's publication, in which he boasted of his SS background. Thereafter he began his political career in the Republikaner party, becoming its chairman in 1985. He was the prototype of a right-wing populist leader whose programmatic demands spoke to the concerns of average citizens. Ambivalent about the Nazi past, he admitted that the Hitler regime brought about the country's destruction and defeat, but he also espoused patriotism and self-sacrifice. Schönhuber's speeches were laced with anti-Semitic references. He said that the Jews themselves were responsible for anti-Semitism in Germany because they had the temerity to meddle constantly in national affairs that did not concern them. He characterized the Central Council of Jews in Germany as "the fifth occupying power" on German soil. He also said that history books needed to be rewritten: "We do not allow that our history be permanently reduced to Auschwitz."[13] Echoing the views of right-extremist historians, he questioned the exact number of Jews killed during the Holocaust, implying that the figure may have been exaggerated.

The party's 1987 nationalist and xenophobic program was directed at German citizens who were affected negatively by a new economic downturn or by high technology modernization. Such citizens were worried that foreigners from poorer countries immigrating into Germany were going to receive jobs, housing, and social services at their expense and would increase the crime rate. The Republikaner program called for limits on foreigners admitted into the country. It was also replete with anti-Europe, anti-West, ultra-nationalist, racist, and xenophobic statements. It characterized its own party as a "community of German patriots."

Yet the program also pledged to preserve the state and the democratic order, and sought to keep out former members of the NPD and the right-extremist German People's Union (DVU). The Republikaner leaders took this position because they feared that the government's *Bundesamt für Verfassungsschutz* might label the party as right-wing extremist and put it under surveillance or that the Federal Constitutional Court might declare it unconstitutional. In 1989, the *Verfassungsschutz* began an investigation into whether numerous Republikaner functionaries had links to the NPD and DVU. At the time it took no further action.

The Republikaner formed a nationwide organization, but their strength lay primarily in Bavaria and Baden-Wuerttemberg. By 1989, the party had chapters in all Länder. Its electoral success peaked that year, when it received 7.5 percent of the total vote in the Berlin Land election, giving it eleven seats in the Berlin legislature. In the same year the party garnered an astonishing 2 million votes, representing 7.1 percent of the West German national vote and over 14 percent in the Bavarian vote, for the European Parliament election. In the European Parliament its six deputies, including Schönhuber, allied themselves with the French National Front and other European rightist parties in a voting bloc. Schönhuber and Jean-Marie Le Pen, the National Front leader, had met in fall 1989 in Berchtesgarden – Hitler's vacation retreat – and praised the solidarity between their parties. They announced periodic joint meetings of their executive bodies, the exchange of guest speakers, and joint publicity.

This unexpected Republikaner electoral strength alarmed some foreign observers who feared that Germany might be on the verge of neo-fascism. Studies showed, however, that the Republikaner had amassed substantial support from moderate conservative voters, especially in the European Parliament election whose outcome had little bearing on the national decision-makers. About two of three of its supporters normally voted for the CDU/CSU or the SPD, but in these elections they switched to the Republikaner as a protest vote against government policies rather than as a permanent commitment to right extremism.[14]

The Republikaner voters were protesting the establishment parties' inability to deal with major issues, such as mass unemployment and high immigration. The party received its greatest support from 18–24-year-old men. They lived in small towns or in working-class districts of large cities, especially in neighborhoods with public housing projects and few social and cultural amenities. Many were workers with minimal education and low incomes or they were unemployed; others were small shopkeepers, salaried employees, civil servants, farmers, and police agents.[15]

The Republikaner had difficulty gaining the support of women, many of whom were repelled by a party that was patriarchical, anti-feminist, aggressive, and ready to use force if necessary. One party plank requested the government to launch a compulsory social year, which would include courses for females "relating to [their] tasks as a woman, mother, and housewife."[16] The party was saddled by numerous internal problems – such as continual feuds among its leaders, expulsions, defections, and litigation relating to the national headquarters and the Länder affiliates – that weakened its position. In addition, the party was unable to find enough candidates for public office in the rural areas. Thus, government intelligence agencies did not view the party as a threat to the democratic order.

The Republikaner had to compete with a new party, the German People's Union-List D (*Deutsche Volksunion*, DVU-List D) formed in March 1987 by Gerhard Frey, a wealthy Munich right-extremist publisher and businessman. Frey, born in 1933, grew up in a conservative business household. He studied law and social sciences, and received a PhD degree. In his subsequent dual career, he mixed publishing and politics. In 1971, he formed a right-wing association, the DVU, which was eclipsed in 1987 by his own new party, the DVU-List D. At its inception it had 12,000 members; by 1990 that number had risen to 22,000. However, most of the members did not come to meetings and restricted their activities to reading Frey's rightist newspapers and party brochures. Within the association and the party, Frey, who had been an NPD member in 1975, unilaterally made the important decisions. Needless to say his actions produced conflicts with lesser functionaries.

In the Bremen Land/city (*Bürgerschaft*) election of 1987, the DVU-List D gained more than 5 percent of the vote because of its opposition to new immigration and because the wealthy Frey had poured DM 2 million into the campaign. This vote entitled the party to *Bürgerschaft* seats, the first such rightist representation in any Land or Land/city election in twenty years. However, the party's *Bürgerschaft* deputies did not distinguish themselves by their parliamentary activities. They quarreled among themselves, were uninformed about the issues, and made few contributions to the legislative debates.

The party switched between an ultra-national and a conservative position. In 1989, it mustered only 1.6 percent in the European Parliament election. Its program had failed to attract enough middle-class voters who normally did not vote for rightist parties or who, if they did, voted for the more moderate Republikaner. Although it maintained strength in several regions, such as Bremen and Schleswig-Holstein, DVU leaders curtailed electoral activities and public meetings as a consequence of leftist counter-demonstrations and harassment of DVU campaign headquarters staff. When party meetings were held, tough neo-Nazis were ready to oust any leftist protesters. The DVU leaders tried to recruit new members and voters by mailing out millions of propaganda leaflets. In the leaflets the leaders equated Nazi crimes and the murder of Jews with Allied "terror bombing" of German cities.

In 1977 Frey invited a leading Holocaust denier, the American Arthur R. Butz, to give a series of public lectures under DVU auspices on the Holocaust topic. In 1983, 1984, and 1985 Frey extended a similar invitation to David Irving, the controversial British historian and Holocaust denier. Such international contacts and the DVU propaganda made it possible for the *Verfassungsschutz*, after an extended surveillance, to include the DVU in its "right-wing extremist" category. The step was a warning to Frey that the Federal Constitutional Court might ban it eventually, unless he moderated his right-wing propaganda.

In West Germany's last year before unification, the DVU and the Republikaner were the chief contenders for right-extremist voters. By then the NPD was a shadow of its former self. Nevertheless, the DVU and the NPD, until then antagonistic, had decided as early as 1986 not to compete against each other in a number of Länder elections but to support each other's candidates.[17]

Neo-Nazi groups

The rise and fall of right-extremist political parties was accompanied by an even quicker rise and fall of neo-Nazi groups and by the emergence of a skinhead movement in the FRG. From 1949 on, those leaders who were not interested in working within the rightist parties formed numerous militant groups of old Nazis, neo-Nazis, and bored youth, most of them men. They were only interested in direct action against the democratic system. The leaders capitalized on the latent neo-Nazi and ultra-rightist views of a small population segment. Some of the leaders preached violence and terrorism. An analysis of those German leaders and members who committed crimes between 1975 and 1985 showed that 39 percent were 14–20-year-old youth and 32 percent were aged between 21 and 30. In 1989, authorities estimated that 220 neo-Nazis were militants who committed political crimes ranging from terrorist actions to threats of force.[18]

The majority of these youths were unskilled laborers, craftsmen or workers, and job trainees, who mostly came from troubled and low-income families. They were angry and fanatical youth who rejected the democratic system and resurrected an idealistic image of Nazism. As a consequence, many of them were willing to fight for such a system. Some criticized Hitler for having turned the NSDAP into a capitalist and bourgeois organization. They preferred the NSDAP's left wing led by Gregor and Otto Strasser or the SA led by Ernst Röhm, which they viewed as more idealistic than the Hitler bloc. During the June 1934 putsch, Hitler had ordered the SS and the Gestapo to assassinate the Nazi leader Gregor Strasser as well as Röhm and other SA leaders who were seen as dangerous rivals to the SS and the army.

In the early 1970s, the neo-Nazi group scene heated up, paradoxically at a time when economic prosperity had led to a decline in the votes for the rightist parties. Many new groups emerged in response to the leftist upheaval of the late 1960s. Former radical members of the NPD's youth branch, the Young National Democrats (*Junge Nationaldemokraten*, JN), often organized the rival groups.[19]

In 1971, the militant leader Friedhelm Busse and colleagues created the Party of Work/German Socialists (*Partei der Arbeit/Deutsche Sozialisten*, PdA/DS). Busse's trajectory in the neo-Nazi movement is characteristic of many others. Born in Bochum in 1929, he was the son of a Nazi who had joined the NSDAP in 1920. Friedhelm Busse became a printer by trade. In 1949, he joined the Socialist Reich Party; in 1952 the German Reich Party; and in 1964 the NPD. But in 1971 NPD officials expelled him as a result of his involvement in an intra-party ideological dispute. Thereupon he formed the PdA/DS.

In 1979, Martin Pape, a rightist activist, founded the Free German Workers' Party (*Freiheitliche Deutsche Arbeiterpartei*, FAP). It had begun as a right-wing splinter group in the Stuttgart area, but soon expanded to the entire FRG. Initially it ran candidates for public office on its party ticket. By 1984 it had stopped being a party and became one of the leading West German neo-Nazi groups, having at its peak more than 400 members. Among its leaders was the highly intelligent and fanatic Ewald Althans, a disciple of Michael Kühnen, who was arrested and fined in 1985 for insulting the democratic system. One year later Althans was convicted in court for wearing a Nazi uniform. He was also fined $6,000 for shouting "Sieg Heil" in public. During the early 1990s he operated a small public relations business in Munich and distributed numerous rightist pamphlets, books, and videotapes. According to Althans, in one year the police raided his home and office sixty-three times, confiscating much of the neo-Nazi materials that he had stored there.

One writer notes that Althans developed a reputation as the "yuppie Nazi" who was media savvy and who was a "café-society fascist dressed in black jeans and boots just like trendy college kids." Althans, about whom a documentary film *Profession: Neo-Nazi* was made, had visions of becoming a new Führer.[20] He often appeared on platforms with David Irving, the British denier of the Holocaust. Althans shared Irving's views about the Holocaust. In the documentary film, he is shown at Auschwitz shouting to a Jewish visitors group that the gas chambers they had just seen were fakes. As a homosexual, he proclaimed the imminent triumph of Nazism as a "lifestyle religion." He had no use for multiculturalism, labeling it a negation of the democratic ideal. When tried for his Auschwitz remarks, witnesses testified that he had been an undercover agent for the *Verfassungsschutz* who had given important information about the rightist leaders to his government employer. After he served his prison term he left Germany and went into hiding to avoid being attacked by neo-Nazis who sought revenge for his activities as an undercover agent. He surfaced in Antwerp, Belgium, where he ran a travel agency specializing in gay tourism.[21] In 1995, the Ministry of the Interior, not surprisingly, dissolved the FAP for its unconstitutional activities.

Some rival neo-Nazi groups claimed the need for an ideological renewal of the rightist scene; others emphasized violence to achieve their ends. By 1982 all groups had a total of about 2,000 members, of whom fanatic racists and anti-Semites were a minority. The groups, often jointly, planned actions to harass foreigners and leftists. At other times they organized demonstrations, such as those honoring Rudolf Hess, Hitler's deputy who was tried in the Nuremberg War Crimes trial and sentenced to life imprisonment. In 1987 he died in the Berlin-Spandau prison. In most of these neo-Nazi demonstrations the groups could muster no more than 100 participants.

The fanatic members idealized the Nazi state and Hitler, contended the Holocaust was a lie, denied the gassing of a single Jew, and said that only pure Aryans, and not foreigners, should be German citizens. Those who espoused violence or terrorism to challenge the establishment amassed an armory of weapons. It consisted of explosives, bazookas, hand grenades, automatic firearms, rifles, hand guns, cutting and stabbing weapons, thousands of rounds of ammunition, and chemical substances. In 1970, some of the neo-Nazis planned a military operation to prevent a meeting in Kassel of Chancellor Willy Brandt and GDR Prime Minister Willi Stoph, who were seeking a détente between the two states. One year later, in 1971, a former NPD member sought to assassinate the Federal President Gustav

Heinemann (SPD), who publicly backed the government's *Ostpolitik*. In short, any liberalization of West Germany's foreign policy or its attempt to produce a rapprochement with the East was anathema to the neo-Nazis.

In 1980 and thereafter the violence escalated. According to the Federal Ministry of the Interior in 1980 a total of six bomb attacks, two murders, fifteen arson attacks, two hold-ups, twenty-seven cases of bodily harm, and sixty-one cases of malicious damage to property took place. These assaults resulted in seventeen deaths.[22] One right-wing extremist member, Frank Schubert, killed a Swiss border guard and a police agent, and wounded two others, who had stumbled on a weapons smuggling operation that Schubert had tried to organize. During the exchange of fire, Schubert killed himself. In 1981, one year later, the Munich police arrested five Nazi terrorists, armed with submachine guns, one of whom had thrown a hand grenade at them. During the melée, the police killed two of the armed rightists. Subsequently the police found a large cache of arms in the garage of one leader.

The plethora of groups that formed, split, and reformed did not necessarily abide by democratic rules. For instance, in the late 1970s a "defense sport group," which normally practiced shooting at a weapons range, in an isolated terrorist act raided a military depot in northern Germany. It also held up two banks in order to amass weapons and money for future use. Among those arrested was Michael Kühnen, born in 1955, who had been active in the NPD's youth branch and then switched briefly to the Communist Party of Germany. There he learned about leftist ideology and revolutionary tactics. He returned to the rightist scene as a result of the strong influence of Thies Christophersen, a former SS agent who was then in Danish exile, and of Manfred Roeder, a leading figure on the right. Kühnen learned quickly from his mentors. In 1977 he was dishonorably discharged as lieutenant from the *Bundeswehr* (Federal Army) because of his right-wing activities. The same year he formed the Action Front of National Socialists (*Aktionsfront Nationaler Sozialisten*, ANS). This revolutionary cadre organization, whose young members had split off from the NPD, maintained contact with fascist groups in other countries. Observers characterized it as the most important neo-Nazi organization in West Germany. During his first jail term from 1979 to 1982, Kühnen, just like Hitler, wrote a book on politics. In Kühnen's case the book was dedicated to the SA leader Ernst Röhm, who was murdered during the 1934 putsch. Upon Kühnen's release, he merged his organization with the National Activists (*Nationale Aktivisten*). But in December 1983 the Ministry of the Interior banned the organization for its illegal activities. Kühnen's new anti-democratic activities landed him in jail again, this time from 1984 to 1988. In jail he renounced politics because other rightists objected to his homosexuality. Once he was released he renewed his political activity by assuming leadership of the Patriotic Community of the New Front (*Gesinnungsgemeinschaft der Neuen Front*).

Kühnen's considerable contributions to the rightist scene consisted of adopting the SA leader Ernst Röhm's ideological struggle against Hitler in the early 1930s. As noted, Röhm had called for the NSDAP to reach out to the workers, just as Kühnen did decades later. From the early 1980s on Kühnen also called on the neo-Nazi groups to emphasize ecological questions. He was a consummate propagandist who knew how to interest the media in the marches and rallies that he organized, especially when he invited internationally well-known neo-Nazis as speakers. Kühnen also granted interviews to television stations, journals, and newspapers. Frequently arrested, he gave the impression of being a martyr to the cause. Yet, despite his prolific activities he was unable to unite the fragmented groups into one powerful association.[23] In April 1991 he died of AIDS.

Violence-prone groups increased their activities, committing 184 acts in 1970 and 1,643 a decade later.[24] The Young National Democrats, the Viking Youth, and the Youth League of the True Homeland (*Bund Heimattreuer Jugend*) were among the groups founded in the 1970s that were nationalist revolutionary and prone to violence. Others engaged in war games. For instance, in 1973, the Nuremberg graphic artist, Karl Heinz Hoffmann, and dissident NPD members founded the Military Sport Group Hoffmann. Organized along military lines, it held field exercises and war game maneuvers in several Länder. On such occasions, its 400 members, who had belonged to numerous neo-Nazi groups, were armed and wore uniforms, comparable to Free Corps members during the early Weimar era. The Hoffmann group's announced purpose was to help quell a domestic disturbance, such as a communist uprising; to protect property and rightist assemblies and demonstrations; and to harass the US forces stationed in Germany. To raise money, the group held up banks five times, using the money, among other purposes, to buy explosives to be used against US soldiers. Governing authorities took action against the group. In several raids on members' lodgings or hideaway areas, the police found an arsenal of weapons and propaganda materials, as well as trucks, military motorcycles, rubber dinghies, personnel carriers, and other equipment. Some members did not shy away from using clubs, steel bars, and tear gas against leftist enemies. In early 1980, in the wake of such terrorist attacks, the Ministry of the Interior banned the Hoffmann group, which by then had shrunk to only a few dozen active members.[25]

The ban did not prevent Gundorf Köhler, a right-wing terrorist with close contacts to the Hoffmann group, planting a bomb at the 1980 Munich *Oktoberfest*. When detonated, it killed thirteen people and injured more than 200, before Köhler was killed by the police. The *Verfassungsschutz* and the police, at the time more worried about left-wing than right-wing terrorist groups, categorized Köhler as a non-political single perpetrator. Clearly, the government did not want to play up the dangers emanating from right-wing groups.[26]

In the meantime, Hoffmann established a link with the Palestinian resistance organization "Fatah." In Lebanon he organized a paramilitary group of his former organization members to prepare for an armed uprising in Germany. While the new Hoffmann group was established overseas, on December 19, 1980 another former group member Uwe Behrendt was suspected of having machine-gunned to death the Jewish publisher Schlomo Lewin and his companion Frieda Poeschke in Erlangen. Behrendt escaped to Lebanon, where he died of natural causes. In June 1981, Hoffmann and his partner Franziska Birkmann, as well as others, were arrested briefly on suspicion of having been involved in the double murder, but then released. In June 1986 Hoffmann was arrested again on the charge of having participated in the murder. He was cleared of that charge, but received a sentence of more than nine years for counterfeiting, grievous bodily harm, and offenses against the Law on Arms and Explosives.[27]

Skinhead gangs

In the Federal Republic, neo-Nazi groups were not the only ones engaged in violence. Skinhead gangs, patterned on those formed in Britain in the late 1960s, emerged in the FRG and other European states in the late 1970s and early 1980s. The West German skinhead groups were divided politically. On the left was the youth gang "Red-Skins" (also known as the "Skinheads Against Racial Prejudice" [SHARP, *Skinheads gegen rassistische Vorurteile*]). On the right were numerous skinhead groups whose members made up a segment of the proletarian subculture. These groups have not shied away from using force. The groups' members wear heavy leather boots (named "Doc Martens" after their manufacturer). The boots are mostly tied with black shoelaces, occasionally with white shoelaces ("proud of the white race"), green shoelaces ("opposed to foreigners"), or yellow shoelaces ("anti-Semites" or "cop killers"). When worn, these boots have often been used to injure or kill opponents. The skinhead uniform also consists of rolled-up blue jeans, wide suspenders, and bomber jackets. The skinheads are adorned with tattoos and have cropped or shaven hair. Their attire and appearance, characterized by the writer Martin Walser as "costume fascism," is designed to frighten their opponents and to make a martial impression on the population.[28] To indicate their nationalistic fervor they have adopted the black, white, and red colors of the German Reich flag, a disguised symbol for the swastika flag. Some wear a "14" patch, symbolic of pure racism. The "14" is based on a fourteen word slogan: "We must protect our race's survival and also ensure the future of Aryan children."[29]

The skinheads have appeared en masse and participated in hooligan riots at football games, one of their favorite venues. They also hang out at bars, discotheques, and public squares, and consume much alcohol. Their terrorized enemies are leftists, gays, the homeless, and foreigners. The skinheads denounce the foreigners for making much money and doing little work or being "dirty." Militant neo-Nazi groups have asked the skinheads to join them, but the groups have had only limited success. The skinheads do not understand or else lack interest in political ideology and strategy. Most of them do not want to be used as the fighting groups for neo-Nazis without having input into making decisions. Rather, they seek opportunities for dealing violently with foreigners and other groups on their own terms. Yet some skinheads make up the security force at right-extremist party assemblies, conferences, and electoral rallies. At times they have roughed up political opponents, who are normally present at such meetings, just like the SA thugs who during the Hitler era brutally beat up political opponents. Until the end of the 1980s, perhaps only 10–15 percent of skinheads, or 250–375 of 2,500, were political right-wingers.[30] These skinheads, then and now, have espoused racism, nationalism, and anti-Semitism. Their views mirror those of a portion of the politically centrist public, although the latter would not engage in violence and terrorism.

There have been two sets of rightist skinhead groups in the FRG: the first are the 13–18-year-old adolescent gangs, who joined for companionship, fun, and action; the second are the older youth aged between 18 and 25. Few skinheads remain in the movement after the age of 25. Most rightist youth come from uprooted working-class families. They have a low educational level, are often unemployed, and many have criminal records. To integrate them into a stable social environment has been difficult. Their eagerness to provoke their opponents and to boost their low feelings of self-worth led them to join the movement. They are ready to injure or kill anyone, even persons met through chance encounters. To these youth, force is the outlet for hate, frustration, and rage.

In the skinhead scene, formal organizational and hierarchical structures headed by leaders are the exception. Occasionally activists may guide a group, which in some instances, such as the "Hammer Skin" groups in Berlin and Brandenburg, will have contacts with their counterparts in the United States, Canada, Australia, and Europe. Viewing themselves as the skinhead movement's elite, their racist aim is to rally the "white, national" forces in the world. But more numerous are the "Fascho" or "Nazi-Skins" and the "Party-Skins" with close links to the NPD and DVU.[31]

The German Democratic Republic

In 1949 officials of the new GDR state claimed to pursue a diametrically different policy toward former Nazis in their territory than their counterparts in West Germany. East German authorities, who had been committed anti-fascists during the Hitler period, charged the West German government with being a stronghold of neo-Nazism. The West German government had appointed numerous former Nazis to leading government, civil service, and professional posts.[32] The GDR leaders said that in 1945, at the war's end, they pursued a much harsher policy. They interned top Nazis in former concentration camps or in Soviet work camps on East German territory. Once the GDR was founded in 1949 its leaders urged former nominal NSDAP members to join a communist-controlled bourgeois party or, in some instances, to accept government positions. Thereby East German authorities could maintain influence over the middle class clustered in the new satellite party.

According to the categorical statements of GDR officials heading the "anti-fascist democratic society," fascism no longer existed in their country. Yet some officials, as was true of their counterparts in Eastern European communist states, expressed anti-Zionist and anti-Semitic views and tolerated jokes about Jews, which fit into a Nazi ideology. The GDR did not recognize Israel until 1990, when it finally accepted co-responsibility with the FRG for the Holocaust.

Moreover, GDR leaders propagated an East German nationalism, reflected in a 1974 amendment to the constitution. It read that "the GDR is a socialist state based on a German nation." The original 1949 constitution had noted that "the GDR is a socialist state of workers and peasants." In speeches, schools, and commemorative meetings, the leaders encouraged the population, but only with minimal success, to link the nationalist views of Martin Luther, Frederick the Great, and Otto von Bismarck to the present. However, they drew a line when it came to the organization of right-wing groups because, except for the church, they did not tolerate a pluralistic society or groups that might threaten their own power base. They also made Nazism and right-wing extremism taboo topics in public discourse. Yet they could not deal with the GDR citizens' negative views of Soviet leaders for the harsh occupation policies and for forcing the merger of the communist and socialist parties into the Socialist Unity Party of Germany (*Sozialistische Einheitspartei Deutschlands*, SED).

The SED functionaries cleaved to a strictly socio-economic interpretation of fascism. Thereby they held capitalists rather than average German citizens responsible for the rise of fascism in 1933. According to some West German writers, the SED functionaries promoted authoritarian and anti-democratic tendencies among many citizens by failing to make them confront their past (*Vergangenheitsbewältigung*) and failing to instill guilt in them for having supported the Hitler regime. The functionaries denied any continuity between the Nazi past and their own GDR regime, and thus any responsibility for the Nazi crimes. The result was that these functionaries pursued a policy of "anti-fascism by decree," in which youth, just like their West German counterparts, lacked objective information about the Nazi past. In addition, the functionaries glorified their own state and the SED, thereby hindering democratic thought and the development of a civic culture.[33] Hence, it is not surprising that in a 1988 survey, 10–15 percent of East German youth concurred with the statement that fascism also had its good sides.[34]

However, one specialist on right-extremist movements, Susanne Backer, believes that West German scholarly critics of the GDR regime, as noted above, were unfairly generalizing their findings to the entire GDR population.

Their theories apply to the GDR's right-wing followers who were ready to support a right-extremist leader. Their theories, according to Backer, do not apply to the rest of the population, which was not authoritarian, or to the GDR's social opposition groups, such as the church-based ecology and peace movements. In 1989 these groups played a key role in bringing down the SED regime. Backer contends that one needs to ask "what are the mechanisms that promote the adoption of authoritarian value orientations in some people but not in others who, after all, live in the same conditions?" Why do some people who are disillusioned with the state become rightist activists, but not others? Her response is that the individual will subjectively interpret events and day-to-day experiences. Such interpretations will vary from one individual to another.[35]

Yet, undoubtedly, the gap between the official glorification of state power and the daily personal powerlessness of individuals, who were expected to conform to the state's dictates, was bound to produce restlessness and resistance, especially among young people. Most of them could not express their views freely other than in their own families. The regime's authoritarian and bureaucratic nature produced young rightist rebels who, bored with the existing society, refused to conform to the policy-makers' dictates.[36] But their number was relatively small within the total population because, even in the 1980s, many citizens were still satisfied with the state, which after all produced a high degree of social equality and material security among the people, even if it limited citizens' freedoms.

Although right-wing extremists hardly organized in groups before the early 1980s, the Ministry of State Security (Stasi), in an unpublished report at the time, recorded that 730 soldiers had been involved in rightist incidents in the National People's Army from 1965 to 1980. Many of these soldiers, whose parents most likely had been Nazis, were accused of glorifying Hitler and the Third Reich and of making xenophobic or anti-Semitic remarks. The Stasi also found that schools were not exempt from some pupils' extremist actions. For instance, in 1978, in a seven-month period, 600 pupils, aged 16 and younger, had spread neo-fascist views and defaced buildings and walls with right-extremist symbols and slogans.[37]

Skinheads

East German government officials blamed the influence of Western skinheads for the emerging right extremism in the GDR. But they said little about the home-grown variety, which in its first phase, during the early to mid-1980s, grew out of GDR soil. According to one poll, many young people, of whom 50 percent were skilled workers and 24 percent apprentices, were eager to create their own identity, autonomy, and space. They did so as a way to differentiate themselves from their parents and the established, stagnating, and to them boring, public institutions and the state.[38] Most of these youth's parents had jobs in industry or government and relatively few were unskilled workers. Thus it was not the offspring of the disadvantaged who made up the bulk of the rightist youth. Distinct youth cultures evolved that were strongly influenced by their Western counterparts, ranging from apolitical or anti-establishment "punk," "heavy metal," and "hippie," to right-extremist groups. The new GDR rightist subcultures consisted of rival skinhead and "Fascho" groups, totaling several thousand individuals.

Initially, the skinheads were apolitical but soon they became more politicized and divided into rival groups. On the left, there were the SHARP-Skinheads, who rejected right-wing extremism and racism, and the "Redskins," who espoused anti-fascism. On the right, there were three groups: the Oi-Skins, the Nazi-Skins, and the Faschos. The Oi-Skins increasingly beat up left-wing punks, gays, and foreigners. The Nazi-Skins protested the government's limits on their freedom. Recognizable by their yellow shoestrings adorning their black boots, they critiqued the state's authoritarian integration of social groups and the limits imposed on their own personal development. They called on the government to tear down the Wall, to allow for unrestricted travel abroad, and to support the two German states' unification, including a return of the eastern territories. Such unification would provide order and security and a strong leader. The Faschos, the more intellectual of the skinhead groups, demanded more discipline and order in the state, as had been the case during Hitler's regime, which they adored. Not surprisingly, they rejected communism, the Soviet Union, and the GDR regimes. During their frequent meetings, held from five to six times a week in the local pubs, the Faschos discussed the historical aspects of the National Socialist era and its leaders, and prepared materials about that era. But they were less prone to physically attack the leftists than the Oi-Skinheads. The three movements became increasingly xenophobic during the early1980s, although at a less aggressive level than in the FRG.[39]

Right-wing extremist groups

In the right-wing extremists' second phase, from 1986 to 1990, a new politically motivated rightist movement emerged from the youth culture. Conspiratorial cadres and groups formed, such as the National Alternative, Free Workers' Party (FAP), German Alternative, and Nationalist Front, with a total of about 1,500 active members. Many of these groups maintained ties with their West German counterparts. But the SED authorities kept the groups' activities a secret, not wanting to give the impression that the government had failed in its anti-fascist mission. In January 1988, right-wing militants in East Berlin organized a *Kameradschaft* (Comradeship), Hitler's term to denote a group with a common ideology. The group called itself the "Movement of 30th January" to commemorate the date when the Nazis came to power in 1933.

Unconfirmed reports surfaced that right-extremist groups formed dueling fraternities in the army and police force. Other rightists organized paramilitary sport groups (*Wehrsportgruppen*), such as one in the Prenzlau region of Brandenburg headed by a 33-year-old man, who was in charge of 16–22-year-old members. The Fascho skinhead groups were less militant or dangerous because they lacked the cohesion of the neo-Nazi groups. The Nazi-Skins, who were anti-social and anarchist, and the rowdy and often drunken hooligans who, adorned with World War Two medals, brazenly shouted the Nazi slogan "Sieg Heil" at soccer games, were even less organized.[40]

Many rightists were young workers or students, who, according to socialist theory, should have been leftists. They did not necessarily live in large cities, but often in small towns of between 20,000 and 50,000 inhabitants. According to one 1988 GDR study of 3,000 youths aged between 14 and 25, 30 percent voiced some understanding for the skinheads, 4 percent sympathized with them, 1 percent believed in them, but 64 percent of respondents disapproved of them.[41]

The rightists, angry at the governing establishment, defaced schools and other public buildings with swastikas or SS runes. They were also hostile to foreigners, even though only about 160,000–190,000 foreigners (1.2 percent of the entire population) lived in the GDR. The rightists were worried that these foreigners, most of whom were contract workers and students from "socialist brother countries," such as Vietnam, Mozambique, Cuba, and Poland, would further worsen the shortage of consumer goods. The rightists were also critical of male foreigners for socializing with German women. But there was a more fundamental bias against foreigners stemming from historical experiences, such as the hostility of civilians in German-occupied countries during World War Two and unpleasant encounters of citizens with forced foreign laborers in Germany. After the war, the bias extended to displaced persons and German expellees from Eastern Europe who had become the new outsiders.[42]

Notwithstanding the government's emphasis on socialist internationalism and brotherhood among people, public officials segregated the foreign workers and the 400,000 Red Army soldiers and their families in housing complexes separate from Germans. This isolation made it difficult for friendships and understanding to develop between the local population and the foreigners. Xenophobic stereotypes about the foreigners arose not only among right-wing extremists but also among average GDR citizens. Whether the rightist youth were merely trying to provoke the authorities, who inveighed against them as "rowdies" or who treated them with benign neglect, or whether the youth were making a political statement, remained unclear. Their numbers were still relatively small, with ten to fifteen members in each rightist group in East Berlin, Leipzig, Dresden, and other cities and towns.[43] However, in the late 1980s the number of members increased significantly.

The turning point for more right-wing activities occurred on October 17, 1987, when thirty right-wing skinheads and hooligans, yelling "Sieg Heil" and "Jewish pigs," severely beat up "red punks," dissidents, pacifists, and members of church groups at a Zion Church rock concert in East Berlin. The right-wing youth had received support from West Berlin skinheads. When the authorities could not cover up this incident, which belied their claim that in the anti-fascist GDR right-wing extremism did not exist, the police arrested numerous rightist perpetrators. Most of them received one- to two-year jail sentences, even though a few of those sentenced had family members in high state positions. Eventually, some of the sentences were doubled, which in turn made the incarcerated youth hate the communist system even more. State authorities officially denied that the skinheads' actions were political, because to acknowledge the skinheads' political bias would have meant acknowledging their own failure to transmit the dogmatic anti-fascist and communist ideology to the next generation. Many residents, and even the police at times, backed the skinheads in their vicious beatings of punks, gays, and foreigners in clubs and barrooms. To these residents the skinheads represented one positive segment of the GDR's political culture. The skinheads were seen as the models of Prussian discipline, industriousness, and tidiness as compared to the alleged "hanging around" attitude and "laziness" of punks and foreigners. These residents, exhibiting a deep xenophobic strain, also criticized the SED regime for allowing Poles to visit the GDR to buy goods not available in Poland; allocating bicycles, sewing machines, and other "luxury" goods to foreigners living in the GDR; and, according to rumors, paying these foreign workers in Western currencies.

To cite the life story of one leading right extremist: Ingo Hasselbach, born in 1967, was among the Zion Church rioters. He became one of the top rightists in later years. His father and mother, living in East Berlin, were professionals who were sympathetic to the GDR regime. Hasselbach did not share his parents' political views. In his rebellious years, he first became a hippie, then a punk, and finally a National Socialist. At a friendship rally for the Soviet military forces he yelled: "The Wall must go." He was arrested and served a one-year prison sentence, which led to a deep hatred for the socialist regime. From the time of the Berlin Wall's collapse in November 1989 and German unification in October 1990, he became "a freelance thug" who roamed the streets with friends searching for trouble.[44] As will be detailed in Chapter 4, his GDR rebellion was but the beginning of a stormy career in united Germany's initial years.

The Stasis

From 1987 until German unification in 1990 the GDR skinheads became more violent, partly as a response to the authorities' increasingly harsh treatment of them. Skinheads not only attacked their weaker opponents but also defaced Jewish cemeteries and memorials to the Nazi victims. In November 1987 a Ministry of State Security senior official sent a secret directive to all Stasi district bureaus requesting them to be on the lookout for skinhead activities in their areas. To identify skinheads, he described their "militant" but clean clothing, consisting of tight blue jeans, bomber jackets, and Doc-Martens high boots studded with iron, and their extremely short hair. He warned that the brutal skinheads were nationalistic, racist, and xenophobic. The communist Free German Youth leaders, also concerned that a segment of their constituency was rebelling against the state, informed SED Politburo members about the skinhead activities. On February 2, 1988, the Politburo issued a report to all district offices directing them to take appropriate measures to quell youthful criminal rowdyism.

In 1988, one incident of rowdyism occurred at an East Berlin soccer match. Erich Mielke, the communist secret police head who attended, was shocked when all at once the skinhead gangs, who had packed the stadium, stood up. They hoisted their arms in the Nazi salute and shouted "Sieg Heil." The match ended when the skinheads and the police slugged it out on the playing field. The government-controlled press did not report this serious incident.[45]

Officials estimated that prior to unification there were 800 skinheads between the ages of 16 and 25 in the GDR, of whom about 350 lived in Berlin and 120 in nearby Potsdam. The report noted that although politically these youth were on the political right, they were models of work productivity and discipline. Most of them were willing to serve in the armed forces as a nationalist "Germania" symbol.[46]

The official warnings had an effect on the police and judiciary. From 1987 to 1989, the state charged 50 skinheads with acts of neo-Nazism and 500 with hooliganism offenses, such as desecrations of cemeteries, or with bodily injury to Stasi officials, punks, and others. More than 80 percent of those charged were aged between 18 and 25 and three-quarters of them came from skilled workers' families or from the university-educated intelligentsia. This was a further indication that many youth grew up in privileged rather than deprived families, against whom, among others, they were rebelling.[47]

The press, which in the past had not been allowed to report on right-wing activities, covered the numerous trials. But still it failed to report on the underlying reasons, noted above, as to why many youth were rebelling against the authoritarian GDR system. The government's crackdown on skinheads produced a retreat into their private sphere. Many skinheads let their hair grow and refrained from violence. Instead, they met fellow group members in their apartments to discuss politics and to read the rightist literature smuggled in from the FRG. But the skinheads' prejudices against leftists, homosexuals, and foreigners remained deeply ingrained. Those skinheads who had served their sentences in prison, labeled by them as "academies," became part of a growing right-wing movement in the GDR. They, or their women friends who visited them in jail, made contacts with rightists in other cities, thus building up a network of rightist groups.[48]

Belatedly, the government officials, representing a closed system that did not encourage democratic and open dialogue, tried to crush the rightist network that had challenged its basic authoritarian governing practice. This practice included a readiness to use force against opponents if necessary. Thus the regime, already in its early years, had projected a tough image, encouraged the sale of war toys, set up a paramilitary Society for Sports and Technology, and scheduled mass rituals, such as torch parades. The skinheads' predisposition toward hatred of certain groups paralleled that of the state, which, for instance, talked of internationalism but ghettoized the foreign workers living in its midst. In one study, Walter Süss noted that the skinheads and Faschos formed merely the tip of an opposition iceberg. Young people increasingly challenged the GDR rulers' ideology. They demanded that the rulers initiate their own Soviet-style perestroika and glasnost policies. In response, the authorities rejected the youth demand because of its "negative-decadent" tone.[49]

Although skinheads and Faschos had little in common with Soviet reform policies, the East German rightists came from a youth milieu in which the critique of the GDR's socialist system had measurably increased in the late 1980s. Before then the critique was almost non-existent, primarily because those who had been critical had left the country. According to a 1985 Leipzig Youth Institute poll, 51 percent of apprentices training for jobs at the time still strongly identified with the state and only 6 percent did not. However, three years later, in October 1988, only 18 percent felt a strong loyalty to the state and 28 percent did not.[50] For some of these disillusioned youth, nationalist and right-wing extremist views provided the answer to their quest for identity. Others turned to the "Red Punks," who formed anti-fascist groups to challenge the right-wing groups.[51]

As the Berlin Wall fell in November 1989 and the GDR's regime collapse was imminent, the right-extremist movement became invigorated. The new GDR authorities amnestied jailed right-wing extremists whose sentences were soon to expire. These and other youth traveled to the FRG to meet their right-wing idols. West-oriented rightist groups, which had been formed in the GDR prior to unification, distributed West German propaganda materials. Until fall 1990, GDR authorities were too busy with pressing political questions to pay much attention to the growing rightist network, which by then enjoyed a new legality. The GDR police were busy trying to catch non-political criminals. Thus the Nazi skinheads committed more street violence and vandalism than in earlier years. They attacked left-wing "Autonomen" who squatted in abandoned old buildings. They openly expressed admiration for Hitler and the Third Reich. Although more moderate skinheads refrained from violence, the scene was ripe for conflict between the neo-Nazi skinheads and the police.

Conclusion

This chapter focused first on right-extremist parties and groups that flourished during the Empire and Weimar eras. These organizations provided some of the ideological bases of Hitler's regime. Soon after the Third Reich's collapse in 1945 neo-Nazi parties and groups in the FRG emerged that successfully wooed unreconstructed Nazis who had no faith in the democratic system and refugees from former German populated areas in Eastern Europe. The latter had been driven from their homes and lost most of their possessions. Many of them perished on the trek to Germany. The conservative democratic parties in West Germany also attracted a share of former Nazis who were eager to shed their past and conform to the new system.

The right-wing extremist parties emerged in the FRG in three cycles. The first cycle began with the rise of the Socialist Reich Party in the late 1940s; the second with the formation of the National Democratic Party in the mid-1960s; and the third with the founding of the Republikaner and the German People's Union in the 1980s. Their electoral fortunes reflected popular dissatisfaction with the national and Länder governments' policies. This was especially true when economic problems and unemployment mounted. Neo-Nazi groups and skinhead gangs emerged at the same time as the neo-Nazi political parties. Imbued by a philosophy of violence, neo-Nazis and skinheads beat up those seen as "the others" – the foreigners, the homeless, the leftists, the gays, the hippies, and the Gypsies. The neo-Nazis and skinheads also desecrated Jewish cemeteries and marched in demonstrations.

Although public attention centered on the visible and virulent neo-Nazism in the Federal Republic, GDR leaders had to cope with right-wing groups that were formed more surreptitiously and did not quite fit into the "anti-fascist democratic society" model that they had propagated. Ironically, these leaders also pursued a German nationalist policy from the 1970s on, which right-wing groups, but not the bulk of the population, supported. The government's authoritarian, heavy-handed, and bureaucratic stance led to a rebellious and rightist attitude among many young people, who often came from advantaged families. Their rightist views mirrored those of their West German counterparts, from whom they eventually received direct support.

In the GDR, numerous skinhead groups emerged in the early and mid-1980s. The groups espoused a nationalist position, backed unification of the two Germanys, and called for a return of the German eastern territories. Right-extremist youth, active in the East German army and in schools, did not shy away from violence or from defacing public buildings. In short, the right-wing scene in the FRG and the GDR mirrored each other to some extent. In both states neo-Nazi and skinhead groups emerged, although in the GDR, given the government's authoritarian nature, the groups could not operate as freely. Right-extremist parties in the GDR obviously were forbidden because they would not have fit into the regime's anti-Nazi ideology.

3
Right-Extremist Parties

Unification of the two Germanys in 1990 produced a momentary euphoria among eastern and western Germans. At last, after forty-one years of painful separation the two sovereign states merged, accompanied by significant changes in the party spectrum. This chapter deals primarily with the development since 1990 of the three major right-extremist parties. It examines their leadership, membership, electoral results, programs, and impact on public policies. Such an overview should provide answers to several questions. Were these parties able to mobilize the dissatisfied youth and their elders? Did their programmatic positions have an impact upon the democratic parties' positions on current affairs? Did their activities represent a threat to the democratic order comparable to the NSDAP during the Weimar era?

The Republikaner

The Republikaner party, as noted in Chapter 2, was one of the key rightist parties in West Germany prior to the unification of the two Germanys. Yet since then the party's membership and its voter support in elections has declined, partly because of the fratricidal power struggles among its leaders. They have indulged in intrigues, vitriolic exchanges, and ousters of their opponents from the party. In the early 1980s, chairman Schönhuber and his lieutenants built up an organization in all West German Länder, beginning in Bavaria. The officials sought to recruit members and mobilize voters during election campaigns. Land, district, and local associations have been strongest in Bavaria, Baden-Wuerttemberg, North Rhine-Westphalia, and Berlin. In other parts of Germany, especially in the new Länder, the associations are weak.

Anatomy of a party

The party chairman is assisted by deputy chairpersons, the secretary general, the presidium, and the federal executive committee (*Bundesvorstand*). Most of the officials serving on these bodies are hardly known to the public.

They include former NPD and DVU members, CDU/CSU activists, leaders of expellee groups, and, after German unification, members of the communist and satellite parties in eastern Germany. The leaders schedule national conventions yearly to discuss and vote on policies.

The party has tried to target specific constituencies, but has not been successful. The Republican League of Women has hardly been active, given the paucity of female party members. In 1989, the party formed a short-lived Republican University Association, which attempted, in vain, to inject a more intellectual atmosphere into the party, to moderate the party platform, and to strengthen the party's national-conservative wing. In 1992, national leaders founded a Republican Youth association to recruit members between the ages of 15 and 30. But, with only about 300 members, it has had little political success, even though reportedly one-third of Republican members are under the age of 30. It replaced a more extremist Young Republicans organization that had a short life span from 1987 to 1989.[1] Republikaner leaders have also targeted government employees as potential members.

Intra-party democracy is lacking. Members and delegates at party conferences have little input into policy questions. The organization has often been in chaos, especially in the former GDR, where there are few members but considerably more sympathizers.[2] The leaders' constant power struggles, intrigues, personal insults, vituperative exchanges, and ideological differences have led to short terms in office for many of them. Schönhuber autocratically fired officials whenever they disagreed with him. In several instances, a Land convention elected officials who the party chairman then ousted several months later.[3]

In 1990 and 1994, Schönhuber himself became the victim of such infighting. The 1990 crisis erupted over a feud between him and Harald Neubauer, the party's secretary-general, Bavarian Land affiliate chairman, and federal press spokesman. Neubauer, a former NPD member, had been groomed to become Schönhuber's successor. But in May 1990, Schönhuber, depicting himself as a moderate rightist, assailed Neubauer for his extremist views. When Neubauer and his friends captured the party's Federal Executive Committee, Schönhuber faced expulsion. To preempt such a move, Schönhuber resigned as chairman, only to be reinstated in his post by a party convention. In turn, Neubauer left the party and formed the *Deutsche Liga für Volk und Heimat* (German League for People and Homeland), which received little popular support.[4]

In 1994, the leadership struggles within the Republikaner party reached their peak. Rolf Schlierer, the 39-year-old deputy chairman, forced the 71-year-old Schönhuber to resign as chairman two weeks before the national election because of the chairman's well-publicized meeting with the DVU leader Gerhard Frey. Schönhuber and Frey had agreed that in future elections their parties would not run two rival slates of candidates for the right-wing vote in any Land election. Schönhuber's critics within the party assailed him for consorting with a right-wing extremist leader and thereby damaging the organization. Schlierer, a lawyer and physician from Stuttgart, took over as chairman. Intending to make the party more attractive to the middle class, he warned other Republikaner officials not to enter into a pact with ultra-rightists. Schlierer's portrayal of himself as a moderate intellectual was inconsistent with his call for the return of former eastern territories to Germany. A disciple of the ultra-conservative constitutional law specialist Carl Schmitt, Schlierer wants the party to be sympathetic to New Right intellectuals. His model of a rightist leader is the Austrian populist Jörg Haider, but Schlierer, a colorless speaker, lacks the populist appeal of Haider, who died in 2008.[5]

Many less well-known officials have quit the Republikaner. In a typical case, in 1994, the party general-secretary, the 31-year-old Martina Rosenberger, resigned, accusing the Republikaner of being a "Führer party," which had no intra-party democracy and whose chairman secretly manipulated the funds. She said bluntly that Schönhuber, then on the verge of ouster, was not a subject for the *Verfassungsschutz* but for the psychiatrist.[6] One decade later, at the 2004 convention, chairman Schlierer's moderate course, alleged support for a parliamentary democracy, and refusal to enter into any electoral coalition with the DVU and the NPD won him reelection. But a sizable number of delegates voted for the party's vice chairman Björn Clemens, a lawyer from Duesseldorf, in his quest to become chairman. He accused Schlierer of causing the party's standstill and criticized him for constantly worrying what the *Verfassungsschutz* would do if the party took an extremist position on national problems. The party, he maintained, should talk with the NPD and not be so "boring."[7]

The party's financial balance has always depended on membership dues, private donations, and government funds. The government reimburses all parties receiving at least 0.5 percent of the vote in Land elections for their electoral expenses. Thus, the Republikaner in 1989 were reimbursed for the DM 16 million that they had spent on the national election. But in 1994 they failed to request in time the DM 3 million that the government owed them. As a consequence, the party was nearly bankrupt and had to close several headquarters in Bonn and the Länder. In more recent years it has been able to maintain its operations.[8]

The number of members, always exaggerated by party officials, grew rapidly in the founding years to a claimed maximum of 25,000 by 1989. Since then, membership has declined to 15,000 in 1996 and to 6,000 in 2006.[9] In 1996, some 2,600 members resided in the new Länder. Most members are over 50 years old, although the 20–30-year-old age group has grown strongly. It is this group that supports a merger of the three right-extremist parties, but Schlierer remains opposed because the DVU and the NPD "pursue anti-democratic goals," an ironic statement given the party's minimum commitment to the Basic Law. The Republikaner officials claim, in order to justify their alleged commitment to the democratic system and their support for law and order and national security, that 20–30 percent of members are civil servants. These comprise police agents, Bundeswehr soldiers, Federal Border Service agents, judges, and prosecuting attorneys.[10]

Although a core of members has remained faithful to the party, in January 1991 dissidents formed the German Alliance-United Right, which ran candidates in the Baden-Wuerttemberg Land election on the slate of the newly constituted League for a German People and Homeland (*Deutsche Liga für Volk und Heimat*).[11] Some Republikaner Länder organizations have considered abandoning the party and joining still another small party, the Free Initiative Germany (*Freiheitlichen Initiative Deutschlands*).

Elections

The Republikaner membership decline has been paralleled by the party's mixed showing in local, Länder, national, and European Parliament elections since 1990. Voters shy away from a party that is beset not only by leadership disputes but also by the incompetence and infighting of its deputies in local or Länder parliaments. In the early 1990s the Republikaner vote in city and district councils throughout Germany was high enough to ensure the election of 402 Republikaner councilors. But as a result of continuing intra-party personal quarrels only 289 remained in the party while they held office. In nearly half of the councils the Republikaner *Fraktionen* shrunk appreciably or dissolved altogether. Usually those who left the party joined another rightist *Fraktion* or formed a new non-partisan group. Those who remained as Republikaner dealt often with issues concerning asylum-seekers, replete with an anti-foreigner bias. In one typical Republikaner query, the mayor's office in a city was asked how many foreigners had contagious diseases.[12] The Republikaner also played the nationalist card, but with mixed effect. In one television spot, the slogan featuring the former CDU and SPD chiefs was "Konrad Adenauer and Kurt Schumacher would vote Republikaner today." A television network refused to air the spot until a Land court, upon the Republikaner judicial appeal, ordered the showing. The judges contended that stations must air political advertisements if legitimate parties sponsored them.[13]

At the Länder level, the one surprising exception to the Republikaner's declining vote was in Baden-Wuerttemberg. There, in the April 1992 Land election, the party mustered 10.9 percent of the votes, most of which were cast by former CDU and some by former SPD voters. This strong support did not mean the Republikaner voters were ideologically identifying with the party but rather that they were casting a protest vote against immigrants and drug pushers, and job losses. The party, as a result of the substantial vote it mustered in large cities, industrial areas, and Catholic regions, gained fifteen Landtag seats. It became the third largest *Fraktion*, trailing the CDU and SPD, which entered into a grand coalition. The solidly bourgeois Republikaner deputies criticized the asylum seekers and foreigners whom they held responsible for criminality, threats to domestic security, and housing and drug problems.[14] Four years later, in the 1996 Baden-Wuerttemberg Land election, the Republikaner mustered 9.1 percent of the vote and gained fourteen seats. However, since the 2000 Land election, the party has not obtained the minimum 5 percent of votes necessary to gain legislative seats.

In Bavaria, the CSU won over former Republikaner voters by moving ideologically further to the right, thus weakening the rightist party. In eastern German Land elections, the Republikaner vote was 2 percent or less. As noted, the party has never been able to gain a following in the former GDR territory, partly because it sought to organize former SED and National People's Army members, whom the voters considered a segment of the GDR establishment, and partly because numerous Republikaner officials, not long in office, resigned for various reasons.[15]

In federal elections since 1990, the party fared poorly. Thus, in the 1990 election, following German unification, it only gained 2.1 percent of the vote. It lacked ideas on the unification question and warned voters of a possible "red-red" coalition, which was not on the cards, allying the SPD and the Party of Democratic Socialism (*Partei des demokratischen Sozialismus*, PDS), the successor party in eastern Germany of the communist-dominated Socialist Unity Party. In the following federal elections the Republikaner party again fared poorly, typically gaining in the 2005 election only 0.6 percent of the vote. The party could not overcome intra-party schisms, a more aggressive NPD, a shrinking core of rightist members, and the voters feeling that the mainstream parties can deal with national problems more effectively than the Republikaner.

Unlike the poor election results in federal elections, in the 1989 German election of deputies to the European Parliament, the Republikaner gained 7.1 percent of the German vote and six seats. Their success marked another protest vote against government policies and approval of the party's electoral demands. These demands rejected giving up any German sovereignty to the European Union and integrating "one-sided" German government policies with those of the West.[16] The Republikaner electoral success proved shortlived. Only Schönhuber retained his European Parliament seat for the entire legislative period from 1989 to 1994. The other Republikaner deputies, dissatisfied with the party's schisms, were ousted from it or left it for a range of reasons. However, when the *Fraktion* was dissolved after one year, the Republikaner deputies retained their seats under a different party affiliation or as independents. Schönhuber, in his Strasbourg legislative career, made only a minimal contribution to EU parliamentary work. He attended few committee sessions, and when he did he hardly ever spoke up or voted on pending bills.[17] In the following elections, scheduled every five years, the party failed to muster the 5 percent minimum needed to gain any seats.

Why did the party not maintain, with few exceptions, the momentum in Länder, federal, and EU elections generated in the late 1980s? The party's espousal of German nationalism and unification, years before the two German states' merger took place, robbed the party of a major campaign issue once unification had been achieved. Many voters supported the Republikaner position on Germany's obligation to restrict immigration, forcing the Bundestag governing parties (CDU/CSU and FDP) and the opposition SPD to confront the issue. In 1993, the three establishment parties, whose conservative wings also favored a cap on immigration, voted to amend Article 16 of the Basic Law. In effect, they limited the right of political asylum seekers to enter the country. Thus, the Republikaner, the DVU, and the NPD had successfully moved the country's political agenda to the right, but in the process robbing them of a major campaign issue.

As a result of declining voter support for the Republikaner and pressure from within the leadership and membership, chairman Schlierer abandoned his earlier decision not to enter into any electoral accord with the DVU. Hence, after the 1998 federal election in which all rightist parties fared poorly, Schlierer met with DVU chairman Frey. They pledged to work together in future elections in order to maximize their influence in Land and national politics. They agreed that the DVU would not put up any candidates in the 1999 Hesse Land election while the Republikaner would stay off the ballot in the Bremen Land election. If necessary their voters would cast their ballot to the other party and thereby, they hoped, gain the minimum 5 percent needed for a legislative seat in each Land.[18] A similar accord was reached for the Berlin Landtag election of 1999 in which only Republikaner candidates and in the Brandenburg election only DVU candidates were on the ballot. The strategy did not pay off; neither party was able to gain any legislative seat. In the 2005 federal election, Schlierer and his top lieutenants were on the defensive. Once again they rejected an electoral alliance with the more militant NPD. The Republikaner officials not only had to worry about their declining electoral fortunes but also about their future as a party. Despite their leaders' claim to support a democratic state, the Federal Ministry of the Interior and its Länder counterparts announced in December 1992 that the leaders' commitment to democracy was insufficient. Thus by classifying the party as right-wing extremist, they authorized *Verfassungsschutz* officials to put the party under surveillance, over the Republikaner's strong opposition.[19] The Ministry officials, in justification, said that the party's brochures, campaign literature, and the leaders' public speeches and contacts with neo-Nazis provided enough evidence to classify the party as right extremist. To buttress their case, the Ministry officials cited leaders' anti-foreigner and anti-Semitic statements, their derogatory stereotypes of minority groups, and their veiled support of violence against foreigners. The *Verfassungsschutz* authorities, who had collected information about the Republikaner for years, made it clear that the party's future as a legal organization was in danger unless it moderated its messages.

However, the Republikaner did not immediately take such a step. At the time of the 1994 fire bombing of the Lübeck synagogue, Schönhuber, then still party chairman, took Ignatz Bubis, chairman of the Central Council of Jews in Germany, to court for slandering him and for accusing the Republikaner of being the "spiritual arsonists" of the violence in Germany. But the court dismissed the charges.[20] The *Verfassungsschutz* authorities produced additional evidence to categorize the Republikaner as an extremist party. To capitalize on many citizens' anti-foreigner sentiments, one author of a Republikaner pamphlet had denounced asylum seekers as an "undesirable category of people" who "should disappear." Another local party publication criticized a proposal to establish a memorial to the half million Roma and Sinti victims of Nazi genocide.

The federal government insisted in its *Verfassungsschutz* reports, which included the Republikaner for the first time in 1993, that the party had continued to maintain an anti-democratic posture. A decade later government spokespersons cited Schlierer's controversial denunciation in the party's newspaper of Allied terror bombing raids that resulted in the mass murder of German women and children. The party chairman demanded that the German government build a memorial to these innocent victims. He also denounced the CDU/CSU-FDP government for excusing the Allied bombing because it resulted in Germany's liberation. He asked at what cost in millions of German lives a defeated country could become once again a member of the civilized community.[21]

However, the government's united front against the Republikaner was broken in the late 1990s. Not all Länder authorities classified the party as right-wing extremist. Administrative court judges in nine Länder ordered the *Verfassungsschutz* to stop investigating the party because there was no proof that it showed anti-constitutional tendencies. The courts cited the party's moderate programs as evidence. However, in some instances they allowed the *Verfassungsschutz* to continue to collect party materials as a monitoring device. In the 2006 *Verfassungsschutz* report a footnote tells of the Ministry of the Interior's decision not to list the party as falling into the anti-constitutional category. The Ministry did not have enough evidence to continue classifying the party as being unconstitutional. However, it warned that some elements in the party were supporting right-extremist goals.[22]

Party programs

The Republikaner have not been hesitant to revise their party programs. Prior to 1990, they revised them twice. Thereafter, in the 1990, 1993, and 2002 programs, party leaders sought to project a moderate national-conservative image. For instance, in the 1990 program, the party called on the Allies to grant the two Germanys full sovereignty as a precondition for unification. In the 2002 program, it insisted that Europe be a continent of sovereign states. Thus it rejected the EU, even though at one time its own deputies were European Parliament members.

The party also advocated the country's neutrality in world affairs. Prior to unification, it insisted that West Germany's integration into Western Europe, including NATO, should not be achieved at the expense of German unity. Demanding that "Germany must come first" it opposed a "one-sided" Western European integration. In 1999, Schlierer denounced Germany's participation in the NATO action against the Serbs in Kosovo. In the 2002 program, the party, like the CDU/CSU, opposed Turkey's admission into the EU because Turkey was not a European country with a Christian heritage.[23] To gain the support of Germans who had formerly lived in Eastern Europe, party leaders demanded the return of the former German territories of Pomerania, Silesia, and East Prussia on the basis of the 1937 German borders.[24]

The party leaders demanded that a distinct German ethnic and cultural identity be maintained to prevent racial integration. The 1990 program asserts: "We say NO to a multicultural society as well as to the ethnically diverse state." The 1993 program calls for an immediate stop to mass immigration into Germany because the country must not become a haven for foreigners. It links their influx to an increase in crime.[25] In speeches, party leaders have called for lifelong jail sentences for convicted drug dealers and three-year limits for the working contracts of foreigners, after which they would have to return to their home country.[26] One high Republikaner official in Bavaria asserted that asylum seekers should not be allowed into Germany.[27] Foreigners residing in Germany should be barred from voting in local elections.

Local actions paralleled national programmatic statements. In March 1993, in Frankfurt/Main, the Republikaner campaigned to block the construction of new housing for, and to stop cash subsistence payments to, asylum seekers. The party also sought to abolish the city's office for multicultural affairs (headed by Daniel Cohn-Bendit, the well-known leftist who had been one of the leaders in the 1968 French political uprising).[28] In national domestic politics, the party's program demands that law and order be strengthened. It supports the free market economy, the right of Germans to choose their workplace, and the right of unions to protect the workers' interests. But it criticizes the unions for their ideological visions and their encroachment into the employer world.

The party's social policy upholds traditional family values and the family's central role, demands tax advantages for families with children and equal rights for women, but opposes abortion. The party's environmental policy indicates that "soil" (a term also used by the Nazis) can be saved only if there is a limit on immigration to ease population pressure. The program, in the agricultural section, attacks the EU policy of forcing farmers to sell their products at dumping prices and calls on the German government to assist small and medium-sized farms. As to the media, they will need to exert more self-control and be less one-sided (i.e. liberal) in their presentation of news in order to further the common good.[29]

If the party in its program, literature, and leaders' speeches was to have an impact on national politics and culture it could not restrict its appeals to neo-Nazis and national conservatives. It would also have to attract the dissatisfied citizenry. But its success has been limited, especially in eastern Germany. There protest voters view the party as representing the wealthier western German Länder, which, for instance, have developed a high-tech economic sector that is less visible in eastern Germany.

German People's Union

In 1987, as already noted, Gerhard Frey, the multimillionaire Munich right-wing publisher and real estate tycoon, founded a new party, the German People's Union-List D (*Deutsche Volksunion-List D*). In 1992, the DVU had about 27,000 members, but then suffered a steady decline, as was true of most other German parties, to 6,000 in 2008. The DVU had difficulty recruiting youth into its ranks, partly because few of them, including deputies, saw a chance to move into leadership positions, which were dominated by Frey and the Old Guard until 2009 when he stepped down as chairman.

In the late 1990s Frey established party branches in all Länder, but they were mostly inactive and had no independence from Munich national head-quarters. Frey, with the assistance of a few top aides, has set the party's ideological positions and goals, thereby crushing any attempts at intra-party democracy. In 1997, Frey, whose fortune was estimated at more than several hundred million DM, said that because he was the sole financier of his party he had a right to control it. He poured millions of DM (more recently euros) into his election campaigns, determining in which one the party should participate. He was also the owner of a publishing house that prints the weekly *National-Zeitung/Deutsche Wochenzeitung* (NZ), with an estimated circulation of 41,000.[30] The NZ serves as the unofficial party newspaper.

Frey organized yearly party meetings in the mammoth Nibelungen Hall in Passau (Bavaria), attended each time by at least 1,000 DVU members. He invited German and foreign rightist leaders and honored some of the latter with a special medal. In 1999, the city's mayor, worried that Passau was becoming known as a "brown" city, sought to ban the DVU's rental of the hall. But the party, in an appeal to the courts, was victorious. The judges ruled that any organization had the right to rent the hall. Stymied by the court, the city's mayor ordered placards bearing the inscription "Right-wing extremists not welcome" to be hung in all districts. When democratic groups staged large demonstrations outside the Passau meeting, Frey, always surrounded by bodyguards, decided to scrap future meetings in Passau and to organize instead four regional assemblies in other cities. Even though he lacks ora-torical skills, he has been the chief speaker at such meetings. However, he allows a few DVU deputies in Länder parliaments and top DVU leaders to address the audience. To appease the critics within the party who demanded more intra-party democracy and the scheduling of monthly meetings at the base, Frey reluctantly consented. But in many cities such meetings have not taken place, except for a few at election time. The DVU remains basically a "phantom party," as some critics have dubbed it.

Elections and *Fraktionen*

Electoral contests are important in the party's activities. Frey and his top lieutenants decide on a pragmatic basis in which Länder and Bundestag elections the party should participate. In some West German elections prior to 1990 Frey worked closely with the NPD. But when that party fared poorly in the 1990 federal election, Frey renounced his agreement with it, only to reverse this decision years later when he realized that the DVU had slim chances of winning seats on its own in Länder parliaments. In 1991, to improve the party's image, Frey struck "List D" from the party's cumbersome name, DVU-List D.

A lack of intra-party democracy marked the election campaigns. Often DVU candidates did not schedule public local meetings to discuss current problems with members or outsiders. When meetings were held, a national representative from Munich rather than the candidate for the Land parliament answered questions from the audience or the journalists.[31] Frey and his associates in Munich headquarters selected candidates for local or Land legislative office. Frey, aware of the paucity of qualified party members running for public office, was obliged to choose candidates on occasion from a data bank in the DVU's central computers in Munich. The data bank had information about citizens who had requested information material concerning the party. In Schleswig-Holstein such citizens thereupon received a letter inquiring about their availability to become candidates. However, most of them had no interest in becoming politically involved.

Not surprisingly given the few programmatic differences between the DVU and the NPD, officials of both parties made deals to support each other's candidates in Land elections in order to enhance the chance of surmounting the minimum 5 percent barrier. In such instances, only one of the two parties appeared on the ballot. Thus the DVU picked up votes from the NPD whenever the NPD did not have its own slate, and vice versa. For instance, in the September 1991 Bremen Land election, in which NPD members were urged to vote for the DVU, the latter gained 6.2 percent of the vote and six seats in the legislature, primarily because of the continuing controversy over immigration and rising unemployment. However, when three DVU deputies quit the party and formed their own group, the DVU lost its *Fraktion* status in the legislature. The party's deputies, as is true of right-wing deputies in other Länder and other rightist parties, did not distinguish themselves in their parliamentary activities. They quarreled, were uninformed about the issues, made few substantial contributions to the legislative debates, and were critical of Frey's leadership. Yet their speeches on the floor were copied from articles in his rightist newspaper. The deputies flooded the legislatures with motions and parliamentary questions that had been prepared at the Munich headquarters. The motions and questions were designed to make the chamber a stage for propaganda, especially on the immigration question. The deputies made few contributions to committee deliberations, partly because they could not meet the intellectual level of other deputies. As a result, they hardly attended committee meetings; if they attended, they remained quiet. Frey's refusal to allow the DVU deputies to have their own *Fraktion* office, for fear that the *Fraktion* would develop its own policy lines, increased the tensions between Frey and DVU deputies.

The party's strength in northern Germany, which was hit hard by the closing of shipyards, was evident again in April 1992, when the DVU won 6.3 percent of the vote in the Schleswig-Holstein Land election, gaining six legislative seats. However, one angry DVU candidate left the party and withdrew his candidacy the day before the election because Munich headquarters had not informed him of his candidacy. Soon thereafter, Frey accused the Schleswig-Holstein *Fraktion* chairman Ingo Stawitz of "treasonous" activities against the party. According to Frey, Stawitz had openly criticized the party program for not emphasizing the positive aspects of neo-Nazi and racist policies. In addition, Stawitz was accused of having misappropriated funds sent from Munich headquarters. Frey also reported that two *Fraktion* secretaries had received excessive salaries in order to spend their time primarily in Stawitz's private house. Frey initiated ouster proceedings against Stawitz, who however received the support of most *Fraktion* members. In May 1993, after one year in office, the DVU *Fraktion* dissolved itself. Its members sought admission to the Republikaner, but were rebuffed for being too right extremist. Thereupon some *Fraktion* members joined the German League for People and Homeland, a small party headed by Harald Neubauer. Two others joined the ranks of those deputies without a party; only one deputy remained in the DVU.[32]

In another unusual case, in the September 1993 Hamburg Land election, the DVU candidate was an NPD member and yet won a seat in the DVU *Fraktion*. She claimed that someone at Munich DVU headquarters telephoned her and said that they needed a candidate. She agreed to run on the DVU ticket. Evidently national officials were desperate to find suitable candidates regardless of DVU membership. The officials selected the list candidates, who were unknown to the voters. These internal problems were compounded by financial irregularities among DVU *Fraktion* members and by Frey's machinations. The members squandered government funds given to the *Fraktion*. Frey forced them to run expensive advertisements in his own newspaper or to take out numerous subscriptions in the *Fraktion*'s name. The party owed Frey DM 8 million. Such a deficit made it certain that Frey would remain master over a phantom-like party, which lacked internal democracy.[33] Despite its well-publicized financial difficulties the DVU once again scored electoral successes in Bremen in 1995 and in Schleswig-Holstein in 1996. The DVU victories reflected the continuing economic problems and fear of foreigners facing the voters.

In April 1998 the DVU most unexpectedly was able to garner nearly 13 percent of the vote and sixteen seats in the Saxony-Anhalt election, its best Landtag results ever. The support of 192,000 voters led to its victory, the first time that a rightist party had gained representation in an eastern German Land. The DVU's unexpected high vote was the result of a mixture of factors. Frey spent DM 3 million (more than the SPD and CDU combined) on an expensive direct mailing campaign, posters on lampposts (mounted high enough not to be torn down), television advertisements, airplanes flying DVU banners, and other publicity. Frey also put forth simple and catchy electoral slogans, such as "German money for German jobs," "Criminal foreigners out," "This time vote for protest," and "Cut politicians' salaries." The DVU program reflected the NSDAP populist demands of Weimar. It was tailored to appeal especially to those voters faced with continuing unemployment and by an alleged crime wave. The slogans had their effect: 27 percent of voters in the under-30 category, especially males, voted for the DVU. In this age group the DVU even trumped the SPD, which gained 22 percent.[34]

According to one study, the DVU received significant support (29 percent) from those who normally abstained from voting and some support from those voters who in the previous election had voted for the CDU, SPD, and PDS. However, in this instance they voted for the DVU as a protest against the government's failure to reduce unemployment and in sympathy with the DVU's racist and nationalist positions. They blamed foreigners for their plight, even though few of the Land's population were foreigners. The DVU scored well in the Halle and Bitterfeld regions where unemployment in the chemical industry was still high. Most of the DVU vote came from male workers, apprentices, and the unemployed.[35] After the election results were announced, the national economic associations warned that foreign investors would be reluctant to invest in the German economy or they might withdraw some of their capital and invest elsewhere. The trade unions, worried that many unionized workers voted for the DVU, called on employers to create more jobs and apprenticeship positions in eastern Germany. The DVU's leftist critics said that the party supporters' racist attitudes reflected those that many average citizens hold.

The Saxony-Anhalt DVU *Fraktion* members, who were hardly known to the electorate, were unprepared for their political tasks and not fit to be Landestag members. The *Fraktion* chairman, an unemployed engineer, was once fined for threatening his former wife with a gas pistol; another member was convicted in court of animal torture. In their legislative functions, the *Fraktion* members had to follow instructions from the party's Munich headquarters. Hence it was not surprising that one year after the election the *Fraktion* dissolved itself.

In the meantime, in the 1998 Bundestag election, the DVU gained only 1.2 percent and all rightist parties 4.4 percent of the total vote. Thus even if these parties had agreed upon one common slate, they would not have received a single legislative seat because they had not broken the 5 percent barrier. To salve their conscience, the Republikaner blamed the Bavarian CSU for pursuing a hard line position on foreigners, which took away votes from their party. Frey made overtures to the Republikaner suggesting that in some Länder the DVU ought to run candidates and in others, such as Bavaria, only Republikaner. But Schlierer was unwilling to enter into such a pact. The NPD chiefs rejected all overtures for electoral deals, partly because a DVU-NPD accord in the late 1980s had gone sour. They viewed scattered efforts to create a united rightist party as utopian.[36]

The DVU, as was true of the other rightist parties, was eager for media exposure. On the eve of the 1999 Thuringian Land election, the Second German Television network had refused to permit Otto Reissig, the DVU list's top candidate, to appear in a round-table discussion with other party representatives. When Reissig took his case to an administrative court, he won. However, the victory was moot because the democratic parties' candidates refused to appear on the same program with him.[37] Although the DVU could not gain any seats in the Thuringian election, in the September 1999 Brandenburg election it mustered more than 5 percent of the vote, thereby gaining five seats. Democratic leaders viewed the results as deplorable, but their failure to wage a strong campaign against rightist extremism, to lower local unemployment, and to denounce racism contributed to the DVU's appeal.

In 2002 the DVU no longer fielded candidates in the Saxony-Anhalt Land-tag election. Instead the splinter Free German People's Party put up a slate, but no one on the list was elected. This volatility in the Saxony-Anhalt voters' support for the DVU proved once again that in eastern Germany party loyalties among voters were not as strongly embedded as in western Germany, although even there party loyalties were evaporating. Yet the DVU managed to maintain some political presence in a few Land legislatures. It continued to have deputies in the Bremen and Brandenburg Land parliaments. In the September 2004 election in Brandenburg, the DVU gained 6.1 percent of the vote and six seats (later reduced to five), thereby winning representation in a Land parliament in two successive elections. This success was the result, by then quite common, of an agreement with the NPD that it would not put up its own slate of candidates in Brandenburg but would support the DVU. Conversely the DVU pledged not to put up a slate of candidates in Saxony, but would support the NPD candidates. During these electoral contests, Frey, in personal columns in his NZ newspaper, appealed to the readers to contribute money for the DVU campaigns. He also sent flyers and party propaganda through the mail, had placards mounted in public places by a commercial agency rather than by the few local party activists, and paid for press advertisements. Once in office, the DVU Brandenburg *Fraktion* did not want to repeat the poor legislative record of earlier DVU *Fraktionen*. It has issued its own newspaper regularly, which also appeared on its internet homepage. Some of its deputies have appeared there in video clips.[38] Yet the dependence on Munich has remained high. One joke circulated that the biggest calamity to befall the *Fraktion* would be if someone pulled the fax machine cord because much of the *Fraktion*'s activity was issuing petitions drafted in Munich headquarters.

At the national level, the DVU could not muster the 5 percent needed for representation in any Bundestag election. The DVU was unable to convince enough voters, who had drifted to the mainstream parties, to cast their ballot for a rightist party. In the 2005 federal election, many protest voters, who might have voted for the DVU or another rightist party, shifted to the left and supported the new Left Party.PDS.[39] The DVU received more than 265,000 votes, constituting 0.6 percent of the total vote.

Program

The party's ideology is reflected in programmatic statements and brochures, issued especially during election campaigns and featured in Frey's weekly newspaper NZ (see Chapter 5). In 1993 the party adopted a new program, which contained few extremist concepts, but reflected a *völkisch* nationalism. For obvious reasons of survival, the party's adherence to the free and democratic basic order is emphasized. As is true of its rival, the NPD, the DVU program reflects a national revolutionary ideology espoused decades earlier by the NSDAP Strasser wing. For instance, the DVP program states that farmers and youth must be helped, the environment must be safeguarded, and popular initiatives and referenda must increasingly be used.[40] Such statements were obviously made to gain public legitimacy and to prevent, in vain, the *Verfassungsschutz* labeling the party as unconstitutional.

The DVU leaders want constitutional rights limited to German citizens and not extended to foreigners. Frey's newspaper prints numerous negative and tendentious stories about asylum seekers and Gypsies. A DVU Bremen legislator, reflecting such a nationalist and racist position, said in all seriousness in the legislative chamber: "Throw out the swindlers, the crooks, the criminals of multinational origin, the heroin Turks and cocaine Negroes, the Gypsy plunderers, the Polish smugglers and automobile racketeers. By tolerating them you are cultivating an anti-foreigner attitude."[41] The party's nationalist position is also reflected in its anti-EU stance, based on the claim that the EU limits Germany's sovereignty. According to the party, the German army should not be used in United Nations-sponsored blue helmet operations until Germany receives a permanent seat on the UN Security Council.

The DVU claims that the Nazi state's cruel excesses have been exaggerated and that from 1933 to 1945 the state had its strengths and weaknesses.

Germany was not guilty of starting World War Two but rather took military action against Poland in 1939 only as a result of Polish nationalist excesses. Moreover, the mass extermination of Jews did not take place. The DVU claims that the Allies were also responsible for grave crimes against Germans, such as the Allied "bombing holocaust." The party does not eschew covert anti-Semitism. It deplored Germany's then continuing reparations payments to Israel and criticized the numerous Holocaust museums in the United States. It also maintains, just like the NSDAP, that the role of women is to marry and bear children for the *Volk* and the nation. Homosexuality is frowned upon. Race is more important than class. But when class plays a role in political conflicts, the DVU is on the side of the employer community rather than the trade unions.

Frey did not hesitate to make contacts with right-wing leaders in other countries in order to increase his visibility and to exchange views on current international developments. He asked the Holocaust deniers David Irving and Robert Brock, an African-American anti-Semite, to many DVU conventions as guest speakers. In 1993 Frey invited Vladimir Zhirinovski, head of the ultra-nationalist Russian Liberal-Democratic Party, to be the honored guest in Passau at the DVU's convention, which at least 1,000 persons have attended yearly. In gratitude, Schirinovski hosted Frey in Moscow where the DVU leader pledged to support the Liberal-Democratic Party. In 1996 Frey invited the former Ku Klux Klan leader David Duke to the DVU convention. In 1998 Frey met Jean-Marie Le Pen, president of the French National Front. Frey's efforts to build up his party through these international contacts have not paid off. However, he was able to convince Schönhuber, the former Republikaner chief, to head the DVU list for the 1998 Bavarian Land election and to be the DVU candidate in a vacant Dresden seat in the 2005 national election.

As a consequence of his autocratic leadership style Frey alienated NPD and Republikaner officials. This situation will ease with Frey's sudden resignation as chairman in January 2009. He has been replaced by Matthias Faust, the 37-year-old Hamburg merchant. Faust had been a long-term CDU and Republikaner member, but DVU member only since 2007. The party's future remains uncertain.

National Democratic Party of Germany

After a spectacular beginning in the 1960s and a lengthy period of inactivity thereafter, the *Nationaldemokratische Partei Deutschlands* (NPD) since 1990 has been on the offensive in several Länder, even though it suffered a temporary decline in members. In 1990, it had 6,700 members but by 1996 it had shrunk to 3,500 members. As a result of a recruitment campaign among eastern German youth, especially in Saxony and Thuringia, the nationwide number of members rose to 7,200 in 2007, of whom about 40 percent were under 25 years old. According to party officials the rise in membership was a sign that the organization was not atrophying. An occupational classification shows that in 1993 workers comprised the largest group, 40–45 percent; small business entrepreneurs and pensioners, 15 percent each; salaried employees, 10 percent; students and apprentices 7.5 percent; and the self-employed 6.5 percent. Perhaps not surprisingly only 7.5 percent of members were women, although in the western Länder they totaled 15 percent of new members.[42]

Of the three major right-wing parties the NPD organization, headed by a chairperson, a presidium and a twenty-member executive, has been the most active since 2000. It has a network of regional and Länder branches, especially in Saxony, Bavaria, Thuringia, and North Rhine-Westphalia. Regional branches are inactive in most of the other Länder. As the party is under *Verfassungsschutz* surveillance, some of the east German local groups meet clandestinely in youth clubs and bars, and on most flyers use west German return addresses.

The NPD, just like other parties, seeks to recruit youth into its organization. It has been successful, as its members' average age stands at 37, a figure lower than any other party (the CDU's average is over 50).[43] As part of the strategy, NPD officials have made it easy for aspiring young leaders, including women, to move to the top in the party. In the early 1990s, the youth branch, the Young National Democrats (*Junge Nationaldemokraten*, JN), had 800–900 members. But by 2007 this number, for various reasons, was down to 400. The party maintains training and education centers where over the years 600 young members have been recruited as leadership cadres. The university affiliate, which issued a journal devoted to political theory and strategy, has had only 40–50 members. Not surprisingly, the JN, to maintain its own profile, has often taken a more radical stance in its programmatic statements and its public activities than the parent organization. The JN has neo-Nazis as top officials, some of whom drifted to it from banned neo-Nazi organizations. It also has cooperated with still existing neo-Nazi groups and local *Kameradschaften* ("comrade" gangs of right-wing toughs), and has organized or participated in neo-Nazi demonstrations.[44] With the closure of some *Kameradschaften*, many of their members have gravitated to the NPD. The JN has also convened a yearly "European Congress of Youth" that brings together 250–300 right-wing extremists from numerous countries. The NPD's ambitious goal, which has not yet been achieved, is to create a European nationalist unity front.

The party did not create a National Women's Division (*Ring Nationaler Frauen*) until September 2006. Its purpose has been to serve as a mouthpiece for the women in the party as well as for non-party women who sympathized with the NPD's goals. In many NPD demonstrations, especially in east Germany, female skinheads and young and older neo-Nazi women wearing either the latest fashions or staid dresses could be seen. The east German women, especially, have participated in the party's affairs, while in west Germany rightist women tend to stay home. Thus at the 1996 party convention, after prolonged discussions east German women forced through an updating of the program chapter on the family. Many female NPD members took issue with the strict anti-abortion provision, but concurred on other issues. One study showed that the more women join the party, the more the men will remain in the party after finding a partner within the NPD. In the past, the men left the party when they were looking for a partner and ready to start a family. When women joined the NPD a softening of the harsh vocabulary also took place.[45]

At least once a year the NPD schedules a party convention; in 2004 it took place under the motto "Work – Family – Fatherland." Intra-party democracy is lacking, despite protests from newer members. Delegates can hardly challenge the top leadership's key decisions. To gain new members and to keep members content, NPD leaders hold major rallies and demonstrations. Typical of these rallies was one held symbolically in the Nibelungen Hall in Passau in February 1998. As is true of any rally or demonstration, the town or city concerned has to give permission. Passau's SPD mayor had sought to forbid the rally, billed as the "Day of National Resistance." But two appellate courts, on NPD appeal, gave their permission. The courts argued that a sufficient police presence could maintain order. A record 4,000 right-wing extremists, most of them skinheads and neo-Nazi youth, attended. Having come from all parts of Germany by train and bus, they made their way through local streets festooned with posters reading "Right-wing extremists not welcome. Signed: The citizens of Passau city." However, in the hall, they felt more welcome. Flags with the German empire's national colors flew and banners reflected the party's ideology. One read "The organized will means power." The rally's official program booklet warned that the government posed great dangers to the German people. More specifically, the booklet accused the government of pursuing "patriots" (read NPD members). The booklet warned darkly that the people's soul was at stake, especially given the increasing number of foreigners. Hence the "day of national resistance" was at hand.[46] Top NPD leaders spoke as well as invited leaders from other neo-Nazi organizations. Among them was Manfred Roeder, who had been jailed for ten years for having founded a terrorist organization and who was a candidate for office in the eastern German city of Stralsund. For old-timers the rally, the atmosphere, and the slogans resembled Nazi-staged events during the Hitler era.

The party's membership dues comprise nearly one-third of its modest income, augmented by donations and public funds in the few instances in which the NPD received more than the minimum percentage of the vote in the preceding Land election. Much of this money goes to the party's employees, staff members, and publications. Despite income from the state, such as 600,000 euros a year for the NPD *Fraktion* in Mecklenburg-West Pomerania, national NPD officials declared in late 2006 that their organization faced a financial crisis and urged all members to donate 100 euros to the party. Those contributing were promised a "solidarity" T-shirt.

Among the party's publications, the *Deutsche Stimme* (German Voice) is the party's monthly journal, with a circulation in 2006 of 21,000. Not unexpectedly it features xenophobic and anti-Semitic articles. Normally once a year the journal holds a press rally that attracts thousands of neo-Nazis and has become one of the highlights of the rightist scene. Leading party officials and foreign neo-Nazis, such as David Duke from the United States, are the featured speakers. Rock bands provide entertainment.

The party's program, revised in December 1996, and strategy papers contain a mixture of nationalist and socialist ideas, as typified in the party's colors of black, white, and red. The documents implicitly call on all Germans to reject the existing democratic political and economic systems. This means abolishing the liberal capitalist system, including the large corporations and banks. Instead, the documents call for the creation of a new German Reich based on a national socialist system. Its political component would be based on a "people's community" (*Volksgemeinschaft*) with the people as the dominant force. However, individual rights would be subordinated to the people's community. Germany's economic system should be based on independent farmers and small and medium-sized crafts and industries, and only German firms could operate in the country. Banks, insurance companies, and big business would be nationalized. The NPD calls for high protective tariffs for German industry and Germany's withdrawal from the EU and the North Atlantic Treaty Organization (NATO) because these organizations protect the interests of "big capital." The United States is denounced for its imperialist policies. Similarly the NPD leaders, cleverly mirroring the German peace movement's critique, assailed the "imperialist NATO intervention in the Balkans." They maintained that no German blood should be shed for foreign interests.[47]

The NPD's emphasis on a socialist economy was designed largely to gain a foothold in the eastern German Länder among the local population that had supported the GDR's economic system.[48] The doctrine's nationalist component provided the framework for an aggressive xenophobia ("close the German borders to Polish and Czech workers"), racism, and anti-Semitism (in the western German city of Bochum, "stop the construction of the synagogue – give the 4 million [euros] to the people"). The NPD leaders have trivialized the Nazi crimes and rejected the Allied accusation that Germany was responsible for the outbreak of World War Two. The German attack on Poland in 1939 was purely for self-defense. World War Two began in earnest when France and Britain entered the war primarily to save "international capital," code words for alleged Jewish domination of the worldwide banking system. In November 2006, NPD leaders in Saxony created a "Dresden School" as a counter to the leftist Frankfurt School. The NPD School intended to establish a revisionist historical understanding among the population. It has also sought to erase the Allied instilled guilt complex held by many

Germans since 1945 for their support of the Nazi regime. But the School's contribution to intellectual discourse has been minimal.

Party leadership

In June 1991 NPD delegates elected Günter Deckert as the new chairman, succeeding Martin Mussgnug who was ready to dissolve the party because of its poor electoral support and declining membership. Deckert wanted to maintain the party intact. Born in Heidelberg in January 1940, he studied English and romance languages at two universities and became a high school teacher, but was fired eventually for his extremist statements in class. In 1966 he joined the NPD. From 1973 to 1975 he became Baden-Wuerttemberg's JN chairman and then the JN's national chairman. As a measure of his personal appeal, since 1975 he has been a city council member in his home town of Weinheim in Baden-Wuerttemberg. There he criticizes immigrants settling in the city. In 1982 he left the party when it became politically too moderate for him. But by 1991 he rejoined and was elected national chairman.

Deckert has made provocative nationalist revolutionary statements. This brought the party into the neo-Nazi orbit and created a haven for neo-Nazis, many of whom had been members of forbidden organizations. Typical of Deckert's *Weltanschauung* was his translation into German of a lecture by Fred Leuchter, the notorious American denier of gas chambers in concentration camps. Deckert also distributed a video on the same subject. In 1992 his illegal activities resulted in a one-year probation court sentence and a modest fine. In April 1995, a Land court in Karlsruhe sentenced him to a two-year jail sentence for hate statements, which he appealed. In June 1995, another court sentenced him to a six-week jail sentence for slandering Ignatz Bubis, president of the Central Council of Jews in Germany. In September 1995 a slim majority of NPD presidium members ousted Deckert as chairman for financial irregularities, making derogatory remarks against foreigners, and organizing meetings for neo-Nazis. They elected, for a brief transition period, Ellen-Doris Scherer, head of the NPD Land Saar organization, as the new national chairwoman. She pledged to work for a "modern nationalism" and to avoid the controversial themes raised by her predecessors. Yet she could not win over a minority of NPD officials, clustered in three eastern German Länder, who supported Deckert. They were ready to leave the NPD and form a new organization.[49]

In March 1996 party conference delegates elected Udo Voigt, a young university graduate, technocrat, and former Bundeswehr captain, as the new NPD chairman. Born in 1952 he belonged to the post-World War Two generation. He joined the NPD at the age of 16, thereafter working his way up in the party hierarchy. He intended to broaden the party's appeal among the citizenry by dealing with national economic and social issues rather than by revising history and glorifying Nazism. Yet on occasion he has said that Hitler was a great statesman who had eliminated unemployment within a few years of gaining power. In a period of rising unemployment and growing uncertainty about the pension system in contemporary Germany, he said that foreigners should be dropped from the social security rolls and that German citizens should receive priority in their job quest. Voigt and top NPD officials did not maintain their pledge to eschew extremism. They have continued to make racist remarks, to talk about German blood, to idealize the NSDAP and Hitler, and in closed rallies to denounce Jews, who do not belong in Germany. In public, these officials cover their anti-Semitism with anti-Zionist remarks. Among their foreign policy objectives, they insist that Germany should lay claim to its erstwhile territories in eastern Europe. Their letterhead showed a map of Hitler's Germany, accompanied by the inscription "Germany is bigger than the Federal Republic." In 1994, the government authorities took the NPD to court over the letterhead issue. The judges decided that the map and the message were unconstitutional and forbade the party to use them.[50]

Voigt has insisted that his party must lead the rightist movement within Germany because the Republikaner and the DVU have failed to assume a leadership role in their parliamentary work. The NPD can make this claim, he notes, because it is the home of the only authentic national party in Germany. The NPD must mobilize youth for a "national resistance" against the existing political system but must not promote violence. It must also be the rallying symbol for the numerous small rival groups that it should absorb.[51] Voigt, in a 2005 interview with a London *Times* reporter, praised Hitler for having been "a great statesman." As a result, he claims that the authorities tap his phone, intercept his e-mail, and film his public meetings.[52] During Voigt's years in power, his colleagues have been increasingly disposed to neo-Nazism. By 2007 they were sitting on the executive committees of eleven of the sixteen Länder branches. However, in 2008 and 2009 a leadership struggle has broken out, partly over serious accounting irregularities and embezzling of large funds, which in 2008 landed the party's treasurer in jail. The subsequent government-imposed fines have pushed the party to the brink of insolvency and may result in the crippling of the party. In 2009, Voigt's continued tenure as chairman hung in the balance as a result of the financial scandals and the normal leadership struggles. He was re-elected by a slim majority.[53]

Three-column strategy

The NPD follows a three-column strategy that encompasses the struggle on the street, the struggle for the people's minds, and the struggle for parliaments.[54] In the first category, it has organized numerous demonstrations in which thousands of members and sympathizers march annually in many cities and towns to mark events commemorating the Nazi past, such as Hitler's army entering Austria on March 12, 1938 or Hitler's deputy Rudolf Hess' day of suicide in Allied captivity on August 17, 1987.

NPD members and sympathizers have also marched and assembled in numerous German cities to protest the traveling German army (Wehrmacht) exhibition, which they labeled as shameful and pure propaganda designed to besmirch the image of the German soldier.[55] The exhibition was assembled by the historian Hannes Heer and other scholars at the Institute for Social Research, Hamburg University, with the financial backing of the Institute's head, Jan Philipp Reemtsa. The exhibition consisted of 1,400 photographs, documents, and letters. It was provocatively entitled "War of Extermination: Crimes of the Wehrmacht 1941 to 1944." The exhibition revealed that during World War Two German soldiers in Eastern Europe, the Balkans, and the Soviet Union had committed countless murders of Jews, other innocent civilians, and Russian prisoners of war. In March 1995 the exhibition opened in Hamburg and then toured in thirty-four German and Austrian cities where an estimated 850,000 people saw it. In protest, the NPD organized marches, with participants holding such signs as "My grandfather was not a criminal" and "Glory and honor for German soldiers." The marches, one held in the historic Berlin Jewish quarter, led to democratic groups organizing counter-marches. In March 1999, right-wing extremists planted a bomb in Saarbrücken to stop the exhibition. This was the culmination of a lengthy debate in the Bundestag and the media. The exhibition shattered the myth widely propagated by right-wing extremists and ultra-conservative CDU/CSU circles that only SS soldiers and extermination squads and East European right-extremist fanatics were the killers. The conservative politicians felt that the honor of the 18 million Wehrmacht soldiers had been smeared. To defuse the controversy ministers of defense forbade Bundeswehr soldiers from seeing the exhibition in uniform.

In 1999 conservative politicians succeeded in stopping the exhibition temporarily. Two foreign scholars had discovered errors in nine photo captions, such as those identifying German rather than Soviet soldiers who had committed massacres. The NPD boasted, falsely, that it was responsible for the exhibition's temporary closure. After an extensive examination of all photos, documents, and letters, and Reemtsa's firing of Heer as the exhibition's director, it was reopened, in a less accusatory form, in 2002.[56]

NPD members have also marched to engender support for their party during election campaigns and to protest the building of the Holocaust monument in Berlin. In recent years, NPD officials have given orders to the young marchers to be well-dressed and not to publicly smoke, drink, or wear Nazi emblems. The marchers are also expected to maintain strict discipline in the hope that such behavior would attract more youth, including skinheads, into the party and would gain the support of those ordinary citizens who can be expected to admire exemplary behavior among "reasonable" young people.

Despite such calls for order and discipline, NPD rallies often end up in confrontations between their own supporters, leftist hecklers, and the police whose primary function is to keep both sides apart. For instance, in September 1998, clashes were bound to occur at a giant rally in the eastern German city of Rostock. About 5,000 NPD members and sympathizers, 10,000 counter-demonstrators, and 6,000 police drawn from all of Germany were in attendance. In the march preceding the rally, ultra-left *Autonomen* members, who had come from several cities, threw stones and other missiles at the NPD supporters. During the melée 127 people were arrested. NPD organizers deliberately chose Rostock for the location of its chief rally prior to the Land election because six years earlier, in 1992, the city had been the center of major violence against asylum seekers (see Chapter 4).[57] NPD officials are not unhappy if the *Autonomen* resort to violence first, as is often the case. They can then picture their party as standing for law and order and the leftists as the "chaotic mob." Moreover, according to the NPD's calculation, the state it hates must protect the NPD's own marchers, who secretly do not mind seeing some action and thrills. Such a strategy often leads to new members joining the party.

Whether the NPD should be free to demonstrate and assemble has been the subject of heated debates in Germany. Those responding in the affirmative point to the need to expand and not limit civil liberties; those responding in the negative point to the NPD's anti-democratic goals. On numerous occasions, the NPD has not received permission from city authorities to stage a demonstration or rally because of the party's neo-Nazi ideology, fear of clashes with counter-demonstrators, or the symbolic target of the march. Then the NPD invariably seeks redress in court. Whether it wins or loses an appeal will depend on whether the judges see a threat to law and order. For instance, the NPD lost court appeals to march on May Day 1999 in Bremen, in a neighborhood settled primarily by foreigners. In this instance, the NPD, considering May Day as "the Day of National Work," had taken its appeal to the Federal Constitutional Court, but lost on legal grounds. On other occasions, courts have ruled that a proposed NPD parade route was unacceptable, but then gave the NPD permission to march in another, less provocative, area.

On January 29, 2000 the party received court permission to march through the historic Brandenburg Gate in Berlin. Five hundred of its members, waving the old imperial war flags and shouting "Germany for Germans" and "Here marches the national resistance," participated in a march that drew world attention for its symbolic value. The parallel to Hitler's parades through the Brandenburg Gate could not be forgotten. Similarly, in November 2001 NPD demonstrators received permission to march through Berlin's historic Jewish district. However, on that occasion, as a result of a Federal Constitutional Court decision, three of its leaders were forbidden to speak because of their past provocative utterances. In May 2005, to memorialize the sixtieth anniversary of the end of World War Two, up to 3,000 NPD members and sympathizers, waving placards reading "Sixty years liberation lie – an end to the cult of guilt" and wearing buttons "Celebrate surrender? No thank you" had planned to march from Berlin's Alexanderplatz to the Brandenburg

Gate. But they were hemmed in at the Alexanderplatz by even more counter-demonstrators, who prevented them from marching. After NPD leaders made a few provocative speeches, the police escorted the rightists back to the subways. The Canadian *Globe and Mail* commented aptly: "As if to assuage their 60-year-old guilt, the people of Berlin did yesterday what they did not do before the end of the Second World War. They stopped the Nazis in their tracks and drove them into a hole in the ground."[58] In the meantime, the government and democratic groups had organized at the Brandenburg Gate a "Day for democracy," including speakers, beer, and sausages.

In March 2005, two months prior to the Berlin confrontation, the Parliament had swiftly enacted legislation limiting the right of assembly as a measure to prevent rightists from marching near symbolic historic sites and permitting the jailing of protesters who glorified Hitler's Third Reich. In June 2007, prior to the meeting of world leaders at the G-8 Summit in Mecklenburg-West Pomerania, the NPD had intended to march in Schwerin while anti-global protesters received a permit to march in Rostock. But the Federal Constitutional Court denied permission at the last minute for the NPD to march. Thereupon NPD leaders swiftly organized illegal marches in numerous German cities, including one through the Brandenburg Gate in Berlin. They outfoxed the police who had not expected such marches and had concentrated their forces in Schwerin and Rostock.[59]

In the NPD's second strategy category, the party has had a mixed record in winning the struggle for the people's minds in its propaganda campaigns. Most German citizens reject the NPD propaganda's neo-Nazi content. Yet at the grassroots level such propaganda speaks to the concerns of the disaffected. To gain more members NPD activists hand out party leaflets in front of unemployment and registration offices, tidy up war memorials, sponsor local soccer teams, organize youth parties, and distribute toys to children on holidays. They try through such populist measures to be on a good footing with small town officials – and are often successful.

The NPD propaganda assumes different forms. In imitation of the democratic parties, the NPD, especially at election time, has opened information stands that are staffed by its members. At rallies and in right-extremist stores party members and sympathizers sell maps showing Germany's 1937 boundaries, including the territories lost in 1945. The maps have a sword across them with the words: "The Reich, our Mission." The shop owners also sell sweatshirts, T-shirts, and blazers emblazoned with the number "88." The eighth letter of the alphabet is "H." Thus "HH" stands for "Heil Hitler," the Nazi greeting forbidden to be used publicly since Germany's capitulation in 1945. A not so subtle anti-Semitism can be seen in the party newspaper, *Deutsche Stimme*. One issue declared that "The Torah is the original document of Jewish hatred of (other) nations."[60]

In eastern Germany, Voigt emphasizes the socialist or Bolshevik component of the party's national-socialist demands as a way to link the present with the GDR's past. Provocatively, he has scheduled rallies on May 1, the socialist and labor holiday. He has also sought to capitalize on nostalgia for a number of GDR socialist programs, such as day-care centers for all children. NPD leaders in the eastern Länder have wooed former GDR officials and praised the GDR as having been more German than the FRG. Such a policy had an unexpected result. In March 1999, in Mecklenburg-West Pomerania half of the 600 members left the NPD and founded, rather surprisingly, a "Socialist People's Party," which sympathized with North Korea and China. Such a leftist radicalization of the party produced an outcry among western German NPD chiefs who had no sympathy for nationalist leftist groups. They would have sympathized more with an NPD secessionist group in Thuringia (eastern Germany) that labeled itself the League of German Patriots.[61] Michael Nier, one of the NPD theorists, said that eastern Germany has become "a mere colony of American financial capital, a place that has lost all identity. Every upstanding German should stand up and fight this."[62]

The NPD's third strategy emphasizing electoral activities has had mixed results. The party's record in national, state, and local elections has varied considerably from one election to another, but with few exceptions has remained poor. In the December 1990 national election, the party could not muster more than 0.3 percent of the vote in western Germany and 0.2 percent in eastern Germany. As a result of its poor showing, NPD officials decided not to enter candidates in the 1994 election. In more recent federal elections the party mustered less than 2 percent of the total vote. However, in the 2005 election, nearly every tenth eastern German voter between the ages of 18 and 24 cast their ballot for the NPD. In local elections the NPD has won some seats in town councils, especially in eastern Germany. As has been true of the Republikaner and the DVU, the NPD receives proportionately more votes in local and Land than Bundestag elections. Protest voters are more apt to express their dissatisfaction in the local and Land elections where the stakes are lower than in national contests. Knowing that the parliamentary strategy cannot produce many victories, the NPD has opted for the slow route of gathering more members and sympathizers by emphasizing social justice issues, thereby competing with the new Left Party.PDS (renamed Left Party in June 2007).

A ban of the NPD?

In 2000, the party's swift radicalization and the increasing number of violent incidents against foreigners led government officials to discuss the question whether they should petition the Federal Constitutional Court to ban the NPD. In the 1950s the Court had declared the rightist SRP and the Communist Party unconstitutional for having violated the Basic Law. On August 1, 2000, the CSU Bavarian Minister of the Interior, Günther Beckstein, requested the SPD-Greens federal government to take a similar step. Even though there were good reasons to ban the NPD, Beckstein's position was politically motivated.

He sought to put the federal government on the defensive, knowing that many of its officials opposed a ban. He also worried that an activist NPD might attract ultra-conservative CSU members.[63]

In Berlin the initial government reaction was mixed. Some officials said that the government should reject the request because civil society, rather than the government, should organize resistance against the NPD. However, in early August the federal and Länder interior ministries decided to form a working group of specialists to look into the legal question and to gather evidence that the NPD had indeed violated the Basic Law's provisions. By then Chancellor Gerhard Schröder sympathized with a party ban if the interior ministries working group, the federal government, and the Parliament agreed. Lower Saxony ministers in the Upper House (Bundesrat), in sympathy with their Bavarian colleague, announced their backing for an NPD ban. In the meantime the working group members, except for Hesse and the Saar, declared their support.

The ban's proponents said that the democratic system must be maintained in the face of the serious NPD challenge. They pointed to an August 2000 poll showing that the public supported the government's case: 65 percent of respondents favored an NPD ban and 29 percent opposed it.[64] Federal Minister of the Interior Otto Schily (SPD) contended that banning the party was essential because it was as dangerous as Hitler's embryonic Nazi movement in 1923, a decade before the Nazis came to power. Schily said: "In a country where there were gas chambers for the extermination of millions of Jews, it is impossible to tolerate organized anti-Semitism."[65] The ban's proponents stated that an NPD ban would end the public campaign funds that the party had received, for instance of DM 1.1 million in 1999. They also said that the government's credibility and image abroad was at stake.

The ban's opponents pointed out that they saw no convincing reason to restrict the right of expression to any political party. A ban merely provides free publicity to the NPD whose members would gravitate towards another rightist party or group. If the members were to go underground, it would be more difficult for the authorities to find them. Thus a ban was not the solution to solve the basic problem of entrenched right-wing extremism and rising racism in the country. Roland Koch, CDU Minister-President of Hesse, said: "We can be more effective in winning hearts and minds by not using constitutional bans on parties."[66] In early November 2000, the Bundestag deputies had a chance to read a short report on the NPD that the Ministry of the Interior had compiled. The report contained a list of criminal offenses that NPD functionaries had committed, references to their anti-democratic statements, and documentary evidence of their willingness to work with rightist *Kameradschaften* that espoused the use of force. In response to the report, the FDP chairman Guido Westerwelle announced that the evidence of NPD guilt was based on insufficient proof. Thus the FDP would continue to oppose a ban, which could lead to greater support for the NPD. The Greens, then in the governing coalition with the SPD, were divided. The ban's opponents feared that should the Court decide not to ban the NPD, the ruling could be misrepresented as a stamp of approval for the party. Others said that the *Verfassungsschutz* reports on the NPD had not cited instances where it had advocated the destruction of the democratic republic. Still others said a ban would run counter to the spirit of a parliamentary democracy in which all parties should be able to organize. One of the Greens' deputies averred that a ban would only increase the NPD's visibility and would not end the violence that NPD members had committed.

Despite these anti-ban views, the cabinet on November 8 decided in the first round of deliberations that the government should petition the Federal Constitutional Court for a ban. It confirmed its decision on January 30, 2001, after having heard from the *Verfassungsschutz* President Heinz Fromm (SPD). He said that his office had sufficient evidence for the Court to find the NPD guilty. According to Fromm, the NPD rejected the Basic Law's guarantee of individual freedoms by espousing a national and racial collectivism. In short, the NPD program and propaganda were replete with anti-Semitic and racist statements, which had a close relationship to National Socialism.[67]

Prior to the final cabinet decision, a majority of Bundesrat members decided to petition the Court to ban the NPD. The Bundesrat rested its case on NPD activities in the Länder and the NPD's linkage to neo-Nazi and skin-head groups, which were committing acts of violence against foreigners and Jews. On December 8 the Bundestag made a similar recommendation to the Court. The government and parliamentary recommendations were bolstered by the submission of seventy-four pages of evidence, winnowed down from a 560-page secret dossier, plus several hundred documents, many of which highlighted the similarity between the NPD and Hitler's NSDAP.

Once the Court received the petitions and the evidence against the NPD, the party prepared its legal defense. Its chief lawyer, Horst Mahler, handed the Court the 388-page NPD response to the government and to the Parliament petitions and documentation. Incidentally, Mahler had been a founder of the left terrorist Red Army Faction and served ten years in prison. He later shifted to the extreme right, becoming for a few years an NPD member. In the NPD documentation, he quotes the remarks of former Chancellor Helmut Schmidt (SPD), who for a time opposed more foreigners immigrating to Germany. He also cites the views of other mainstream politicians to indicate that the NPD position against more foreigners coming to Germany is shared by the masses and by the establishment parties, which have warned that further immigration will lead to violence. Mahler weakened his case when he alluded to a Jewish-American world dominance that continues to wage a battle against the German people – arguments that Hitler and the NSDAP had made decades earlier. He also accused the German government of advocating a multiethnic society that will lead to the end of the German race. He called for a national revolution in the country.[68] Parallel to Mahler's response to the Court, NPD chairman Voigt ordered his staff to cleanse the party's web pages of materials that the Court might find incriminating. He also requested party members to look less aggressive and to wear ordinary clothing. He ordered a temporary end to demonstrations.

In February 2002, one year after the Court received the petitions from both sides, it invited NPD officials to appear for oral hearings. The case was suddenly postponed when it became known that the government had often relied on information provided by at least two dozen *Verfassungsschutz* agents who had infiltrated the party and who had become active in neo-Nazi groups as *agents provocateurs* rather than as passive observers.

In the government petitions, the agents' statements, among others, were used as evidence for the NPD's aggressive position against the Basic Law. Minister Schily defended the use of agents because they revealed much valuable information, including statements reflecting the party's position on key issues. In response, Mahler said the court must stop the proceedings because the agents had influenced the party ideology. In the meantime the government revealed that 30 of 200 NPD functionaries in national and Länder headquarters, including North-Rhine Westphalia chairman Udo Holtmann, had been well-paid intelligence agents. Mahler contended that at least two of them, whom he characterized as *agents provocateurs*, had been influential in setting national party policy. Other agents organized NPD marches. Independent observers contended that by using agents the government had strengthened rather than weakened the party. NPD officials said that this was an absurd affair. They accused the *Verfassungsschutz* of steering the party from the outside, creating a false image of the NPD, and using it as a scapegoat against rightists. In reply, one Bundestag deputy said that the NPD's hostility to the Basic Law was evident in its program, speeches, and publications, even without quotations from agents who had infiltrated the party.[69] Within the NPD, an angry minority unsuccessfully sought to oust the top NPD leadership for knowingly allowing the agents to stay in the party.

In March 2003, the Court, obviously angered by the Ministry of the Interior's gaffe, stopped the proceedings. It said that the state's evidence was tainted by using informants who had gathered intelligence on the party, who had an opportunity to influence its policies, and who had strengthened it. The presiding judge, Winfried Hassemer, said that the government's case had been compromised by its use of agents who created "a lack of clarity that can no longer be overcome." In effect the Court, concurring with Mahler's legal arguments, felt the government had duped it. The Court's decision ended a two-year government campaign to ban the party. Schily expressed regret at the ruling, which had not been unanimous.[70] The government had suffered a major defeat. It would have to seek other ways to combat the NPD, which it still characterized as the most active and dangerous right-extremist organization. The NPD celebrated the end of Court proceedings as a major victory.

The episode reopened the question of how best to fight a neo-Nazi party. The option to ban it turned out to be a failure. Most likely the option will not be used again, although some SPD politicians have called for a ban. Other politicians and academics, with some logic, said that it would suffice to observe and analyze such a radical party by establishing a public scientific documentation center, through which intelligence agencies could gather most of the available data. The ban's opponents contended that the use of well-paid covert government agents, who supported the NPD programmatically and financially, only strengthened it by their membership. The opponents also said that there must be greater parliamentary control of intelligence activities.[71]

Saxony elections of 2004

The NPD was buoyed by the Court decision and by its growing strength in eastern Germany where it embarked on a right-populist course. It participated in weekly marches that unionists, the PDS, and leftists had organized to denounce government cutbacks in social welfare made under the government's Agenda 2010 and Hartz IV programs.[72] The march organizers were not happy about the uninvited right-extremist guests.

The NPD's strength in Saxony was the result not only of economic and social factors but of a successful membership recruitment campaign among youth, many of whom were unemployed. Few women became members, partly because of the party's macho atmosphere and partly because a number of the women, more mobile than the men, had resettled in western Germany. The NPD, as a result of its recruitment effort under the tutelage of the party's deputy chairman Holger Apfel, had 1,200 members in Saxony, the highest number in any Land.

In June 2004 the NPD fared well in local and regional Saxony elections. In the picturesque Saxon Switzerland, located near the Czech border, and the Erzgebirge areas, the NPD received seats in twenty-two out of twenty-seven local councils. In Dresden, the capital city, it headed a "National Coalition" of rival rightist parties' candidates who, just like the leftist PDS, protested the dismantling of the social welfare state. The rightists captured more than 4 percent of the vote to gain three seats in the city council.[73] In September 2008 they introduced a resolution commemorating the September 11, 2001 "terrorist" attack on the World Trade Center in New York and other US targets. In this instance they won the support of CDU and Left councilors, assuring passage of the resolution.

The NPD's surging strength was most evident in the Saxony Landtag election of September 2004. This was partly the result of the already cited agreement made in June with the DVU that it would not put up candidates in Saxony while the NPD pledged to do the same in the Brandenburg Landtag election. Prior to the Saxony vote, Minister-President Georg Milbradt (CDU) sent out a mailing to all households warning voters of the negative economic consequences of an NPD success. He implied that the tourist industry and US foreign investments would suffer. Other democratic groups called on voters not to support the NPD.

Nevertheless, the party scored a spectacular victory in Saxony. It gained 9.2 percent of the vote or the support of 190,000 voters. As a result the party had twelve deputies in Saxony's Landtag, its first representation in any Land election since 1968. Once again, the party's strength lay in Saxon Switzerland. There 18 percent unemployment produces disillusionment with the established parties for not solving economic and social problems and for cutting unemployment benefits. The NPD had assiduously built up a local base in numerous towns and cities, which, for instance, resulted in a vote of nearly 20 percent in the town of Königstein. As a result, the town's mayor feared that tourists, worried about rightist violence, would not come. In the wake of the NPD vote, Edmund Stoiber, then the conservative CSU minister-president of Bavaria, made political capital out of the electoral result. He accused Chancellor Schröder of failing to reduce unemployment, thereby driving voters into the NPD's arms.

In the Saxony legislature, deputies from the democratic parties have ostracized the well-dressed and polite NPD deputies, who are mostly in their thirties. However, several CDU deputies voted with the NPD in two secret votes on legislative bills. Whenever the NPD legislators speak on the floor, the Greens deputies turn their backs to them. No democratic party representatives will eat with them in the parliamentary canteen. The NPD deputies have been involved in several controversies since the election. In January 2005 they walked out of the chamber when other legislators commemorated the sixtieth anniversary of the Auschwitz death camp liberation with a one-minute silence for its victims. NPD Land and *Fraktion* chief Holger Apfel said that the party deputies had walked out because the Landtag had no plans to mark a few weeks later the Allied "bombing Holocaust" of Dresden. The party issued a statement equating Auschwitz with abortion. On its website it said: "Since the end of Auschwitz, 18 million unborn people have been murdered in Germany ... is Auschwitz really over?"[74]

In February 2005, the NPD organized a public "funeral march" to memorialize the death of at least 35,000 Germans killed during the British and American bombers' "terror" attack on Dresden in February 1945, close to the war's end. The march was attended by 5,000–6,000 NPD demonstrators and sympathizers, many waving black flags. The NPD Saxony deputies joined the march. Among the speakers was Apfel, who characterized the Allied attack as an "act of gangster politics" and a "bombing Holocaust of Germans."[75] Peter Marx, the NPD's chief whip in the *Fraktion*, a lawyer, and one of the party's leading ideologues, insisted that there had been no military need for the bombing. He said that any talk of the Germans' war crimes needs to be balanced by the Allied war crimes committed against the Germans; young Germans are fed up with being told that they are guilty of war crimes.

Democratic leaders called on concerned citizens to take to the Dresden streets in a counter-march to denounce the NPD demonstrators. The democrats held up signs with the slogan "This city is sick of Nazis." Chancellor Schröder remarked in Berlin: "Sixty years after the end of the war we are seeing attempts by a small minority to take this instance of human suffering out of its historical context and to instrumentalize it. We will do everything we can to oppose these attempts to falsify history. We will not allow cause and effect to be reversed."[76]

In response, NPD leader Marx complained that FRG President Horst Köhler had attended events commemorating the Auschwitz liberation and forty years of cordial relations between Germany and Israel. Marx asked whether there was only selective memory: "Does the younger generation have to be collectively responsible for the past? This sense of guilt creates a sense of inferiority."[77] Such provocative comments resonated with a segment of the public.

Some NPD critics, such as an official from the Central Council of Jews in Germany, demanded anew that the Federal Constitutional Court should ban the NPD, but the CDU minister-president of Land Saxony, Georg Milbradt, among others, argued against a ban. He warned against reacting in a "Pavlovian" way to everything the NPD does. The party, he said, would exploit such a ban. More important is to lower unemployment and to address the question of how jobs are lost to German companies building plants in Eastern Europe where costs are lower.[78] Many minister-presidents also opposed a ban because they did not want to withdraw their agents working within the NPD. In the meantime the NPD *Fraktion* in the Saxony Landtag had shrunk from twelve to eight deputies as one died in an automobile accident, two members resigned from the *Fraktion*, and another was ousted by the party for financial irregularities rather than for his public support of Hitler.

Despite such problems, the NPD scored well in the June 2008 municipal elections in Saxony. The party received 160,000 votes, a 400 percent increase from the votes amassed in the 2004 municipal election. As a result, the party won seats in every county council in Saxony. In two counties, the NPD received more votes than the SPD.

Mecklenburg-West Pomerania election, 2006

The topic of a renewed NPD ban arose again in the wake of another Land election in eastern Germany. On September 17, 2006, the NPD gained 7.3 percent of the vote in Mecklenburg-West Pomerania, thereby capturing six seats in the 71-seat Land parliament. Reflecting a lack of party loyalty, about a quarter of the NPD votes came from citizens who had voted for the SPD or the Left Party. PDS in the previous election, and another half of the votes came from former CDU voters or non-voters. This NPD victory, in an economically deprived Land that adjoined Poland, embarrassed Chancellor Angela Merkel (CDU) who grew up in Mecklenburg-West Pomerania and who began her political career there fifteen years earlier. At Land election time, she headed a ten-month-old national coalition government with the SPD in Berlin. The national government's failure to reduce the almost 20 percent unemployment in eastern Germany, its infighting, its tax hike, and its failure to deliver promised reforms produced much popular discontent. As a result, in the Mecklenburg-West Pomerania election, the SPD, which had led a coalition government with the Left Party. PDS, lost ten seats.

After the election, tourist officials were worried that in a Land heavily dependent on an influx of summer visitors, the economy, with its 160,000 unemployed, would suffer even more should tourists stay away. These tourists might fear that the NPD would pursue its violent course against foreigners. The NPD's election posters, "Tourists welcome, asylum-swindlers out" and "Work first for Germans" presaged possible NPD clashes with foreigners on the Baltic Sea island of Usedom, the chief destination for summer tourists.

Many rural residents and 18–24-year-old youth, of whom 70 percent were unemployed, voted for the NPD. It had plastered the Land with election banners calling on citizens to "Defend Yourself." The residents signaled their dissatisfaction with the status quo and the "arrogant" establishment parties that "have done nothing." Other residents, often the women and the well-educated, have left the area to seek employment in western Germany or in neighboring countries. Remaining are young and less educated men and the older residents, many of whom voted for the NPD or stayed at home on election day.[79] The older voters were especially worried about the government freezing pensions and raising the retirement age from 65 to 67. According to one opinion survey of NPD voters, 80 percent of respondents said that they had voted for the NPD because of their disappointment with the mainstream parties rather than as an ideological commitment. Astonishingly, in eight villages, most of them located in the economically depressed area of Pomerania, the NPD became numerically the strongest party. It gained between 24 and 38 percent of the vote, repeating successes in earlier local elections.[80]

In reaction to the NPD victory, hundreds of anti-Nazi citizens marched in mourning in the capital city of Schwerin. Minister-President Harald Ringstorff (SPD) said that the NPD vote was a disaster for his Land. Hubertus Heil, the SPD's national secretary-general, compared the NPD's campaigners to brown-shirted thugs in the paramilitary SA during the Nazi period. He accused them of intimidating mainstream party members and of using violence. Peter Struck, SPD Bundestag *Fraktion* chairman, said that the government should take further measures against the NPD, such as checking on its finances. He favored a ban on the party if it appeared likely to succeed. Christian Wulff, the CDU minister-president in neighboring Lower Saxony, asserted that "In view of German history, this is a disaster."[81] Gideon Botsch, on the staff of the Moses Mendelssohn Center for European-Jewish Studies at the University of Potsdam, contended that the NPD's close alliance with the neo-Nazi Free Comradeship Groups (see Chapter 4) produced much of the violence.

Toralf Staud, a specialist on right-wing movements, said that the NPD successfully projected an image of the nice Nazi from next door who has become an integral part of civil society and who has launched civic programs for children and youth. Much of the NPD's success was due to the absence or closing of democratic structures, such as religious communities, schools, and clinics. The NPD ran a successful election campaign in areas where the democratic parties had given up and where the NPD officials became involved in citizens' initiatives, parent councils in schools, youth groups, and the organization of concerts. The NPD officials backed the opening of low-enrollment rural schools, which the mainstream parties had not supported. The NPD deputies decided to open citizens' bureaus in order to develop a close link to the population.

Udo Pastoers, who owned a clock and jewelry shop and who heads the NPD *Fraktion*, said, "We will not be a protest party. We will be an opposition party. We are going to lead a tough opposition because for the last few years, they have all been asleep in the parliament here."[82] Such a statement had a kernel of truth to it, even though it came from a man who had been sorry that an Adolf Hitler was only born every thousand years. Pastoers made headlines when he opened the first citizens' information office in his small town of Lübtheen.

No doubt, the governing parties, SPD and Left Party. PDS, in Mecklenburg-West Pomerania had failed to address some Land and local problems and were being punished by the voters. If these parties were to regain the voters' confidence they would have to pour more financial and personnel resources into economically weak regions. The Mecklenburg-West Pomerania 2006 election was the fourth one in eastern Germany in which rightist deputies had captured seats. As noted, the DVU had gained parliamentary representation in Brandenburg and in Saxony-Anhalt, and the NPD in Saxony. On the day of the Mecklenburg-West Pomerania election, the NPD amassed sufficient votes in Berlin to gain seats in four of the city's twelve local councils. But the party failed to win enough votes to gain seats in Berlin's Land assembly.

The party's future course will partly be shaped by the success that its chairman Voigt achieves in his goal to form an alliance of all rightist parties, dubbed "Popular Front of the Right." Such an alliance is unlikely in the near future, however, given personal rivalries and Voigt's intention to recruit leaders of the radical right *Freie Kameradschaften* into top NPD positions. As many of the *Kameradschaften* members are militant neo-Nazi fighters, most Republikaner or DVU members would not welcome their presence in the NPD.[83]

Although a merger of the three parties is most unlikely, despite a Stuttgart Declaration signed by their representatives in February 2005, electoral alliances have taken place on occasion. Thus in October 2004 NPD and DVU leaders decided in a Germany Pact not to run candidates against each other in the projected European Parliament and Bundestag elections. The NPD was to field candidates of both parties in the Bundestag election and the DVU in the European Parliament election. Although the 2006 Bundestag election took place already in September 2005, none of the rightist parties were able to gain enough votes to win a seat. Yet by gaining more than 0.5 percent of the votes they were able to receive some public financing. Such funds were desperately needed when the NPD's national treasurer Erwin Kemna was arrested in February 2008 on suspicion of embezzling $913,500 for private use. At the same time the Bundestag demanded that the NPD repay over $1 million for false filings for public financing. The future of the party hung in the balance, especially when the party's top leaders were openly feuding.[84] Hajo Funke, a political scientist at Berlin's Free University, said in May 2008: "This milieu, this scene is not broken. It's a smoldering fire underground that always breaks out again."[85] He noted that the NPD could become a collection of isolated nationalists or the hub of a dangerous rightist scene.

Conclusion

This survey of the rightist parties in Germany indicates that especially since the late 1980s they have been able to attract enough votes in several Länder elections to gain a minimum of parliamentary seats. In most of these instances they have not been able to repeat their success in the following legislative period. Thus the cycle of a few significant gains and numerous losses in any one Land marks the three rightist parties' electoral record. They achieved a modicum of success when the degree of popular dissatisfaction with government policies, especially on immigration and employment, rose. Then, one of the three right-wing parties fielding candidates in a Land legislature might win seats. But even gaining such seats did not ensure that the few policy statements made by the rightist deputies would carry any weight with the other deputies, except possibly on immigration issues.

Republikaner leaders, especially, have sought to unite all rightist parties into one new party in order to increase their electoral chances. In the mid-1990s a few round-table meetings between the parties took place, but the Republikaner chiefs have been wary of associating too closely with the far right NPD and DVU. In addition, personal rivalries and turf wars between the parties make it unlikely that a new single rightist party will be founded in the coming years. However, the NPD and DVU agreement in 2004 and 2005 to support each other's slates could be the first step in an eventual unification of the two parties. But it is doubtful that that will happen until the NPD becomes less fanatic.

In the meantime the rightist parties have continued to push their legislative agenda. In 2005 they had 313 politicians serving in local councils where they had varying degrees of influence.[86] Since 1990, the rightist parties gained votes and legislative seats in some Land elections. One 2004 survey indicated that in fourteen years (1990–2004) there were sixty-eight Land, federal, and EU Parliament elections in Germany. The three rightist parties managed to surmount the minimum 5 percent barrier only eight times.[87] In the 2005 federal election, the three rightist parties mustered 1 million votes, which seems high, yet accounts for only a fraction of the nearly 48 million votes cast. Most of the time legislative representation in a Land was not repeated, indicating volatility in the voting for rightist parties. In recent years, eastern German voters gave more electoral support to these parties than western German voters. This demonstrated dissatisfaction with the ruling elite in national and eastern German Länder politics, especially concerning job losses and immigration policies. A key item in the right extremist parties' propaganda and in their deputies' speeches in the Land legislatures has been the danger of allowing too many foreigners and asylum seekers into the country. Their warnings have not been in vain as polls show significant support for their position. Among the three rightist parties, the NPD, with its glorification of Nazi ideology, has emerged as the most dangerous and aggressive in its actions.

4
Neo-Nazi Groups, Skinheads, and Violence

As noted in Chapter 3, right-extremist parties have not played any significant role in national politics and only a minor role in Länder politics since German unification in 1990. While leaders of right-wing parties have held seats in Land parliaments and city and town councils, their contributions to political discourse have been minimal. However, on the immigration question, they have reinforced or reflected an anti-foreigner bias among a significant segment of the population. We must now assess the role played by the neo-Nazi groups and the skinheads to complement the study of the three major right-wing parties. In the 1990s, the government's ban of many neo-Nazi groups that had openly operated in western and eastern Germany, as well as the jailing of neo-Nazis and skinheads, must be evaluated. As will be noted, the ban did not mean an end to the formation of new groups. These groups, partly forming the social base of the parties and partly separate from the parties, were again involved in violence against their traditional disadvantaged enemies – the dark-skinned foreigners, leftists, gays, homeless, and Gypsies. The new groups were small and more loosely organized than their predecessors, partly in response to the infiltration of government undercover agents. But in both instances they received significant support from conservative citizens. The causes for this support must be assessed to see why right-wing forces feel confident of eventual victory.

To understand the right-wing movement since 1990, we must turn first to the neo-Nazi groups and skinheads, including the role of women in the movement. Then we assess the numerous outbreaks of right-wing violence committed by individuals and groups, especially in eastern Germany. Given the country's Nazi past, many criminal acts have received wide publicity beyond its borders and have had an effect on its image, economy, and tourism.

A splintered movement

The number of neo-Nazi organizations has varied from year to year and declined significantly when the government banned a number of them in the 1990s. According to the Federal Ministry of the Interior, in 1990, in eastern Germany, there were about 1,500 right radical activists and 10,000 sympathizers. The activists embarked one year later on an unprecedented wave of violence primarily against dark-skinned foreigners. By 1992, the number of right-wing individuals had climbed to 2,000 activists and 15,000 sympathizers. At the end of 1992 there were eighty-five neo-Nazi organizations, including the three right-wing parties. They had 41,900 members, of whom 6,400 were militant right-wing extremists, including skinheads. Among these extremists, 3,800 lived in eastern Germany and 2,600 in western Germany. There were also 1,200 organized neo-Nazis who were non-violent and 800 neo-Nazis who did not belong to any organization or who had belonged to an illegal organization.[1]

By the mid-1990s, about thirty neo-Nazi organizations were active, in each case ranging in membership from a few to several hundred. Most members were under 30 years old. Some of the *Kameradschaften* (see below) have even attempted to recruit 10–16-year-old males. In the decade from 1997 to 2007 the total number of members in the 110 surviving neo-Nazi groups rose from 2,400 to 4,800, a far lower number than the 21,500 members in the three major right-wing political parties.[2] In the neo-Nazi groups, the number of women members was less than 10 percent, and most of them played the traditional role of supporting the men. The groups received much of their income from membership dues and contributions. Ingo Hasselbach, a founder of the National Alternative party, revealed in his book that West German doctors, lawyers, and other professionals provided financial support to his group, which also received money from the media in exchange for interview and photo opportunities. In addition to the neo-Nazi group members, there were an estimated 10,000 violent unaffiliated neo-Nazis and skinheads, living mostly in eastern Germany. In 2008, according to official figures, they were involved in nearly 20,000 incidents, a significant rise over 2007. The number of violent attacks increased in 2008 to 639 and the incidents of anti-Semitism rose to 797.[3]

The neo-Nazi groups have political aims and pursue strategies that hardly differ from each other. They have displayed contempt for the Federal Republic's democratic system because it is seen as degenerate and corrupt. They have opposed ethnic pluralism and rejected independent civic institutions. Instead they have talked about "Germany for Germans" and espoused totalitarian values. They would not hesitate to support a new Führer who would be capable of uniting the plethora of rival neo-Nazi groups. In foreign policy, they have opposed a stronger European Union because it would narrow Germany's sovereignty. They have clamored for a restoration of lost territories in eastern Europe.[4] Some of them have been attracted to the radical ideas expressed decades earlier by the NSDAP's left nationalist or SA wing under the leadership of Gregor Strasser, Otto Strasser, and Ernst Röhm.

To achieve their goals, at times contradictory, a few neo-Nazi leaders have openly asserted that extra-legal means will have to be taken to gain power. In August 1993, Christian Worch, the prominent head of the neo-Nazi National List, asserted "I do not believe in the parliamentary process, but rather in a national movement from below. I do not think that we will come to power through the parliament, as in 1933. People right now are hit by the economic crisis. They are screaming and in their desperation turn on foreigners. We will achieve power only when Germany becomes ungovernable."[5]

A neo-Nazi leader in Chemnitz, who preferred to remain anonymous, told a foreign reporter: "People here have no jobs and no hope, and meanwhile our government is giving money to foreigners for nothing. It's time to stand up for Germany. We're going to clean up this country. No foreigners, no filth, no drugs, no pornography, and work for everyone. Germany is going to be great again."[6] Left unsaid was the popular resentment against a western German dominated central government that in 1990 forced a quick unification process. As a result, eastern German youth no longer had the certainty of gaining jobs in a chosen profession and of receiving full social protection that existed under the GDR regime. They felt disoriented and overwhelmed, and blamed primarily the few foreigners in their midst for their problems. Although the GDR had provided jobs for all, they looked to the Hitler regime as their model for a state that would provide full employment.

Given the serious economic and social problems in the former GDR, it is no wonder that 40–50 percent of right-wing supporters were found in eastern Germany. They joined neo-Nazi or skinhead groups in the early 1990s because they had many grievances against a political system that could not resolve them satisfactorily. For similar reasons much of the right-wing violence took place in eastern Germany, despite the region's much lower population size and the few foreigners. Often the violence, fueled by boredom and drinking, stemmed from the skinheads rather than the neo-Nazis. To achieve a new order the latter often preferred peaceful actions because they did not want to be subject to incarceration or to lose the sympathy of potential members.

Comparable to the often feuding right-extremist political parties, a number of competing neo-Nazi groups existed, which weakened the movement. The chief reason for the competition was that local leaders were striving for power at the national level but could not gain the support of rival groups. A brief examination of the most important groups shows the diversity in the movement.

The Free German Workers' Party (FAP)

As described in Chapter 2, the FAP, founded in 1979, cleaved to a neo-Nazi philosophy. Although it fielded candidates for some elections, it never showed any voting strength. Martin Pape, the founder, began to lose influence among his erstwhile followers as the FAP restricted its organization after

1990 to Baden-Wuerttemberg, North Rhine-Westphalia, and Lower Saxony. Politically isolated, Pape quit the FAP and in 1990 founded a new organization. Friedhelm Busse took over as FAP chairman. In 1992 the FAP gained new members in eastern Germany where it worked with numerous local groups and skinheads. The group even gained some recruits among skinheads. In 1993, it claimed 996 members, of whom 518 were active. Federal authorities viewed these totals as highly exaggerated.[7]

A membership analysis indicates that as many new members, mostly male, resided in eastern Germany as in western Germany. In eastern Germany only 8 percent of the new members were women; in western Germany the corresponding figure was 13 percent. Workers were well represented among the new members, totaling 48 percent in western Germany and 69 percent in eastern Germany. Among the other new young members, many were pupils and apprentices; only one was a university student.[8]

Members committed numerous acts of violence. In January 1994, fifteen FAP activists in the small Rhineland town of Rheinbach pounced on a group of leftist youngsters on the central square, who then fled into a bar. The FAP members pursued them into the bar, fired tear gas, and shot wildly with their pistols. The youngsters fled in panic through the emergency exit. The police eventually arrested the FAP Bonn district chairman. On another occasion, in Munich, Busse was set upon and severely beaten by militant anti-fascists. He had to be hospitalized. In May 2001, at an NPD demonstration in Essen, Busse declared, "Once Germany is free of Jews, then we do not need Auschwitz any more."[9] The judges, in sentencing Busse to prison, said that he was promoting hate toward Jewish co-citizens and thereby endangering the public peace.

Within the movement Busse had made enough enemies that many former members viewed him as a caricature of a right-wing leader. For instance, Siegfried Borchardt, FAP vice chairman and North Rhine-Westphalia chairman, repeatedly told his members that the government was bound to dissolve the FAP and that they should reorganize into autonomous *Kameradschaften* (see below). Then they could maintain contact with each other via high-tech communication.[10] Borchardt's prediction proved correct.

In February 1995, the Ministry of the Interior had enough evidence, after a nationwide raid of over fifty FAP members' apartments and offices, to put the FAP on the prohibited list of right-wing organizations. In the raid, the Ministry confiscated the FAP's wealth and property, including computers, diskettes, printed material, and tapes, which included one describing the Auschwitz "myth."[11] It ruled that the FAP had not supported the democratic order but was close to the Nazi philosophy, revered Nazi leaders, and fostered Nazi rituals. The Ministry did not have to petition the Federal Constitutional Court for an FAP ban because the Court had ruled that the FAP was not a traditional party. It did not have enough local and regional organizations and not enough members to qualify as a party.[12]

The Ministry realized that a ban of the FAP and other right-wing groups would not spell the end of the right-wing menace. The ban would spawn the formation of loosely organized *Kameradschaften*, greater underground actions, and increased terrorism. It justified its action by saying that fellow-travelers would more readily quit right-wing groups and that youth interested in neo-Nazi views would more likely be deterred. It remains to be seen whether such optimism was warranted.

National List

The FAP prohibition did not spare the National List. In 1989, in Hamburg, 38-year-old Christian Worch and his wife Ursula organized the regional group. He was one of the most influential neo-Nazis in Germany and a driving force behind efforts to create a neo-Nazi network. The National List fielded candidates in two Hamburg elections, but Worch considered the group more a movement than a party. In November 1994, he had been indicted for neo-Nazi activities and appealed the decision. Worch maintained close links to Gary Rex Lauck, the American neo-Nazi leader who headed the overseas organization, NSDAP/AO.[13] Lauck was well known in neo-Nazi circles for sending stacks of written propaganda materials to neo-Nazi organizations in numerous countries and raising money from prominent Nazis who had fled to South America and South Africa after the war. Given the National List's anti-democratic orientation, Ministry of the Interior authorities decided in 1995 to prohibit the organization, giving the same reasons as the FAP ban.[14]

Nationalist Front

The Nationalist Front (*Nationalistische Front*, NF) was one of the numerous right-wing groups that neo-Nazi leaders had organized in West Germany before the two Germanys merged in 1990. Chairman Meinolf Schönborn and others founded the NF in 1985, soon claiming eighty members. After unification they organized groups in numerous eastern German cities and towns, bringing the membership up to 400 by 1992, of whom half lived in eastern Germany.[15] From its beginning, the group's main enemy was the foreigners. In April 1991, Jürgen Rieger, a lawyer from Hamburg and the man behind the scenes of several right-wing organizations, asserted at an NF national meeting in Niederaula (Hesse), that "we must make the stay of foreigners as uncomfortable as possible." Delegates approved a nine-point plan concerning foreigners. It demanded that the government repatriate foreign "criminals," impose an integration tax of DM 50,000 per year on employers who hire a foreigner, and forbid foreigners to live in apartments reserved for low-income Germans and to receive subsidies for children and their education.[16]

Such proposals were bound to reinforce the members' xenophobic views. Some NF members participated in attacks on hostels housing asylum seekers in and near Bremen; two others beat up and burned to death a German who they thought was Jewish, as detailed below. The NF saw itself as a successor organization to the Nazi SA and the NSDAP Strasser wing. Its members characterized themselves as "fighting nationalists" who propagated an anti-imperialist and anti-capitalist "people's socialism."

The NF was an organization based on neighborhood cells and small cadres, providing ideological indoctrination in special schools for some of its members. In imitation of the Nazis, it organized fire rituals. It also set up paramilitary summer camps, at times using the former East German army's abandoned training field facilities. There they learned how to handle automatic rifles, grenade launchers, and other weapons. In June 1991 the NF sought to hold an international congress in Roding (Bavaria) to deal with the "Auschwitz lie," but authorities refused permission because a Holocaust denial would be illegal. The NF's publications (*Aufbruch* and *Revolte*) were blatantly racist, showing in one instance a caricature of skinheads stomping a prone Turk.[17] The NF encouraged skinheads and hooligans in eastern Germany to join the organization.

When the NF's secretary general, Meinolf Schönborn, who had been a leading aide of Michael Kühnen, secretly proposed that highly mobile "National Mission Commandos" be trained that would plan central actions against the government, the NF had gone too far. A government agent, who had infiltrated the NF, reported on the plan to the authorities. The agent's report provided evidence that the NF had no intention of supporting the democratic system. On November 27, 1992, soon after the federal attorney general had begun an investigation of the NF, Federal Minister of the Interior Rudolf Seiters promptly dissolved the organization. In house searches of NF members throughout the Federal Republic, police agents seized propaganda materials, weapons, dynamite, and a death list of opponents. As leading NF officials were not arrested immediately, they had time to go underground. In hiding, Schönborn asserted that the NF prohibition indicated the absolute correctness of the group's *Weltanschauung*.

In February 1994, when authorities feared that the NF was continuing its activities underground, they searched the premises of Schönborn and other former NF leaders. In the "German Toys Publishing House," which he owned, the police found a list of clients who had ordered materials, such as forbidden swastika stickers. Needless to say, the police confiscated the list.[18] In 1995, the authorities imposed a mild jail sentence on Schönborn for having resuscitated the NF with a different name but the same political players. Once released Schönborn opened a store selling pamphlets and religious objects, but he could barely make a living. Although he still had fifty loyal followers in a few major cities, the group was no longer politically important. When Schönborn built a house in Denmark in exile, left extremists demolished it.[19]

German Alternative

On May 5, 1989, Michael Kühnen, the prominent neo-Nazi leader, founded in Bremen a new nationalist protest party, the German Alternative (*Deutsche*

Alternative, DA). One of its goals called for Germany to reclaim the "stolen" German territory of Poland and the Czech Republic. Before and after unification, the organization's leaders swiftly recruited new members in East Germany. About 350 persons joined, including 200 from Cottbus, its chief base in eastern Germany. In September 1991, after Kühnen's death, eastern Germans captured the DA's leadership at a Duisburg convention. By 1992, the neo-Nazi group, with about 700 members, had become the largest in eastern Germany. Many students, including those in academic high schools (*Gymnasien*), found a home in the DA.

Frank Hübner became chairman. Born in 1966 in Cottbus, Hübner was eventually arrested and expelled from the GDR in 1985 when he wrote letters to prominent West Germans seeking asylum. In the FRG he joined a soldier's association, which in turn led to contacts with right-wing leaders. For a while, he worked for the DVU and neo-Nazi organizations in Hesse. In 1989, Hübner renewed contacts with former right-wing "comrades" in Cottbus and sought to recruit and politicize skinheads. Although the DA did not engage in violence, the Federal Minister of the Interior in December 1992 dissolved it for its failure to support the democratic order.[20]

National Alternative

In January 1990, in East Berlin, Ingo Hasselbach, supported by neo-Nazis and skinheads who had been right-wing rebels during the GDR era, founded the National Alternative party. As chairman of a small group of three dozen right-wingers, many of whose parents were GDR functionaries, Hasselbach received the counsel of his close friend, the veteran West German neo-Nazi leader Michael Kühnen. In January 1990 the West German leader came to Hasselbach's apartment in East Berlin with a party program and statute for the National Alternative, as well as a legal application to the government for its approval to constitute the National Alternative as a political party.[21] Prior to the party's founding, Hasselbach, the blond, tall "Aryan poster boy" who wore army parachutist boots, had become a contact for West German neo-Nazis. After the fall of the Wall the neo-Nazis recruited young eastern German men housed in refugee camps in Hanover and Hamburg.

Once the party was founded, Hasselbach and his supporters became squatters in an empty Berlin apartment building, which ironically belonged to a Jew. To ward off leftist *Autonomen* attacks, the right-wing occupiers kept in readiness a flame thrower, a bazooka, and 400 liters of gasoline for Molotov cocktails. They organized street battles against the *Autonomen*, which often turned bloody. Finally in late 1990 the police stormed into the building and forced out the squatters. Hasselbach also scheduled military sport exercises in the Brandenburg forests and on the island of Rügen, where the instructors were former East and West German soldiers.[22] He participated in right-wing demonstrations throughout the FRG. He ordered one member to grow his hair long and infiltrate leftist groups to collect intelligence on their activities.

He planned terrorist actions using an array of weapons against top German political leaders, but the actions were aborted. For three years, Hasselbach, modestly calling himself *"Führer* of Berlin," met with right-wing leaders of other European countries and the United States. In 1993 Hasselbach quit the right-wing scene in protest against the 1992 firebombing of a house in Mölln, western Germany, resulting in the deaths of three young Turks.

In 1991 the federal government banned the National Alternative for not supporting the democratic system. By then the group had about 800 members. Its dream of becoming a major right-wing party had vanished.

Viking Youth (*Wikinger Jugend*)

This group was the oldest and largest right-wing youth organization in West Germany, in which its rank and file was subject to considerable ideological influence. It was founded in 1952, in Wilhelmshaven, by the Socialist Reich Party's youth members. Wolfram Nahrath, who has headed the organization since 1991, welcomed Germany's unification as a way of broadening the group's appeal. Yet he also characterized the Federal Republic in negative terms as "the democracy of the victorious powers." The organization was virulently anti-Semitic, even advocating that Jews wear the yellow star. It had about 400 members, mostly over the age of 21. Its strictly hierarchical organization and ideology resembled that of the Hitler Youth. Viking Youth began its educational work as early as the kindergarten and ended with the "Fighting Community" (*Kampfgemeinschaft*). At the age of 15, members had to pass a test, which included knowledge of the German Reich's lost territories. Viking Youth set up summer vacation tent camps where propaganda about Nordic superiority was disseminated. The organization also provided paramilitary training at sports camps during winter vacations, but the police, who knew about the camps, eventually closed two of them.

To broaden their outreach, Viking Youth officials worked closely with the NPD's youth division and placed advertisements in the NPD's official journal. The Viking Youth and other right-wing organizations also frequently used the Heide-Hems Association educational facilities located in northern Germany. The Hamburg lawyer Jürgen Rieger was the educational center's chairman. A fanatic ideologue, he headed the right-wing Society for Biological Anthropology, Eugenics, and Behavioral Research. He also defended numerous top neo-Nazi leaders in court for having stated that Auschwitz was a lie.[23] The Viking Youth maintained ties with its counterparts in several West European countries.

In 1994, Minister of the Interior Manfred Kanther (CDU) outlawed Viking Youth because it wanted to scrap the Basic Law and instead "recreate a National Socialist state in Germany." He said that Germany would not accept National Socialists undermining the democratic order through propaganda and political activities. According to Kanther, "Germany is not a playground for extremists, no matter which sort."[24]

Homeland Loyal German Youth

More than a decade later, a successor to the Viking Youth surfaced. A right-wing leader, Sebastian Räbiger, who had been a Viking Youth official, formed a new organization, known as *Heimattreuen Deutschen Jugend – Bund zum Schutz für Umwelt, Mitwelt und Heimat* (HDJ, Homeland Loyal German Youth – League for the Protection of the Environment, the Present Generation, and the Homeland). He received the support of other former Viking Youth and current NPD officials. The HDJ was founded to bring children and youth between the ages of 7 and 25 into the right-wing movement. One of its chief activities has been to operate a camp in a large meadow owned by a sympathetic farmer near the town of Südheide, Lower Saxony. In 2007, the police, in allowing camping to take place, insisted that no one wear a uniform as had been planned. The leaders instilled in the enrolled youth a homeland nationalist propaganda and emphasized rigorous sports activities, such as forced marches. The HDJ was also active in other Länder. In 2007 a Potsdam state prosecutor investigated a charge that Räbiger and other HDJ leaders physically attacked journalists at one of the HDJ meetings. Leftist Bundestag deputies called on the Ministry of the Interior to intensify its observations of the HDJ.[25]

National Offensive

On July 3, 1990, in Augsburg, Michael Swierczek and other former members of the Free German Workers' Party (FAP) founded the neo-Nazi group, National Offensive. It was designed to keep disillusioned FAP members in the movement. Kühnen, until his death in 1991, influenced the group's leaders. Then the Austrian Gottfried Küssel assumed the leadership. Soon thereafter, the Ministry of the Interior banned his entry into Germany. The National Offensive achieved a certain fame in the neo-Nazi scene for its unusual actions. In June 1991 it launched a campaign demanding freedom for a former top SS official, Josef Schwammberger, who was being tried in a Stuttgart court for his criminal activities during the Nazi era. As part of its tough image, the National Offensive organized demonstrations in eastern Germany calling on judges to send drug dealers into work camps. In December 1992, one week before the government outlawed the National Offensive, criminal police agents raided members' apartments in North Rhine-Westphalia. But the group's leaders had been advised, presumably by friendly agents, that a crackdown was in the offing. Warned in time, they removed most of the evidence of a conspiracy against the state. The agents did not find much political material, although they did uncover some ammunition, arms, and dynamite, which seemed to have been forgotten.[26]

National Movement

Some regional groups played an important role in the right-wing movement. In Potsdam and surrounding area, the National Movement acknowledged participating in sixteen actions from January 2000 to January 2001. One such action was setting on fire the Hall of Sorrow of the Jewish cemetery in Potsdam; two others consisted of torching Turkish fast food establishments. Aware that the firebombing of the Hall of Sorrow drew international attention, the Federal Attorney General Kai Nehm, rather than the Land attorney general, took over the case. Suspects were not found.

The National Movement also sent out threatening anti-Semitic and racist letters to democratic group recipients. The Brandenburg head of the Office for the Protection of the Constitution, Heiner Wegesin, was urged to resign in the wake of another incident. In February 2001 one of his agents who had secretly become a member of the National Movement had revealed to a prominent neo-Nazi in the group that the police were planning a raid on the premises of some members. When the police were informed of the leak, they conducted the raid earlier than planned but with meager findings. The agent was tried for betraying a state secret.[27]

The Help Organization for National Prisoners and their Dependants

In order for neo-Nazi and skinhead organizations to maintain close links to their members who have been jailed, the *Hilfsorganisation für nationale politische Gefangene und deren Angehörige* publishes a monthly newsletter with a circulation of 700 copies, which is given to the organization's members and sent to all right-wing political prisoners. The *News* lists the names of prisoners who can then be contacted upon their release from prison. The government is unable to forbid this legal, non-profit organization, financed primarily by all neo-Nazi parties and groups, because it is doing "humanitarian work." Thus, neo-Nazi leader Kühnen sought the support of elderly Nazi widows for young neo-Nazis who were serving time in prison. The widows have sent prisoners food and cigarettes, as well as propaganda materials.[28]

Free Comradeship Groups

After the government's ban on numerous neo-Nazi groups and the arrest and imprisonment of leading neo-Nazis in the early 1990s, the remaining leaders sought an alternative way to keep the movement going. Beginning in Berlin and then spreading to other cities, on the model of left-extremist groups, they formed about 160 small Free Comradeship Groups (*Freie Kameradschaften*), based primarily in local eastern German areas. Each group, normally consisting of up to twenty-five neo-Nazis, including politicized skinheads, can act independently. In order to have some coordination concerning actions, demonstrations, and campaigns, the comradeships communicate with each other over the internet. Local leaders have met on occasion at district or regional conferences. The Action Bureau North in Hamburg and the *Kameradschaft South*, until its ban in 2003, served as coordinating bodies. *Kameradschaft München* succeeded *Kameradschaft South*. In addition, an Action League

(*Aktionsbündnis*) replaced the *Fränkische Aktionsfront* (prohibited in 2004) at the national level. It too had primarily coordinating functions. The neo-Nazi leaders Christian Worch and Thomas Wulff of Hamburg were among the founders of the *Kameradschaften*. According to the *Bundesamt für Verfassungsschutz* report of 2003, approximately 3,000 neo-Nazis have joined the *Kameradschaften*. In 2008, about 200 groups were in existence.[29]

Such a change in the neo-Nazi scene from national groups into primarily "unorganized" organizations without firm structures made it more difficult for government agents to infiltrate the small units. The comradeships, often founded by western German NPD functionaries seeking to strengthen their own youth division, are financed by dues and the sale of trinkets, jewelry, tapes, and flags. The groups seek to promote a right-wing ideology among their members. In some instances, they oppose violent actions against their foes. Instead they emphasize those cultural leisure-time activities, such as soccer, camping, and paramilitary games, which will appeal to youth. Many group leaders are eager to organize public demonstrations to commemorate, for instance, the death of Rudolf Hess, as a symbolic gesture to recruit more members and to publicize their organizations.

The *Kameradschaften* have used their right-wing positions on current foreign and domestic policy issues to provide a group identity and to politicize the movement. Thus they denounce US policies in the Middle East, which, according to them, reflect the power of Jews in Washington's policy-making circles. They emphasize the need for Germany to pursue its own nationalist policies rather than be sucked into the relentless globalization drive. In the domestic sphere, in 2004 they supported local leftist and union initiatives to defeat the German government's Agenda 2010 legislative measures cutting back on government social welfare plans. Although, in a populist spirit, they joined demonstrations against Agenda 2010, to the discomfort of leftists, the PDS, and the unions that had sponsored the demonstrations, the neo-Nazis maintained their own profile. Under the Hamburg neo-Nazi chief Christian Worch's leadership, militant *Kameradschaften* members held a protest rally at one of the US bases in Germany. However, a leading leftist activist warned the peace movement that no joint actions with neo-Nazis should be scheduled. Flyers at peace rallies were distributed saying that neo-Nazis were not welcome. If they joined, the police should remove them.[30]

In June 2007 the *Kameradschaften* and NPD officials, working together, planned a massive demonstration in Schwerin, the capital of Mecklenburg-West Pomerania, on the eve of the G-8 Summit meeting dealing with global issues. At the last minute the Federal Constitutional Court forbade the march. The neo-Nazis thereupon staged illegal demonstrations in numerous other German cities. They had planned to march in Schwerin with banners urging priority for German social rather than global issues. Their slogan, "Beware, social instead of global," did not differ from that of the leftist opponents of globalization, who received permission to march in Rostock. Hidden under the veneer of some joint goals between the right and the left was the NPD's emphasis on the old nationalism, which it did not share with the left. The NPD's nationalism was reflected in its slogans "Globalization is the death of people; National Socialism produces the turning-point" or "Homeland is not an object of trade." Right-wing leaders denounced leftist *Autonomen* for injuring police agents, burning cars, and plundering shops in one of the authorized Rostock leftist demonstrations.[31]

The *Kameradschaften* have been active in large cities and small towns. In groups containing skinheads, they have been eager to engage in violence against their enemies. A few have even adopted the leftist *Autonomen* black uniforms and Palestinian kerchiefs to befuddle their leftist enemies and the police. Some carry red flags, although most carry black flags. In some small towns, where the right-wing groups have been especially active in citizens' initiatives and cultural clubs, they have sprayed symbolically the number 88 (as H is the eighth letter in the alphabet, HH stands for Heil Hitler) as graffiti on the walls. At other times they hail each other with the perfectly legal greeting "Heil Hiller."

The Dresden suburb of Gorbitz is the site of a typical *Kameradschaft* group. The setting is already forbidding. High-rise prefabricated concrete buildings erected during the GDR era house 45,000 residents, many of whom are without jobs. In the project, with few facilities for recreation and social assistance, young men organized the *Kameradschaft* Gorbitz, with a hard core membership of forty to fifty persons. The *Kameradschaft* meets in a local bar in which outsiders are definitely not welcome. The group has close contacts with other organizations in the militant right-wing scene. Most have been involved in violence against foreigners in Dresden. *Kameradschaft* members are expected to have "real opinions, courage, and an unconditional comradeship." The first test of courage is "roughing up foreigners." In November 1990 the Gorbitz members squatted in an old tenement house in order to have a central office. The house owner had to telephone the police on three occasions until they came to clear out the right-wing squatters. Once again, the police showed that they were less concerned about rightists than leftists. The Dresden mayor, Herbert Wagner (CDU), was unhappy that the mass media labeled Dresden as the "capital city of the right-extremist movement," although he admitted that it has offered a fertile ground for the right's ideology.[32]

Whether a *Kameradschaft* uses violence or not against its foes depends on its leaders and members. Some violence-prone rightists hold weekly military sport exercises in forests near Munich and the Czech frontier, and store dynamite and weapons for future terrorist actions. This happened in the case of *Kameradschaft Süd* (South). This group, which included a number of militant skinheads, was founded in late 2001 in Munich, by NPD activist Norman Berdin. When he had to serve a fifteen-month jail sentence for nearly murdering a Greek citizen, 27-year-old Martin Wiese, one of the top neo-Nazis in southern Germany, took over the group.

Less than two years later, in 2003, the government banned *Kameradschaft Süd* after having received information from one of its agents that Wiese and other key members had planned to bomb the site of a new Jewish community center to be built in downtown Munich. When arrested, one 18-year-old female member told the police that an alternative plan had also been developed. She had volunteered to blow herself up on Marienplatz, the well-known square in front of the city hall. The original plan, an attack at the dedication, was planned for November 9, 2003, which also marked the commemoration of the *Kristallnacht* (Crystal night) in 1938. It was to be attended by top politicians, including Minister-President Edmund Stoiber of Bavaria, German President Johannes Rau, and Paul Spiegel, President of the Central Council of Jews in Germany. In September 2003, two months before the ceremony, government agents arrested leading neo-Nazis in the *Kameradschaft* for having illegally stored weapons and ammunition in the Munich area, and preparing to use them. The police also found a hit list with names of politicians who might be attacked, as well as Munich mosques and other targets.[33] Thus on the dedication day of the Jewish community center, at which the top politicians appeared, the neo-Nazis were in jail. Nearly one year later, in October 2004, in a trial lasting five months, they faced criminal charges in court of plotting the attack and of being members of a terrorist association. They received sentences of up to seven years imprisonment. The government was able to prove the case based on information supplied to it by one of its agents who had infiltrated the fifty-person group.[34]

Most *Kameradschaften* have pursued their goals more peacefully. In the latter instance, comrades meet at least weekly and often follow a set routine. They have a beer at their accustomed table in a bar, discuss politics from a Nazi perspective, organize occasionally an information booth on the central square, plan trips to skinhead concerts, and on Sundays participate in army sport exercises. Some groups have abandoned their formal organization as *Kameradschaften* with membership lists and dues, but continue to meet informally. The government has disbanded still others for a variety of reasons, such as glorifying the SS or making anti-Semitic statements.

National liberated zones

In eastern Germany the youthful neo-Nazi gangs, many organized in *Kameradschaften*, are often no longer a subculture, but have become dominant in numerous villages and small towns. In at least twenty-five towns, they have proclaimed central urban sections as "national liberated (or freed) zones" or "no-go zones." Foreigners in Germany have named them instead "zones of fear." In these zones, the groups pride themselves on offering a "leaderless resistance" against the democratic establishment. Foreigners and leftists are not welcome in the bars, discos, and clubs that neo-Nazis and skinheads frequent. If the leftists dare to trespass a zone, which has no signs or well-defined borders, they may be beaten up, especially at night. Some foreigners and their families have had to leave the towns in fear.[35]

The zones concept stems from a five-page manifesto that an unidentified NPD writer published in 1991 on the neo-Nazi Thule Net computer site. According to the manifesto: "We must create the space in which we exercise real power, in which we are capable of imposing sanctions – that is, we punish deviants and enemies, we support comrades in the struggle, we help fellow citizens who are oppressed, marginalized and persecuted."[36] The author prophesized that ten or twelve determined right-wing individuals could accomplish much in a town to realize rightist goals. The rightists would need to act in such a manner that "average" citizens would show a "sea of sympathy" for them or be too intimidated by them to fight the neo-Nazi goals openly.[37] The rightists would communicate with one another through neo-Nazi mail boxes, organize local meetings, and perhaps open a right-wing bookstore that carries books, pamphlets, and flyers not available elsewhere. In some towns, a right-wing publishing house, an advertising agency, a travel agency, an internet café, or a record store might be opened that would offer services and goods, which would parallel the left-inspired social movement to establish an alternative economy and culture. The neo-Nazis also sponsored sports competitions and dance parties in order to reach youth. In one town a right-wing lawyer set up an advisory office for people on social welfare, a function that normally could be expected to be performed by a leftist lawyer.

The national liberated zone in Wurzen may serve as a typical one among the twenty-five towns that neo-Nazis had "captured" by 1997. In the CDU-governed Saxony town of 16,000 people, neo-Nazis and skinheads planned to beat up foreigners, punks, and hippy-looking leftists, collectively known as the "alternative scene." In 1991, in one such incident, skinheads fell upon Portuguese workers who were peacefully building a high school. Neo-Nazis also beat up members of an out-of-town football team that was camping near the town. In still another incident, on a train from Berlin to Wurzen, eight skinheads entered a car that was almost empty. Two of them put on black masks to hide their identity and stomped on two leftists with their boots, causing serious injuries. The frightened ticket-inspector did not appear. These incidents were carried out by some of the town's estimated sixty rightists, of whom about two dozen were 16–30-year-old skinheads. The average town residents, including some SPD supporters, sided with the rightists rather than the leftists. The rationale was based on sweeping generalizations. The rightists worked while the leftists chose to be unemployed; leftists took drugs while the rightists only drank alcohol; the rightists were clean while the leftists, especially women, looked slovenly. In short, to be a rightist was to conform to venerable German values.

In January 2001, a scholarly committee of German language and media experts declared the concept of "nationally liberated zones" as the "Unwort" (non-word) of the year 2000, even though it had been used for a number of years. The experts considered it a non-word because it celebrates and inflates a violent form of sectarianism by calling it "national," and because ironically it refers to the persecution of people as "liberation."[38]

Skinheads

Since the early 1990s, but especially since the mid-1990s, the number of right-wing skinheads has increased appreciably, especially in eastern Germany, Berlin, and Hamburg. In late 1992, the Ministry of the Interior estimated that there were about 6,500 skinheads, of whom 4,500 were rightist, in Germany. An astonishingly high number of 3,000 lived in eastern Germany. By 1997, the figure rose gradually to 7,000 skinheads, of whom some had already joined the right-wing scene in the GDR era prior to 1990.[39] By 2003, the number of skinheads had risen to 10,000, but figures fluctuate constantly and are based on police estimates that often seem on the low side.

The German sections of Blood and Honor, whose international headquarters are located in the United States, and of Hammer Skinheads, which originated in Great Britain, were the most active in Germany. They have propagated the superiority of the white Aryan race and called on "patriots" to be ready to fight the enemy. The Blood and Honor groups, with a membership of about 300, formed anti-anti-fascist cells to battle ultra-leftist anti-fascist groups. The latter have often marched in demonstrations against skinheads and neo-Nazis, and are ready to fight the rightists and the police. In turn, some skinhead groups have resorted to armed and terrorist underground activities. A number of western German skinheads, who had moved to eastern Germany after 1990 because it represented less of a decadent Western culture and more of an authoritarian culture, moved back west after witnessing the brutal skinhead attacks on their foes.

In September 2000, the Federal Ministry of the Interior outlawed Blood and Honor and its White Youth division as a result of the skinhead violence. Individual members remained active in the skinhead movement and maintained ties with the NPD. However, the nationalist and racist Hammer Skinheads, with about 120 members, as well as a skinhead group *Furchtlos und Treu* ("Fearless and True"), with several Länder branches, were allowed to operate. The latter has been seeking to unite all right-wing skinheads under a populist umbrella. It has wooed young people who are at a loose end with concerts, ballad evenings, laying of wreaths, and political courses to give them a sense of belonging.[40] Occasionally regional skinhead groups have been formed. In September 1995, the Bavarian Skinheads Allgäu was founded only to be banned in July 1996 by the Bavarian Ministry of the Interior for its violent activities.

Other skinhead groups include the *Deutsche Alternative* (DA), which initially began as a neo-Nazi group (see above). Its leader Frank Hübner also became active in the skinhead scene, soon becoming one of the movement's chiefs. The DA's news-sheet, the *Brandenburgische Beobachter* (a name that invokes comparison to the notorious Nazi newspaper *Völkischer Beobachter*), contained strident anti-Semitic materials. In 1992, Hübner pledged that his organization of about 700 members, led primarily by former GDR youth, would not engage in the violence so prevalent at the time.[41]

One year earlier, in 1991, Dresden youth formed the German National Resistance after a west German skinhead leader, Rainer Sonntag, was killed in the city. He had declared his intention to close the sex shops and clubs that had opened in eastern German cities upon the GDR regime's demise. To avenge Sonntag's killing the local right-wing youth smashed the windows and signs of the offending shops and clubs. Other skinhead groups in eastern Germany set their sights on closing gay bars and clubs. In eastern Berlin, skinheads shouting Nazi slogans broke up a gay street festival.[42]

One of the most active skinhead groups was the Skinhead Saxonian Switzerland (SSS), named after an eastern German tourist region near Dresden known for its beautiful landscape. The group was founded in 1996 in the aftermath of the ban on the Viking Youth. Its 100 members and 200 sympathizers, closely linked to the NPD, were attracted to the organization through its rock music evenings, armed sports maneuvers near the Czech border, camping retreats, hikes, and songfests.[43] However, the members have committed numerous violent acts against their political foes, resulting in three trials involving forty-two members. The trials, in which the members showed no remorse, have resulted in prison sentences of up to two years. In April 2001, the Saxonian State Minister of the Interior dissolved the SSS and its auxiliary organization as a consequence of the violence, the attempt to clear foreigners from liberated zones, and the military-nationalist ideology.

Many skinheads receive moral support from their parents and grandparents, some of whom were World War Two veterans. The older generation talks little about the Nazi era, knowing that the vast majority of them were guilty of collaborating with the Hitler regime. But this guilt is not voiced openly. Instead the skinheads see it as their mission to continue, in their view, a fine tradition in which in effect they rehabilitate their elderly family members, who in turn approve of their offspring's brutal actions. Such views are accompanied by an ethnic-cultural and a racist Aryan superiority, mixed in with Germanic-pagan elements.[44] In this *Weltanschauung* the victims are the foreigners, the leftists, the gays, the homeless, and the Jews. At soccer matches the skinheads have been ready to engage in violence or yell racist slogans and throw bananas on the field as a symbolic hate gesture if a player is black. But they have not been interested in long-range political work, which they leave primarily to the neo-Nazi groups.

Although most skinheads still wear their typical bomber jackets and menacing Doc Marten boots as a way to raise their self-esteem and to suggest power and authority, the modern skinheads tend to blend into the crowd in large urban areas in their chic sports clothes and adoption of the latest cultural trends. Yet skinheads, often using symbols and codes, tend to recognize each other, especially if some of them wear winter jackets made by the Norwegian manufacturer Helly Hansen, whose initials HH are identical with the Heil Hitler salute. Another favorite is a British-made Lonsdale sweatshirt. German rightists put open bomber jackets over the shirts, making sure that only the NS of Lo"ns"dale is visible, which in their imagination stands for "National Socialism," or the letters NSDA (Lo "nsda" le), which stands for "National Socialist German Workers." Regardless of their appearance, the skinheads have been intent on demonstrating their power and authority, and their willingness to attack.

The German Thor Steinar Company fashion label is on sweatshirts, sweaters and baseball hats that are popular among right-wing teenagers, especially in eastern Germany. The company logo shows an arrow bisected by a lightning flash, symbols of nationalism and force. According to the state prosecutor Gerd Schnittcher, the logo is a combination of the Tyr rune, worn on the armbands of graduates from Nazi academies in the 1930s, and the Wolfsangel, the emblem worn by several *Waffen* SS units during the Nazi era. If the logo is shifted toward the right it looks like the runes worn by all SS members. In addition, the state prosecutor contended that one of the company's clothing lines, named "Division Thor Steinar," referred to the SS division that had been commanded by General Felix Steiner, who had become a cult figure among neo-Nazis. The state prosecutor called on a judge presiding in a court near Berlin to crack down on such clothing. Concurring, the judge ordered the police to confiscate logos and clothing as part of a strategy of zero tolerance for right-wing extremism. Nazi insignia such as the swastika and SS flashes had been banned since 1945, but even variations of the emblems were to be outlawed. According to the judge, to produce, display, or distribute emblems in public can lead to a jail sentence of up to three years. The Thor Steinar Company, in a counter-claim for damages, told a judge in a different court that "It's not for us to look inside people's heads." But police were ready to raid boutiques and factories across Germany to abide by the judge's ruling, which also supported the prosecutor's arguments.[45]

While controversies broke out over what may seem as a trivial sartorial issue, several skinhead political demonstrations held in 1999, 2005, and 2006 are typical of the ways in which right-wing forces have been able to mobilize their followers on numerous occasions. The 1999 demonstration, staged on Cathedral Square in Magdeburg, Saxony-Anhalt, was attended by hundreds of young men, wearing White Brotherhood jackets, who chanted "Glory and honor to our *Waffen* SS." The police, who outnumbered them by a two to one ratio, warned them to desist from chanting a slogan that exalts Nazi deeds or face immediate arrest. Thereupon, as a substitute slogan, the demonstrators yelled, "Work for Germans first," which appealed to many onlookers living in an area where unemployment hovered around 20 percent. One 56-year-old construction worker, out of work for six months, told a reporter that in the past he had voted for the CDU but now was ready to vote NPD. He said that "people my age no longer have a chance, and foreigners are pouring in." At least these people, the demonstrators, "stand for German ideals."[46]

Typical of skinhead participation in demonstrations was the rally on November 11, 2005 of about 2,000 skinheads who had gathered in Halbe, Brandenburg. The town is located about thirty miles south of Berlin. The largest World War Two military cemetery is located in Halbe. It contains the graves of about 28,000 German army and SS soldiers, most of whom died in April 1945 in the defense of Berlin. The cemetery has become a rallying point for neo-Nazis and skinheads, who gather there annually on the eve of the national day of mourning to commemorate the German war dead of the two world wars. In 2005 almost as many counter-demonstrators, including several prominent politicians and personalities, appeared on the scene. Earlier in the day, these counter-demonstrators had held a rally outside of the cemetery in honor of the victims of Nazi crimes. Brandenburg's Minister of the Interior Jörg Schönbohm said at the rally that "we cannot allow Halbe to become a regular place of pilgrimage for the neo-Nazis." After the rally the counter-demonstrators blocked the skinheads from entering the cemetery. In turn, the skinheads charged the police cordon separating the two sides, causing injuries to several police officers. However, the skinheads failed to gain entrance to the cemetery, a minor triumph for the democratic forces.[47]

In March 2006, in another right-wing demonstration at the Halbe cemetery, organized by the Hamburg leader Christian Worch, the police checked the identity cards of all leftist counter-demonstrators but not of the rightists. Leftist leaders were incensed at this bias of police officials. In November 2006 a court banned a neo-Nazi rally at the Halbe cemetery but allowed the right-wing demonstrators to gather at a smaller military cemetery in Seelow sixty miles away. On the same day, about 6,500 leftist demonstrators rallied at the Halbe cemetery. Greens' co-chairperson Claudia Roth, who took part in the rally, accused the neo-Nazis of seeking to "denigrate the memory of the dead."[48]

Skinheads and neo-Nazis, forbidden to march with swastika flags, have carried the old imperial war flag as a symbol of their support for Germany's imperial era in numerous demonstrations and rallies throughout Germany. In 1993 Land Brandenburg forbade any person to carry the old Reich flag.

Women in the movement

Until the late 1990s female neo-Nazis and skinheads did not organize their own groups, with a few exceptions such as the *FAP-Frauenschaft* and *Skingirl-front Deutschland*. Not yet imbued with the feminist movement's demands, the women saw themselves primarily as aides to the chauvinist male members, who did not encourage their participation in the movement.[49]

Given this attitude it was not surprising that there were almost no women in top policy-making positions in the neo-Nazi and skinhead groups. Many women still characterized their role in traditional terms of hearth and pro-creation. Although the right-wing women in the Federal Republic formed interest groups within the movement, these were restricted to the assistance type, such as those helping "national" prisoners, "the Brown Cross," the "National First Aid," the "Association of German Women," and the "Free Girls League" for women without children.[50]

Since the late 1990s, partly because of the delayed influence of the feminist movement, right-wing women have become more self-assertive and have formed their own political groups within the NPD, the *Kameradschaften*, and the skinheads. They constitute a growing minority within this movement, especially in eastern Germany. In 2002, the total number of female skinheads was estimated at 1,500, a significant increase from earlier years. In Bavaria, for instance, the percentage of rightist women in the movement rose from 10 percent in the mid-1990s to 16 percent in the early 2000s; in Thuringia the corresponding rise was from 20 to 30 percent. It remains to be seen whether this increase in female membership will correspond to an increase in their political activities and effectiveness.

There are a number of leather-jacketed young female skinhead militants in cities and towns who identify themselves by shaving their heads, except for a blond fringe above their foreheads. These women have the same national goals – order, discipline, and racial purity – as their male counterparts. They meet on their own to show that they are not merely auxiliary members of male groups. They do not elect officers as a sign that all women are equal. These young right-wing women, labeled by one author as "Femi-Nazis," reject the traditional images of women, propagated by numerous right-wing males, as home workers and producers of children. Tensions rise in young right-wing families in which these women become the chief breadwinners and the men are unable to find a job. An increasing number of women, whether they are at home or at work, commit themselves to political work. Just like their male counterparts, they seek to recruit new members for their groups, engage in propaganda, make banners, and plan demonstrations at which some of them might speak.[51]

Thus, in their programmatic demands, the right-wing women take the same position as the men. For instance, in polls, a majority of right-wing women, imbued by xenophobia and racism, said that they oppose their chil-dren marrying a Jew, Turk, or a person of color. According to one 1993 Lower Saxony study of young people in apprenticeship training programs, a major-ity of young women had xenophobic leanings. By contrast, only about a third of the male respondents showed similar sentiments.[52]

According to other polls in 2001, the number of women in right-wing organizations, such as a political party, a youth clique, or a *Kameradschaft*, ranges from 7 to 33 percent. Of these women, perhaps 3–5 percent engage in violent acts against foreigners and leftists. Among the women are some who have been raped in their youth and who then took revenge by joining gangs to beat up male foreigners. In Thuringia, a surprisingly high 10 per-cent of right-wing females participate in violent acts.[53] Most women reject violence but are conscious of the need to organize politically and to cre-ate a network of women's groups that will coordinate actions above the local level. In Thuringia, for example, NPD and *Kameradschaften* women activists have formed a Land organization, *Mädelring Thüringen* (Girls Circle Thuringia), whose members have assumed a leading role in their organ-izations. Some of the coordinating group activists are speakers at major right-wing rallies and demonstrations. In October 2000, the *Gemeinschaft Deutscher Frauen* (Community of German Women) was founded to replace the defunct *Skingirlfront Deutschland*. The new national organization of women has established regional groups in Berlin-Brandenburg, Bavaria, and Mecklenburg-West Pomerania. Its members meet regularly, organize hikes, and take part in political education. Their view is that women can no longer rely only on men to achieve their objectives of creating a new order.[54]

Eastern Germany: prelude to violence

Once the GDR collapsed in 1990 the western neo-Nazi groups and East German youth who had fled to West Germany had a golden opportunity to fill a political vacuum. They swiftly formed new groups in eastern Germany, even though some, such as the Fascho gangs, had already existed clandes-tinely during the final GDR years. The western neo-Nazi groups' efforts paid off in the face of mounting citizen dissatisfaction and frustration with the Federal Republic's political economy. As was true of some other postcommu-nist societies, the eastern German economy was in tatters, unemployment was nearly twice the level of western Germany, and social services were cut back drastically. Many of the restless youth were willing to join the newly formed Party of Democratic Socialism (PDS) on the left or neo-Nazi groups on the right as a protest against a West German neo-capitalist system that was swiftly imposed on them and that did not meet their needs. These youth, and their elders, had hoped in vain that a democratic regime would retain some of the GDR's egalitarian practices and institutions. But the FRG government did not accept this proposal.

Instead the authorities treated the eastern German population as second-class citizens, producing still another source of conflict, disappointment, and resentment. Many older eastern Germans could not continue in their careers because their jobs were scrapped. Numerous young people could not get into apprenticeship programs or find full-time jobs. As a result the youth espe-cially were easy targets for the emerging right-wing movements. However, not all young rightists were without jobs; many came from well-off families and were gainfully employed.

Western German rightists played primarily on the fears of those nega-tively affected in eastern Germany and provided them with moral and other support. As a result, eastern German youth, who could not fit into a pluralist modernization process mirroring the neo-capitalist western German model, found a new home in the right-wing milieu. Still imbued with a GDR authoritarian, anti-pluralist, anti-American, and anti-Zionist outlook, these troubled youth then looked for scapegoats for their own restlessness and joblessness and found them especially among the foreigners.[55] There were not that many foreigners in eastern Germany because of the repatriation of more than 100,000 foreigners to their homes in Third World countries in the wake of German unification.[56] After July 1990 foreigners totaled only 80,000 guest workers, in addition to a relatively small group of asylum seekers, within a population of 15 million east German citizens.

In a Federal Ministry of Labor poll conducted in late 1990, xenophobia was found to be more common in the five new Länder (eastern Germany) than in the eleven old Länder (western Germany). Seventy percent of the foreigners in eastern Germany, including eastern Berlin, told the interviewers that Germans had insulted or reviled them. This figure includes 20 percent who reported physical abuse. Many foreigners stated that they were afraid to walk alone during the day to the supermarket or to leave their apartments in the evenings. Not surprisingly, the majority of respondents said that xenophobia had increased since unification.[57] According to still another study, the risk of a foreigner being assaulted was twenty-six times higher in eastern Germany than in western Germany.[58]

The many causes of this striking imbalance between eastern and western Germany can be traced back to a deficit in the GDR's social development. This produced strong xenophobia among many East Germans who viewed the foreigners as class enemies. It also resulted in the isolation of Soviet soldiers in their military bases and of foreigners working on a contract basis in the GDR or studying at its universities. Most citizens viewed the foreigners as competitors for scarce housing and social services. This view encouraged the right-wing attitudes found among many eastern Germans after unification.[59]

In eastern Germany, from 1996 to 1999, three times as many right-wing extremist crimes per inhabitant were committed as compared to western Germany. Similarly in 1999, although eastern Germany's population was only 21 percent of Germany's total population, the percentage of political crimes that eastern German rightists committed totaled 51 percent of all such crimes in Germany.[60] As noted, the causes were youth's dissatisfaction with the unification's negative effects, such as 20 percent unemployment and the loss of some welfare programs. However, in one study, scholars at the Universities of Bonn and Zurich noted that, contrary to common belief, the unemployed youth did not carry out most of the crimes. Rather, employed male youth, who were afraid of becoming unemployed, and apprentices, who had other fears, committed them.[61]

According to Bernd Wagner of the Center for Democratic Culture in Berlin and a former East German policeman who has been monitoring neo-Nazi activities in the new Länder, "the people in the east live in a values system that is very vulnerable to right-wing extremism because it connects with their previous experiences."[62] Their xenophobic views, he writes, have taken on the insidious form of a "cultural subversion," which burrows into their daily life and takes on the attributes of normalcy. Thus the neo-Nazis and skinheads receive moral support in their anti-foreigner and anti-left activities from older citizens and even on occasion from the established political parties, which have been backpedaling on the rights of asylum seekers to enter the country.

Violence

In the early 1990s neo-Nazis and skinheads committed numerous acts of violence against their enemies in western and eastern Germany. The number of such acts was significantly higher when compared to the pre-unification period in West Germany. This increase in violence included injuries and deaths and acts of damage to property. According to federal and Länder *Verfassungsschutz* surveys, in 1985 in West Germany neo-Nazis and skinheads committed 123 violent crimes; in 1990 the figure for the united Germany rose to 306 and in 1992 to a high of 2,639. Thereafter there was a significant drop-off in violence to 759 in 2003, but then it rose sharply to 1,047 in 2006.[63] The earlier drop-off was partly due to the democratic parties toughening the country's asylum laws, which the rightists had clamored for, and partly due to the shock of fatal arson attacks on Turkish women in 1992 and 1993 (see below). Most of the violent crimes, often committed on weekends, were directed against foreigners; fewer against minorities and political opponents; the fewest against Jews. The number of other punishable right-wing offenses rose from 8,328 in 1993 to 10,929 in 1997, dropped to 10,036 in 2003, and rose to 19,900 in 2008. Up to two-thirds of these punishable offenses involved the distribution of illegal propaganda materials.[64] In 2006, more rightist offenses were committed than leftist offenses, which was not surprising given the degree of right-wing activities since German unification.[65] A 2007 government analysis of the ages of those committing violence indicates that the highest number consists of the 18–20-year-olds, followed by the 21–24-year-olds, and then by the 14–17-year-old youth. Ministry of the Interior officials called for public and private initiatives to win over these youth to the democratic cause.[66]

Much violence took place in the five new Länder, although western German Länder also had their share of violence. In 89 percent of cases it was committed against foreigners. The other cases included attacks against homeless persons, punks, leftists, gays, the handicapped, and Gypsies. The high degree of violence was caused primarily by the 600–1,000 skinheads who had lived in the GDR in the 1980s and who at the time confronted the communist regime. From 1990 on, their principal new enemy became the foreigners living in eastern Germany.[67] In 1997, for instance, 40 percent of right-wing acts of violence occurred in eastern Germany, even though only 20 percent of the population lives there. From 1990 to 2007, as a result of xenophobic and racist attacks in both parts of Germany, 130 persons, but none Jewish, perished in arson attacks on asylum hostels or were murdered.[68] This total was challenged by the government, which said that in the first decade of a united Germany (1990–2000) 26 people died. Two newspapers claimed in a detailed study that the official data were false.[69] Obviously the government was trying to minimize the degree of violence, but agreed in 2000 to set up a commission of specialists to review the data. These specialists concurred with the higher figure of casualties. Although the degree of violence is high in eastern Germany, a 2006 government survey shows that, with the exception of east (and west) Berlin, which had the highest number of cases (25) in which victims were injured, western German Länder scored higher on the violence scale than eastern German Länder.[70]

Most rightists who have been prosecuted for punishable acts are males in the 18–20-year-old age group. The 15–17-year-old group is the second largest one, followed by the 21–24-year-old group. The smallest group consists of older 25–29-year-old individuals, some of whom have a following of younger disciples. According to two academics who have undertaken opinion surveys, the older rightists, although ideologically unchanged, lose interest in using force against their opponents and prefer to engage in political work. At their age, many have a family and a job, and are more locked into the system than is true of their younger age cohorts. Often the female partners are the ones who insist that, given job scarcities, the males stay at home while they seek jobs. But once at home, some males beat up their partners in another manifestation of violence and boredom.[71]

A chronological survey of several cases of violence that occurred in both parts of Germany shows that its nature has changed. For instance, there have been fewer arson attacks against foreigners' hostels in recent years. Yet the violence continues. In 2004 neo-Nazis and skinheads committed about 600 acts of violence in eastern Germany alone. Typical of the hostility and violence toward foreigners in the former GDR is the case of Amadeu Antonio Kiowa, a guest worker from Angola, whose death marked the first among foreigners after German unification. During the night of November 25, 1990, in the town of Eberswalde, a large group of skinheads marched to a discotheque frequented by foreigners. When the owner saw the skinheads, he decided to close early. On the streets the fleeing foreigners were easy prey for the skinheads. Several foreigners were seriously injured. Kiowa was surrounded by fifteen skinheads who beat and kicked him so severely that he died in a local hospital three weeks later. Human rights groups criticized not only the skinheads' brutality but the police passivity and bias. Three armed police officers had watched the attack from a distance. At the trial one officer said: "I immediately called both of my colleagues back, because I wanted to prevent their getting into any conflict with the group." One witness testified in court that a police officer had said: "I am not doing anything for an African. I won't risk my own life."[72] Five right-wing youth received varying light sentences, ranging from four years in jail to two years' probation.

Bonsu Jones of Ghana was lucky not to be a death victim of the skinheads. In early 1991, as a potential target of political oppression in his home country, he fled to eastern Germany and asked for political asylum. He was housed in Magdeburg, the capital of Saxony-Anhalt. In the first six months of his stay, he was threatened by rightists at knife point, chased down a street, called a "nigger pig," and told to "go home." In July 1991 fifty neo-Nazis scaled a fence surrounding the hostel where Jones lived. They hurled rocks, broke numerous windows, and shouted Nazi slogans. One refugee had to be hospitalized.[73]

Dark-skinned foreigners fear living in eastern Germany. For instance, in 1991, one survey showed that seven in ten non-Germans living there had been abused by Germans, four in ten were discriminated against or treated unfairly while shopping, and one in five had endured physical assault.[74] At times, there have been heroic stories in which Germans have come to the assistance of foreigners whom rightists had assaulted. But in most instances the local population has been too fearful to intervene.

Hoyerswerda and Rostock

Some of the violence against foreigners probably could have been avoided if eastern Germans had been better prepared to absorb asylum seekers in their cities. According to Bernd Mesovic, a Workers Benevolent Society (*Arbeiterwohlfahrt*) staff member in Frankfurt am Main:

> The distribution of refugees to the East went too fast. There was no thought, no overall concept, no organization. These refugees were viewed as solely a problem of order by the authorities. They were worried about protecting the German population from the foreigners. It was only later that they realized that it was the foreigners who needed protection ... The speed with which reunification and these transfers occurred contributed to the violence. The population was unprepared for the refugees. They were too preoccupied with themselves. The problems were obvious. Predictable. It was clear that their (the foreigners') security could not be guaranteed. But the government sent them anyway.[75]

Asylum seekers are not allowed to work and must remain in their home district while government staff members review their application, a process that may take up to a year because asylum seekers must prove that in their home countries they were politically persecuted. The frequently bored asylum seekers receive about $190 a month from the state, in addition to free housing and health care, until their case is decided. Thus it is not too surprising that hatred and prejudices develop between the two groups, although the blame for violence rests most of the time on the rightists.

On September 17, 1991 the first major outbreak of right-wing violence in eastern Germany occurred in Hoyerswerda, a small town in Saxony whose coal mining industry had closed after unification. A number of guest workers from Mozambique, Angola, and Vietnam had worked there from the early 1980s on in low-paid jobs, but were slated to be repatriated in the near future. After unification, city authorities admitted 230 asylum seekers from twenty-one countries to live in Hoyerswerda hostels until decisions had been made in each case whether or not they could settle in Germany. Numerous residents opposed the authorities' arbitrary edict to have the foreigners stay temporarily in their town.

On the first day of violence, racist skinheads systematically vandalized Vietnamese goods being sold on the market square. Then, in the following days, in an escalation of violence, they threw bricks, Molotov cocktails, and other projectiles at a hostel housing the foreigners, as ordinary citizens in houses near the hostel clapped and shouted their approval. The foreigners were in terror; the police removed them from the hostel by buses to other shelters in Saxonian small towns under cover of darkness. Once the foreigners were removed, the skinheads and local citizens celebrated their victory. The skinheads received further support from other cities' skinhead groups. Each evening they attacked still other hostels housing foreigners. The skinheads also paraded through the city with their German empire flags and forbidden straight-arm *Sieg Heil* salutes. The police, many sympathizing with the rightists and feeling outnumbered, made few arrests at the height of the disturbances. Belatedly, heavily armed Federal Border Guard (*Grenzschutz*) units arrived to help restore order.[76] National soul searching ensued as to how such a disturbance could have occurred and why so many people were right-wing supporters. One mother of three children provided an answer: "The asylum seekers were dirty. They threw their rubbish on the streets. We all work hard and yet they get clothes and a free flat. It's just not fair."[77]

In 1991 the escalating violence spread to Zittau, Halle, Cottbus, and other eastern German cities. That year more than 1,000 acts of violence against foreigners took place throughout Germany, including 383 arson attacks and three deaths. In Dresden, an immigrant from Mozambique was killed when neo-Nazis threw him from a streetcar. In Berlin subways, neo-Nazis and skinheads assaulted so many blacks that the city's transportation commissioner urged blacks not to use certain subway lines at night. Violence increased the following year, with an unprecedented seventeen reported deaths, including seven foreigners.

From August 22–28, 1992, large-scale violence against foreigners erupted in Rostock, a port city on the Baltic with a population of 210,000. It was plagued by high unemployment and had to cope with a closed shipyard and clothing factory and cutbacks to its deep-sea fishing fleet and merchant marine. In this instance, skinhead leaders were eager to see a repetition of the Hoyerswerda riots. They notified their members of the pending actions against foreigners.

Many of the hundreds of rioters (some estimates ranged up to 1,000 participants) came from several western and eastern German cities; the others were local skinheads, neo-Nazis, hooligans, and sympathizers. However, the right-wing leader Ingo Hasselbach, who was on the scene, wrote that "Rostock hadn't been organized (by the neo-Nazis); it was a spontaneous affair that had escalated."[78] The violence was directed against the 200 Roma (Gypsy) asylum seekers who were living in a city shelter. Each evening the youth threw flagstones and Molotov cocktails at the shelter. They clashed with about 500 local police, causing injuries to many. On the third evening, city authorities decided that the asylum seekers should immediately be evacuated by buses to other shelters in the area. This was a victory for the skinheads and for the 2,000 lower middle-class residents who encouraged the rioters. The residents shouted slogans such as "Hang Them," "We Will Get You All," "Foreigners Out," and "Germany Remains Ours."[79]

As the riots continued, city authorities did not relocate the 150 Vietnamese guest workers who lived in a building next to the shelter. By 9.30 p.m. on August 24 the police units had withdrawn from the area and were stationed on a hill located some distance from the building. Thus it became an easy target for the skinheads who had surrounded it. They lobbed Molotov cocktails, setting it on fire. Firefighters arrived at the scene but could not approach the building because rightists attacked them. When the police did not come to the rescue of the firefighters, the latter withdrew after ten or fifteen minutes. In the meantime, the Vietnamese guest workers were trapped in the smoke-filled building. They managed to make their way to the roof and from there to balconies and fences. When a police officer was asked after the riot why the police did not intervene to save the building, he said that there had been no order given to move in.[80] Such an order probably was not given because the police at the time were poorly equipped and had not been reinforced. Mass arrests took place only when 1,500 agents of the well-equipped Federal Border Guard units arrived in Rostock to restore order after battling some 500 skinheads and hooligans, many of whom had overturned and torched cars.

Eventually 235 skinheads and neo-Nazis were arrested and tried for firebombing and other criminal offenses. Many juveniles received eight-month jail sentences. The CDU mayor of Rostock blamed the tension in the city on "an uncontrolled influx of foreigners," a statement that was hardly helpful under the circumstances but which reflected the bias among many policy-makers.[81] In a similar vein, Minister-President Berndt Seite (CDU) of Mecklenburg-West Pomerania, in defending the rioters, said that "they are in no way anti-foreigner, but they are not prepared to accept the abuse of the right to asylum."[82] Minister of the Interior Lothar Kupfer (CDU) asserted that if 200 asylum applicants have to live together in cramped conditions, this was bound to cause aggression among German neighbors. After Kupfer had made similar remarks on other occasions, Seite asked him to resign his post. Clearly Seite, whose views coincided with those of Kupfer, feared that his own political future might be endangered if he did not act.[83]

The Land government had been warned about the possibility of violence, but had done nothing to ward it off. After the Rostock riots, Land legislature members set up a special committee to prepare a report. They were lackadaisical about gaining details to prevent similar future incidents. Instead they were ready to discuss the general asylum issue. The international press gave full coverage to Rostock, which had become another symbol of the right-wing threat and the xenophobia among a segment of the populace and the governing authorities. Anti-fascists viewed the xenophobia, especially manifested in right-wing attacks on asylum homes, as equivalent to "ethnic cleansing" in former Yugoslavia.

Violence in western Germany

Although violence was most extensive in eastern Germany as a result of the unification's negative economic and social consequences, western Germany was not spared the neo-Nazi and skinhead attacks on foreigners, the desecration of Jewish cemeteries and synagogues, and the provocative marches and demonstrations in large and small cities. No doubt much of the violence in western Germany was inspired by that committed in eastern Germany. In western Germany, the two most widely publicized attacks against foreigners, in these instances Turks, occurred in Mölln and Solingen. In November 1992, two young rightists set fire to two apartment buildings housing numerous foreigners in Mölln, a small town in Schleswig-Holstein. The inhabitants of the first building were able to escape, but in the second one a Turkish woman, her granddaughter, and her niece burned to death. Other Turks were seriously injured.

Newspaper reports indicated that the 26-year-old Michael Peters, an unemployed handyman, had called the police from a telephone booth to claim responsibility, closing the call by shouting "Heil Hitler." Reporters pieced together his and his friend Lars Christiansen's life. Peters had been a school dropout who hardly ever worked, who was often drunk, and who gave loud parties in his apartment. When his guests staggered out before dawn some flashed the Nazi salute and shouted "Heil Hitler." At home, Peters liked to listen to recordings of Hitler's speeches. The police put him on a "watch list" of rightists. His neighbors did not dare to challenge him or his friends. For five days Peters had participated in the Rostock riots and came back home injured and limping. He formed a coterie of young disciples, including the 20-year-old Christiansen, who worked in a supermarket in Mölln. Christiansen apparently had been a member of the neo-Nazi organization FAP and collected pictures of Hitler. The two friends made trips to World War Two battlegrounds, where they dug for weapons, Nazi insignia, and other souvenirs. Bernd Wagner, the Berlin specialist on right extremists, wrote: "These are normal types. They are small people, not very intelligent, who for various reasons feel like outsiders. For them Nazism is not an ideology but a structured system of simple, traditional beliefs. It is a place of refuge, something like a religion."[84] After a court trial, the two perpetrators, Peters and Christiansen, received a life sentence and ten years respectively.

In May 1993, in an even worse incident, a group of neo-Nazis firebombed a house in Solingen in the Ruhr area. It resulted in the death of five Turkish girls and women, ranging in age from 4 to 27, and injury to eight other Turks. In response, angry Turks residing in numerous western German cities held protest marches, which resulted in the smashing of shop windows, the vandalizing of cars, and battles between rival Turkish groups. The mayor of Solingen offered a deeply felt apology. Chancellor Helmut Kohl (CDU) denounced the torching of the houses in Mölln and Solingen, but declined to travel to the two cities. He said that such trips would only represent a symbolic "grief tourism." SPD and FDP leaders criticized the chancellor for his failure to maintain peace. When Kohl appeared publicly in Berlin one week later, leftist demonstrators chanted "Coward!" and threw eggs at him.[85] In Turkey, German flags were burned amid cries of "Down with Skinheads!" and "Death to Murderers!" at the funeral for the three victims of the Mölln firebombing. The German foreign and interior ministers traveled to Turkey to attend the burial of the five women and girls who had perished in Solingen. Civic groups in West Germany also organized vast candlelit demonstrations and rallies to show their support for the Turkish population in Germany. Eventually, in October 1995, a State Superior Court in Duesseldorf found four suspects, two of whom had been only 16 years old, guilty of the Solingen firebombing and sentenced them to 10–15 years in prison, some of which they had already served. While the nation was shocked at the deaths of the Turks, right-wing violence against foreigners rose precipitously in the weeks after the bombings, as in a chain reaction, but then subsided.[86]

However, the decline of violence did not contribute to a diminution of xenophobic attitudes among rightists or the general public. There were always some unreconstructed neo-Nazis in western and eastern Germany who stored caches of munitions and weapons, Nazi propaganda sheets, swastika insignias, and busts of Hitler in their apartments or garages, which on occasion the police raided. As a result the *Verfassungsschutz* established a special unit to counter neo-Nazi activities and, as noted, dissolved a number of neo-Nazi and skinhead organizations. Yet such an action did not signify an end to the violence as the number of political asylum seekers arriving in Germany reached a high of 439,000 in 1992. The major parties decided that an amendment to the Basic Law was necessary to limit the number of foreigners seeking asylum. Accordingly, legislation was passed that made it much more difficult to gain admission into the country, a policy that the rightists and segments of the CDU/CSU had demanded for years. Despite this governmental action, the degree of violence hardly tapered off.

American blacks traveling in Germany have not been spared the violence against dark-skinned foreigners. In October 1993 a group of US athletes, members of the US national luge team, were training in Oberhof, Thuringia, to prepare for the Winter Olympics in Norway. When one evening they went to a local discotheque a group of fifteen skinheads from a nearby town shouted racist insults at Robert Pipkins, the sole black team member. Thereupon one of his white teammates, Duncan Kennedy, defended Pipkins. This infuriated the skinheads who in turn beat up Kennedy. Five of the skinheads were subsequently arrested; two eventually received tough jail sentences under the juvenile code. The government, embarrassed at the worldwide attention the case had received, issued a statement condemning the attack. Chancellor Kohl noted that Germany was a country that was hospitable to foreigners and committed to international cooperation among athletes. The Oberhof mayor warned that any further attacks in the town could ruin it financially because it relies almost entirely on sport-related tourism. One German newspaper wrote that "the right-wing riffraff in Oberhof have given a strong boost to Germany's increasing isolation."[87] Another stated: "Either all foreigners can visit Germany without courting the danger of being beaten, stabbed, thrown out of the streetcar or drowned in a lake, or we must live with the taint of racism."[88] Still other German newspapers urged the government to do more to curb racist violence.[89]

Although foreigners were most often the victims of violence, western German youth and school classes vacationing on the North Sea coast or the eastern German lakes area were targets of violence because they represented the country's wealthier classes. Western German school administrators advised teachers to have emergency phones with them when camping out. Neo-Nazis and skinheads also targeted leftists as the "enemy." For instance, in February 1997, a neo-Nazi, Kay Diesner, irritated by the taunts of leftist *Autonomen* and acting alone, shot and severely wounded a Berlin leftist book dealer whose store served as one center of the city's PDS scene. In flight in Schleswig-Holstein, a panicky Diesner subsequently killed a policeman and injured another who had approached the parked car that he was driving.[90] In a well-publicized court trial, Diesner received a life sentence in prison.

Rightists often lay claim to the space in and outside of railroad stations. In November 1997, in Angermünde, a small town located near the Polish border, five rightist women beat a 16-year-old girl to the ground and stubbed a lighted cigarette in her face, apparently for loitering in a hall that the rightists controlled. To counter this territorial claim, the leftist youth club opened the Alternative Literature and Info Café, adorned with Che Guevara and anti-Nazi murals. Fearing neo-Nazi attacks, the café resembled a bunker with boarded-up windows covered with steel mesh to shield against firebombs, and an iron grille over the door. When the café was firebombed once, the police failed to investigate the incident.[91] Such an anti-left and pro-right-wing bias on the part of the police is not unusual.

Violence is committed by neo-Nazis and skinheads, as well as by approximately 440 rightist *Autonomous Nationalists*, clad in black clothing and black sunglasses. They ruthlessly beat up or kill foreigners and leftists whom they do not like. Right-wing demonstrations and rallies often produce violence because leftist *Autonomen* or leftist counter-demonstrators will in many instances appear on the scene. To keep a precarious peace between the two hostile forces, the police, many wearing riot gear, are charged with keeping both sides apart. The situation often escalates into violence. Numerous demonstrators and the police sustain serious and lesser injuries from thrown rocks and bottles, while demonstrators are also injured by police use of water cannons and tear gas. Such battles took place on May Day 2008 in Hamburg in which 1,500 rightists battled 6,000 leftists.

Although the rightists have ceased large-scale arson attacks on hostels, they have continued to prepare for more violence. In February 1998, acting on tips of government agents who had infiltrated neo-Nazi and skinhead groups, the police in Jena, Thuringia, found in a garage a workshop in which pipe bombs filled with TNT had been fabricated. Three rightists in their early twenties, including one woman, who had installed the workshop and whom the police had observed for months, had fled the scene in time.[92] In 1998, in three other cities, the police discovered hidden guns and explosives. The authorities feared that right-wing extremism could escalate into terrorism. Reports surfaced that German neo-Nazis were buying handguns, automatic weapons, and explosives in the Ukraine and the Czech Republic. In Mecklenburg-West Pomerania, neo-Nazi terrorists were planning to use 9-mm semi-automatic Makarov pistols against "criminal" foreigners and sex offenders.[93]

The use of deadly weapons has been rare, but old-fashioned violence has continued to erupt. On February 13, 1999, another typical attack against a foreigner took place in the East German city of Guben, located near the Polish border. As a result of its location, foreigners frequently enter eastern Germany illegally and ask for asylum in Guben. They are then given housing in a dormitory for asylum seekers. Fueling the city's problem is the high unemployment rate of 23 percent, the result of the closure or downsizing of several factories. On the evening of the fateful day, an altercation between eleven bored and drunk 17–21-year-old rightists and a 28-year-old Algerian refugee, Omar ben Noui, broke out at a dance club.[94] It was preceded by an incident in which a Cuban refugee apparently injured a German right-wing youth, which precipitated a brawl between refugees and Germans. Ben Noui, accompanied by two other foreigners, ran out of the club in panic, chased by the angry rightists in cars who shouted "Foreigners out." Ben Noui thereupon accidentally crashed into the glass door of an apartment house and bled to death in fifteen minutes. A number of neo-Nazi youth were arrested on charges of manslaughter and breach of the peace. Authorities laid a memorial stone near the scene of the tragic crime. On seven different occasions rightists defaced the stone, urinated on it, or crushed the commemorative flowers.[95]

Violence spread to Dessau, renowned as the cultural home of the Bauhaus architectural movement during the Weimar era. On June 11, 2000, three youths, two of whom were 16 years old, brutally and without cause murdered Alberto Adriano, a black man from Mozambique. Adriano had lived in eastern Germany for twelve years, having come to the GDR under an exchange agreement between the GDR and the Mozambique government. He had worked as a meat packer, had married a German woman, and had three children. The night of the murder, the three youths had met by chance in the railroad station, had a drink, and had gone for a walk while waiting for their train. They stumbled on Adriano, who was returning from a party. Christian Richter, one of the young assailants, had not even been a rightist and was not interested in politics. But his friend Frank Mietbauer, whose father was dead and whose mother was hospitalized with mental illness, was drawn to the movement. In Mietbauer's apartment the police found Nazi flags and memorabilia. Mietbauer, in defense of his action, told a defense lawyer that foreigners needed to be restrained.

On occasion, homeless men have also been the objects of violence. In one instance, in July 2000, young neo-Nazis entered an abandoned house at 4 a.m. looking for homeless men who might have some money on them, which the neo-Nazis could then use to buy beer at an open gasoline station. When they found that their 52-year-old victim did not have any money on him, the neo-Nazis injured him so badly that he soon died from his injuries. In a 2001 trial, the ringleader Gunnar Doege was sentenced to life imprisonment; his three accomplices received jail sentences ranging from three to twelve years.[96]

Although the German neo-Nazis and skinheads initiate most of the violence, on occasion foreigners who felt threatened have lashed out at the rightists. In one such incident, in December 2000, in Bautzen, Saxony, three drunken Germans harassed a 15-year-old Vietnamese youth, damaged goods at his stand on the central square, and yelled anti-foreigner epithets at him. Thereupon the angry Vietnamese youth went home, picked up two kitchen knives, and returned to the market. He plunged one knife into each of the two young Germans still on the square, killing one and injuring the other. He was immediately arrested, tried, and sentenced. In this instance, the harassed Vietnamese youth became the aggressor and the skinheads the victims, in a tragic twist of incidents in which rightists and foreigners are involved.[97]

On numerous occasions in 2003 and 2004 groups of right-wing teenagers in Havelland, northwest of Berlin, staged a series of arson attacks late at night against Turkish and Vietnamese-owned snack bars and small restaurants. In one instance, a fire spread to a nearby shopping mall, causing extensive damage. In a Potsdam court, the judge, labeling the youth as terrorists, sentenced the group's leader to four and a half years in prison. The other eleven youth, ranging in age from 14 to 19, received various terms of probation for their involvement.[98]

In October 2004, an instance of police indifference occurred in the city of Gera, Thuringia. Three neo-Nazis severely injured one leftist youth who, with friends, was standing in front of a club frequented by leftist and foreign youth. The friends notified the police who, after a four-minute telephone conversation, told the youth to look into a history book for the proper definition of a Nazi before making accusations about the right-wing perpetrators. After a second phone call a police cruiser finally showed up forty-five minutes later. The rightists of course had fled by then. This incident was one of several that put the city on the map as another center of right-wing activity. In one of the attacks in Gera, after chanting anti-foreigner slogans, forty neo-Nazis attacked two asylum seekers from Iraq in the central railroad station. In this instance the police responded quickly, arrested three ringleaders, and confiscated iron pipes and other non-lethal weapons.[99]

Still another case of violence occurred in Potsdam, the capital of Land Brandenburg. In the early morning of Easter 2006 two presumed rightists assaulted a 37-year-old hydraulic engineer, Ermyas Mulugeta, at a trolley car stop. He was a naturalized German citizen born in Ethiopia, married with two children, who was completing his PhD studies. The two perpetrators first called the dark-skinned man "dirty nigger" and "pig." Then they attacked him with a bottle, beat him to the ground, and repeatedly kicked him in the head and body. He remained in a coma in one of the local hospitals; for three weeks his life hung in the balance. The federal government was aware of the damage to Germany's image that such an attack had caused. In an unusual move restricted to exceptional cases, Germany's Federal Prosecutor Kay Nehm, rather than a local prosecutor, immediately began an investigation. The police announced a $6,000 reward for information leading to the culprits' arrest. Two suspects were arrested as the possible perpetrators, but in June 2007 charges against them were dropped for lack of sufficient evidence.

Soon after the assault on Mulugeta an Italian citizen claimed to have been assaulted by rightists in Berlin. In this instance the claim was false. He was drunk and had hurt himself falling on trolley tracks. The authorities brought charges against the Italian for feigning an incident, which is rare compared to the thousands of proven rightist-inspired violent incidents.

In preparation for the World Cup soccer matches in Germany in June 2006, the police made plans to minimize violent incidents. One plan was to bar entry to Germany of foreign skinheads and hooligans who might clash, because of national rivalries, with German rightists at the games or thereafter. The World Cup organizers warned British fans planning to come to Germany that those caught flashing a Nazi salute to insult German spectators would be arrested. Television networks were requested to turn off the sound or interrupt the broadcast should a racial incident take place during the games. Organizers were also worried that rightists would sing racial monkey chants in the stadiums, as they have done in German soccer matches, to taunt black soccer players.

The Africa Council, an umbrella organization of African community groups and activists in Germany, in reaction to the Potsdam incident, warned black visitors to the games to avoid certain Berlin and eastern Germany districts, especially in Brandenburg and Saxony-Anhalt. There violence had broken out in the past. According to Moctar Kamara, president of the Africa Council, his group planned to set up a website and to distribute brochures with maps of the "no-go" areas and with lists of bars, clubs, and other establishments where black and other foreign visitors could be at risk of racist attacks. Länder and local German officials were upset that their areas were singled out. According to a police spokeswoman in Magdeburg, the capital of Saxony-Anhalt, "There are xenophobic incidents, but they happen everywhere. I do not know why Herr Kamara picked our state as the worst example." In response, the Africa Council president noted that politicians were trying to ignore the problem. He said "The majority of victims of racism are outside the statistics, as African people often do not dare to go to the police. Violent assaults motivated by racist hatred are therefore registered as 'normal' incidents."[100] To the dismay of Brandenburg and Saxony-Anhalt officials whose Länder were singled out as dangerous territories, Uwe-Karsten Heye (SPD), a former government spokesman, publicly agreed with Kamara's warnings. In the wake of further criticisms of Heye, Daniel Cohn-Bendit, a Green Party deputy in the European Parliament, said: "The reality is school classes with many immigrant children question whether it is safe to go to Brandenburg or Mecklenburg-West Pomerania for camping trips." Ekin Deligöz, a Green deputy in the Bundestag with Turkish roots, said of right-wing extremists: "That's what they want. They want foreigners to stay home and not even come to Germany in the first place."[101]

The World Cup games turned out to be peaceful. However, the well-publicized violence in eastern Germany on other occasions led to a decline in foreign investments and tourism in that territory. The authors of foreign travel guidebooks warned dark-skinned foreigners and homosexual tourists to be extremely cautious in walking through small cities, towns, and isolated low-income areas after dark. The tourists were also advised to be cautious on suburban trains at night and to avoid areas near the railroad stations, where right-wing assaults frequently take place. The US State Department issued an unprecedented warning to American travelers to be wary of drunken skinheads and hooligans.[102] Several foreign professors who had been invited to teach at eastern German universities declined the offers, fearing violence against them. Similarly, some foreign students at these universities, which were eager to build up an international reputation, were the targets of rightist violence, but not on the campuses.

One incident received worldwide publicity in August 2007. In the small town of Muegeln in Saxony a group of fifty rightists chased eight Indian nationals during a local festival through the market place and brutally attacked them in a pizzeria whose windows were smashed and doors kicked in. The rightists shouted "foreigners out" and "Germany for Germans" during verbal altercations between the two groups. The town's citizens did not protect the Indians. The conservative mayor accused the media of whipping up a campaign against the town and criticized leading politicians for their malicious comments. Chancellor Merkel condemned the attack and urged citizens to show personal courage. She sent a similar message in the wake of an incident in Passau, Bavaria, where a suspected neo-Nazi in December 2008 inflicted near-fatal stab wounds on the police chief, Alois Mannichi, who is committed to fighting neo-Nazis and skinheads.[103]

As noted, rightists have targeted primarily foreigners, leftists, homosexuals, and the homeless. But they also have been hostile to the Gypsies. Romani Rose, the chairman of the Central Council of Sinti and Roma in Germany, alerted Germans about the rising violence against his people. He said that after the Nazis exterminated more than 20,000 Gypsies, mostly in Auschwitz, it was a cause for alarm for a democratic system if the Holocaust survivors among the Gypsies had to fear for their lives once again.[104]

Violence has marred the traditional May Day holiday demonstrations and rallies organized by left political parties and the trade unions to celebrate the gains of the past and to protest governmental policies that have hurt the working class. In recent years, on that day, the NPD has organized counter-demonstrations, which have led to serious clashes between the opposing forces and the police. For instance, on May 1, 2007, nearly 2,000 people participated in a protest against right-wing extremists in Dortmund (western Germany). Right-wing groups marshaled 650 members in a different area of the city. The demonstrations and rallies led to more than 300 ultra-leftist rioters setting fire to train tracks, streetcars, and buses. The police arrested numerous participants. In Erfurt, eastern Germany, about 1,300 NPD members marched through the city center, some hurling bottles and cobblestones at police. The demonstration produced clashes with ultra-leftists, who in turn caused some damage to property.[105]

German neo-Nazi groups and individuals have been active in foreign countries. In December 1993, the police investigated the possible involvement of German neo-Nazis in the series of mail bombings that swept Austria. Thereafter the German *Bundesverfassungsschutz* sent a liaison official to Austria on permanent assignment. German neo-Nazis also became involved in foreign conflicts. During the first Persian Gulf War in 1991 several neo-Nazis offered their services to Iraq as mercenaries. Others volunteered to travel to the Balkans to join the Croatian Defense Force.

Anti-Semitic acts

Since unification, there have been relatively few incidents involving Jews when compared to the numerous serious attacks on foreigners. This has not been due to a lack of anti-Semitism among rightists or a segment of the general population, however. Rather it is because there are relatively few Jews in Germany and they are not easily recognizable, unless they are orthodox Jews. Occasionally non-Jewish persons have been taken for Jews and have been assaulted. In one such attack, in November 1992, two skinheads were drinking in a pub with a 53-year-old man. When the bartender told them in error that the man was Jewish, they beat him, set him on fire and then, in a car that the bartender lent them, dumped the charred corpse across the border in the Dutch town of Venlo. The two perpetrators and the bartender received long prison sentences.[106]

The possibility of prison sentences has not stopped neo-Nazis and skinheads from attacking Jewish sites and spreading anti-Jewish propaganda, especially since the early 1990s. For instance, to taunt the Jewish community in Erfurt (Thuringia), skinheads on occasion have stood in front of the local synagogue, their faces visible to the surveillance camera, singing Nazi songs, and yelling "Jewish pigs." Neighbors, either afraid or in sympathy with the skinheads, did not call the police. At times, prominent Jews, especially members of the Central Council of Jews in Germany, have received insulting telephone calls or mail threats.[107]

Most of the offenses have consisted of vandalizing Jewish cemeteries. From 1945 to 1989 an average of eighteen cemeteries per year were desecrated. Since 1990 the number has risen to forty per year. One specialist has calculated that from 1945 to 1999 in West Germany and in the GDR, and thereafter in united Germany, more than 1,000 acts of vandalism have taken place in Jewish cemeteries. In many cemeteries, vandals repeatedly smeared slogans, such as "Death to the Jews", "SS," or "Jews Out," and painted swastikas on the smashed or overturned gravestones.[108] The number of gravestones damaged in anti-Semitic actions has risen since 1990. For instance, in early October 1999, vandals in one night damaged 103 gravestones in the Jewish cemetery of Berlin-Weissensee, the largest in Europe. Earlier, in December 1998, an unknown vandal or vandals used a homemade bomb to destroy Heinz Galinski's marble tomb, located in the Jewish cemetery in Berlin-Charlottenburg. Galinski had been head of the Berlin Jewish Community since 1949 and head of the Central Council of Jews in Germany from 1988 until his death in 1992. Leading German politicians, including the Federal Republic's President Roman Herzog, condemned the bombing and called on Germans to fight anti-Semitism. As happened so often in cemetery vandalism, the police were unable to find the guilty person or persons, primarily because Jewish cemeteries are normally located in isolated areas on the outskirts of cities and towns, based on old municipal regulations. However, in some cemeteries there is a caretaker, video cameras have been installed, and the police occasionally have sent patrols.[109]

Ignatz Bubis, who had succeeded Galinski as president of the Central Council of Jews in Germany, decided that he would be buried in Israel rather than in Germany after having heard of the attack on Galinski's tomb. Months before Bubis' death in August 1999, in reflecting on his past, he felt that he had not contributed measurably to an increase in fraternal relations between German Jews and non-Jews. After his death, Chancellor Schröder, in a message to the Bubis family, wrote that on the contrary Bubis, more than most, made it possible for Jews to see a future for themselves in Germany. Bubis' wish to be buried in Israel was honored. German President Johannes Rau and Minister of the Interior Otto Schily took part in the ceremonies in Tel Aviv, which leading Israeli politicians also attended.[110]

In September 1992, to combat anti-Semitic actions, one Land criminal police official urged that all Länder criminal offices contribute information on anti-Semitic acts to a new databank set up by a special federal office in Berlin. Since then the office has coordinated moves to fight anti-Semitism. This action was taken after the torching of the "Jewish barrack" located on the Sachsenhausen concentration camp memorial site. Yet despite the government's initiative, firebombings of synagogues and Holocaust memorials, some located in former concentration camps, have continued. In 1994 and again in 1995, the Lübeck synagogue was firebombed, causing damage in each instance. The 1994 attack was the first one against a synagogue since the Nazi era. One memorial to the victims of Nazism in Berlin-Kreuzberg was vandalized four times.

Anti-Semitic acts have peaked on certain historic occasions. In November 1998, on the eve of the 60th anniversary of the November 9, 1938 Jewish pogroms in Germany, rightists damaged a memorial in Berlin and a Jewish community house in Potsdam, and sprayed Nazi slogans on houses in Schwerin and on a deportation memorial in Berlin-Tiergarten. On April 20, 2000, the day of Hitler's birthday, rightists threw Molotov cocktails at the synagogue in Erfurt. Neighboring residents extinguished the fire in time. On July 27, 2000, unknown terrorists detonated a hand grenade at a crowded elevated train station in Duesseldorf in western Germany. Seven women and three men, students at a nearby language school, were injured, many severely, including a woman who sustained a miscarriage as a result of the attack. Seven of the ten victims were Jewish immigrants from Russia. The police interrogated more than 1,400 persons and offered a high reward for any information on the assailants, who might have been right-wing extremists and anti-Semites. But nine years later the police still have not found any suspects. According to Paul Spiegel, chairman of the Central Council of Jews in Germany, Jews in Germany have become more fearful and cautious than ever before. On another occasion he said that "After such repeated attacks on synagogues, one is justifiably entitled to ask whether it was right to rebuild Jewish communities in Germany."[111]

In January 2001 the Potsdam Jewish cemetery's memorial hall and in April 2002 the Berlin-Kreuzberg synagogue were firebombed, but the latter fire was quickly extinguished. As a result of these anti-Semitic acts and the parallel to the Nazi past, police officers are stationed around the clock at some Jewish sites or patrol there frequently.[112] On June 24, 2006, seven suspected neo-Nazis, members of a dissolved right-extremist group, first burned a US flag and then threw a copy of *The Diary of Anne Frank* on to a bonfire at a village summer solstice festival in Pretzien, near Magdeburg. About eighty villagers, including the mayor, witnessed the incident, but no one protested at the time. Prosecutors claimed that the neo-Nazi men, aged between 24 and 29, ridiculed Anne Frank "and all those who died in the concentration camps." The men used language praising Nazism and chanted "German youth, German blood." The men face up to five years imprisonment under the same laws that cover Holocaust denial and racial incitement.[113] In February 2007 unknown assailants threw a smoke bomb into a Jewish nursery in Berlin and smeared swastikas and the slogan "Jews out" on the building's façade. No children or staff members were inside the building at the time.[114]

The numerous and increasing anti-Semitic incidents and acts of violence committed by rightists led Charlotte Knobloch, president of the Central Council of Jews in Germany since Paul Spiegel's death in 2006, to compare these "blatant and aggressive" acts with those after 1933 when Hitler came to power. She urged the police and the courts to take a hard line toward extremists whose message "has become firmly entrenched in certain spheres of our society." On another occasion she said that right-wing violence reminded her "of the time after 1933."[115] Shimon Stein, Israel's ambassador to Germany, viewed the right-wing parties as no longer marginal. He said that he was concerned that Jews do not feel safe in Germany.[116]

This chronological survey of anti-Semitic acts must be supplemented by statistical data. In a typical three-year period 1993–1995, there were 217 anti-Semitic incidents (more than one per week), of which 69 consisted of damage to property; 60 physical injuries; 48 cemetery desecrations; 38 threats to individuals; and 2 breaches of the public peace. Of the right-extremist participants, 95 percent were primarily 17–24-year-old men. One 81-year-old fanatic Nazi was involved in thirty-one judicial inquiries. The largest group of those involved in anti-Semitic physical violence and anti-Semitic propaganda were the neo-Nazis (36.9 percent), followed by the skinheads (16.6 percent).[117] In 2005, rightists committed 1,658 anti-Semitic offenses, of which most involved banned propaganda. However, the offenses also included forty-nine acts of violence. At some soccer games, anti-Semitic youth shout "Referee-Jew" if a referee makes an unpopular decision. During a game in Leipzig the local right-wing fans arranged themselves in the stands in the form of a swastika.[118]

On occasion, Palestinians and Arabs from North African countries residing in Germany, rather than native rightists, have been guilty of anti-Semitic acts in Germany. In October 2000, two youth, one a Palestinian and the other a German citizen who was born in Morocco, hurled three firebombs at the Duesseldorf synagogue during the night before the Day of German Unity, in a symbolic protest against Israeli policies. A neighbor living next to the synagogue put out the flames before they caused extensive damage. Five days later, thousands of Palestinians in several German cities peacefully demonstrated against the Israeli government's actions against Palestinians in the occupied territories. However, in the North Rhine-Westphalia city of Essen, about 250 demonstrators attempted to attack the Old Synagogue. When the police blocked them, the demonstrators threw paving stones and base plates at the synagogue, causing considerable damage to the stained glass windows. The police arrested 175 people to check their identity cards.[119] The Muslim Federation in Germany has urged its members not to join the anti-Semites. However, in 2003, immigrant Arab youth attacked a 19-year-old orthodox American Jew wearing side burns, a yarmulke, and a Star of David in the Berlin subway. In beating him up, they called him a "filthy Jew." He was able to flee the attackers. Two other attacks against orthodox Jews occurred in Berlin in the same year. In each instance the police were unable to find the assailants.[120]

Government actions

In the early 1990s the federal government was worried about the escalating violence and the racist outbursts, especially in eastern Germany. The result was considerable damage to its image abroad, declining foreign investments, and a slump in tourism. Thus it publicly denounced the mounting incidents and demanded vigorous judicial prosecution of the rightists. The Federal Ministry of the Interior and its Länder counterparts forbade a number of demonstrations and meetings. They also banned seventeen neo-Nazi groups, primarily between 1992 and 1998.[121] In justification of its bans, the Federal Ministry said the groups failed to support the constitutional order, were anti-Semitic, opposed to foreigners living in Germany, honored Nazi leaders, and adopted Nazi rituals. Ministry officials also confiscated right-wing literature, weapons, and membership lists in the leaders' homes. Judges sentenced a number of activists to considerable jail sentences for having broken the law. However, despite these measures, violence was not stamped out, partly because the neo-Nazi movement changed its tactics and partly because the skinheads, despite the bans on some of its groups, continued to use violence against their foes.

Conclusion

Significant organizational changes have taken place in the neo-Nazi movement from the time of German unification to the present. The formal neo-Nazi groups, many of which the government banned during the early 1990s, were supplanted by loosely organized *Kameradschaften*. These often operate in so-called "national liberated zones" located in small conservative east

German towns. Government authorities have cracked down on some right-wing groups and, partly in response to pressure from the rightists, on the flow of illegal immigrants. Such moves were made in order to increase domestic tranquility and security and to meet legitimate charges that the government's tough response to leftist terrorism in earlier decades was not matched by its response to right-wing violence and terrorism. As one German newspaper put it, "There is no justification for murder, manslaughter and arson, regardless of who commits it and who the victim is."[122] However, despite crackdowns on rightists the degree of their violence and brutality toward powerless social groups, especially toward foreigners and the homeless, has hardly decreased. The violence has escalated, partly because a new generation of young neo-Nazis and skinheads has taken over from the old guard. These youth once again act out their boredom, their racism, and their xenophobia by hitting out, injuring, and killing the defenseless. In their violent deeds they have no empathy for the victims. The old guard in turn consists now of veterans of violence who have graduated into non-violent political support for the right-wing parties. Immigrant youth of the second and third generation, to protect themselves from the right extremists, have formed defense groups, which at times take the offensive against the right extremists.

Right-wing violence has meant that the government leaders have had to cope swiftly with the country's image problems. They have had to counter the adverse effects on foreign investments and tourism, especially in eastern Germany. For instance, Dresden's business leaders who had planned a trip to the United States in 1993 to find new investors scrapped their trip knowing that their search would end in failure. In the early 1990s, up to 10 percent fewer tourists, especially from Japan, Great Britain, and the United States, visited eastern Germany, which resulted in substantial losses to the tourist industry.[123] Even the Goethe Institutes that operate German language schools and cultural centers across the world reported that enrolment in their language courses had dropped significantly because of an "enormous wave of antipathy" toward Germany. Such attitudes were reinforced when foreigners read reports, for instance, about some neo-Nazi groups, such as the *Stahlhelm-Kampfbund für Europa* (Steel Helmet – Fighting League for Europe), recruiting 10–16-year-old youth into "children circles." The group had also organized summer camps for the 17–21-year-old youth, some of whom even received marksmanship training at former military rifle ranges.

In the early 2000s, the right-wing terrorist threat assumed another dimension. The government was wary of a neo-Nazi group, the German National Party, which had formed links with an alleged Islamic terrorist group, *Hizbut-Tahrir* (Party of Liberation). The Islamic group has members in numerous European countries and purportedly has had contacts with one of the September 11, 2001 planners. In 2001, two members of the German National Party attended a meeting of *Hizbut-Tahrir*. The German government intelligence officials were worried that the country's right-wing groups would join forces with Islamists in their common hatred of Israel.

In December 2001 the German government banned twenty Islamic groups. In January 2003, it banned *Hizbut-Tahrir*, but in the meantime other groups have become active.[124] However, the degree of cooperation between German right-wing and Islamic groups is likely to be minimal because of the German rightists' xenophobic and racist views toward foreigners.[125] To illustrate: in June 2000 four rightists in the city of Gera (Thuringia) smashed a window in the local mosque. This kind of an anti-Muslim action may be the forerunner of more in the coming years, such as the right populists' protest in September 2008 in Cologne against the construction of a giant mosque in the city. After left extremists threatened the rally's supporters, the police forbade the rally that the Citizens Movement pro-Cologne had organized. The Movement plans to help found similar right-populist groups in other German cities. In opposition to such plans, democratic citizens can be expected to show their support for the Islamic community and for a multicultural Germany.[126]

Observers of the German political scene are worried about the degree of public support that the neo-Nazi and skinhead activities have received from the more conservative segment of the public. In some towns the local conservative politicians have suggested that the police should not act too harshly toward bored right-wing youth, some of whom have joined the Hells Angels motorcycle gangs, because the real enemy lies on the political left. Many citizens support skinheads because they uphold German values of orderliness, unlike punks and leftists.[127] As a result, victims of neo-Nazi terrorism feel that the authorities are not providing them with enough support. Indeed numerous authorities have taken the same position, as have the rightists, against more immigration into Germany. Thus, when the rightists engage in violence against their foes, they feel that they are on the winning side. After all, local authorities and the police often side with them in their demands for legislative restrictions on the number of immigrants coming into the country or other issues affecting immigrants. This feeling of victory in turn reinforces the feeling among rightists that they can force changes by escalating their violent actions. On the table remain their long-range goals of achieving a national socialist revolution in which a revived NSDAP would flourish.

5
Tools of Propaganda and Recruitment

Any organization seeks to attract more members and followers to achieve its objectives. German neo-Nazi parties and groups, as well as skinheads, have had a checkered record in gaining significant support from their potential target groups such as high school students, apprentices, fraternity members, and soldiers. The right-wing organizations, never too strong when compared to catch-all parties, have used an array of propaganda and recruitment tools in the cultural realm, ranging from their own newspapers, journals, and publishing houses to cultural organizations, television, the internet, rock bands, and even fanzines. In this survey we explore the various tools and attempt to gauge their effectiveness.[1] As Armin Pfahl-Traughber notes, right extremists realize that in order to achieve a political victory, be it a street demonstration or an electoral success, an ideological victory must precede it.[2] The question arises how successful have such efforts been, especially in the new youth-oriented media, in shaping the minds of others. There is no easy answer.

Although the focus of this volume is on the period since 1990, in West Germany many extreme right-wing publications date back to the decades since the 1950s when the bitterness of a lost war was still uppermost in the minds of many Germans.

Newspapers

In the print media, newspapers play an important, although declining, role. In 2005, according to the Ministry of Interior reports, the number of right-extremist publications totaled 90, a decline from 103 in 2004. Fifty-one of the journals appeared at least quarterly.[3] The leading right-extremist newspapers have been those owned by the multimillionaire DVU chairman Frey. In 1951 he and former Nazi and army officials published the *Deutsche Soldaten-Zeitung*, which, for instance, glorified German army battles against the Soviets during World War Two. The US administration, in its anticommunist crusade, partly financed the *Deutsche Soldaten-Zeitung* from 1951

117

until 1953. When it stopped payments, Frey turned to the German Federal Press Office for financial support. The government subsidized the paper for a brief time but then stopped payments when it realized that the paper's revisionist theses were becoming too controversial.

Beginning in 1963 the *Deutsche Soldaten-Zeitung* appeared as the *Deutsche National-Zeitung,* Frey altered its frequency of publication from monthly to weekly.[4] In 1999 the *Deutsche National-Zeitung* and the *Deutsche Wochen-Zeitung* merged, but retained their names. In 2006, the weekly circulation stood at 35,000. Frey's newspaper contains few stories based on the reporters' own research. In his newspapers, Frey has constantly sought to recruit new DVU members. Advertisements have featured books printed in his publishing firms.[5] To maximize his yearly profits Frey, who owns numerous apartment houses in Berlin and Munich, also set up a book buying club, a travel agency, and a shop selling Nazi era trinkets.[6]

In addition to Frey's newspaper empire there are independently owned regional right-wing newspapers, such as the *Berlin-Brandenburger-Zeitung der nationalen Erneuerung* (BBZ; *Berlin-Brandenburg Newspaper for National Renewal*). The BBZ has appeared once every six weeks. Its editors have been able to recruit top neo-Nazis to contribute articles.[7] Other neo-Nazi propaganda organs have surfaced, such as *Sturm* (*Storm*) in Schleswig-Holstein, which denounces anti-fascists, criminals, and drug dealers. In 2003, Joachim Siegerist, the German Conservatives chairman, founded the monthly *Konservative Deutsche Zeitung,* with a circulation of 40,000 copies and an estimated readership of 100,000. From 1993 to 1994 the journal *Einblick* (*Insight*) was distributed in Germany from a post office box in Denmark because its contents would have been cause for criminal proceedings against the journal's editor. For instance, in its November 1993 issue *Einblick* printed the names and addresses of 250 "Red Front" individuals and "anarchist-*chaoten*" who, according to the journal, should be prepared to spend "restless" nights at home. The list also included the names of well-known unionists, teachers, lawyers, writers, and social workers, as well as the names of leftist bars, bookshops, youth centers, and copy shops. This tactic of intimidation was another step in the right-wing attempt to "smash the antifascists" in an "anti-anti-fascist" campaign.

Journals

Numerous right-wing German journals seek to spread rightist ideology.[8] In 1950 Arthur Ehrhardt founded the *Nation Europa* publishing house, which printed a monthly journal, *Nation & Europa*. In 2007 it had a monthly circulation of 18,000. Ehrhardt, a former SS officer, made *Nation & Europa* the most important right-wing periodical in West Germany and one of the top ones in Europe. He was an admirer of the British fascist leader Oswald Mosley who had proposed to form a European volunteer army against Bolshevism.

Most of the journal's young authors supported the concept of nationalism and opposed European integration in which Germany would lose some of its sovereignty.[9]

Upon Ehrhardt's death in 1971 Peter Dehoust, a high NPD official, took over as publisher. In January 1990 *Nation & Europa* bought out the journal *Deutsche Monatshefte* (*German Monthly Brochures*). The editors called on all patriots to create a true people's party. In 1992 Karl Richter, who had been on the Republikaner top staff until 1990, became editor-in-chief. In 2006, circulation stood at 18,000. Two prominent right-wing leaders, Harald Neubauer and Adolf von Thadden, joined the journal's editorial board. As a result the journal has become increasingly an NPD mouthpiece under their influence.[10]

The publishing houses of these publications often performed the services of a mail order company by selling Reich war flags, calendars, posters, jewelry, compact disks of Nazi leaders' speeches, right-wing CDs, DVDs, video cassettes, and other neo-Nazi, folk, and Germanic-mythological paraphernalia.

Herbert Grabert, who during World War Two had been a high official in Alfred Rosenberg's Reich Ministry for Occupied Territories, founded in 1953 the Grabert publishing house in Tübingen. From 1955 on, he edited the *Deutsche Hochschullehrer-Zeitung* (*German Professors Journal*), which sought the reinstatement of Nazi professors in their former positions and which praised the Nazi regime's foreign policy. In 1972 it was renamed *Deutschland in Geschichte und Gegenwart* (*Germany in History and the Present*). After Grabert's death in 1978, his son Wigbert took over the journal, which has appeared quarterly and has a circulation of 8,000. Rolf Kosiek, a former NPD theoretician, became editor-in-chief.

Publishing houses

In 2006, thirty-three right-extremist publishing houses and marketing companies brought out books and other printed media. Among the publishers was Herbert Grabert who was one of the earliest right-wing publishers in West Germany. He has printed books by nearly all prominent German rightwingers. Udo Walendy published a book whitewashing the Hitler regime. Later the author became a high functionary in the NPD. In 1978 publisher Herbert Grabert's son Wigbert, taking over the publishing house, continued to issue revisionist books. Thus in 1992 he printed the chemist Germar Rudolf's brochure, which allegedly proved that no cyclone-B gas could have been used in Auschwitz. The neo-Nazi leader Otto Ernst Romer sent the brochure provocatively to the "Jewish Führer" Bubis (then head of the Central Council of Jews in Germany) and to numerous German scientists.

Other writers insisted that the Holocaust's official account was based on falsified historical facts and Allied reeducation efforts and that no Jews were gassed at Auschwitz. In 1994 one opinion poll indicated that the writers received considerable support for their historical revisionism. Approximately 1.9 million Germans believed that Auschwitz had been a "lie."[11]

In Toronto, the German-born Ernst Zündel, who had emigrated to Canada in 1958, denied the Holocaust in propaganda materials that he sent by bulk mail to Germany. In one two-year period West German authorities intercepted 200 shipments, most of which came from Canada. In 2005, a Canadian judge ordered that Zündel be deported to Germany. He was detained in Mannheim prison to await trial for inciting racial hatred. In 2007 he was sentenced to five years in prison for stirring up hatred against a minority of the population. He has appealed the sentence.[12] Earlier, in the 1970s, the British author David Irving, another Holocaust denier, made several illegal trips to Germany at the invitation of neo-Nazi leaders. He was arrested on a few occasions and had to pay modest fines.

In recent years, the Grabert publishing house has become more restrained in the themes of its publications. Thus it has not stepped over the threshold of glorifying Nazism, which under the Basic Law is a crime and would result in court actions. However, the Arndt publishing house has issued a number of books and video documentaries detailing the Hitler regime's alleged achievements.[13]

Grabert also manages the Hohenrain publishing house in Tübingen. This publisher seeks to sell not only books aimed at the right-extremist market but also at the broader public. Many of the books deal with contemporary foreign and domestic issues. In 1991 Gert Sudholt, stepson of the NSDAP Reich deputy press chief, founded Berg and Druffel publishers in Bavaria.[14] Berg's publication lists contain numerous memoirs by former Nazis, with anti-Semitic and pro-Nazi content. As a result, Sudholt was prosecuted on at least three occasions and jailed for six months in 1993.

In the 1990s some of the right-wing publishers distanced themselves from the propaganda reflected in the many books that had appeared under their imprint in earlier decades. They were aware that once the government put a book on the prohibited list, all unsold copies had to be destroyed. Often the publishers appealed the lower court decisions, but most of the time they lost their appeals.

In addition to a number of right-extremist publishing houses, marketing companies sprouted. They distributed numerous books, pamphlets, compact disks, and videos praising Hitler, the Hitler youth, the SS, and other Nazi organizations. The Hohenberg publishing and media house was one of the largest purveyors of such right-wing materials. In its online catalogue "World Net Shop" it has offered, among numerous items, a booklet "From National Resistance to National Attack"; a CD *Prussian Blue – For the Fatherland*; a map "Dictate of Versailles"; jewelry containing a Celtic cross or a Viking ship; a pin "White Power"; and numerous other right paraphernalia. In late 2006, the government began legal proceedings against Hohenberg seeking to put its catalogue items on a prohibited list. In turn Hohenberg initiated a legal counter-offensive. It asserted that the items for sale did not fall into a prohibited list.[15]

From 1980 on, video cassettes, including those praising Hitler, entered the underground market. In 1982, the Federal Ministry of Youth, Family, and Health prohibited a video film called *Trilogie*. This was a copy of a 1938 Nazi propaganda film in which the German masses are shown enthusiastically greeting Hitler.[16] Since the early 1990s fanzines and comic books with neo-Nazi themes in pictures and short statements have appeared as well as comic books approving the killing of neo-Nazi opponents as a step to Aryanizing German society.[17]

Various neo-Nazi parties and groups distributed propaganda materials at information stands and to passers-by in towns and cities. For instance, in 1991 the neo-Nazi group Nationalist Front handed out 400,000 flyers about the Auschwitz "lie." Other flyers dealt with the power of world Jewry and with the Jewish appeals for Germans to remember the Holocaust. Whenever liberal or conservative newspaper editors in Germany ran stories supporting the Jewish point of view, they would receive flyers and brochures from neo-Nazi organizations that publicized the neo-Nazi position.[18]

Cultural organizations

Right-wing leaders set up a number of cultural organizations to gain support among conservative national opinion-makers. In 1950 Herbert Böhme, a former high SA functionary, founded the *Deutsche Kulturwerk Europäischen Geistes* (*German Cultural Work of European Thought*). It issued the *Klüter-Blättern* and assisted the publication of works by former Nazi authors.

In 1960 the right-wing publisher Gert Sudholt and erstwhile Nazi functionaries founded the *Gesellschaft für Freie Publizistik* (*Society for Free Communication*), which grew to a membership in 2005 of about 500 journalists, editors, writers, academics, book dealers, and publishers. The Society, which has become the leading right-wing cultural organization, has promoted the works of authors of different right-wing views, supported right-wing journals, created working groups, and held meetings, seminars, and yearly conventions. The Society, with close ties to the NPD, has issued a quarterly newsletter and has scheduled numerous well-known rightists as speakers.

The right-wing political parties have sought to establish congresses, education, and social centers for their members and sympathizers in various German Länder. They are interested in buying old hotels, inns, and farm houses in order to convert them into such centers. The parties have run into trouble when negotiations to purchase real estate properties become public knowledge. Then the citizens, worried that their towns will be known as "brown (fascist) centers," might petition the authorities to buy the real estate instead. However, even when right-wing educational centers are established, as is true of the NPD's Dresden School, which claims to be a counterpart to the leftist Frankfurt School, their intellectual contributions to political discourse are minimal. Peter Dehoust and Karl Richter, editors of *Nation & Europa – Deutsche Monatshefte*, who head the Dresden School, are veteran ideologues but lack enough vision and support among their followers to make the School a threat to democratic values.[19]

Not surprisingly, the various cultural centers' organizers also have made use of the internet as another propaganda tool. But, unlike the cultural centers, there is little intellectual dialogue on this expanding communications link. Similarly, in the publishing world not a single right-wing book appeared on the market in 2006, except for a translation of a book by the French New Right author Guillaume Faye.[20]

The visual media

German television, as is true in other countries, is one of the most important media as a news and entertainment source. The increased number of private stations competing with the government stations gives the right-wing parties an opportunity to be seen and heard on the airwaves. One television talk show host invited, for instance, the neo-Nazi leader Udo Voigt and the SPD theorist Peter Glotz to a debate. Glotz had no difficulty scoring points in their policy disagreements. In a 2004 poll of Berlin viewers, 55 percent of respondents said that DVU and NPD representatives should be invited to talk shows; 40 percent answered in the negative.[21] Rightists made a video, shown on a television station, about Nazi leader Rudolf Hess. They labeled him as a "peace flyer" when he flew to Scotland on May 10, 1941. He intended to negotiate peace with the British, but the flight resulted in his capture and long-term imprisonment.

The public station producers represent a liberal and left-of-center orientation, which is reflected at times in their choice of programs. In one instance, in 2000 they showed a documentary film in which they interviewed government specialists of the right-wing scene. The film surveys the internet and warns about the racism and anti-Semitism visible on the computer screen. At other times the producers have shown the American *Holocaust* series, the film *Schindler's List*, and Art Spiegelman's *Mouse* comic strip. However, television viewers can also see a number of soap operas on private television stations that show a right-of-center but not extremist point of view. The programs emphasize the pre-modern *Volk* and *Heimat*, the family, the authoritarian father figure, nature, and the soil. These are concepts that have an uncanny resemblance to aspects of Nazi ideology.

The fake violence and murders, especially on police shows, portrayed on some television programs play into the hands of neo-Nazis and skinheads who see their own violent actions as justifiable and legitimate. In the police shows the neo-Nazis are often portrayed as psychopaths who are beyond the pale socially and who are negligibly important.[22] Rightists, to offset some stereotypes and to gain more exposure, are eager to appear on television's nightly news programs and on magazine, interview, and talk shows. At election time the right-wing parties get an opportunity to show provocative brief television advertisements. Directors have made a few feature documentary films, such as *Profession: Neo-Nazi*, about the neo-Nazi movement that depicts the life of the photogenic neo-Nazi leader Ingo Hasselbach. The film, subsidized by several Länder governments, shows him visiting Auschwitz. There he asserts that the ventilation system made gassings technically impossible. Whether such films, some shown on German television, make the neo-Nazi and skinhead scene more rather than less interesting to potential young recruits is difficult to tell. The anti-Nazi film director Winfried Bonengel deliberately did not want to make a film that would show the neo-Nazi culture, the violence, and the leader's blind followers, for fear of making it a cult film that would attract teenage youth who may then be prone to join an extremist group. Rather, Hasselbach's eventual break with the neo-Nazi movement was shown in the documentary film as a positive move on his part, but relatively few neo-Nazi members, as will be seen, have followed the government-initiated strategy to help them break away. Despite the director's effort to make a balanced film, he did not succeed. Bubis, head of the Central Council of Jews in Germany, asserted that "the film is a horror. It's pure Nazi propaganda." In the wake of further protests, officials of the four sponsoring Länder reviewed the film. Hamburg and Mecklenburg-West Pomerania took no action against the film, characterizing the protests as excessive. Brandenburg urged the addition of a commentary. In the toughest response, Hesse demanded the return of its subsidy and banned the film's showing. The spokesman for the Hesse prosecutors said that the film failed to rebut the neo-Nazi lies and the propaganda. Given this controversy, the film's distributors decided to withdraw the film for a short time in Germany. However, Hasselbach and his supporters reportedly distributed copies of the film abroad. The controversy surrounding the showing of the Hasselbach film was reflected by the staff of the Berlin's leftist daily newspaper *die tageszeitung*. According to its editor Michael Sontheimer, his staff had a mixed reaction. "The people in the culture department are all against the ban, but the people who cover politics are for it." In August 1995, as a consequence of Hasselbach's demagogic remarks concerning Germany's democratic system and his denial of the mass gassings at Auschwitz, he received a three and a half year prison sentence.[23]

The director Franziska Tenner made another documentary film *No Exit*. For one year she attended neo-Nazi meetings, which proved to her how neo-Nazis were unable to articulate Nazi ideology. By not glorifying the neo-Nazis she may have contributed to a rejection of their attempts at recruitment of new members.[24] In August 2007, a Mainz television channel aired on its *Panorama* show the YouTube's collection of neo-Nazi clips and World War Two propaganda films, despite considerable protest by politicians and officials of the Central Council of Jews in Germany. However, one month later, a popular television commentator, Eva Herman, had to resign from her position at the North Rhine-Westphalia network. She had said on air that she regretted seeing family virtues nurtured by the Nazis being swept away. The family values included women staying at home, rearing children, and looking after their husbands. In reacting to her remarks, one specialist on neo-Nazism pointed to a recent Forsa poll that showed about 25 percent of Germans thought that the Nazis had "some good points."[25]

The electronic network

As noted in Chapter 4, the government's dissolution in the 1990s of numerous national neo-Nazi groups for having violated the Basic Law led to the formation of small local and decentralized groups. As a consequence isolated neo-Nazis and skinheads have found it important to communicate with one another and to coordinate activities through the rapidly changing electronic network.[26] An extensive right-wing system has been built up on internet websites, e-mail servers, chat rooms, and a national information telephone system (*National Info-Telefone*, NIT). The number of right-wing websites varies constantly, but one government report estimates that the number mushroomed from a mere 32 in 1996 to 350 in 2000 and to 950 in 2003. In 2000 the government would have begun legal action to close down eighty websites that had illegal contents, but it could not discover the sites' initiators.[27]

Although the websites have become more professional, right-wing organizations often prefer to contact their members personally. Nevertheless the organizations have used the internet and e-mails as a communication medium to issue press releases, prepare position papers, form news groups, encourage chat rooms and individual blogs, and send e-mails that contain hate messages against foreigners, Jews, and leftists. In their propaganda campaigns, neo-Nazi and skinhead groups have called attention to foreigner-free zones in eastern Germany. They warn foreigners to keep out of certain discos and cafés. Normally 150–200 participants use the rightist chat rooms on an ordinary day but occasionally up to 1,000 persons have opened the sites daily.[28] The chat rooms have led to rightists stating their extremist views, such as denouncing the "J State," an abbreviation of "Jewish State" or Israel. They can also view the uncensored materials that appear on foreign sites; especially those in the United States and Canada. E-mails are sent to interested right-wing youth who are kept informed of coming events and receive propaganda materials.

In 1996, at the German government's request, *Deutsche Telekom* blocked access through its network to a Canadian site operated by Ernst Zündel. As noted above, he had sent out pro-Nazi materials that were illegal under German law. In Germany a new website must first be registered with a provider and then with the central German Network Information Center (*Denic*) for a domain name. A right-wing site could easily remain undetected because *Denic* receives 200,000 reservations for domain names per month. As a result the Center, without knowing it, approved such sites as "Gestapo," "Heinrich Himmler," and "Hitler Youth." Some of these sites were blank, but were registered for future use. Ironically, rightists discovered that when they wanted to open the site "NSDAP" or "Nazis," an anti-fascist group had already registered it to block them from using the title. NSDAP site visitors were confronted with content of utter nonsense, while those opening the "Nazis" website in 2006 were informed about the World War Two disasters in which 4.7 million German soldiers perished.

In 1999 the Federal Criminal Police Office and the private Bertelsmann Foundation, with the support of numerous German internet and technology firms, developed a filter system in which materials that appeared on foreign right-wing websites could be blocked in Germany if the materials were deemed to be illegal under German law. The Internet Content Rating Association administered the filter model system.[29]

The government agents, many inadequately trained for the computer age, have found it difficult to trace the location of domestic sites, which sprout and die with some frequency. Most right-wing sites, however, provide no legal ground for the government agents to close them because they operate within legal boundaries. In February 2001, the Central Council of Jews in Germany sued those providers who were hosting extreme right-wing or racist web pages. The Council also criticized the German government's "snail's pace" in applying anti-Nazi laws to eliminate racist and anti-Semitic content on the internet. However, soon thereafter, in the United States Yahoo closed forty-four US websites that were beaming programs in German to Germany. In the ensuing two years the German government, prodded by the Central Council of Jews and anti-Nazi initiatives such as "Together against the Right in the Internet," was able to close 173 right-wing websites, including White Youth of Germany and North Front.[30] In March 2008 the Central Council of Jews intended to file a law suit against Google for "citing racist anti-Jewish ideas." The Council objected to a video clip published on YouTube in which a former Council president appears to be burned with Nazi symbols in the background.[31]

Since 1999 the Federal and Länder Offices for the Protection of the Constitution have been greatly concerned about the publication of right-extremist black- or hate lists of so-called leftist enemies with their names, addresses, telephone numbers, occupations, and photos. Some right-wing groups have publicized such lists, stored on disks, to harass their opponents who include anti-fascists, state employees, and trade unionists. The lists contribute to anxiety among potential victims of violence, especially if there is the occasional naming of people who should be shot on sight. Other right-wing disks provide details on how to construct explosives from everyday materials.

The explosives can then be added to the arsenal of weapons that some rightists have already stored secretly. The government has sought to block such sites, but often without success.

As noted, neo-Nazi and skinhead groups have used the internet, including e-mails and web blogs, as a communications and electronic warfare medium. They are not the only ones. Skinhead music bands, right-wing publishing houses, and mail order firms (selling, for instance, Walküre perfume) have been dedicated users. In addition, some individual activists seek to find a romantic partner on the web. Right-wing individuals who have computers, and not all have, can sign up on e-mail lists to receive automatic mailings from right-wing organizations.

Right-wing "guerrillas" have hacked into e-mail boxes of an FDP Landtag deputy, among others, and left messages, such as to vote for the NPD or to support a right radical political system rather than the tired-out FRG system. Horst Mahler, the right-wing lawyer for the NPD and former leftist lawyer, sent an e-mail to all Bundestag deputies, titled "Appeal to the German Reich citizens." He warned that Germany was in danger of being overrun by foreigners. His message was not the only one; an avalanche of right-wing propaganda reaches all Bundestag deputies. Unknown persons with fake names have transmitted some of these e-mails, many containing viruses.[32] Similarly, on one occasion thousands of rightists sent e-mails that jammed the homepage of a Jewish organization.[33] In the global network, the German government has put pressure on the internet auctioneer eBay Web to close sites that, according to German statutes, were selling illegal music CDs and videos. The company agreed to purge all such materials from its server list.

The content of internet sites has expanded rapidly. In addition to text, photos, and music, site developers in recent years have made more use of animation, video sequences, and radio and television broadcasts. These can be downloaded onto computers, often without cost. For instance, the right-extremist press service *Politische Hintergrundinformationen* (*Political Background Information*) offers on its home page videos of singers familiar to a right-wing audience. "NIT Radio" and "Radio Germania" in their videos combine traditional German music with commentaries. Users can then make their own compact disks and distribute them. They can also subscribe to online magazines and download videos of the 1930s. Internet chats provide a swift method of members communicating with one another or with the general public. When pictures of the attack on the World Trade Center and other targets in September 2001 appeared on the screens, rightists were jubilant that finally their chief enemy, the United States, had been hit. One right-winger wrote that at last the American people could learn first-hand what a war looked like.[34]

A restricted number of right extremists, estimated at 250 neo-Nazi cadre members and activists, made full use of the mailbox Thule Network, which the NPD and right-wing groups established in 1993 in Nuremberg.

The network was named Thule after a mythical island inhabited in prehistory by superhuman beings of the Nordic race. Other interested persons, considered "guests," had access to the network and received basic information, but only about planned authorized demonstrations, rallies, and meetings. The Thule Network was a personal computer exchange and database, with a secret entry number. Not linked to the internet, it was designed for users to share propaganda, shape ideology, make plans for demonstrations and meetings, provide information on how to make bombs and engage in other illegal tactics, prepare to go underground for a possible civil war, and publicize lists of leftist enemies. Of seventeen mailboxes in the Thule Network, three (Norway, Netherlands, and Austria) operated from abroad. In 1997, as a result of personal internal discords, the Network expelled two mailbox enterprises. Thereupon these enterprises, joined by one functioning Thule mailbox, formed the rival *Nordland-Netz*.[35] The government found it difficult to penetrate the two networks, with their connections to foreign neo-Nazi groups, because right-extremist technicians made use of sophisticated encryption techniques. The approximately 250 users, with cover names, who were linked to the two networks, used them primarily as a discussion forum. The users were able to download forbidden works, such as Hitler's *Mein Kampf* or the *Protocol of the Elders of Zion*. In mid-1999, the top decision-makers in the two networks decided to dissolve their organizations because the goal to build up a broad right-extremist network had not been achieved.[36] At the same time the Simon Wiesenthal Center in Los Angeles called on the online Barnes and Noble, as well as Amazon booksellers, to stop selling Nazi books to customers in Germany. The Center contended that the booksellers were violating German anti-hate laws. In response an Amazon official said that its German-based site would not sell any literature that was banned in Germany but if a German tourist in the United States bought *Mein Kampf* in a bookstore there was no violation of the law.[37] In December 2007, a Left Party deputy leader, Katina Schubert, filed a charge with the Berlin police against the online encyclopedia Wikipedia for frequently promoting the use of banned Nazi symbols in Germany. In response a Wikipedia official said that the symbols were used only for educational and artistic purposes. Schubert's colleagues in the Left Party convinced her to withdraw her charge. They contended that Wikipedia had its own procedures for filtering out unsavory content.[38]

As indicated, right extremists can quickly send hate materials and information about meetings, demonstrations, and skinhead concerts by e-mail, but this method is not as secure as national and regional "info-telephones," which also have a chat room component. For instance, whenever public authorities denied permission for a concert and it was going to be held elsewhere, the message would then be posted only hours before the event was scheduled. Organizers would communicate further by cellular telephones. To weed out the merely curious telephone callers, one such recorded message began with the statement, "Unwanted listeners are hereby informed that this connection is for friends and is not public."[39] In many instances rock concerts were scheduled without state authorization. To prevent the police from observing the proceedings, concertgoers in convoys of cars were not informed of the final destination until the last minute. They would then receive a series of instructions from organizers through the info-telephones, of which there were sixteen in 2006.

The electronic highway has major advantages of low cost and speed over its predecessors, such as flyers and pamphlets. As a consequence the right-wing parties also established their own websites, especially when in February 1996 internet provider America Online (AOL) closed the NPD home page. In the same year, the NPD's youth division, a major user of the electronic revolution, organized two national internet congresses.

To counter right-wing use of the internet and propaganda, young democratic opponents have launched a network of websites containing information about the rightists. The youth provide details about their experiences with human rights violations, but also seek to establish a dialogue with the more moderate rightists. The police have repeatedly raided the homes of rightist suspects who have been involved in the sale of right-wing literature and audio materials on the internet. The police have confiscated computers, memory devices, and rightist CDs and LPs.

The global nature of the internet has made it inevitable that international organizations also take cognizance of it. In November 2001, the 43-nation Council of Europe added a protocol listing web page content and hate speech over computer networks to the list of cyber crimes. The United States, which is a signatory to the cyber crime convention, said that it could not sign because doing so would conflict with the free-speech protections in the First Amendment to the Constitution. However, a Council of Europe spokesman said that the Council hoped that the United States would honor the protocol. According to an American internet company executive, he doubted that the protocol would have any effect in the United States given its freedom of speech tradition.[40]

Electronic games

Since 1987 ideological neo-Nazis of a technocratic bent have developed illegal electronic games that in most instances can be downloaded for free. The games' architects, who make ample use of forbidden Nazi symbols, have glorified war, racism, and nationalism in a much more blatant way than appear in right-wing publications. These games teach violence and dehumanize the victims effectively. Since 1993 companies provocatively named "Anti-Negro German Association," and "Adolf Hitler Software, Ltd." and others have developed more than fifty games with such titles as "Anti-Turk Test," "Aryan Test," "Adolf Hitler," "Clean Germany," "Concentration Camp Manager," and "Sieg Heil." In one game a Hitler portrait appears on the screen with the text "I am coming back! And then I put all Turks into the gas chamber."[41] The Federal Agency for the Corruption of Youth has put computer games that glorify the Nazi regime or are blatantly xenophobic or anti-Semitic on its youth endangered list. But as the games' manufacturers and distributors have been operating in secret, government agents can only confiscate such games when seizing computers and disks in raids of shops or apartments of known neo-Nazis.[42]

On occasion, journalists have unmasked the programmer of a game. This happened to a young Berlin student Burkhard. He denied being a neo-Nazi, yet developed the game "Anti-Turk Test." When asked how he felt about Turks, he responded that they behaved as if they were in a jungle and could not adjust to the German realities. Burkhard made similar anti-Semitic remarks. However, in his case, and those of many other young men, the challenge to successfully devise a game was more important than the political message. True, his remarks could have been those made by a neo-Nazi, yet he had no interest in a restoration of the Nazi era and was unable to make historical connections.

Dedicated neo-Nazis, who are steeped in Nazi ideology, have devised a second category of games, including "Concentration Camp Manager II – A Game for the Whole Family," written by "Firefox." The game's object is to construct a concentration camp, located in West Russia. It included barracks for the SS and for inmates, and a gas chamber. According to the game's instructions, not too many inmates should remain alive because then the danger of a mass escape is heightened. The player wins the game if the building of the camp is completed and 3,000 inmates are gassed. Thereupon the player receives a Knight of the Iron Cross medal, first class, from the Führer Adolf Hitler. Another grisly game called "Pogrom" was modeled on "Monopoly." The purpose of the game was to rid Germany of Jews by collecting concentration camp chips and purchasing German gabled houses. SA and SS cards rewarded winning players.[43]

A third category of games has been devised by neo-Nazis who excel at writing games that use graphics and provide digitalized original sound for Hitler's speeches and Nazi songs. Typically, players, who are mostly 8–15 years old, may spend two to three days, five hours each day, to complete a game. For every original copy of a game, there may be as many as ten to thirty stolen copies. According to estimates 100 million copies of right-wing and non-right-wing games may be in worldwide circulation, of which the great majority are stolen copies. Even if most players do not have Nazi games, it is still a significant minority that does have them.[44]

For democratic groups and the government the challenge is how to minimize the hate and propaganda forthcoming daily on the internet and in cyberspace. In 2000, then German President Johannes Rau (SPD) and Justice Minister Herta Däubler-Gmelin (SPD) urged delegates to an international conference on the digital components of racism, anti-Semitism, and xenophobia to consider ways of minimizing the hate content of internet sites. Däubler-Gmelin said: "What is forbidden off-line must be forbidden on-line. Our goal must be to achieve a global value consensus and to agree on an international minimum of regulation."[45] In that spirit, Däubler-Gmelin announced that German authorities had successfully blocked applications for the domain names *Gestapo.de* and *Heil Hitler.de*.

The German government has put pressure on the internet auctioneer eBay to close sites that, according to German statutes, were selling illegal music CDs and videos. The company agreed to purge all such materials from its auction site. Yet, as noted, the government had to contend with an avalanche of right-wing propaganda addressed to all Bundestag deputies.[46] There is no doubt that the internet has become one of the central propaganda tools for the extreme right, which has poured considerable funds into it. Anti-Nazi sites have also increased in numbers, but how effective they have been in countering neo-Nazi propaganda is difficult to calculate.

Music as a propaganda tool

In the cultural realm, music has been the chief recruitment and propaganda tool for the skinheads and neo-Nazi groups. It has become the focus of a youth pop culture that has its own language and clothes, and believes in German nationalism, xenophobia, anti-Semitism, and a runic and Aryan mysticism. Youth are often first exposed to right-extremist music by the distribution of CDs within their groups, by downloading music from the internet, and by attending concerts. Politicization of rightist music began in the late 1970s and early 1980s. At the time, different styles of music originated primarily in Great Britain and the United States, to which eventually rightist German musicians added their inflammatory texts. In western Germany, punk rock and dark wave groups emerged. Many were strongly influenced by British skinhead bands, of whom a few made appearances in Germany. At the time a number of German punk and heavy metal bands played the British derived "Oi" music ("Oi" representing a British working-class greeting).[47] Incidentally, the British band Skrewdriver, allied with the British right-wing National Front party, was banned from playing in Germany in 1991 because five of its followers were charged with injuring a black man during a neo-Nazi demonstration in Cottbus in eastern Germany.

After German unification, well-known rock and rap skinhead bands attracted committed rightists and apolitical youth to their concerts in both parts of the country. The German branch of the British Blood and Honor skinheads, from their birth in 1994 in Berlin until the ban of their organization in 2000, and the competing Hammerskins were the chief organizers of right-wing concerts. At many of these concerts audience members came not just from the local right-wing scene, but also from different parts of Germany and neighboring countries. In 1999, for instance, 105 major right-wing concerts took place, some of them featuring foreign bands. By 2007, the number of concerts had increased to 163; usually most of them drawing between 70 and 250 audience members. Proportionately more concerts took place in eastern than in western Germany because of the fewer cultural offerings in eastern Germany and because the NPD and the *Kameradschaften* made concerts a part of their electoral strategy.

In 2007, the *Verfassungsschutz* counted a total of 146 bands that had performed in Germany that year.[48] Typically they sang the music with simple guitar chords, in a piercingly loud and rapid staccato style, with the lead singer hoarsely screaming the lyrics. Such performances led to audience members breaking out into a mesmerizing "Pogen" dance after having consumed much alcohol and drugs. The bands' singers lauded German nationalism, racism, and a mystical pagan and Nordic history. They sang of the white master race superiority, which must be maintained against its Zionist, communist, and capitalist foes. They warned the skinheads to be aware of the dangers to their movement and to be ready to fight their enemies. Occasionally the singers used coded words to prevent the police from breaking up a concert on the pretext that the Basic Law had been violated.

The primary audience at weekend concerts has been teenagers. They are attracted to such German rappers as Fler, who as a trademark has worn thick gold chains and baggy jeans. A rhyme from one of his songs reads "Black, red, gold, hard and proud . . . believe me, my mom is German." This nationalist song, referring to the flag colors, quickly became one of the most popular in the German hit parade. Many of his other songs have lyrics that are violent and suggestive of neo-Nazi goals. Yet, to deflect criticism, Fler said to a reporter: "I don't want to put down other minorities. I'm just saying that I think it's cool to be German."[49] Such a statement does not match the advertisement on Fler's compact disk that uses a pre-Polish invasion quotation by Hitler: "On May 1st, we'll shoot back."[50]

Other famous rappers, such as Sido and Bushido, who is half Tunisian and half German, have emulated American gangster-style hip-hop music with lurid lyrics that glorify violence, crime, and neo-Nazism. In one best-selling album, Bushido rapped "Salute, stand at attention, I am the leader like A." When critics said that the "A" reference was to Adolf Hitler, Bushido denied it. Yet he was willing to sign his name on the shaved heads of skinheads who attended his concerts. Although skinheads and neo-Nazis approved the hip-hop lyrics, they identified the music with African-American roots.

There have been numerous occasions when the police broke up a concert because of the far-right content of the songs and ballads, the violence among the listeners, or the Heil Hitler salutes of inebriated spectators. To give one example of the violence that accompanies some concerts: in September 2000, in the West German city of Laave, near Lüneburg, 500 police officers received the order from their chief to disband a weekend concert held in a large hall filled with 500 right-wing spectators. The ensuing violence led to forty-six injured police agents and the arrest of thirty-two skinheads. The police chief accused the prohibited skinhead group "Blood and Honor Division Germany" of having organized the concert.[51] Yet even when the police are not present concerts often end in violence among those in attendance or in violence against foreigners who happen to be on the streets after the concerts.[52]

Since the 1990s the right-wing music scene has been vibrant. Many young people are attracted to hard rock or heavy and black metal music played at concerts and on recordings. In 1992 a few right-wing bands issued twenty-six LPs and CDs. But by 1998 the number of bands had grown to fifty-five, which released 136 records that year. In another tally, in the decade from 1991 to 2001 more than 100 right-wing bands produced about 500 CDs. In 2006 the number of bands stood at 152.[53] The impresario of recorded right-wing music has been Herbert Egoldt, who founded the firm Rock-O-Rama, with headquarters near Cologne. Originally, the firm pressed and sold numerous records of skinhead and leftist bands. When Egoldt had more commercial success with the albums of right-wing bands, sold throughout the world, he dropped the leftist bands. In the 1980s he targeted a growing audience of working-class youth who were alienated from the democratic system and had drifted to the right. He had a near-monopoly position as few right-wing bands made their music available under other labels. In the course of time he became more cautious in releasing albums that had a strong right-wing message for fear of governmental seizure and his own possible jail sentence. In addition, he lost his monopoly position when smaller competing companies successfully shared in the rich market. One specialist calculated that from 1991 to 1999 about 1.5 million copies of right rock CDs had been sold in German record stores.[54] The Anti-Defamation League of B'nai B'rith in New York charged Rock-O-Rama with serving as an international clearing house for right-wing bands, including several in the United States. Abraham Foxman, the League's national director, urged Chancellor Kohl to close down the company, but the prosecutor's office in Cologne said that a probe of the company had been concluded because of lack of evidence that any law was violated.[55]

Although the government did not take any action against Rock-O-Rama in that particular instance, over the decades it considered numerous lyrics of songs at concerts or on disks, produced in 2006 by ninety-one companies, to have violated existing laws. Some of the lyrics called for violence against women and foreigners, and for genocide. A typical song that the government banned was called "Kanaken," a racial epithet for a Turkish foreigner: "When you see a Turk in a tram; And he is looking at you annoyingly; Just stand up and give him a good punch; And stab him seventeen times."[56] Since the 1980s the Federal Inspection Office for Media Endangering Young Persons, which was set up in 1954 to monitor neo-Nazi music, has put more than 450 songs and albums on a list that forbids their being advertised or sold to any person under the age of 18. Once the songs and albums are on the Index, most large record stores do not bother to stock them. However, youngsters can easily buy them illegally in small record stores, video shops, and army and weapons stores, which the police rarely check, or download them onto their computers.[57]

Manufacturers, sellers, and distributors of albums can be prosecuted if titles of their recordings are on such an Index list. Thus most bands have lawyers check the lyrics to ensure that they are within constitutional bounds and that the CDs would not appear on the Index list. A few bands have chosen the underground route by recording their music abroad and smuggling their CDs into Germany. In one instance, in 2006, customs officers in Wroclaw, Poland intercepted a parcel containing 300 neo-Nazi CDs that had been shipped from the United States and was destined for Germany. Most records had pictures of Hitler, barbed wire from concentration camps, or a canister of cyclone-B, the gas that was used in the death camps, on their covers. Ironically, some of the confiscated CD songs were anti-Polish, with one proclaiming that "Gdansk, Wroclaw, and Szczecin are German cities just like Berlin."[58]

In February 1993, in one successful government campaign, the police confiscated 30,000 records, tapes, and compact disks, many recorded by Rock-O-Rama. The government also investigated the popular *Störkraft* (Disturbing Force) band for having played songs that incited audiences and listeners. In one of its songs, the lead singer warned that the white race was threatened by a flood of foreigners, but that as only the skinheads recognized such a danger they will purify Germany. Another band, *Radikahl* (a pun on the words "radical" and "kahl," meaning in this instance close-cropped hair) was charged in connection with a song "Swastika." One stanza read: "Give Adolf Hitler, give Adolf Hitler, give Adolf Hitler the Nobel Prize; Raise the red flag, raise the red flag, raise the red flag with the swastika."[59] The first stanza of another of its songs, "Saviors of Germany," read: "O my poor Germany, you've come to this; And there's no one, no one near or far to free you; But things can't go on this way; I can't stand this filthy breed any longer." The song called on Germany's saviors to awake and fight for their homeland "like a wild beast."[60] In one interview, a band member said that "we must fight for the white race in Europe, America, and all over the world. It is our culture and we must save it and break the Jewish plan to destroy the white race and culture."[61]

In 1997 the police confiscated 500,000 right-wing music CD copies, which was but a fraction of the total number owned by rightists.[62] Two years later the police raided the offices of distributors of black metal music CDs. Among those arrested was the 23-year-old Satanist Hendrik Moebus, who had already been accused in 1993, with two accomplices, of the murder of 15-year-old Sandro Beyer for having made fun of the "Children of Satan" group to which Moebus belonged. Moebus justified the murder as being part of an "archaic sacrificial ritual."[63]

In 2003, a Berlin court ruled that the extreme-right rock group *Landser* ("Foot Soldiers") had been guilty of inciting racial hate and violence by targeting foreigners and Jews in Germany. One lyric read: "Turks and commies and all that scum will soon be gone forever" in a song titled "The Reich will be back." The band's two CDs had similar provocative titles. Under court order the rock group had to disband; the first one in Germany to be given such an order. Michael Regener, its lead singer who wrote most of the band's songs, received a jail sentence of over three years for his provocative songs, for planning an "Aryan Revolution," and for operating in a secretive manner. Two other band members were given suspended sentences. In March 2005 Regener filed an appeal with the German Supreme Administrative Court to have his sentence lifted, but the appeal was denied. In 2006, the NPD organized a rally attended by about 750 neo-Nazis who demonstrated outside a Berlin jail demanding Regener's immediate release. Several hundred anti-Nazi protesters also turned up, chanting the familiar slogan of "Nazis out," although in this instance not wanting Regener to be out of jail.[64]

In the meantime, in 2004, the police raided the homes of more than 300 people in the FRG who were suspected of posting neo-Nazi music files on the internet for others to download free. The music contained lyrics that could incite racial hatred against Jews and foreigners, and thus could be ground for imprisonment. In 2009 German police seized thousands of recordings of suspected neo-Nazi music in raids of more than 200 homes and businesses. The government actions obviously had an effect on the content of songs that punk band members belted out publicly. As already noted, following government pressure, the internet auctioneer eBay agreed to remove from its lists any music CDs and videos that were illegal under German law.

Recording artists and musicians had to be careful to remain within constitutional boundaries. They switched to the safer themes of nationalism, national identity, and pride in one's own country that swept Germany after 1990, but especially after 2000. Thus, in 2004 the single record "We" was high in German pop music charts. The song proudly recalled German post-war history with lyrics such as: "I ask myself who we are. We are we. Divided, defeated but, nevertheless, in the end, we're still alive." The song does not mention the war, the Holocaust, or the Third Reich. Instead, it celebrates the country's reconstruction and reunification.[65]

One of the top hard rock bands, Rammstein, also well known outside of Germany, initially sang neo-Nazi lyrics and then switched to safer nationalist themes. In more recent years, the band members have asserted that they were fed up with national soul-searching and self-reproach. One band member said: "It's time to stop being ashamed about what comes out of Germany and to establish a normal way of dealing with being German."[66]

Despite public and private efforts to stem the outpouring of right-wing music, illegal CD copies still circulate among skinheads and neo-Nazis.

Concerts, usually organized by the NPD's youth division and other right-wing organizations, continue to take place, especially in eastern Germany where there are fewer distractions for youth. But in many instances the concerts are falsely registered with innkeepers as a birthday or wedding party, or are hastily and secretly arranged to prevent a police presence. At these concerts, youth from different parts of Germany make contact with one another and buy CDs and fanzines (see below). Thus the music scene serves as an important tool of bonding individual skinheads who come from different localities.

The right-wing bands, whose mostly male members are responsible for the hard beat and provocative songs, continue to play a role in the German musical scene. The lyrics lead some audience members to use the illegal "Heil Hitler" and "Sieg Heil" salutes and to stir up violence during and after rock concerts. The concerts serve as the primary means to attract youth into the right-wing subculture and to instill a sense of camaraderie among them. But it is difficult to estimate how many of those who have attended the concerts have actually joined the movement. On numerous occasions authorities have forbidden a concert in advance because of the danger of violence or because the band has been known to sing prohibited songs.

Undoubtedly the lyrics in the rightist music scene have become less political because of the danger of being banned in advance. But there are exceptions, such as CDs being manufactured in neighboring countries. On these underground CDs, the rightist ideology expressed in numerous pop songs has become a part of popular youth culture. This is especially true in eastern Germany where in some small towns and rural areas right-wing culture has become close to being dominant, if not wholly dominant. The neo-Nazi and skinhead groups have discovered that they can attract more youth into their ranks through music than by scheduling political meetings. Or, in an increasing blend of the two subcultures, a band might be scheduled to play at a political meeting. Music not only plays a powerful role in recruitment of potential rightists, but produces among concertgoers a feeling of being part of a collectivity.[67] To offset the attraction of right-wing bands to teenagers, cities, towns and groups have hired prominent non-right-wing rock bands to perform at concerts and to produce CDs with democratic messages.

Fanzines and youth

Among youth the simultaneous development of comic books propagating right-wing propaganda and the publication of fan magazines (fanzines) has paralleled the attraction of right-wing music. The comic books and the fanzines reflect a changing culture among bored teenagers who are growing up in a society increasingly oriented to the visual scene, which contains numerous pictures and few words. The fanzines, originating in Britain, spread to Germany in the early 1980s. In Germany skinhead music fans found the fanzines invaluable as a way to find out about upcoming concerts, to exchange views, to instill an ideology among their readers, and to help recruit new members. From 50 to 1,000 copies of one issue of a fanzine is normally distributed to a coterie of group members and hangers on. Each issue, often appearing irregularly, is meant for a group's internal consumption and thus is not available at newspaper kiosks. More than sixty fanzines, with such provocative titles as *Der Aktivist, Attacke, Blood and Honour, Division Deutschland, Sachsens Glanz (Saxonian Sparkle)*, and *Volkstreue (People's Loyalty)*, have appeared in Germany. Some published a few issues and then disappeared; others have published for many years. Some fanzines have a niche audience, such as *Aryan Sisterhood* and *Das Treue Mädel (The Loyal Girl)*, which target women as potential readers.

Although not professional looking and printed on a shoestring budget in the local communities, fanzines consist of action reports, interviews with members of skinhead bands, political columns, and reports about national and international events. The fanzine editors have established regional networks in order to send propaganda material to persons likely to join the cause and to instill a feeling of camaraderie among readers.[68] In some instances the government has confiscated a fanzine issue if it crossed a legal boundary.

Conclusion

To sum up, youth who feel socially and economically disadvantaged and who suffer from a loss of orientation and misdirected politics can be expected to be more attracted to the right-wing illiberal subculture than other youth. They will be more prone to read right-wing newspapers and other print media, attend the offerings of neo-Nazi cultural centers, look at right-wing websites on computers, attend skinhead concerts, or listen to Oi music in their homes. Although the government has attempted to limit the propaganda emanating from many members of these subcultures, it has had only limited success. The evidence points to the continuing attraction of such propaganda tools. This youth is more prone to accept diffuse nationalist, xenophobic, and anti-Semitic *Weltanschauungen*, some of it premodern, than their more democratically oriented peers.

It is hard to measure the effect of these propaganda tools on the youth, especially the uncommitted ones. A reading of one propaganda leaflet or an attendance at one Oi concert does not mean that the right-wing movement has gained one new supporter. However, if such a youth is exposed to an array of propaganda then it is more likely that the movement has gained a new recruit. The New Right's emphasis on changing Germany's culture prior to changing its political system, as noted in Chapter 6, is reinforced by these tools of propaganda and recruitment.

6
The New Right

A survey of the right-extremist scene in Germany since the country's unification in 1990 would not be complete without examining the intellectual contributions that New Right (*Die Neue Rechte*) academics, writers, publicists, and journalists have made. They number several hundred individuals, of whom many are organized in small discussion groups and projects. They have positioned themselves as a bridge between right-extremist parties and groups, on one side, and the conservative wing of the mainstream political parties, on the other.[1] They have provided some, but still limited, intellectual nourishment to the right-wing extremist cause since the 1960s, but particularly since the early 1980s. They have sought to make the right-wing extremist ideology and politics relevant and influential. They have had little in common with the Old Right generation that had enthusiastically supported Hitler and that after 1949 had received a number of important political posts in the West German establishment. However, the Old Right played no significant role in West German intellectual circles. In this chapter we examine how much influence the New Right adherents have had on both the right-wing extremist and the ultra-conservative groups. Have the New Right ideas and concepts percolated to these two groups? How successful have they been in making an impact on Germany's domestic and foreign policies?

The German rightist intellectual model is the French *Nouvelle Droite* (New Right), which surfaced in France in the 1960s as a counter-cultural revolt against the New Left. Its founder, Alain de Benoist, has had a major influence on his German counterparts in *Die Neue Rechte*. In France, the movement emerged out of a male political club in Paris whose members were former activists in the nationalist student groups of the 1960s. On the political agenda they battled Charles de Gaulle's decision to grant Algeria independence in 1962. They also questioned the left's emphasis on individual human rights and social equality. They sought to break the left's alleged cultural hegemony by emphasizing their own cultural priority. After the 1968 leftist uprising, the approximately 3,000 *Nouvelle Droite* members, consisting of intellectuals, journalists, teachers, politicians, and university staff, narrowed their intellectual activities to a Research and Study Group on European Culture (GRECE); two journals, *Éléments* and *Nouvelle École*; and the publishing house Éditions Copernic. In the late 1970s, a number of members joined the editorial staff of *Figaro Magazine*, the daily newspaper's weekend edition. Since then the French movement has declined because of internal conflicts and a failure to develop new perspectives. As a result some members became active in the newly founded Synergies Européennes movement or in Jean-Marie Le Pen's rightist Front National party.[2]

The roots of the German New Right models go back to the Weimar anti-democratic nationalist and conservative movements whose supporters wanted an authoritarian state based on the Old Right concepts of the *Volk* and *Heimat* (Homeland). In the FRG the New Right adherents, loosely organized since the 1970s, have also clustered in journal and theory circles, cited in Chapter 5. In scholarly articles or at conferences, they have discussed the works of the pre-Nazi nationalists and conservatives, such as Friedrich Nietzsche, Edgar Julius Jung, Arthur Moeller van den Bruck, Oswald Spengler, Ernst Jünger, Carl Schmitt, Georges Sorel, and Julius Evola.

A glance at Schmitt's contributions, to which the New Rightists are strongly indebted, shows that his Weimar parliamentary system critique had an influence on national conservatives during that era. He maintained that only the German president could stop the political parties' fratricidal struggles, which threatened to destroy the constitution. Between 1930 and 1933 Schmitt was a confidant to the conservative governments. He did not criticize President Paul von Hindenburg's appointment of Adolf Hitler as chancellor in 1933.[3] Jung tried to make the conservative positions palatable to the Nazi elite but without success. In short, most national conservatives did not support the Weimar democratic governments. But a minority actively opposed the Nazi regime and were murdered as a result.

Birth of a movement

The New Right movement's origins can be traced to the late 1960s and early 1970s. At the time young NPD members became disillusioned with the power of the Old Right in their party. The young members formed several groups that were the forerunners of the New Right. One group was the National Revolutionary movement headed by Henning Eichberg, a cultural sociologist and historian. Born in 1942 in Silesia, he studied at Bochum and Hamburg universities. He received a postdoctoral degree at Stuttgart University, where he taught sociology and the culture of sports from 1971 to 1982. He launched a journal *wir selbst* ("we self") and was a prolific author, original thinker, and organizer. His movement took national and social revolutionary positions that, in some respects, bordered closely on New Left ideological territory. In the early 1970s he was active in the "Action Resistance," which denounced

Chancellor Brandt's Eastern policy. In 1972 he drafted the manifesto of the newly created Action New Right. In 1974 he was one of the founders of *Sache des Volkes/Nationalrevolutionäre Aufbauorganisation* (SdV/NRAO) (A Matter of the People/National Revolutionary Reconstruction Organization). Its position was not to support the left or the right but rather to follow the Weimar's National Bolsheviks' revolutionary course.[4] Such a position meant opposing a pluralistic society and supporting instead an ethnically pure Germany.

Whereas the leftist movement peaked during the late 1960s, the New Rightists or Young Turks began their counter-offensive against the New Left establishment and the SPD-FDP coalition in power from 1969 to 1982. As their long-term goal, the New Rightists sought to overcome the Western capitalist and Eastern communist systems and embark on a third way. They wanted to first gain a cultural hegemony in Germany, which would be the forerunner of a new political order. In contrast to the anti-intellectualism of the neo-Nazis and skinheads they emphasized the need for an intellectual approach. They formed small discussion groups and cadres at the base and founded more than one hundred newspapers and journals. They recruited a number of professors, journalists, and politicians, some of whom moved from the left to the right camp, to write for their publications. Horst Mahler, a prominent lawyer, began his career on the left. He had defended leftist Extra-Parliamentary Opposition (APO) and Red Army Faction members, but then switched to the right and became the chief defense lawyer for the NPD.

The swing from left to right was not that difficult for some individuals because of ideological overlaps in the two camps. New Left and New Right individuals had studied with the same professors. Thus, the rightist National-Revolutionaries supported the worldwide struggle for national liberation of oppressed people and opposed globalization because of its alleged negative effects on the German economy. The left and the right camps denounced the United States' hegemonic policies in the international arena. Both supported environmental protection and criticized cutbacks to the German welfare state. Yet these New Right positions also contained dangerous nationalist and racist components, such as tough restrictions on immigration and opposition to multiculturalism, which the left did not share.

Ideological components

Two decades after the Nazi regime's downfall in 1945 the New Right founders in Germany expressed theoretical and conceptual ideas that right-extremist party leaders have generally accepted. Some of these right extremists, especially in the NPD, are clustered in the Old Right. They still believe in the discredited Nazi ideology. Other rightists, such as the neo-Nazi skinheads, imitate the violence of Nazi Storm Troopers. If a comparison is made between the contemporary New Right and its Weimar counterpart, then the New Right's limited ability to shape the current political discourse in the FRG era pales in comparison to the high influence its counterpart exerted during the Weimar era.

From the New Rightists' point of view the discourse has had some problems. For instance, in the immediate post-1945 era, and to some extent since then, it has been unacceptable or illegal for German citizens to openly praise any aspects of the Hitler regime or improper to criticize the US and British mass bombings of German cities. Once the Federal Republic achieved sovereignty, New Right and right-extremist parties' members have, with few exceptions, voiced criticisms of the bombings without being punished.

The German New Rightists have emphasized the need for a more nuanced appraisal of the Nazi regime. Most of them have disassociated themselves from it partly out of conviction and partly as a means to curry favor with the conservative mainstream. But they also have criticized the Allies who in 1945 had split the German nation into four occupation zones and who had denied Germans full sovereignty. In recent years they have said that Germans need to step out of Hitler's shadow and to become as normal as citizens of other countries. To accomplish this the New Right theorists see the need for a historical revisionism. As one example, they cite the imperative to jettison the Allied talk about the Germans being solely guilty for the Nazi catastrophe and instead to reeducate the citizenry to the fact that other states shared in the twentieth-century disasters.

As to contemporary problems, the New Rightists have concentrated their attention on the immigration issue. They have reinforced the mainstream German parties' view that immigration from Third World countries must be restricted. They assert that such a policy must apply especially to foreigners seeking political asylum in Germany. The New Rightists also state that the country's primarily German labor force needs to demonstrate such qualities as diligence, discipline, and order, especially in the business and technology sectors, if it is to compete successfully with other states. In addition, the New Rightists have stressed certain conservative virtues, such as honor, loyalty, morality, and comradeship, which should govern the public discourse.

As to long-term goals, the New Rightists reject the democratic state's foundations, such as human rights and pluralism. They denounce liberal school curricula that emphasize democratic rather than "national" education. They bemoan the lack of full German sovereignty, some of which has been lost to the European Union. They opt for a strong authoritarian state, headed by a president with full powers and with the authority to restrict political parties. Voters would need to approve such a radical proposal by a national plebiscite.[5]

The author Michael Venner argues cogently that the New Right, which he labels "conservative-revolutionary," seeks to serve as the conduit between, on the one side, ultra-conservatives in the mainstream democratic parties and, on the other side, right-extremist forces. As these two camps on the New Right perimeter are not rigid, CDU/CSU and FDP ultra-conservatives, on the one hand, and Republican, DVU, and NPD leaders, on the other, can have an influence on the New Right or can support its emphasis on the nation and nationalism. Thus, for example, the ultra-conservatives, aware that they concur with some of the New Right doctrines, will not automatically label the New Right positions as anti-democratic.[6]

In unified Germany, most New Right disciples have distanced themselves tactically from the right-extremist parties, although the views of both camps rest on the anti-democratic "conservative revolution" ideas propagated during the Weimar era and, for some of them, on Nazi and anti-Semitic concepts. The New Rightists call on the German ruling elite to sever the country's close ties to the culturally decadent United States and the West. These countries stand for an unacceptable universal egalitarianism that has spread to other countries via Christianity, liberalism, or Marxism. Egalitarianism, which provides free rein for consumerism, capitalism, and big business, needs to be supplanted by a return to pre-Christian times in a neo-pagan setting. Thus, the New Rightists call on the German government to pursue a policy of "ethnopluralism," which means the separation of ethnic groups and a denial of multiculturalism. In essence, ethnopluralism has a racist component because it implies that the world is populated by a superior Caucasian race and lesser Negroid and Mongol races. A *Volksgemeinschaft* – a group of biologically similar human beings – constitutes the body politic.[7]

Ethnopluralism is also meant to link geopolitics with population and environmental protection policies, the latter in conformity with the Greens' philosophy. Professor Jonathan Olsen points out, in a study of German right-wing views on ecology, that for rightists "multiculturalism and immigration, on the one hand, and environmental destruction on the other are grouped together as a threat to nature."[8] According to the scholar Hans-Gerd Jaschke, some New Right adherents believe that "genetic and cultural factors must serve to prove national identity, racial segregation and the autonomy of the peoples."[9] Thus New Right theorists emphasize the need to study cognitive theory, biology, social anthropology, and psychology. The American author and journalist Paul Hockenos, based in Berlin, notes that the New Rightists emphasize the bonds of family and *Volk* as their answer to modernity. They support an ethnic nation, which is "an organic, folkish community, bound not by a common legal code or state borders but by descent, tradition and fate."[10] Such a nation will also be guided by German mysticism and Nordic myths. In this ethnopluralist vision, a greater German Reich would arise once again that would include the lost territories in Eastern Europe. Other groups seeking independence, such as the Basques, the south Tyrolean, and the Flemish and Walloons in Belgium, would be assured of German support.[11]

In sum, the New Right has a number of ideological concepts that lack a unified whole. This lack is caused partly by the New Right intellectuals' fear that German authorities would prosecute them if they were to advocate establishing an authoritarian system that would supplant the existing democratic system. There are differences among New Right adherents in details, such as the half-hearted opposition to Christianity or the support for right-extremist political parties. Many of them know what policies should be pursued but few have fully sketched out details as to what they want. This New Right vision would remove the legitimacy of the current constitutional system and lead to its death. Such views obviously border on a challenge to the existing parliamentary system and thus will not be expressed too openly.

A plethora of authors and journals

Numerous New Right writers who admired the Weimar's national conservative movement led the battle first for cultural and second for political hegemony. They wanted to publicize their ideas, which included a revision of German history, greater national self-consciousness, and the formation of an elite governed authoritarian state. In the face of a hostile leftist dominated media, as they saw it, they have written a multitude of books that appeared under the imprint of conservative publishers and numerous articles in conservative journals (see Chapter 5). In addition, the Carl Friedrich von Siemens Foundation has served as a New Right transmission organ. Armin Mohler, its secretary from 1964 to 1985, edited numerous books that articulated the movement's views. His successor, Heinrich Meier, was active in the 1970s in the right radical youth scene and edited the journal *Im Brennpunkt (Focus)* that mirrored many NPD goals based on New Right ideology. From 1974 on, Gerd-Klaus Kaltenbrunner (not related to the high SS official) was the publisher's reader of the Foundation. He edited numerous manuscripts that New Right authors had written under the auspices of the ultra-conservative Herder Publishers in Freiburg.

A survey of some of the leading New Right authors indicates that most of them were born in the 1950s, with only a few born in the 1920s and 1930s. Armin Mohler is among the movement's grey eminence. Born in Basel, Switzerland in 1920, he first espoused left radical and pacifist views during his university studies. Later, at the University of Basel, he studied German language and culture, art history, and philosophy. He was called into the Swiss army during World War Two, deserted, and crossed the German border in order to enlist in the *Waffen*-SS. Mohler was greatly influenced by the works of Spengler and Jünger, whose private secretary he became for four years. Mohler wrote a number of books, such as *Die Konservative Revolution in Deutschland 1918–1932*, which was published in 1950. It was viewed as path-breaking and widely read within ultra-conservative and rightist circles. Mohler contributed numerous essays and articles to a wide range of conservative newspapers and journals, but also to the liberal *Die Zeit*. As a result of his writings, Mohler influenced a younger generation of conservative intellectuals. As foreign correspondent in Paris, he became enamored of Gaullism. After his stint with the Siemens Foundation, he supported Minister-President Franz Josef Strauss of Bavaria and the CSU. In 1967 Mohler received the Konrad Adenauer Prize of the *Deutschland-Stiftung* (Germany Foundation) for his work in journalism. Given to the authors of works that "contribute to a better future," it is one of Germany's most prestigious literary prizes.

Mohler backed the Republikaner for a brief time, but did not see much of a future for them. In 1983 he founded the *Deutschlandrat* (Council for Germany) with the support of a number of conservative university professors. The council never became a viable institution. Mohler also organized a number of conferences under the auspices of the Siemens Foundation at which speakers often touched on topics that corresponded more to the CDU/CSU's ultra-conservative wing than to the New Right position. Shortly before his death in 2003, he acknowledged that he had been an admirer of Italian and Spanish fascism.[12]

Hans-Dietrich Sander, born in 1928, stayed from 1952 to 1957 in the GDR as a committed leftist. In 1957 he fled to West Germany and soon became a New Right journalist and literary critic for *Die Welt*. He was in close personal touch with Carl Schmitt. During the 1960s and 1970s he taught at the Technical University in Hanover and from 1978 to 1979 he was guest lecturer at the Free University in Berlin. Sander achieved recognition in rightist circles when his book on the national imperative for a united Germany was published in 1980. He maintained that unification would end United States and Soviet influence in German affairs. At the same time a united Germany must lead to a revival of a Teutonic "furor" and pride in one's country. From 1983 to 1986 Sander was editor-in-chief of *Deutsche Monatshefte*. In his writings he contended that Hitler's personality and the NSDAP's political immaturity caused Germany's downfall.

In the late 1990s, members of the NPD and other groups discussed Sanders' model of a future Reich. A majority of rightists abandoned his call for a new Reich and a new Prussia based on a conservative revolution. In the journal *Staatsbriefe* (*State Letters*), which appeared under his editorship from 1990 to 2001, they opted instead for the vaguer concept of a "constitutional patriotism." The SPD accused him of anti-Semitism and anti-Americanism. On occasion he became isolated in right-extremist circles, especially when he denounced the NPD for its corruption, incompetence, and narrow-mindedness. In turn the editors of the neo-rightist journal *Junge Freiheit* (*Young Freedom*) assailed him for his reactionary views. In 2003 Sander sought a rapprochement with rightist circles. He became a founding member of an association to provide support to those who have been criticized as Holocaust deniers.

Hellmut David was another veteran of the right-wing scene. Born in 1929 he eventually received an appointment as professor of history at the University of Erlangen. In 1978 he published *Geschichte der Deutschen* (*History of the Germans*), which became a seminal work in the ultra-conservative and right-extremist circles. In numerous essays and articles he emphasized the mythical rather than the political Germany. He was also a chief author of the Republikaner platform preamble.[13]

Gerd Klaus Kaltenbrunner was among the New Right authors who belonged to the older generation and had a great influence on the younger rightist academics, publicists, and journalists. Born in Vienna in 1939, he studied philosophy and law at the University of Vienna. In 1962 he immigrated to the Federal Republic. As noted above, he was a reader for several publishing houses, including Herder, which printed over sixty conservative books. In the 1970s he authored several volumes on conservatism as a means to combat, as he saw it, a deficit in the movement's theoretical base. His books and his edited ones each had a printing of over 10,000 copies. His writings in prominent New Right journals contributed to the movement's challenge to the 1968 New Left theories. In 1988, two years prior to German unification, Kaltenbrunner predicted the two German states' inevitable merger. He wrote that the concepts of a new nation and a German loyalty were becoming increasingly important. He claimed that young Germans, whether on the left or the right, whether socialists or conservatives, were breaking with the tradition of self-accusation in coping with the Nazi past. As to ecological issues, he emphasized the need to preserve the natural, societal, and cultural conditions for the earth's survival. Since the mid-1990s Kaltenbrunner has become interested in religious and philosophical questions. As a result of his prolific and original contributions to the New Right philosophy, he won several awards, including the Konrad Adenauer Prize for Literature in 1986.[14]

Most of the New Right authors were born after World War Two and thus did not experience the Nazi rule. Ulrich Schacht was born in 1951 in the GDR. At an early age he was active in groups that opposed the communist regime. In 1973 he was arrested and imprisoned for nearly four years. Upon his release the West German government paid the East German regime to have him resettled in the FRG. He chose Hamburg as his domicile. There he received a position at the prestigious cultural affairs desk of *Die Welt*. He was also the author of several poetry and fiction books. Schacht, initially an SPD member, broke with the party when it established closer ties to the GDR regime. Yet he applauded unification of the two Germanys, especially because it promoted the concept of *Heimat*. In 1998 he settled as an émigré in Sweden because the Federal Republic had become too left wing for him.[15]

Heimo Schwilk has been another pillar of the New Right establishment. Born in 1952 in Stuttgart, he became a paratroop officer in the Bundeswehr and then studied philosophy, German literature, and history at Tübingen University. Upon graduation in 1981 he became a journalist for *Die Welt* and then editor-in-chief of *Welt am Sonntag*, a conservative weekly. During the 1980s and 1990s he published numerous books and articles on German history and politics. Schwilk was a close friend of Ernst Jünger and wrote and edited numerous books about him. Schwilk in his writings was critical of the mass media for catering to the population's lowest intelligence level and critical of the economic system for furthering the irresponsible managers who were out to take advantage of the workers.

He coedited with Ulrich Schacht the well-known "selbst" anthology *Die Selbstbewusste Nation* (*The Self-Confident Nation*), published by Ullstein in 1994. According to the two authors, self-confidence means that Germany must play a more significant role in international affairs because the country has the largest population in Europe and significant economic strength. Contributors to the volume assailed the post-1945 culture of the occupying powers, the New Left movement, political correctness, media democracy, societies built on the pleasure principle, and cosmopolitanism. A critic wrote in *Die Zeit* that the book represented a declaration of war on the Federal Republic's basic consensus.[16]

Klaus Kunze, born in 1953, was one of the New Right architects but never achieved the reputation of the old-timers. In his youth Kunze founded a science fiction fan magazine, joined the police in North Rhine-Westphalia, and completed his law studies in 1979 at the University of Cologne. During his studies he was an active *Germania* fraternity member who contributed to its right-wing orientation. He also was a founding member of the *Ring Freiheitlicher Studenten* (Circle of Free Students), whose orientation ranged from national liberal to right extremist. He wrote for the student newspaper from 1977 to 1979, thereafter for *Heimat* journals and for the conservative weely *Junge Freiheit*. Kunze had numerous contacts in right-extremist organizations. He joined the Republikaner and in 1990 became its candidate for the Lower Saxony Landtag election. Thereafter he was editor of a regional Republikaner newspaper and a founding member of the Franz Schönhuber Foundation. As a lawyer he defended neo-Nazi activists before the courts and the Republikaner Länder organizations in their attempt not to have the Federal Constitutional Court tag them as being unconstitutional. In his writings, he leaned on the political sociologist Robert Michels and Carl Schmitt for his argumentation. He denounced the German mainstream political parties' power in the parliamentary system and called for a direct election of the president, who would act as a counter to the parties. Kunze has opted for a strong state with fused executive and legislative powers.[17]

Rainer Zitelmann, born in 1957, was another leading New Right scholar, with a leftist background. He studied history and political science at the University of Applied Sciences in Darmstadt and received his doctorate in 1986. The title of his dissertation, which was published as a book, was *Hitler: Selbstverständnis eines Revolutionärs* (English edition: *Hitler: the Politics of Seduction*). It dealt with Hitler's social, economic, and domestic policies from the perspective of the system's modernization. Zitelmann became a research assistant at the Free University of Berlin, then in 1992 editorial director for the publishing houses of Ullstein and Propylaeen. In a not so veiled attempt to capture a strategic post to influence the country's cultural life, he became head of the desk for contemporary thought and later for contemporary history of *Die Welt*. In 1994, when he used his position as a platform for right-wing articles, fifty editorial staff members petitioned the publisher successfully to have him removed from his position. A prolific writer, he published a dozen books on history and politics. As a long-time FDP member, he insisted that daily politics should no longer be determined by the Nazi past's memory. Rather, "a line has to be drawn against this permanent self-flagellation and self-hatred, which produces neo-Nazis in the end. We must become normal."[18] He expected the FDP to become a nationalist party that would exert enough influence on the CDU/CSU to jettison its liberal social and pro-Europe policies. In 1998 he lost interest in history and politics, and became a specialist in real estate economics.

Karlheinz Weissmann ranks high among the younger rightist intellectuals. Born in 1959, he studied history and theology, and taught history in a Lower Saxony *Gymnasium*. The author of several controversial books on German history, such as *The Way into the Abyss*, he also edited a short-lived ultra-conservative journal *Phoenix*. CDU officials put enough pressure on Weissmann to jettison the journal. Thereupon, he wrote numerous articles in *Criticón* that lauded an authoritarian state. According to Weissmann, National Socialism in Germany failed because it was not anti-capitalist enough and because it did not collaborate with Nazi parties in other European states. In his books he acknowledges the Nazi crimes committed against the Jews but devotes more space to the Allied bombardment of German cities and to the Red Army's murders in East Prussia.[19]

The filmmaker Hans Jürgen Syberberg wrote a book *Vom Unglück und Glück der Kunst in Deuschland nach dem letzten Krieg* (*On Misfortune and Fortune of the Arts in Germany after the Last War*) that had anti-Semitic undertones. Syberberg assailed a "Jewish left aesthetic" that produced an unholy alliance with "throwaway products like punk, pop, and junk." Similarly, the playwright Botho Strauss wrote innovative and revolutionary plays in the 1970s, but in the early 1990s blamed the left for having created a moral and intellectual vacuum in the country. He assailed German high culture's debasement, blaming it on television and commercialism.[20]

New Right journals

To publicize their views, New Right authors, as noted, have written numerous books as well as essays and articles in several journals founded by them. These include *Criticón*, *Junge Freiheit* (*Young Freedom*), and *Europa vorn* (*Europe in Front*). In 1970 Caspar von Schrenck-Notzing founded the quarterly *Criticón*, which soon became the German New Right's leading theoretical organ. Just like its French counterpart GRECE, its aim was to establish a cultural and historical base that would challenge the New Left ideology and serve as the first step for New Rightists to capture the cultural scene and then political power. The authors, who saw themselves as a bulwark against liberalism, represented an array of ultra-conservatives, New Rightists, national revolutionaries, and nationalists. Their articles dealt with the urgent need for a law and order state in which immigration and social welfare would be cut back, the nation and nationalism would rank high, and the German *Volk*'s declining birthrate would be reversed. The authors provided a strong theoretical component to these topics. In the 1970s and 1980s they sought to bridge the differences between ultra-conservatives and right extremists. They supported Professor Ernst Nolte in his dispute with progressive historians (cited below). In its ideological position the journal straddled the space between national conservatism and fascism. The editors, who wanted to draw a line under the establishment's continuous denunciation of Nazism, maintained that Germans should finally jump out of Hitler's shadow.[21]

In 1980 *Criticón* merged with the Protestant-conservative journal *Konservativ heute* (*Conservative Today*). From 1994 to 2005 it appeared quarterly with a circulation of approximately 8,000. In 1998 Gunnar Sohn, formerly an official of the conservative League of Free Citizens, became the new publisher and the Bonn political scientist Amsgar Lange the new editor-in-chief. They abandoned the New Right philosophy and transformed the journal into a mouthpiece for libertarians and employers. In 2005 they changed the journal's name to the blander *Neue Nachricht* (*New News*) and made it an online databank for journalists and researchers.

Junge Freiheit has received much publicity since its founding in May 1986 in Freiburg, primarily because journalists for the democratic press did not envisage rightist young intellectuals capable of publishing a stimulating journal. It has carried interviews primarily with New Rightists but also with conservative CDU and FDP politicians, and with German and foreign right extremists. On occasion it has interviewed SPD and Green politicians in order to provide a respectable veneer to its ideological offensive. It has a strong cultural section. In short, it has become the New Right's most successful organ.

Editor-in-chief Dieter Stein's political career has been typical of a small group of young rightist intellectuals. He was born in 1967 in Bavaria, studied political science and history at Freiburg University, joined the CDU youth branch, and in 1984 switched to the Republikaner. One year later he joined the Free People's Party (*Freiheitliche Volkspartei*), a leftist splinter group of the Republikaner, and remained a member for three years until its dissolution. Thereupon he rejoined the Republikaner but initiated contacts with the ultra-conservatives in the CDU/CSU and with rightist circles. He began to publish *Junge Freiheit* as a 400-copy multigraphed tract, which appeared every two months. It was designed to be the journal for young rightist students and intellectuals who sought to respond to the dominance of the 1968 youth generation. Originally it was the organ of the Free People's Party youth division but soon it abandoned its party moorings and appeared independent of any party. In 1993 Stein moved its editorial offices to Potsdam and in 1995 to Berlin. Since 1994 *Junge Freiheit* has been published as a weekly with an initial average circulation of 10,000, which increased to at least 15,800 by

2007.[22] The articles in each issue deal with domestic and foreign affairs, and with cultural commentaries.

The ten editors, who had been members of conservative-nationalist fraternities and right-extremist university clubs, support the goal of a Weimar style conservative cultural revolution. Stein and associates believe that once the rightists have gained cultural hegemony in the nation, political power will fall into their hands like an overripe fruit. Thus the paper seeks, just like the New Right, to bridge the gap between neo-conservatism and right extremism. However, although the *Junge Freiheit* utopias are not clearly defined, Alain de Benoist of the French *Nouvelle Droite* movement, who frequently writes for *Junge Freiheit*, provides an intellectual base. He and other writers seek to define a "national opposition without Nazis and without those who propagate remaining in the West community."[23] Thus many articles denounce the German leftist, feminist, and liberal communities. In 1992, as part of its ideological offensive, Stein announced, with the support of *Criticón*, the creation of up to fifty readership circles in the larger German cities. The readers discuss political and cultural developments and the works of classical theorists. The groups also schedule lectures open to the public.

On one occasion the North Rhine-Westphalia *Verfassungsschutz* put *Junge Freiheit* under its right-extremist category because, under the cover of supporting democracy, the journal had eroded the barrier between democracy and extremism.[24] Lawyers for the *Junge Freiheit* appealed the ruling on the basis of the constitutional right to freedom of speech. In 2005 the Constitutional Court ruled in the paper's favor. At the federal level, the paper was often cited in the Federal Ministry of the Interior (BMI) reports but without putting it into the right-extremist category. The BMI took issue with articles that found merit in the arguments of revisionist historians. The *Junge Freiheit* editors usually distance themselves from the views of radical NPD and DVU officials. But being partly dependent on them and their followers as subscribers and being open to a variety of views on some issues they do not automatically reject articles supporting, for instance, Holocaust revisionist positions. Yet the editors, eager to occupy the grey zone between ultra-conservatism and right extremism, often reflect the more moderate views of Republikaner, CDU/CSU ultra-conservatives, and the right-populist Austrian Freedom Party.[25]

Another journal that occupies the grey zone is *Europa vorn* (*Europe at the Front*), which, however, is more right extremist than *Junge Freiheit*. Its slogan has been "Nothing for Us – All for Germany." In 1988 Manfred Rouhs founded it as a fortnightly publication. It seeks, among other goals, to bridge the gap between rightist youth functionaries and skinheads as part of a yet to be created "patriotic" youth organization. Editor-in-chief Rouhs' political biography is typical of young university-trained intellectuals who have gravitated toward the political right but then have not found a permanent political base. Born in 1965, Rouhs joined the CDU youth organization in

1979. Two years later he switched to the NPD Young National Democrats and soon became Land chairman of the North Rhine-Westphalia branch. In 1987 he was the party's candidate in Krefeld for the Bundestag election. Later he joined the Republikaner party, eventually holding party office. But when in 1989 regional Republikaner leaders ousted him from office, he joined a rightist citizen's movement in Cologne.

Already two years earlier, in 1987 he had founded the Rouhs publishing house, which prints rightist books, CDs, and *Europa vorn*. The journal, with a circulation of 5,000, is an organ of the German League for People and Home, a small rightist association. The young editors of *Europa vorn*, who claim that German citizens are alienated from their political establishment, have supported German unification, the creation of a German cultural and national identity, ecological renewal, and closer links to Eastern Europe and Russia. The journal provides news about skinheads and rock and Oi music. It issues special reports on key topics and prints 30,000 copies of a student journal *Hoppla* that are sent to right-extremist parties and organizations. The editors have organized round-table discussion groups and have circulated petitions demanding that right-extremist leaders end their fratricidal feuds. They have called for a well-organized opposition to the federal government, but without the support of Hitler fanatics. Yet Rouhs has also printed racist articles, which led to court proceedings against him.

The Heidelberg Manifesto and the Thule Seminar

As noted, the New Right authors were responsible for an outpouring of books, pamphlets, and articles. A number of them became involved in political actions. On March 4, 1982, fifteen conservative Heidelberg professors who were members of or stood close to the academic association *Bund Freiheit der Wissenschaft* (League for the Freedom of Science) issued the Heidelberg Manifesto. Its blunt opening statement, couched in racist and xenophobic overtones, dealt with the key issue of immigration: "It is with great concern that we observe the infiltration of the German people through the influx of many millions of foreigners and their families, and the undermining of our language, our culture, and our nationhood by foreign influences."[26] The Manifesto urged a tightening of immigration. Mirroring the Nazi philosophy, it called on German families to have more children in order "to preserve the German people and its spiritual identity on the basis of our occidental Christian heritage." It notes in language that sets the tone for some of the New Right literature:

> In biological and cybernetic terms, peoples are living systems of a higher order, with distinct system qualities that are transmitted genetically and by tradition. The integration of large masses of non-German foreigners and the preservation of our people thus cannot be achieved

simultaneously; it will lead to the well-known ethnic catastrophes of multicultural societies.[27]

The Manifesto notes that any people have the natural right to preserve their identity; hence there should be no melting together of people of different national origin. Europe should be preserved as an organism of peoples and nations that are worthy of preservation. Implicit in the statement was the need to preserve the white race.

According to the Manifesto authors, several of whom were CDU or CSU members, the FRG Basic Law is based on the concept of a people (*Volk*). Consequently they called on the German government to limit immigration by assisting foreigners to return to their home state. The foreigners' return will provide social and environmental relief in Germany.[28] The Heidelberg professors urged organizations that agreed with the Manifesto to form an umbrella organization.

Many professors also worked closely with members of the Thule Seminar, a cultural study group that Pierre Krebs founded with other rightists in 1980 in Kassel. The Seminar was designed to serve as a German counterpart to GRECE, the New Right organization in France. The Seminar has issued a newsletter *Thule-Briefe* and a magazine *Elemente*. Krebs has described Thule as a research group based on a study of the Indo-European culture that strives to bring about an all-encompassing European rebirth. Many of its members have written books and articles dealing with New Right themes. Krebs, who chairs the Seminar, was born in 1946 in Algeria and later moved to France where he was active in right-wing politics. Thereafter he emigrated to Germany and studied at Göttingen University. In Germany he publicized the ideological contributions of the French New Right members. He is the author of numerous books in which literature, philosophy, and politics intersect. In his writings he has sought to create the premises for a cultural revolution. This means that egalitarianism is replaced by differentiation, Judeo-Christianity by Indo-Europeanism, Enlightenment humanism by organic humanism, and racial mixing by separation of national groups. The Grabert publishers in Tübingen printed his book *Die Europäische Wiedergeburt* (*The European Rebirth*).[29] In 2003 Krebs founded the publishing house, edition de facto, to print books that were politically correct and thus not subject to government censure.

Krebs bases his views on, perhaps surprisingly, the Italian Marxist Antonio Gramsci who insisted that the state should not be restricted to a political apparatus but must gain the civil and psychological consensus of the masses. According to Gramsci such a consensus must be achieved at the cultural level. For Krebs, who obviously rejects Gramsci's political views, this means that the people, in this instance Germans, must reject the egalitarian ethos and global view of their political establishment. Instead the people should be exposed to a new educational and value system that will be the base for a peaceful cultural revolution. Once the people have begun to back such a revolution then the German establishment's political power will begin to crumble and be replaced by an authoritarian state. Krebs also pleads for a cultural rebirth of Europe as the harbinger of a political change that rejects American and Russian hegemonic designs. In his utopian vision of new alternatives, left and right political parties and ideological dogmas will play no part. The Thule Seminar's members contributed to the dialogue on the right, but Krebs' dominant personality had a negative effect on the Seminar's plan to become an ideological factory comparable to its French counterpart GRECE.[30] When Krebs, who had espoused a European neo-fascism, became politically inactive in 1990, the German seminar had become too esoteric for some earlier participants and it ran into organizational difficulties. Currently, it is hardly active.[31]

Historians' dispute

New Right historians received ideological support from ultra-conservative professors who sparked the famous *Historikerstreit* (historians' dispute) of the mid-1980s. At the time these professors relativized and decriminalized Germany's responsibility for World War Two and the Holocaust. They asserted that it was important to put the Third Reich in a proper historical context and that Hitler sought to protect Germany from the "Bolshevik hordes" and "Asiatic terror." Their chief spokesperson was Ernst Nolte, professor of history at Mannheim University (1965–1973) and the Free University in Berlin (1973–1991). He insisted that the Nazi Holocaust was a consequence of the Bolshevik-inspired genocide in the Soviet Union. He wrote that Stalin's gulags (forced labor camps), established to wipe out the Russian bourgeoisie and the peasants, served as a dress rehearsal for Hitler's concentration camps. In short, Nolte was deflating the horrors of Auschwitz and the other Nazi camps. Jürgen Habermas, then professor of philosophy and sociology at the University of Frankfurt, Heinrich August Winkler, professor of history at Humboldt University in Berlin, and other academics sharply attacked Nolte's theses.[32]

In June 2000, in a postscript to the historical debate, Nolte was awarded the Konrad Adenauer Prize. The Prize came from the conservative *Deutschland Stiftung*, a CDU foundation that in this instance showed its sympathies for historical revisionism. Horst Möller, director of the *Institut für Zeitgeschichte* (Institute for Modern History), gave the honoring speech. He praised Nolte for his "life's work of high rank" and agreed with Nolte that National Socialism was a reaction to communism and other ideologies. Möller assailed Nolte's critics who sought to censor an open debate on the Holocaust in Germany. In turn, the critics demanded in vain Möller's resignation as director of the Institute. Professor Winkler, one of the critics, wrote in a letter to the liberal weekly *Die Zeit*: "Herr Möller allowed himself to become party to an intellectual political offensive aimed at integrating rightist and revisionist positions in the conservative mainstream." According to Winkler, Möller's decision to make the speech had been a "big mistake."[33]

Frankfurter Allgemeine Zeitung advertisements

In 1995, fifty years after the war's end, the New Right took the offensive. On April 7 the *Frankfurter Allgemeine Zeitung* published a controversial political advertisement entitled "Against Forgetting," which Schacht, Schwilk, Zitelmann, and Weissmann had drafted.[34] It was signed by 281 prominent and less prominent Germans, including not only conservative politicians from the CDU/CSU, SPD, FDP, and the DVU, but also one former and one current cabinet member, a former federal prosecutor, active and inactive duty military officers, Germans expelled from Eastern territories in 1945, a few aristocrats, and a number of writers, academics, and journalists. As Jay Julian Rosellini points out, "What is unusual about this action is that two conservative literati, Schacht and Schwilk, played a major role in its organization. This would have been inconceivable before 1989, and it harks back to the Weimar Republic."[35]

The advertisement said that May 8, 1945 was not only the day of liberation from the Nazi dictatorship, as the media and the politicians kept saying, but also the "beginning of the expulsion, terror, and new oppression in the East and the division of our nation."[36] The advertisement's intent was to rewrite history. It implicitly equated the terror of Nazi Germany (which led to millions of casualties during World War Two) with the Red Army's expulsion of Germans from eastern territories (which resulted in the killing of two million Germans), with the "new oppression" in Eastern Europe, and with the Allied carving of Germany into four occupation zones. Among others, Rita Süssmuth (CDU), the Bundestag president, and Ignatz Bubis, the Central Council of Jews in Germany president, objected strongly to the advertisement.

On May 5, 1995 the *Frankfurter Allgemeine Zeitung* printed another political advertisement, signed again by Schacht, Schwilk, and three other New Right adherents. It objected to the cancellation of a memorial service for Germans killed in World War Two planned for May 7. At the service the ultra-conservative CDU leader Alfred Dregger was supposed to have spoken. According to the advertisement's signers, the cancellation occurred because of "an aggressive (defamation) campaign by the leftist media." On June 10, 1995 the *Frankfurter Allgemeine Zeitung* printed a third advertisement in which the anti-communist signers urged that June 17 be retained as a national holiday. This was the day on which East Germans rose up en masse in 1953 against their communist regime.[37] However, after German unification in 1990, the government decided to move the holiday to October 3, the date of Germany's formal unification. In May 2006, another advertisement appeared in the *Frankfurter Allgemeine Zeitung*. One hundred academics, publishers, journalists, and book dealers signed an appeal warning readers about the government's curtailing of basic freedoms, including research and teaching.[38]

The 1995 and 1996 advertisements typify the *Weltanschauung* of the New Right practitioners, who are currently saying that Germany's history and its role in world politics need to be reassessed. Their goal is to counter what they see as the left's cultural and political hegemony. (In reality, the media's political spectrum ranges primarily from liberal to conservative.) The New Right practitioners, despite their lack of an organized movement, have been successful in creating a more conservative climate in which government officials, such as Chancellor Kohl, have made some decisions that skirt closely to the right of the political spectrum. Many instances can be cited. In May 1985 President Ronald Reagan, at the invitation of Kohl, laid a wreath at the cemetery in Bitburg, West Germany, where over 2000 *Waffen* SS and Wehrmacht soldiers were buried. Kohl's goal, supported by Reagan, was to transform the image of German killers, especially the SS soldiers who had died for the Fatherland, into war victims. In 1992, Kohl was one of the few foreign leaders who did not shun a meeting with Austrian president and former United Nations Secretary-General Kurt Waldheim, the erstwhile Wehrmacht officer whom the US government had accused of having participated in "acts of Nazi persecution" during the war. In 1993, Kohl nominated Steffen Heitmann, a CDU ultra-conservative and minister of justice in Saxony, for the post of German federal president. Heitmann's nomination was withdrawn after he made damaging remarks about women who should remain at home and mind the children rather than go to work, about Jews, and about foreigners who were "overrunning" the country and being responsible for many crimes. He also said that Germans should not be held eternally in thrall to their past. According to Bubis, if Heitmann had become president it "would make anti-Semitism respectable in Germany again."[39]

New Right links to ultra-conservatives

CDU

There is an ultra-conservative faction in the CDU that takes domestic and foreign policy positions somewhat akin to the New Right adherents. This faction advocates that the CDU should move to the right, which has been the case on the issue of immigration. The CDU at times puts more weight on the state guaranteeing security, order, and unity than individual rights, freedoms, and a reduction in hierarchical class and societal income differentials. From the CDU viewpoint, but publicly denied, it makes sense for the party to woo supporters of the right-extremist parties by taking positions on policies, such as immigration restrictions, that are acceptable to its own members.[40] However, in the CDU, which can be considered the prototype of a conservative party, most members are moderate conservatives who support the democratic parliamentary system, an independent judiciary, and civil rights. The party's social liberal wing, headed in different periods, among others, by Heiner Geissler, Rita Süssmuth, and Richard von Weizsäcker, has sought to counter the programs of ultra-conservative supporters. The CDU programs show that leaders and members have accepted the central elements of a democratic conservatism.

The New Right practitioners have sought to cement ties to the CDU's ultra-conservative wing. However, most ultra-conservatives have maintained their distance. The more moderate Republikaner was able to make contact with a number of CDU ultra-conservatives, especially after the Republikaner's strong showing in the Berlin legislative election of 1989. Republikaner chairman Schönhuber sought to gain greater support among the ultra-conservative intelligentsia. He moderated the party's program, as on the asylum issue, thereby lessening the distance between his party and the CDU. Yet he had little success in attracting more young intellectuals into his party, as evidenced by the relatively few university students who joined the Republikaner.[41] He also could not gain support from Chancellor Kohl and the CDU presidium in order to enter into a coalition accord with the Republikaner.

Numerous CDU politicians have been in the ultra-conservative camp. Among them was Alfred Dregger whose career included Wehrmacht duty during World War Two, and serving as mayor of Fulda from 1956 to 1970 and as Bundestag deputy from 1972 to 1998. For nine years he headed the Bundestag CDU/CSU *Fraktion*. He was known as a staunch conservative who became a prominent founding member of the Stahlhelm *Fraktion*. This group represented the party's ultra-conservative wing in the Bundestag. Dregger pushed hard for the party to restore the country's national identity.

Hans Karl Filbinger rose in CDU ranks to become minister-president of Baden-Wuerttemberg. In 1978 he had to resign his post when it became known that as a high naval judge during World War Two he pronounced death sentences on the Nazi regime's opponents. One year after his resignation, he founded the Study Center Weikersheim, located in Baden-Wuertttemberg, which had a strong rightist orientation. The think tank, having received grants from German government and industry funds, saw as its mission the strengthening of the Christian national-conservative wing within the CDU/CSU. Many Center presidium members, such as Wolfgang Schäuble, held high CDU posts and spoke at the Center's conferences. A few of the invited speakers at its meetings were journalists from conservative newspapers. The 400-member Weikersheim Center spawned conservative think tanks in other parts of Germany.[42]

In a sequel to the Filbinger affair, Günther Oettinger, the CDU minister-president of Baden-Wuerttemberg since 2004, spoke in 2007 at a memorial service for Filbinger. Oettinger described Filbinger as a Nazi regime opponent who, like millions of others, had no chance to flee the regime's tentacles. According to Oettinger, Filbinger did not wield power during the Nazi era as suggested by his critics. In turn CDU opponents accused Oettinger of whitewashing the Nazi dictatorship. Chancellor Merkel, who rejected any ties with rightists, admonished Oettinger for his remarks. For tactical reasons he eventually withdrew them.

Another ultra-conservative CDU member was the former Bundestag deputy Heinrich Lummer who in 1981 became Berlin Senator of the Interior. *Junge Freiheit* characterized him as the "rightist *enfant terrible* of the CDU" who supported rightist youth financially if they put up campaign posters against the SPD. He was one of the founders of the Christian Conservative Germany Forum designed to promote Christian and conservative values within the CDU. He was also a founder of the ultra-conservative Berlin Citizens Association, created to defeat the SPD in the city's elections. Lummer became honorary president of the German Conservatives and was a frequent contributor to *Criticón* and *Junge Freiheit*. He was also the author of a book entitled *Germany Should Remain German*, which opposed mass immigration. He had no objections to the CDU forming a coalition with the Republikaner in order to gain their votes.[43]

In a 1989 Frankfurt/Main city council election campaign, the CDU sought to gain the votes of NPD supporters by waging a veiled anti-Semitic campaign against Daniel Cohn-Bendit, the erstwhile French-German radical student leader running on the Greens ticket. The campaign was not successful; the SPD-led administration appointed Cohn-Bendit as the city's deputy mayor in charge of multicultural affairs.

From 1998 on, CDU Bundestag deputy Martin Hohmann of Hesse made headlines. He opposed legislative tolerance for homosexuals, a change in the immigration laws to allow double citizenship for foreigners, restitution grants to former forced laborers who had worked in German plants during World War Two, and governmental funding for a memorial to the Holocaust victims in Berlin.[44] On October 3, 2003, the Day of German Unity, Hohmann gave a virulent anti-Semitic speech to his constituents that produced banner headlines in Germany and abroad. It led to the immediate dismissal of the Bundeswehr General Reinhard Günzel who had publicly endorsed Hohmann's remarks. According to press reports the CDU deputy had said that "one could with a certain justification in regard to the millions of dead in the Russian first revolutionary period call the Jews a race of perpetrators." Hohmann meant that prominent Jews had instigated the Bolshevik Revolution of 1917 and had conducted the civil war from 1918 to 1921, which led to the deaths of millions of Russians. He acknowledged that his remarks about the Jewish domination of the Bolshevik Revolution were gleaned from a book *The International Jew: the World's Foremost Problem* that Henry Ford, the notorious anti-Semitic automobile magnate, had authored in 1920.

Hohmann regretted that the Germans were still laboring under the burden of responsibility for the Nazi crimes, while other people who have committed atrocities present themselves as innocent lambs. His remarks caused consternation among top CDU officials and anger among the Central Council of

Jews in Germany officials. The latter threatened to bring a suit against him for violating Germany's laws against inciting racial hatred. The CDU officials put pressure on Hohmann to apologize for his remarks. Thereupon he said that his words had been taken out of context. He had not intended to disparage Jews or to deny the Holocaust's uniqueness.[45] Yet, as Professor Jeffrey Peck notes, Hohmann sought to equalize guilt on both sides and take the burden of collective shame off German backs and put it on the Jews. According to Peck, "As the saying goes, Jews will never be forgiven for the Holocaust as long as Germans are made to suffer for it."[46] Hohmann's remarks reflected Professor Nolte's arguments in the historians' dispute of the mid-1980s. Not surprisingly, Hohmann had close links to the Working Circle of Conservative Christians, whose platform mirrored the New Right philosophy. Eventually the CDU, after heated internal debates and negative reactions from Israel and other European states, forced Hohmann out of the party.

Roland Koch, minister-president of Hesse, must be included in the ranks of CDU ultra-conservatives. In 1999 he initiated a signature campaign in his Land that opposed pending national legislation, introduced by the governing SPD-Greens coalition in the Bundestag, easing dual citizenship requirements for foreigners. His xenophobic campaign gained him many votes and contributed to his becoming minister-president in 1999 and the party's vice chairman in 2006. In the same year, the CDU campaigned in the Land North Rhine-Westphalia election that immigration be more limited. The campaign was characterized by slogans, such as "more education than immigration" and "children instead of Indians." The latter slogan referred to the SPD-Greens national government proposal to allow 20,000 qualified computer specialists, including those from India, to work in Germany for a limited time period.[47] Obviously the CDU sought to capitalize on a strong feeling among voters wanting to restrict immigration. In the 2001 federal election campaign Koch demanded that the CDU make the Germans' national identity one of its principal themes. He asked pupils to show more respect for the German flag and joy in the national anthem. SPD and Green leaders accused him of promoting a policy of bashing foreigners.[48] In the 2008 Land Hesse campaign he ran on a populist anti-foreigner theme, repeatedly citing an incident in which a Turkish and a Greek youth severely beat up an elderly German man in the Munich subways. He used this attack to justify a call for tougher penalties for juvenile immigrants who commit serious crimes. Immigrant groups, the Jewish community, and the SPD denounced Koch as a xenophobic populist.[49]

Many federal ministers of the interior, such as Wolfgang Schäuble (CDU), have supported tough law-and-order legislation allegedly to fight terrorism, but in the process reducing individual rights. For instance, in 2007 he proposed controversial legislation that would allow the federal government to carry out assassinations of terrorist suspects, and outlaw the use of the internet and cell phones for people suspected of being terrorist sympathizers.

CSU

Not surprisingly given Bavaria's political conservatism, a number of top CSU leaders have taken an ultra-conservative line that has not been too distant from the New Right and right-extremist positions. Franz Josef Strauss, erstwhile minister in numerous Bonn cabinets and minister-president of Bavaria (1978–1988), made nationalism the party's political doctrine. He deemed it important that there should be no party on the right of the CSU. Thus, the party took over the nationalist and racist positions of the right extremists. In May 1998, former federal finance minister Theo Waigel, in addressing CSU convention delegates, said that "We do not live in a multi-cultural society, we remain a German nation!" He added that "foreigners convicted of criminal acts should be deported and . . . deportation proceedings be speeded up."[50] SPD, FDP, and the Greens strongly criticized the CSU's policy on immigration.

In 2000, the CSU secretary-general Thomas Goppel granted an interview to the neo-Nazi publication *Zentralorgan*, the organ of the Free Comradeships. In the same year the CSU Landtag deputy Klaus Gröber invited Thomas Prinzhorn, a leading official of the right-populist Freedom Party of Austria (FPÖ), to speak in his district.[51] SPD leaders warned CSU leaders to stop their support of the FPÖ and its then chairman Jörg Haider. In 2002, Edmund Stoiber, the CSU chief who had been CDU/CSU chancellor candidate in the national election that year, used the New Right vocabulary. He spoke of the threatened miscegenation of the German people unless immigration was curtailed.[52] In 2005, he accused the SPD-Green national government of failing in its economic policies, thereby causing an NPD electoral victory in the Saxony election. He drew a parallel to 1932 when the Nazis gained strength during the Great Depression. The conservative Israel-born history professor Michael Wolffsohn, teaching at the Bundeswehr University in Munich, concurred with Stoiber's position. Wolffsohn claimed that millions of Germans had supported the NSDAP not to produce the Holocaust but to overcome a massive unemployment and political crisis. SPD chief Franz Müntefering, in a rebuttal to Stoiber, warned the CSU chief not to blame the SPD for the strengthened right-extremist scene, but to blame the voters who voted for the NPD. Müntefering called on all democrats in the mainstream parties to resolutely oppose the right-extremist parties.[53]

Günther Beckstein, former interior minister and minister-president of Bavaria since 2007, has been another staunch law-and-order official who has favored fewer immigrants streaming into Germany. He, like Schäuble, has demanded an immediate expulsion of immigrants who are suspected of being terrorists and has called for a tightening of the security system.

FDP

The FDP has had numerous intra-party schisms. In the early 1950s, the national-conservative wing, concentrated in Hesse, Lower Saxony, and North

Rhine-Westphalia, issued a "German Program." It lauded nationalism, the middle class, the peasants, and the family. It demanded restitution for persons prosecuted by the authorities as former Nazis. It had visions of forming a new German right, but did not succeed because rival rightist political groups had similar objectives. In addition, in January 1953 British intelligence arrested Werner Naumann, who had been a state secretary in the Reich Propaganda Ministry, and six other ex-Nazis for their plan to infiltrate the FDP and take over its leadership. Two prominent FDP members, Ernst Achenbach and Wolfgang Diewerge, who had been secret supporters of Naumann, had fed him high-level information about FDP leaders. In later years, FDP conservative leaders in Berlin became increasingly powerful. They saw an ideological model in the Austrian FPÖ which, under the leadership of Haider and others, was pursuing a right-populist and national-conservative course.

In the meantime, the FDP's liberal wing called for economic deconcentration and more cultural freedoms, and denounced extreme nationalism. The two antagonistic wings, which had equal strength at party conventions, were forced to compromise. As a consequence the party pursued a middle course. This enabled the FDP to become the junior partner of the CDU/CSU or the SPD in most federal cabinets in Bonn. When the conservative CDU/CSU was in power, the FDP as the liberal junior coalition partner sought to block or weaken some conservative proposals emanating from the CDU/CSU. The liberal FDP leaders were dismayed by the conservatives' program within their own party. Among the liberals, Hildegard Hamm-Brücher, state secretary in the Foreign Office from 1976 to 1982, even supported, in vain, their ouster from the party. Among the national conservative wing's members were the writer Rainer Zitelmann, the former federal attorney general Alexander von Stahl, the former communist Klaus Rainer Röhl, and the North Rhine-Westphalia chief, Jürgen Möllemann.

The latter was the most outspoken and flamboyant leader in the FDP whose right-populist views were close to the New Right. In 2002, Bundestag deputy Möllemann, on the basis of his anti-immigration position, sought to attract right extremists to vote for the FDP in the national election. Möllemann and FDP leaders in Berlin attempted to transform the FDP into an openly racist and right-wing party comparable to the FPÖ in Austria, the Danish People's Party, and the Swiss People's Party. Möllemann even made anti-Semitic overtures to gain more support. He accused Michel Friedman, the Central Council of Jews in Germany's vice president, of encouraging anti-Semitism in Germany with his "intolerant, spiteful manner" and "unbearable, aggressive and arrogant behavior." Möllemann combined criticism of the Israeli government with statements that had anti-Semitic undertones. He refused to distance himself from right-extremist groups that expressed enthusiasm for his 2002 campaign. In June 2003 when the state prosecutors began an investigation into his involvement in alleged fraud and illegal party funding,

Möllemann committed suicide by not opening a parachute while making a jump in Germany.[54]

This brief survey of the mainstream democratic parties CDU/CSU and FDP shows that in each one of them there was a minority whose political or social views were not that far apart from the more moderate New Right theoreticians. This was especially true of a number of CDU/CSU politicians and intellectuals who had a chance to realize some of the New Right programs when their party was in power. The SPD had a moderate conservative wing, while the Greens, the PDS, and the Left Party did not.

Coming to terms with the past

Certain historical and political themes emerge from the New Right publications. The rightist authors have written that Germans should be proud of their country's many achievements since World War Two and not focus on the Nazi leaders' crimes. The authors have decried the fact that since the Federal Republic's founding in 1949, Germans had been expected to cope with and overcome the past (*Vergangenheitsbewältigung*). When New Right adherents condemn the Hitler regime they do so with reservations or cite other authoritarian governments to indicate that the Hitler regime was not that unique. Most of them have acknowledged that the Holocaust was one of many horrible events in world history but that the Soviets were equally if not more guilty of murdering millions of Russian citizens. The New Rightists do not accept the thesis that Germany was solely responsible for World War Two. They also contend that historical events must not be viewed primarily from the perspective of Germany coming to terms with its past.

After the war ended in 1945 Germans were too busy foraging for food and reuniting scattered family members to make pronouncements about the evils of Nazism. Rather, the mood was one of apathy and lethargy. The New Right authors objected to the constant Allied reminders that the Germans were guilty of having supported the Hitler regime. Such reminders meant that the Germans had "one strike" against them, which would not be the case of the victorious powers' citizens. The authors contended that even though Germany has become a major European state it was still at a disadvantage in being blamed unfairly for instigating two world wars in the twentieth century and producing a Hitler. Some of the authors praised Hitler's domestic policies up until World War Two and approved of his annexing Austria in 1938. One author (Mohler) reminds his readers that other states have been guilty of expansionist moves, such as Britain in Ireland.

Once West Germany became a state in 1949, its democratic leaders sought popular acceptance of the Basic Law. Polls indicated that only a bare majority of Germans approved the "temporary" constitution. Few citizens could muster a sense of pride in the Federal Republic's civic symbols, such as the national flag and the anthem, because in the post-Hitler era they lacked a national consciousness and identity. To instill such feelings, mainstream leaders echoed some of the New Right authors' sentiments. Eugen Gerstenmaier (CDU), Bundestag president from 1954 to 1969, wrote: "If we (Germans) want to survive as a nation, we must once again begin to know who we are and what we want."[55] He warned that unless such feelings emerged Germany would not become an important state in the European Community. By 1972 Willy Brandt, the SPD chancellor candidate in the electoral campaign, had coined the slogan "Germans, we can be proud of our country." When public opinion polls in 1974 and 1975 showed that most voters, but not the younger ones, were comfortable with the terms "fatherland" and "patriotism," CDU leaders Kohl and Kurt Biedenkopf, minister-president of Saxony, coined the slogan "Out of love for Germany." Similar themes have emerged in more recent elections.[56] In 1985, President Richard von Weizsäcker (CDU) declared that pride in one's country must be balanced by the need for Germans to confront "the unspeakable truth of the Holocaust." In the same vein, the Israeli ambassador to Germany, Avraham Primor, praised the Germans' new attitude toward their own country as shown in the number of people attending memorial services for the Holocaust victims.[57]

Prior to German unification in 1990 the New Right authors claimed that the victorious Allied powers continued to have a monopoly over the FRG and GDR even though the two countries had nominal sovereignty. According to these authors a German state must be created that has full sovereign rights. Some of the New Right writers even contended that one of the East German Länder should once again carry the name of Prussia, the symbol of German power. In addition, Germany must carry out a policy of regaining the eastern European territories that in 1945 were ceded to Poland, Czechoslovakia, and the Soviet Union. The New Right writers, in viewing global developments, emphasized the need to strengthen Europe in order to stem immigrant "hordes" from Third World countries and implicitly to maintain a racial superiority.

In terms of domestic policies, Günter Maschke, one of the New Right publicists, decried Germany's extensive network of basic and social rights, which will lead to a moral and hedonistic degeneration of the *Volk* and to a "total" democracy. He sees the United States and its decadent way of life, its melting pot, and its mass culture as a further threat to the declining German ethos. Such a negative development within Germany encourages useless disputes among its political parties, tough bargaining among them, and injurious pragmatic decisions. According to Maschke, the New Right's goal should be the creation of an authoritarian state that acts decisively to stem a democratic tide.[58]

The Martin Walser controversy

The well-known German novelist Martin Walser has become controversial in the country's literary and political circles. Some of his current views have received the support of New Right and right-extremist intellectuals. At one time he supported the leftist extra-parliamentary opposition, but during the 1980s he was criticized for having become a conservative and "crypto-nationalist." He denies such a charge and considers himself as a man of the intellectual and moral center. Although certainly not viewed as a New Right writer, Walser touches on the anti-Semitic theme that has preoccupied many of these writers for a long time. On October 11, 1998 Walser won the prestigious Peace Prize of the German Book Trade in Frankfurt. Frank Schirrmacher, editor of the conservative *Frankfurter Allgemeine Zeitung*, presented the award in the historic Paulskirche, in front of 1,200 guests, including Germany's top political leaders. They gave Walser a standing ovation at the end of his speech. Walser, in his acceptance speech, made remarks that could be construed to be anti-Semitic and that sparked a national debate. He accused foreigners of repeatedly bringing up Auschwitz and the Holocaust. According to Walser, Auschwitz had become to the Germans "a routine threat, a tool of intimidation, a moral cudgel or just a contemporary exercise."[59] He said: "No one who can be taken seriously denies Auschwitz; no one still in full possession of his faculties splits hairs regarding the horror of Auschwitz; when in the media, however, this past is held up to me every day, I notice that something inside me resists this continuous presentation of our shame."[60] Walser also objected to the huge Holocaust memorial to be built in the center of Berlin. He said that it was time to stop letting Germans know how guilty and disgraced they had been for supporting the Nazi regime.

Walser's views were shared not only by German right extremists, who had made similar charges in earlier years, but also by a significant number of mainstream Germans. According to Micha Brumlik, the director of the Frankfurt-based Fritz Bauer Institute, which studies the Holocaust's impact on German society, more than 50 percent of Germans polled no longer wished to be reminded of the Hitler era that had tarnished their country's honor and integrity.[61]

On November 9, in response to Walser, Ignatz Bubis, then the president of the Central Council of Jews in Germany, a Holocaust survivor and FDP member, spoke at a ceremony marking the sixtieth anniversary of the Nazi burning of synagogues (*Kristallnacht*) in November 1938. The top German political leaders also heard Bubis' speech. He bluntly accused Walser of being an anti-Semite and committing "intellectual arson." He also asserted that Walser on this and later occasions had encouraged neo-Nazi groups, had stimulated a new intellectual nationalism, and had betrayed the memory of Auschwitz. Bubis noted with alarm that ideas once considered extremist, as expressed by DVU chairman Frey and former Republikaner chairman Schönhuber, have recently become mainstream. According to Bubis, the desire to return to normality overlooks the dark past. Such growing intellectual nationalism, as was also voiced by a growing number of right-wing intellectuals, was not devoid of an anti-Semitism, which gives comfort to neo-Nazis.[62]

Bubis' remarks in turn infuriated Walser and his supporters. The writer Monika Maron said that Walser had not gone far enough: "I, for my part, neither think nor feel that young Germans must carry the shame of their nation. For me young Germans are as little incriminated as young Danes or young French."[63] Rudolf Augstein, editor of the weekly *Der Spiegel*, also came to the defense of Walser. He wrote that non-Germans had no right to participate in the decision about a Holocaust memorial to be built in Berlin. Professor Michael Wolffsohn of the Bundeswehr University of Munich denied that Walser's remarks would provide respectability to ultra-nationalists and that anti-Semitism was growing in Germany.

After numerous protests of Bubis' position, the *Frankfurter Allgemeine Zeitung* editors arranged a private meeting of Bubis and Walser in their editorial office. At the December 11 meeting, Bubis admitted that his comments might have been too strong and that he did not mean to suggest Walser was anti-Semitic. Bubis retracted his arson statement. Walser claimed that he had expressed the views of a majority of Germans. Paradoxically Marcel Reich-Ranicki, a well-known literary critic, chief of the *Frankfurter Allgemeine Zeitung* literary bureau, and Holocaust survivor, initially defended Walser. Reich-Ranicki said that Walser was not an anti-Semite. While this debate was continuing, a Mannheim court convicted Günter Deckert, an NPD chief, of calling Bubis a "Jewish Führer" and of threatening to kill a policeman. Deckert received a four-year prison term.[64]

In 2002, four years later, Reich-Ranicki changed his mind about Walser not being an anti-Semite when Walser published a novel titled *Death of a Critic*. In the novel, the literary critic happened to be Reich-Ranicki who, metaphorically, under a pseudonym, was murdered by a writer. Walser parodied the critic who in the novel and in real life was born in Poland and whose parents perished in the Holocaust. In this instance Reich-Ranicki condemned the "truly monstrous" book for its blatant anti-Semitic references.

Editor Schirrmacher had intended to publish the novel in serial form in the *Frankfurter Allgemeine Zeitung*, but then decided against publication. In an open letter to Walser, the editor wrote that the novel was full of anti-Semitic clichés and finished off "what the Nazis did not accomplish." According to Schirrmacher, "your novel is an assassination in which you settle the score with Reich-Ranicki . . . Your book is nothing but a murder fantasy . . . This is about the murder of a Jew." In reply, Walser wrote that the novel was less about the Holocaust than about the critic's power in the television age. He was referring to Reich-Ranicki who in 1988 had become host of a popular television program in which he discusses important books. During the years that Reich-Ranicki was host he was increasingly critical of Walser's books, which would account for Walser's negative attitude. Incidentally the rift between the novelist and the critic had flared up years earlier when Walser, in the autobiographical novel *A Bubbling Well*, acknowledges his mother's decision to join the Nazi party as early as 1932. Reich-Ranicki accused Walser of having played down the persecution of the Jews. In a conciliatory response, Walser acknowledged that the past, especially the Holocaust, can never be trivialized or manipulated.[65]

On May 8, 2002, the anniversary of Germany's capitulation to the Allies in 1945, Walser and Chancellor Schröder met at the SPD national headquarters in Berlin to publicly discuss Germany's past and present under the rubric "nation, patriotism, democratic culture." The SPD did not want to let the right-wing extremists take the lead in these highly sensitive topics. Walser and Schröder discussed the implications of Germany having become a "normal" nation, which subsequently triggered a feeling of pride and patriotism among German citizens.[66] Normalcy also included a modicum of anti-Semitism and anti-Israel feelings among a significant segment of the German public. The SPD meeting's purpose was to win over Walser to the party's goals. This was not achieved, especially when the novelist implied that the Jews' memory of the Holocaust prevented Germans from living a normal existence.[67]

National pride and *Leitkultur*

One of the psychological traits that has emerged among Germans in the last decade is pride in one's own country. New Right and right-extremist writers had been the first to break the unwritten rule that Germans could not feel proud of their country given the country's Nazi past, its hegemonic rule over its neighboring states, and the crimes committed under its name. In the post-1945 era the right-wing extremists declared that Germans should henceforth be proud of their achievements and not focus on the alleged crimes committed during Nazi rule. Indeed, they denied or minimized the Nazi crimes, such as the Wehrmacht atrocities committed in Eastern Europe during World War Two. They denounced the American-dominated "Holocaust industry," convinced that Germany had paid and done enough to atone for its alleged sins.

By the 1980s FRG officials were eager to signal to the country's Western allies that Germany was not a threat to its neighbors and that its future lay in a peaceful Europe. The officials realized that a West Germany that acknowledged its Nazi past would have more credibility in relations with its allies. Thus in 1985 President Weizsäcker (CDU) declared that it was time for Germans to confront the Holocaust's unspeakable truth. In the 1990s, many Germans, especially youth, began to look at the past and recognized the horrors committed in the country's name. They visited former concentration camps, bought books, and looked at films on television depicting the Nazi era.

Yet party politics surfaced time and again. During the 1990 national election campaign Helmut Kohl (CDU), running for reelection, insisted that it was proper to refer to Germany as the "Fatherland." His rival Oskar

Lafontaine (SPD) retorted that he could not use the term because he associated it with an outdated nationalism and the Nazi Storm Troopers. In 1995, fifty years after Germany's defeat in World War Two, Chancellor Kohl, once again mirroring the New Rightist arguments, commemorated the war's anniversary by suggesting that ordinary Germans were the victims of a Nazi rule of their state. By 1999, mainstream politicians of both major parties began to speak of pride in one's own country and a return to normalcy. However, in March 2001 Federal President Johannes Rau (SPD) said in a television interview that the Germans can be glad and thankful to be Germans, but not proud given the country's history. He added that "One can only be proud of something one has achieved." He was obviously worried about a resurgent German nationalism. CDU/CSU and FDP leaders protested his remarks. Thomas Goppel, CSU secretary general, said "one must ask whether a president who does not have this pride can represent a country of 80 million citizens." He accused Rau of polarizing the country.[68]

In the same vein, CDU leader Wolfgang Schäuble asserted that "the bond holding a community together and creates identity is the nation."[69] The FDP general secretary Guido Westerwelle, bluntly criticizing Rau, said "We must not allow neo-Nazis and skinheads to define what national pride is. We democrats, from conservatives to social democrats, must show pride in our country." The NPD officials reminded CDU/CSU and FDP voters that years earlier the NPD had printed red posters with the picture of a German eagle and the statement "Show German pride."[70]

The shift toward increased pride reflected a greater patriotic feeling. It was caused partly by the two Germanys' unification in 1990 when demonstrators in East Germany chanted "We are one people." At the time, 17 million East German citizens became FRG citizens. They had been raised on expressions of pride and the exaggerated notion that during the Nazi era they had been good socialist citizens opposed to Hitler and his capitalist supporters. Pride was further nurtured when FRG officials decided in 1990 to shift Germany's capital from sleepy Bonn to bustling Berlin. Such a shift facilitated a united Germany becoming the center of a united Europe and an important player in economic globalization. Pride in one's country was also triggered by the Germans' desire to stop being tagged as an eternal villain for the Nazi crimes and instead to have the opportunity to join the ranks of fully-fledged sovereign states. According to this view, Germany had earned the right to be normal.[71] In a 2001 poll, 71 percent of German respondents were proud of their nationality while an even higher 78 percent voiced pride in being European.[72]

As noted, New Right authors had also been pushing Germans to be more self-assertive, to be proud of the country's achievements, and to shed their contrition for the twelve years of Nazi rule. But most Germans could not easily draw a line under the country's history without seeming to discard it. They had to face the fact that there was no statute of limitations on how long the unborn generations needed to atone for the sins of their ancestors.

The American author Daniel J. Goldhagen argued in his much debated book *Hitler's Willing Executioners* that ordinary Germans had been anti-Semitic for generations and were the perpetrators of genocide.[73] Numerous German and American historians took issue with Goldhagen's thesis. CDU leader Angela Merkel, espousing a compassionate conservatism, supported the national pride concept when she said that she was proud to be living in Germany.

Yet a 2006 University of Chicago 33-nation study indicated that Germans were at the bottom of a scale measuring national pride.[74] Paradoxically just as the concepts of nationalism and patriotism emerged in German history when it was all right to voice such sentiments, leftist intellectuals sought to minimize the feelings of patriotism and nationalism, deeming them to be outdated. More important, they argued, were supranational European perspectives. But many Germans did not share such sentiments, including Chancellor Schröder who said that he was proud of the achievements of Germans and their democratic culture. He added that "in this sense I am a German patriot who is proud of his country."[75] Similar sentiments arose after Germany's third place in the World Cup soccer games of 2006.

Leitkultur

In 1992, Rolf Schlierer, Republikaner chairman, was the first to publicly write in his party's journal about the *Leitkultur* (defining or guiding culture) to which all immigrants should subscribe. The slogan meant that immigrants would have to give up their own culture and fit into the German culture, including fluency in the German language. In March 1999 Dieter Stein, editor of the *Junge Freiheit*, picked up on the theme in his journal, based on a contribution by the ultra-conservative Brandenburg minister of the interior Jörg Schönbohm (CDU) who proposed an annual immigration limit of 200,000. CDU leaders in a 2001 position paper wrote about the need for foreigners to adhere to "the values of our Christian culture" and avoid "parallel societies." Given its nationalist connotation, *Leitkultur* received support from other New Right authors and right-wing extremist leaders.[76]

In defending the *Leitkultur* concept, CDU leaders sharply criticized SPD and Green officials for attempting to link the CDU/CSU to right-extremist parties. Environment Minister Jürgen Trittin (Greens) said that CDU general secretary Laurenz Meyer had a "skinhead" mentality after Meyer had professed pride in being German. In turn, furious CDU leaders demanded Trittin apologize, which he did. However, Reinhard Bütikofer, the Greens' federal party manager, asserted the CDU wanted to defame its political foes with its "unspeakable 'I am Proud to be a German' debate." In turn, Chancellor Schröder (SPD) and politically moderate CDU leaders assailed the ultra-conservative CDU deputies for producing this controversy. Paul Spiegel of the Central Council of Jews in Germany said in reference to rightist violence against minorities: "Is it German guiding culture to hunt down strangers, set fire to synagogues, and kill homeless people?"[77] After numerous protests from the other democratic parties, CDU leaders abandoned the *Leitkultur* concept, but still opposed the concept of "parallel societies." In adult education courses for foreigners they intended to set up cultural integration courses emphasizing German language, values, and customs.

Nationalism and patriotism

Given the memory of Nazi aggression, the Holocaust, and the Nazi regime's support among Germans there was no outpouring of nationalist and patriotic feelings within Germany until the unexpected breaching of the Berlin Wall in 1989 and then again during the 2006 World Cup games held in numerous German cities. During the intervening years the major manifestation of nationalism occurred among right-wing extremists and neo-Nazis who were chanting "I am proud to be German" in their demonstrations.

However, in fall 2003 democratic leaders began to use the concept of patriotism once again. Foreign Minister Joschka Fischer (Greens) said: "I belong to a generation that still flinches when it hears the word 'patriotism,' but if patriotism means respect for democratic values, overcoming nationalistic prejudices and protecting minorities, then I am happy to call myself a patriot."[78] One year later CDU chairwoman Merkel announced that the party convention would deal with the patriotism question. CSU chief Stoiber asserted that expressions of patriotism would prevent political crises. However, many SPD and Greens members, wary of the emphasis on patriotism, felt that the right-wing extremists would be the primary beneficiaries from such a discussion. After all, the extremists had been responsible for voicing the patriotism theme decades earlier.

Nevertheless patriotic feelings surfaced during the European soccer championships and especially during the World Cup soccer matches in 2006. In that year, the British *Daily Telegraph* newspaper expressed such feelings succinctly: "Football, it seems, has achieved more for Germany in the space of just a few weeks than sixty years of soul-searching since the end of the Second World War."[79] Patriotism surfaced in the many tri-colored black, red, and gold flags shown outside private homes, flapping on car windows, and wrapped around women's waists. The patriotic frenzy reached a peak once the World Cup started and Germany moved up to the semi-finals. In Berlin, an estimated 1 million people watched the games on giant screens along a mile-long zone near the Brandenburg Gate and chanting "Deutsch-land" (clap, clap, and clap). Federal President Horst Köhler (CDU) remarked on German radio: "It is a sign that the country is increasingly returning to normal, that one can show uninhibited pride in your national flag and drape yourself in it."[80]

The World Cup games marked a turning point in legitimizing expressions of patriotism and nationalism. Charlotte Knobloch, president of the Central Council of Jews in Germany since 2006, said "One should support and not obstruct this joy. It must not be that youths feel in any way a debt for what their ancestors did sixty years ago."[81] Thus the younger generation should not be responsible for a "culture of contrition" and repentance for the Holocaust. According to Knobloch, young people had not been responsible for the older citizens' support of the Nazi regime and the terrible crimes committed by many of their elders. As an antidote to the Nazi past and to improve its image, the German governments have pushed for détente on the international level, increased respect for human rights, and greater ecological safeguards.

An appraisal

The German New Right movement has made theoretical and conceptual analyses of the country's history and its politics, but which perhaps for tactical reasons have not been rooted overtly in the discredited Nazi ideology. The New Right's members have sought links with their ideological brethren in the CDU/CSU ultra-conservative wing and the FDP national-conservative wing as well as with the Republikaner, the DVU, and, especially, the NPD. Thus, as the New Rightists straddle the divide between the democratic parties and the right-wing extremist parties, they seek to exert influence upon both camps. In their aspirations many New Rightists have striven for a strange mixture of historical revisionism, a cultural hegemony, the creation of a neo-socialist system, and an end to US imperialism and globalization.

Specialists on right-wing extremism agree that during the Weimar period nationalist and conservative revolutionary movements, as well as Carl Schmitt's constitutional law doctrine, had a significant impact on the unstable political situation that led to the rise of Hitler. The specialists also agree that the degree of influence the New Right has exerted and is currently exerting on the FRG government, society, and culture is much less than during the Weimar era. Yet some influence has been exerted. Young bright intellectuals have written a number of provocative books and are publishing, among others, *Junge Freiheit*, which has become a successful political and cultural weekly. The country's continuing restrictions on immigration and the emerging feelings of patriotism and pride in Germany are important milestones in the country's recent history. These developments were caused by overlapping pressures from the New Right, the mainstream parties, and the right-wing extremist parties, especially the NPD.

However, most New Right specialists, despite these achievements, feel that the movement has had a negligible and declining influence on the body politic.[82] They contend that the movement has not captured the key political or cultural editorial offices of conservative newspapers and is not represented on the boards of private radio and television stations. Hardly any well-known university professors have been active in the New Right movement, while the less well-known ones have not had the prestige to make an impact on the political landscape.

Conversely, there have been individuals, often retired, in the CDU/CSU's ultra-conservative wing who write for New Right publications, but their influence within the CDU/CSU mainstream has been limited. New Right members, unlike their Weimar counterparts, have had no significant access to funds from big business circles. Rather, some funds flow into the movement from small and middle-sized economic enterprises and from wealthy alumni of conservative university fraternities. Furthermore the current New Right adherents, who serve as a bridge or grey zone between CDU/CSU and FDP ultra-conservatives and nationalists, on the one hand, and Republikaner, DVU, and NPD right-wing extremists, on the other, have not contributed much to debates concerning the existing parliamentary system and possible alternatives. One reason for this gap is the low level of right-wing intellectual discourse, especially compared to those in some other European states.

In short, the New Right authors have had a minimal impact on Germany's domestic and foreign policies, except on the crucial immigration and less quantifiable patriotism issues. On the immigration issue, the New Right authors were able to have an impact because the major democratic parties, especially the CDU/CSU, failed to vigorously push the issue of integrating foreigners into German society. The democratic parties caved in to the rising anti-foreigner sentiment in the general population, a sentiment that the New Right fanned successfully and that led to constitutional restrictions on the number of political asylum seekers streaming into Germany. But even on the immigration issue, the New Right authors have not been able to block Germany from becoming a multicultural state that maintains strong links to the United States, NATO, and the European Union. On another issue: most of the New Rightists are careful not to question the Holocaust's existence, unlike some of the right-wing extremists. Yet in their revisionist views the New Rightists attempt to lessen German guilt for the Nazi horrors and to push aside the memories of that tragic period.[83]

7
Responses: Public and Private

This chapter covers the array of public and private responses to the right-extremist scene since Germany's unification in 1990. In the public sector the federal, Länder, and local governments have sought to stem the violence with varying degrees of success. The chapter first describes the legal system that provides guidance to judges who must deal with breaches of the law. Second, the role of the police in maintaining law and order is discussed. Third, the anti-rightist policies devised by the top government officials are assessed. What has been their response to the anti-democratic statements of the right-extremist parties and to the violent acts committed by the neo-Nazi groups and the skinheads? What kind of moral and financial support have the federal, Länder, and local governments given the numerous civic initiative groups, youth leaders, social workers, teachers, religious leaders, and union and business officials in their struggle against neo-Nazism? How effective have the programs initiated by public and private groups been? Have the groups succeeded in producing a more democratic climate in the German polity? Have the degree of violence and the number of neo-Nazis and skinheads decreased as a result of a multitude of public and private initiatives?

The law and the courts

In 1949, the West German government authorities signed the Basic Law (the constitution). It included clauses designed to maintain the democratic system and to guarantee the inalienable rights of individuals, whether Germans or foreigners. It declared the inviolability of a person's dignity and the duty of all state authorities to respect and protect it. The Basic Law also noted that everyone shall have the right to life and physical liberty. It emphasized the equality of all persons before the law and stated that no one may be disadvantaged or favored because of their sex, their parentage, their race, their language, their homeland and origin, their faith, or their religious or political opinions.[1] Yet, as noted, the Federal Constitutional Court, under Article 21 of the Basic Law, has the right to ban anti-democratic political parties. The minister of the interior has the power under Article 9 to ban extremist organizations. The Federal Office for the Protection of the Constitution, created in 1950, and its Länder counterparts have the power to collect and distribute information on unconstitutional political activity.

On February 2, 1967, the German government signed the United Nations International Convention on the Elimination of all Forms of Racial Discrimination, which it ratified on May 1969. The signatory states pledge "to prohibit and eliminate racial discrimination in all its forms and to guarantee the right of everyone without distinction as to race, color, or national origin, to equality before the law, notably in the enjoyment of the right to security of person and protection by the State against violence or bodily harm, whether inflicted by Government officials or by any individual, group, or institution."[2] In addition, "The participating States ... commit themselves to take appropriate and proportionate measures to protect persons or groups who may be subject to threats or acts of discrimination, hostility or violence as a result of their racial, ethnic, cultural, linguistic or religious identity, and to protect their property."[3]

As noted in earlier chapters the German legal system makes it difficult in practice to ban a political party or suppress a political activity. The Basic Law's authors were aware that the Nazi dictatorship's legacy demanded the rigorous right to protect political protest and dissent. But where to draw the line between these democratic rights, on the one hand, and the right of the state to protect itself by limiting these rights, on the other hand, is not easy. There are several provisions in Germany's Criminal Code that give authorities the power to limit these rights. Article 86(a) prohibits the wearing of anti-constitutional symbols, such as the Nazis' swastikas and SS runic pins. Articles 90(a) and (b) prohibit disparaging the state, its symbols, and constitutional institutions. Article 111 considers the open encouragement of illegal acts against persons a punishable offense. Article 125(a) grants authorities the power to arrest individuals in cases of civil disorder. Article 129(a) refers to the illegal founding, membership, and support of a terrorist organization. Article 130 states that incitement of hatred between people or calls for violence is a punishable offense for which a sentence of up to five years' imprisonment could be meted out. Thus it has been illegal to sell Hitler's classic *Mein Kampf* in Germany. However, the book is readily available on the internet from the United States. Article 131 categorizes the incitement to violence and racial hatred as another punishable offense.

The interior ministers, who initially had used many of these legal provisions primarily against left terrorists, hoped belatedly to reduce neo-Nazi and skinhead violence by extending or strengthening these articles. In September 1992, Parliament passed a law increasing the maximum sentence from three to five years for a punishment involving bodily injury. Murder has been punishable by a life sentence but if committed by a youth less than twenty-one years of age (as is true of many neo-Nazis and skinheads) then lighter sentences are meted out. Police officials were given wide authority to use wiretap information stemming from the Federal Intelligence Service. The purpose was to make it easier for the police to identify right-wing extremists. On December 1, 1994, Parliament enacted another bill that outlawed the use of any Nazi-like flags, badges, uniforms, slogans or gestures. This provision supplemented the 1945 ban on producing and distributing Nazi memorabilia and propaganda, including leaflets, posters, and newspapers. The 1994 law also stipulated a maximum five-year jail sentence for any person denying the Holocaust. At the same time the Parliament sharpened the law against "popular incitement" to make it apply more directly to "Holocaust denial." The new amendment made it a crime for a person "in a manner that could disturb the public peace, publicly or in a meeting" to "approve, deny or whitewash" genocidal actions carried out under National Socialist rule.

In September 1995, as a result of such legislation, the American neo-Nazi Gary Rex Lauck was extradited to Germany after his arrest in Denmark. In a Hamburg court he faced charges of distributing over a period of twenty years a plethora of illegal racist and anti-Semitic propaganda materials and Nazi symbols that he had produced in Lincoln, Nebraska and shipped illegally to Germany. He considers himself the propaganda leader of the National Socialist German Workers' Party – Overseas Organization (*Auslands- und Aufbauorganisation der NSDAP*). He was given a four-year prison sentence and was returned to the United States upon his release. Other Holocaust deniers received varying light sentences ranging from fourteen months in prison for Germar Rudolf to eighteen months for Ewald Althans who had made Holocaust denial statements while visiting Auschwitz. In 1999, Jean-Marie Le Pen, the French National Front leader, was convicted in a Munich court of inciting racial hatred and was ordered to pay an undisclosed sum in fines. At a Munich news conference in 1997 he had referred to the Holocaust as a "detail in the history of World War Two."

In March 2005, the Bundestag approved a ban on neo-Nazi marches at Holocaust sites and memorials to Third Reich victims, as well as marches that glorify or play down Nazi crimes. The new law was designed to ensure that the NPD and other organizations would not be able to upstage the sixtieth anniversary ceremonies marking the end of World War Two. Minister of the Interior Schily (SPD) welcomed the law, but criticized the fact that protests at the Brandenburg Gate would still be allowed because the Gate has no bearing on the Holocaust or on Third Reich victims. However, Schily noted that Nazis frequently marched through the Gate during the Hitler era and that an NPD march in the same place would reflect negatively on the country's image.

The courts on numerous occasions dealt with cases involving freedom of assembly and the right to demonstrate. The balance between protecting individuals' civil rights and maintaining the democratic system meant in practice that freedom of assembly could only be restricted if, for example, right-wing demonstrators called for racial hate or if there was a danger of violence. To give but one example, in 1998 a Leipzig court overruled the mayor's ban to allow the NPD to demonstrate on May Day. He had feared that a clash between NPD supporters and leftist opponents would present a danger to the public order. The presidents of Germany's Jewish community and the police union, in support of the mayor, criticized the court decision but had to abide by it.[4]

When a criminal offense has taken place the police in judicial proceedings have to investigate every reported crime and send all investigations to the office of the public prosecutor (*Staatsanwaltschaft*) who decides whether to indict the accused or halt the proceedings. The prosecutor's office has in theory the duty to investigate and pursue any matter in its jurisdiction as soon as it learns that a criminal offense has been committed. Prosecutors are authorized to perform investigations themselves or can request the police to do so. The investigating judge only reviews the interrogation's legality and must comply with the prosecutor's request if it is legal. However, the police conduct the majority of criminal investigations on their own. Cases are normally turned over to the prosecutor's office only when they are considered solved or all leads have been negative. Police also contact prosecutors when significant publicity is expected in a case, when they need help gaining a judicial arrest or search warrant, or when the investigating judge is to interrogate a witness.

Chapter 4 has chronicled some of the acts of neo-Nazi and skinhead violence and the subsequent judicial proceedings. Most judges have followed the law but many conservative judges have given lighter sentences to right-wing extremists than to left-wing extremists. The writer Jane Kramer notes that only about one-third of the skinhead crimes were ever sent to a judge for a trial.[5] In the 1960s especially, when the left was treated more harshly than the right, most of the older judges had been NSDAP members during the Hitler era. The sentences that they meted out to rightists reflected their continuing bias, at times clothed in remarks that the crimes were but youthful pranks or that a rightist bias could not be proven. However, in recent years when rightists killed an individual then, absent the death sentence, a younger judge, who had grown up in the 1960s or 1970s, would more likely mete out a life sentence for an adult and ten years' imprisonment for a minor than their counterparts in the 1960s.[6]

A few conservative judges have even belittled the severity of Holocaust denial. For instance, in December 1994 one judge acquitted two rightists who had sent copies of the book *Auschwitz Mythos* to customers from their mailbox in Hamburg. He ruled, in a narrow legal interpretation, that the use of the term "Auschwitz myth" could not be equated with a Holocaust denial. His ruling provoked anger in democratic circles.[7] Rainer Voss, the chairman of the German Union of Judges, told the press that "the public has thought us inappropriately lenient" in dealing with extreme right-wing law breakers. He urged judges "to confront decisively the enemies of humanity and democracy."[8]

In 2007, Saxony-Anhalt and Brandenburg government officials, in response to numerous racist violence incidents, urged the federal cabinet to propose a change in the law in order for judges to mete out harsher sentences where a racist motive was involved. Whether the federal government will change the law remains to be seen.

Critics of sending youth to prison, especially if the crime is light, contend with some justification that imprisonment will not solve the youth's problems and that their psychological makeup and their social status will be damaged further. Imprisonment means that the group of jailed rightists will become more cohesive and that society will further brutalize them. Consequently once such individuals are released from prison, they may participate even more in violent acts rather than in joining a socially acceptable group. The latter alternative is within reach, however, because many of the youth stem from supportive families.[9] In January 2001, the Federal Ministry of Justice developed a program to have judges and public prosecutors visit schools to talk about the constitution, the judicial system, and the dangers of right-wing extremism and intolerance.[10]

The police

Among public authorities, the police have played an important role in combating right-wing extremism. Police powers reside principally with the Länder and local authorities, although there is a Federal Criminal Police Office (*Bundeskriminalamt*), which is the country's national investigative agency, and the German Federal Border Guard (*Bundesgrenzschutz*), renamed the Federal Police (*Bundespolizei*) in 2005, which handles domestic security matters and guards Germany's borders, airports, and rail system.

The police, whether federal, Länder, or local, cannot be expected to tackle the deep-seated causes for the rise and staying power of the right-extremist movement. However, the failure of Länder police authorities to coordinate their own activities and eastern Germany's personnel shake-up after unification in 1990 meant that police resources in eastern Germany were woefully inadequate to meet the right-extremist threat. In eastern German cities thousands of police officers quit the service, while higher police officers were dismissed for having been loyal GDR state officials. As a result, police officers, who were often undermanned in confrontations with rightist youth, injured and in a few instances killed the unruly rightist youth. The police version of such confrontations was that they used firearms in self-defense.[11] Bernd Wagner, the former GDR police official, charged the eastern German state authorities with major delays in not making more resources available to the police.

Police bias against leftists but not rightists has also surfaced. For instance, in October 1990 rightist leaders organized a major demonstration in Dresden against drug dealers. The police assured the leaders that the marchers would be protected against the leftist *Autonomen* who were expected to break up the march. In another incident, when a journalist asked the Dresden police to do something about the neo-Nazis who in the railroad station raised their arms in a Nazi salute and yelled Heil Hitler, a police officer retorted that he saw no one who shouted.[12] When the radical leftist Antifa organization dialed the emergency phone number about rightist violence incidents, the police hung up.

As detailed in Chapter 4, the federal, Länder, and local governments had to take a stand against the mounting right-extremist violence committed in the early 1990s against foreigners in Hoyerswerda, Rostock, and other cities and towns. In May 1991 plans were made to coordinate governmental programs in a single Federal Action Program against Aggression and Violence. On October 17, 1991, immediately after the Hoyerswerda riots, all Länder interior and justice ministers convened a joint conference, at which their federal counterparts were also present. The ministers agreed, among many measures, to strengthen the police to protect the homes of foreigners and German émigrés who had returned to Germany, to intensify the exchange of information between the security forces, and to utilize information that *Verfassungsschutz* officials had made available. Judges were requested, partly as a deterrent effect, to promptly handle cases in which violence was used.[13]

In the Rostock area, no extra police were put on duty between the neo-Nazi attacks against foreigners in autumn 1991 and the more serious attacks one year later. If there had been, the latter attacks might have been avoided. To meet these rightist threats, Federal Minister of the Interior Rudolf Seiters (CDU) belatedly suggested that the Länder governments establish "rapid reaction squads" consisting of officers from the Federal Police and the Länder, to break up serious disturbances. The Länder top police officials rejected the suggestion. They perceived it as an intrusion into their sovereignty in police matters. They contended that constitutional provisions allowed the then Federal Border Guard to assist the police only in threatening situations. Although Seiters' proposal was not accepted, he was able to ban several neo-Nazi organizations that had participated in racist violence.[14]

Hans-Ludwig Zachert, the Federal Criminal Police Office president, admitted at the time that police and judicial authorities did not react sufficiently to right-wing violence. The Federal and Länder offices of the *Verfassungsschutz* shared this failure. According to Zachert, law authorities were too fixated on left-wing extremists, some of whom were clustered in the terrorist groups of the 1970s. In October 1992 the Rostock police had to face a different kind of law and order situation. They arrested a group of French Jews who sought without permission to put up a banner in the city hall reading "Germany, don't forget history." The group was also protesting the Rostock racist incidents, which did not endear them to the local police.

Although measures to increase friendship with foreigners may have had some effect on the citizenry, in 1992 the Federal Ministry of the Interior

Working Group for Internal Security recommended new measures to the federal and Länder governments to combat right-wing criminality. The measures included the setting up of a special commission or group to investigate such crimes and to make back-up police available. The Working Group also recommended that the police launch an information campaign aimed at the public and that shelters for asylum seekers be made more secure.

On August 31, 1992, the Bundestag Committee for Domestic Affairs held a special session to discuss the violence in Rostock and other cities, but it could not reach an agreement on additional measures to be taken. On September 19, 1992, the Kohl government announced that it would increase the police presence in eastern Germany and send the Federal Border Guard to back up local police departments whenever riots broke out. The government also intended to establish a special hotline for persons to report incidents of violence against foreigners.

In 1993 the western Berlin police were known to contain many right-wing extremists who had voted for the law-and-order Republikaner Party. At the time the courts handled fifty cases of racism in the Berlin police department. In May 1994 Federal President von Weizsäcker expressed dismay when after large-scale rioting had taken place in Magdeburg fifty rightists were arrested but all were released the same evening. The city's chief of police blamed the violence on the heat and alcohol consumed by "boys who will be boys." In September 1994, twenty-seven police officers in Hamburg were suspended for beating foreign detainees.[15] In short, the bias against leftists and foreigners was strong not only among rightists but also among a number of police agents. As a result, police responses to reports of rightist violence were often slow and the assailants could not be found.

Amnesty International reports in May 1995 and July 1997 severely criticized such police attitudes and behavior. The organization cited a pattern of police abuse against foreigners. The Standing Conference of the Länder interior ministers rejected the 1995 report findings. However, the ministers reached an accord that politicians and senior police officers need to create a climate of opinion that would not tolerate human rights abuses. In an attempt to be balanced the ministers also emphasized that not only rightists engage in violence but some young foreigners who are members of immigrant gangs commit crimes or engage in violence against other foreign gangs and German right extremists. The gang warfare was especially pronounced between Turkish and Kurdish groups.[16]

The police bias against foreigners decreased somewhat in the late 1990s after numerous acts of rightist violence had taken place, partly because in some police schools lectures against bias were held. In Hamburg the police authorities opened an internal bureau, entitled "Do not look away – Help," for its officers. The Federal Ministry of the Interior initiated a public campaign, "Basta – No to Violence," which dealt with the causes of violence against foreigners and ways in which to counter them. In addition, politicians urged the police to respond more swiftly to acts of violence, although at times it was difficult to gain evidence against rightists when public witnesses were too fearful to provide details.

The flow of information increased rapidly between local police and the Federal Border Guard. In addition, special police liaison officers were appointed to communicate with asylum seekers living in hostels and to improve links between local residents, refugee administrators, and the local police. The hostels were linked directly to police stations to ensure swift police action to protect the foreign residents.[17] The police in a number of cities, aware that their image was tarnished, sought to create a greater rapport with local groups whose members could assist the police in finding suspects or witnesses to crimes. Whether the tension between police and foreign groups can be deescalated through greater police recruitment of ethnic minorities remains to be seen.[18]

In 1998, after numerous incidents of rightist brutality against foreigners in Brandenburg and Thuringia had taken place, the Land governments formed a special mobile rapid reaction commando squad against violence and xenophobia. In Brandenburg forty-five specially trained agents, making use of helicopters and police dogs if necessary, were deployed in urban areas between 6 p.m. and 3 a.m. weekdays and around the clock on weekends. They were expected to patrol forty areas, such as railroad stations, where the rightists met on frequent occasions.

In 2000, the Federal Criminal Office accused the police of listing the many crimes committed by right-wing extremists as criminal rather than political. Such manipulation of statistics is often done in order not to give a town, city, or Land the reputation of being a "brown" neo-Nazi stronghold. In addition, accurate data collection is difficult at best, especially when foreigners in Germany do not speak the language. They have problems in communicating with the police, which makes their case even more difficult. In 2001, the Federal and the Länder ministers of the interior, aware that existing police registration systems were not satisfactory in counting politically motivated crimes, introduced the concept of "hate crime," with two sub-categories "xenophobic" and "anti-Semitic." In addition, numerous non-governmental victim support organizations collect information on right-wing violent hate crimes. In turn, the European Monitoring Centre against Racism and Xenophobia tabulates the data.

In January 2001, in Cottbus and Guben (Brandenburg), where rightists were especially active, a special police group met with representatives of youth and social welfare offices, judges, and prosecuting attorneys to collect the personal data of known rightists. Public officials had to contend with another type of crime. Many rightist meetings throughout Germany were scheduled in public halls or pubs under false names as a means of circumventing the police.

In February 2001 the Saxony mobile squad was supplemented by a special eighty-person unit of the Federal Border Guard charged with fighting right-wing extremism. It established a hotline for persons to report on violent incidents. Its task was to patrol especially railroad stations and trains, where a number of incidents had taken place that produced fear among foreigners and leftists. The patrols were to increase pressure on the rightists to refrain from violence.

In numerous Länder and cities, police on patrol pay frequent unannounced visits to rightists' apartments and warn them not to engage in any illegal activities. Such a warning, it was hoped, might serve as a deterrent to individuals who also know that Land criminal offices transmit personal data, including automobile license plate numbers and previous convictions, to a central information collection office. In 2004, after years of discussion, the *Bundesverfassungsschutz* received authorization to open a central office in Berlin to act as a central point for the collection and analysis of intelligence information from a host of federal and Länder agencies, including the police. The central office could issue orders for investigations, raids, and arrests. Critics warned that the separation of the police and intelligence services, in place since 1949 in West Germany, would thereby come to an end and give too much power to the new office. Defenders retorted that the continuing violence against foreigners and rising Islamic terrorism required maximum security.[19]

Despite some Länder resolutely dealing with right-wing violence, this was not the case in Saxony-Anhalt and Mecklenburg-West Pomerania, which suffered from a peak eastern German unemployment rate of close to 16 percent. Thus it was not too surprising that in Saxony-Anhalt the highest incidence of right-extremist attacks in Germany took place. In 2007 the Greens and the Left Party recommended to the Land parliament that it set up a special committee, which was to include parliamentary deputies, specialists in police work, and members of a mobile advisory body for victims of right-wing violence. The committee was formed and charged with making recommendations as to how the police can more effectively combat such violence.

The numerous incidents of rightist violence in which the police were criticized for being biased clearly showed that they needed additional training. In addition, critics said that the police and prosecutors were too passive in the light of the racist threat and were too slow to bring cases to court. In 2006, the police trade union federal chairman, Konrad Freiberg, defended the police record in dealing with right extremists. He asserted that the police was the only institution that confronts these extremists day and night. Its presence in dangerous areas has been increased, but financial support has been limited.[20] In 2007, Bundestag Vice-President Wolfgang Thierse (SPD) charged the police, especially in Berlin, with often letting right-extremists go free rather than arresting them.[21]

The federal, Länder, and local governments

In the 1970s the federal, Länder, and local authorities in West Germany sought to confront teenagers with the Nazi era horrors that their parents and grandparents had lived through. Such a confrontation, including teenagers' visits to concentration camps and interviews with Holocaust survivors, was designed to ensure that never again would there be another German-initiated Holocaust. In the 1980s, as noted in Chapter 6, some ultra-conservatives and right extremists sought to relativize the Holocaust. They asserted that the Soviets were equally to blame for mass murders in their state and that it was time to draw a line under the past.

Since 1983 German trade unions, church groups, civil right organizations, and political groups have sponsored a yearly "Week of Foreign Fellow Citizens" (*Woche der ausländischen Mitbürger*). The thousands of events that have been scheduled, such as cabaret performances, film programs on youth violence, and literature readings, focus on the contributions to society made by persons from the diverse national and cultural backgrounds living in Germany.[22]

Until the time that major outbreaks of rightist violence against foreigners took place in the early 1990s, public authorities were slow to act against right-wing extremists who were flouting the law. Chancellor Kohl was singularly reluctant to side publicly with foreigners seeking political asylum in Germany and, with a few exceptions, to denounce mounting right-wing violence. However, Federal President von Weizsäcker, who spoke out publicly about the rightist threat on several occasions, made a point of visiting hostels that rightists had torched.

In May 1991 plans were made to coordinate governmental programs in a single Federal Action Program against Aggression and Violence. On October 17, 1991, immediately after the Hoyerswerda riots, all Länder interior and justice ministers convened a joint conference, at which their federal counterparts were also present. The ministers agreed, among many measures, to protect the homes of foreigners and German émigrés who had returned to Germany, to intensify the exchange of information between the security forces, and to utilize information that *Verfassungsschutz* officials had made available. Judges were requested, partly as a deterrent effect, to promptly handle cases in which violence was used.[23]

In 1991, Cornelia Schmalz-Jacobsen (CDU), the federal government's Commissioner for Foreign Affairs, announced the beginning of a campaign to promote friendship between Germans and immigrants. The campaign was held under the slogan "Foreigners need friends, we do too." Twenty-eight organizations, including trade unions, employer associations, economic and public welfare associations, and the media, signed up for the campaign. Yet at the same time Schmalz-Jacobsen, mirroring the CDU/CSU position, suggested that Germany should adopt immigration quotas to limit the number of non-political refugees.[24]

Private efforts complemented public anti-discrimination efforts. In fall 1991, sixteen mainstream rock bands organized a ten-hour "solidarity concert" in Berlin under the motto "I am a Foreigner," which 10,000 fans attended. Celebrities, such as tennis champion Steffi Graf and film director Wim Wenders, appeared on posters with the same "I am a Foreigner" message. In Krefeld, officials promised that in each asylum hostel there would be a first-aid kit, a fire extinguisher, and a telephone to call the police in an emergency. The residents also demanded that Chancellor Kohl strongly condemn the rightist violence sweeping the country. Instead he denounced the "misuse of the right to asylum."[25]

In 1992 the Berlin House of Representatives, supported by the Council of Europe, initiated the Youth with a Future program. Its mission was to prevent endangered individuals from falling foul of the law. It sought to improve the range of leisure activities for youth who were encouraged to produce their own plays, music, graffiti, films, and fashion. In these initiatives the struggle against violence, racism, and xenophobia would be emphasized.

As noted in Chapter 4, on November 23, 1992, three Turkish citizens perished in a fire in Mölln that right-extremist youth had set. The CDU/CSU-led government reacted swiftly, partly because of negative reactions abroad and at home. On December 2 the cabinet met to coordinate measures against extremists. Chief Federal Prosecutor Alexander von Stahl was given the power to take over the Mölln case. This was the first time that he dealt with the prosecution of right-wing extremists, a task that Länder chief prosecutors normally handled. In addition, Federal Minister of the Interior Rudolf Seiters convened an urgent meeting of the Länder interior ministers. They concurred on a series of measures to stem the right-extremist violence and terrorism that had assumed alarming proportions. They created a new inter-departmental unit that would deal only with right-wing violence. Finally, they made it a priority to combat right-wing extremism rather than, at least for the time being, to stem the immigration of foreigners or to fight the extreme left, whose remnants lived on in the *Autonomen*.[26]

Soon after the cabinet meeting, the Standing Conference chairman of the Länder interior ministers announced that the members had reached agreement on other measures. They set up special police units that could be deployed rapidly, created new commissions to coordinate actions against racism, and formed Special Forces on a standby basis in Rostock and other trouble spots. The federal government also allocated modest additional funds to combat racism and xenophobia among German youth. For example, the Federal Ministry for Women and Youth and the Federal Ministry for Family and Senior Citizens allocated DM 20 million for the years 1992 to 1994 to fight xenophobia. For 1992 the federal budget also included DM 50 million for projects dealing with special political education for eastern German youth.[27] This authorization meant that up to 144 youth projects in eastern German urban areas could be launched in areas that had been especially prone to violence against foreigners and leftists. The projects, staffed by over 400 professionals, included counseling centers, residential programs, leisure time and cultural centers, youth clubs, the media, social training, and workshops.[28] In eastern Berlin 300 youth were able to work for three years at the state's expense. The aim was to integrate a work program with suburban improvement and renewal plans. Although some of the plans sounded ambitious numerous civil rights leaders denounced the government for its slow response to the rightist threat.

In 1993 the Federal Ministry for Labor and Social Affairs allocated DM 92 million for various programs designed to speed up integration of foreigners and Germans. Once again the western Länder gave an additional DM 52 million to their eastern counterparts. In turn, cities and towns were free to distribute the funds to various organizations. Yet despite some boondoggling most projects were worthy of support. Seminars, vocational projects, and binational training projects were launched to promote integration. Regulations were eased for foreigners to receive a monetary compensation if they had become victims of violent crime.[29]

In a speech on September 2, 1993, Chancellor Kohl finally condemned the numerous acts of violence and declared that the authorities must use democratic means to repel such attacks. He urged all citizens to defend the country's fundamental values and democratic principles without which domestic harmony was not possible. At the same time the federal government, in order to reduce citizens' racial prejudice and hostility toward immigrants, instituted a massive public information campaign that included advertising, television programs, and the dissemination of school materials.

In February 1993, prior to Kohl's speech, the federal cabinet issued its first interim report followed in January 1994 by a sequel report. The reports noted that to reduce hate and violence the federal government and the Länder must pay more attention to education, employment, and information efforts dealing with political extremism. Moreover, the government should speed up the integration of foreigners and initiate legislation to confront right-wing extremism.[30] The January 1994 report sought to pinpoint the challenges, such as the traditional family breakdown and changing roles and structures facing youth. It noted that the media attention given to the violent incidents against foreigners and leftists may have encouraged other youth to commit similar acts. Furthermore, it emphasized that the public concern about the massive flow of political asylum seekers into Germany provided right wingers with a sense of legitimacy. In eastern Germany the sudden shift from a communist regime to a Western democracy made it difficult to provide for an effective reeducation program. The difficulty was compounded by a severe shortage of qualified social workers in the initial post-unification years. The report called on the authorities to educate youth for a democratic life, meeting their employment goals, providing support for those with special needs, accentuating non-violent alternatives in schools, and scheduling more leisure time activities.

The government launched programs to reduce violence among young right-wing extremists. Youth directors initiated a range of anti-hate and anti-violence programs. The media were urged to cover hate incidents in such a manner that they would not encourage more violence. The federal, Länder, and local governments financed additional child, youth, welfare, and social work services based partly on the advice of government experts, academics, and youth project specialists and partly on a spate of books and articles on the subject. Not unexpectedly the various reports came to different conclusions as to how best to tackle the subject. In 1994 the non-governmental Documentation and Information Center for Racism Research was founded in Marburg to coordinate the work of numerous grassroots organizations. In the same year broadcast industry professionals created a Media against Racism organization. They produced a number of radio and television anti-racist advertisements to counter the right-extremist propaganda.

The federal government also provided financial support for counseling services and German language classes for foreigners and their families. It urged the media to emphasize the contributions that foreigners have made to the German economy. Such contributions have meant that the foreigners are consumers, pay taxes, and contribute to the social insurance funds. Many have started their own businesses; others work in factories and stores, where integration of foreigners into German society has made some headway. In numerous instances, local governments have organized seminars, vocational projects, and binational training projects. In addition, Foreigners' Councils (*Ausländerbeiräte*) were created at all government levels to advise policymakers. German authorities chose prominent migrants to sit on the councils, although in some areas migrants elected their own council members.[31]

While these measures and recommendations to curb right-wing extremism were announced, the Ministry of the Interior took a controversial step that limited the civil rights of numerous foreigners seeking political asylum. It concluded a treaty with Romania that authorized the German government to speed up the deportation of Romanians whose asylum applications had been rejected. The accord primarily affected Gypsies, who comprised 60 per cent of Romanian asylum seekers. But it also led to the deportation of a number of Africans who feared torture and death upon their return. Right-wing extremists were pleased by the government's action and viewed it as a victory for their cause. Leftist groups, which supported a multicultural society and a maximization of civil rights, were highly critical.[32]

By the mid-1990s the Länder had initiated a host of anti-right extremist programs. For instance, in 1997 the Brandenburg Land government (CDU-SPD) created an Action League against Violence, Right-wing Extremism, and Xenophobia, which sponsored numerous local initiatives. But three years after its founding, the League faced an identity crisis. The Ministry of the Interior's state secretary (CDU), backed by the Catholic Church, called on the League to also tackle left extremism. The German Trade Union Federation, the Land Youth League, and the Land SPD opposed the proposal, contending that the Land has an image problem for failing to mobilize the population against right-wing extremism. The League's officials threatened to resign. The Commissioner for Foreigners, Almuth Berger (Greens), also criticized the CDU proposal, stating that the rightists committed almost all acts of violence. A decision was postponed.[33]

In the meantime mobile advice teams for the prevention of right-wing extremism and regional centers for inter-cultural understanding, education, and schools were created. The centers organized numerous projects in kindergarten, youth clubs, schools, and communities. In addition, they provided counseling for refugees, migrants, and other victims of violence. They strengthened networks between social workers, teachers, local councilors and government officials, mayors, and the police. The centers also supported youth cafés, youth clubs, and citizen initiatives. Other Länder also had a broad range of programs.

In 1998, nearly a hundred human rights groups in the FRG formed a Network against Racism – for Equal Rights. They demanded in succeeding years that the government support an anti-discrimination law to facilitate victims of racist violence receiving financial assistance. They also demanded a liberalization of the right to asylum for foreigners and the right of foreigners to have double citizenship. They criticized the conservative position of Minister of the Interior Otto Schily (SPD) who opposed liberalizing the government's immigration policies.[34] In the same year, 1998, the international Jewish organization B'nai B'rith supported the founding of an Anti-Defamation Forum in Berlin to complement the work of the American Jewish Committee's Berlin office. The Forum's leaders met with top German government officials to voice their concern about the country's numerous racist and anti-Semitic incidents. The Forum planned to work directly with German youth organizations and to establish a research and documentation center.[35]

Over the years, federal authorities have given financial support to public and private agencies to create new youth and welfare services. One of the chief agencies was the Amadeus Antonio Foundation, which chairwoman Anetta Kahane had founded in 1998.[36] The Foundation has been concerned especially by the rise of anti-Semitism and racism in Germany. It seeks to strengthen the democratic civil society. It financially supports local projects and initiatives, and organizes training sessions and workshops for social workers, parents, and teachers in regional advisory centers.

In 1998, in the wake of the DVU electoral victory in Saxony-Anhalt, the Land government supported the creation of a Land initiative against rightists, as well as the convening of numerous round tables at which representatives of local governments, trade unions, business associations, schools, youth groups, and culture met to discuss ongoing and new projects. Two years later, in 2000, in the aftermath of a bomb detonation in Düsseldorf in which ten immigrants from Russia were injured, government state secretaries examined the efficiency of federal programs, many financed by the European Social Fund, to combat violence. The Fund was set up to assist structurally weak regions in the European Union. Heiner Geissler, one of the few liberal CDU officials, blamed the German democratic political parties for not stopping rightist influence in the federal administration and the courts. Renate Künast, Greens chairwoman, blamed the SPD, then in a governing coalition with the Greens, for not doing enough to minimize the rightist menace.[37] In response the SPD noted that the Bonn-based Federal Agency for Civic Education, charged with supporting local initiative projects and supplying teachers with pedagogical materials, had done a commendable job.

In 2000, the SPD-led federal government founded the League for Democracy and Tolerance against Right-wing Extremism and Violence. In its initial year the League suffered from lack of funds and qualified personnel but in the following year it hired experienced staff. The League's purpose was to provide assistance to the 900 local groups affiliated with it and to publicize the more successful initiatives.[38] The government also supported a Youth for Tolerance and Democracy program and a Democracy Learn and Live model program that financed some 3,600 projects. Many of these were located in the cities and towns suffering from unemployment and social problems. Unemployed youth, including those who dropped out of high school, were given a chance to work in hospitals, retirement homes, social agencies, and sports clubs. Once they became experienced in their work they had a better chance of finding full-time jobs. It was hoped that the right-wing scene would then be less attractive to them.

In February 2000, the government-sponsored association *Gesicht Zeigen!* (literally "Show Your Face!"), with the assistance of the Central Council of Jews in Germany, produced film and television advertisements opposing racism and xenophobia. Their purpose was to spread awareness that citizens standing up for others were brave and good, and what the citizens had done should be done as a matter of course. The film clips were shown in 800 movie theaters. Five hundred groups and individuals became "Show Your Face!" members.

In 2001, the federal government, in another round of fighting right-wing extremism, founded "Xenos" (foreigner), "Civitas" (city), and "Entimon" (dignity and respect) programs. It committed $30 million of its own funds as well as those of the EU, Länder, and communities. The Xenos program financed projects designed to minimize xenophobia and racism among vocational trainees and workers in shops and companies. Advice teams were to be formed to deal with such biases. Bus and trolley car drivers were to be trained in conflict resolution to avoid serious incidents in which right-wing extremists threatened foreigners on the public carriers.[39] The Civitas program was designed to fight right-wing extremism and strengthen democratic culture specifically in eastern Germany. The Entimon program provided support for innovative projects to strengthen democracy in all Länder. The EU sponsored its own programs designed to fight racism and xenophobia and to strengthen democratic cultures in its member states.

The CDU/CSU had reservations about the effectiveness and the expense of the German programs and consequently made financial cuts in Länder that it controlled. Occasionally an advertising campaign to reduce, in this instance, anti-Semitism, can misfire. In 2001, the Berlin Holocaust Memorial sought donations of $2 million for the Memorial's construction. As part of its campaign it paid for newspaper advertisements and billboards with the deliberately false but eye-catching motto "The Holocaust never happened." Under the slogan and the picture of a lake and a snow-capped mountain a smaller type said "There are still many people who make this claim. In twenty years there could be even more." Democratic organizations protested and the Memorial committee withdrew the advertisement.[40]

In February 2005, Federal President Horst Köhler (CDU), in an address to the Bundestag, asserted that "attempts to play down the Holocaust are a scandal that we have to confront."[41] In February 2006 Charlotte Knobloch, a Holocaust survivor and Central Council of Jews in Germany president, said that authorities appeared at a loss as to how to cope with the popularity of neo-Nazi parties in eastern Germany. She called for a "democracy summit" to discuss further measures to deal with the growing problem of right-wing extremism.[42]

In the following years, new problems arose at the national level when a few ministries once again cut funds to some of the well-publicized projects. For instance, in 2006 the Federal Ministry of Family, Senior Citizens, Women, and Youth, then headed by a CDU minister, did not renew all the funds that it had allocated since 2001 to the innovative projects of the Advisory Office for the Victims of Right-Extremist Violence. These projects included mobile advisory or crisis intervention teams and victims' counseling. The specialists' intention was to promote democratic values among moderate rightists rather than to win over the fanatic rightists. The Federal Ministry put the financial burden instead on the already strapped municipalities.

A number of academic institutes received financial support from the federal and Länder governments to survey violence data as well as individual and institutional discrimination against foreigners. The institutes were to assess the success or failure of projects designed not only to reduce the right-wing violence against foreigners and other target groups but also to reduce the prejudices against foreigners among the general population. Academic and other specialists sent out reports to social workers and other specialized personnel on their findings. They also met to assess intervention strategies, such as attempts to reduce discrimination against foreigners among public officials.[43]

For years, the Anne Frank Center in Berlin has mounted traveling exhibitions warning viewers about right-wing violence. The Center trains teenagers from the communities in which the exhibitions will be shown to work as guides. Surveys have shown that teenagers in these communities are more interested in the subject if the teacher is one of their peers. According to Uwe-Karsten Heye, an official of the anti-racism organization, *Gesicht Zeigen!*, the time had come to think about implementing a national action plan against right-wing extremism. He said that whoever takes seriously the integration of foreign teenagers must invest heavily in kindergarten, school, and social work projects.[44] *Gesicht Zeigen!* has sponsored an annual campaign against racism, discussions on racism in cooperation with different embassies in Berlin, and an exchange program between foreign and German students.

From 2001 to 2007, according to German government officials, about 80 percent of the 4,500 initiatives against racism and intolerance proved successful. The officials viewed their high cost as justified, especially when resources are allocated for vulnerable people affected by racist crimes.[45] However, many specialists were more critical in assessing the success of the initiatives, particulalry in eastern Germany. Some critics called on law-makers to invest even more funds to combat right-wing extremism, especially among youth, on the local level rather than allocating money to the well-endowed Federal Agency for Civic Education, the national welfare associations, and the Land sport organizations. In October 2006 an SPD deputy, Sebastian Edathy, supported by Greens and Left Party.PDS deputies, urged the scheduling of a "democracy summit" that would bring together representatives from political parties, religious groups, unions, and grassroots associations to develop an anti-rightist strategy. A CDU deputy, Wolfgang Bosbach, rejecting the idea, contended that a better solution to the rightist threat was a combination of stringent court sentencing and political education.[46]

Top government officials voiced support for the anti-right projects. In June 2006 Chancellor Merkel chaired an integration conference. In January 2007, on the Holocaust Memorial Day, she urged "all courageous democrats" to stop the rise of the right extremists and anti-Semites. In Brussels, the European Parliament's president, Hans-Gert Pöttering, warned that the Nazi crimes must never be repeated. He condemned the intolerance and hatred of other religions and races among a segment of the German population.

Grassroots actions

In the early 1990s, and especially in winter 1992–1993, the waves of rightist violence were countered immediately by impressive ad hoc mass demonstrations, candlelit vigils, and chains of light. Millions of Germans were on the streets in Berlin, Munich, Hamburg, Bonn, and other cities. The demonstrators, many carrying "Nazis Out" banners, sought to show their backing for foreigners living in Germany. Although some demonstrations were spontaneous, most of them had the support of political parties, trade unions, churches, and other groups. As symbols of protest these demonstrations and vigils were designed to show that a democratic system cannot tolerate such right-wing excesses. However, one author contended that the demonstrations and vigils made no political demands on the policy-makers.[47]

Yet in the aftermath of the violence, politicians and specialists did discuss how future violence could be curbed. An array of different programs and projects was launched, including international youth meetings, intercultural youth projects, round table meetings, local history projects, and street work that included mobile youth teams. Representatives of parties, unions, and churches, as well as academics, pedagogic specialists, police officers, journalists, and social workers, established networks to strengthen democracy and tolerance. In many cities and towns, shopkeepers put stickers in their windows saying "We provide protection and information for racist and fascist excesses."

The democratic parties targeted apolitical youth who were not yet committed to the rightist cause. The parties urged their members to write letters to local newspaper editors, organize dances and other entertainment for Germans and foreigners, provide support for asylum seekers, organize multinational sports teams, erase rightist graffiti on buildings, and convince newspaper dealers in kiosks not to carry right-wing newspapers and journals. Should a neo-Nazi organization schedule a major rally in a city or town, anti-fascist organizations were urged to organize a counter-rally as a means of protest against the right-wing extremists. But specialists also said that the democratic organizations should send individuals to rightist assemblies to challenge the speakers and gain the support of uncommitted individuals. The SPD, for instance, warned its members not to heckle right-wing speakers who would then gain the support of uncommitted audience members. In regions where the right extremists hardly play a role they should not be invited to public forums. But in regions where rightists are strong it is crucial to have a dialogue with them in order to expose their dangerous ideas.[48]

The German Trade Union Federation (*Deutscher Gewerkschaftsbund*, DGB) and its affiliated unions, such as the powerful Metal Workers Union (IG *Metall*) with 3.6 million members, also waged a campaign in factories to integrate foreign workers into the local labor force, to end all discrimination against them, and to provide more openings for them in company-sponsored vocational training programs. Companies or shops that pledged not to practice discrimination were allowed to post publicly a sign saying "Company friendly to foreigners." In a DGB study, published in 2001, attention was drawn to a reverse phenomenon, the numerous union members, many of them young, who had supported a right-extremist political party. Several polls indicated that young union members were more apt to back rightist parties than non-union youth. The DGB deemed it crucial to find ways to bring such members into the democratic sphere. Not all unions supported the DGB position; for instance, the Transport Workers Union did not view right-wing extremism as a pivotal area of concern to the labor movement. Even in the left-leaning Metal Workers Union, an estimated 70 percent of members were hostile to foreigners who might take away their jobs. Consequently the DGB study was hardly discussed in most unions.[49]

The Federation of German Industry, worried about the nation's reputation and the reluctance of foreign companies to invest in German industries at a time when rightist violence was high, urged its member firms to fire right-wing employees. In the Volkswagen firm, for instance, managers were trained to spot employees who were sympathetic to the rightist cause. Conversely, employees who felt discriminated against could ask for assistance from managers on a hotline.[50] Other companies required their employees to attend one-week anti-racist and tolerance training sessions. The national Chamber of Industry and Commerce hired a specialist on foreigners' issues who made contacts with foreign firms interested in launching a new company in Germany. In December 2006 numerous large companies, such as Deutsche Bank, DaimlerChrysler, Deutsche BP and Deutsche Telekom signed a "Diversity Charter" in which they committed themselves to promoting diversity in their firms.

Citizens' initiatives, civil rights, and religious groups sought to recruit citizens who were willing to defend foreigners and Jews from attack. The citizens could join telephone networks that mobilized people to protect sites that might be in danger of rightist attack.[51] Protestant church leaders in Berlin-Brandenburg sharply criticized Federal Minister of the Interior Schily (SPD) for his demagogic remarks concerning asylum seekers. Konrad Raiser, the World Council of Churches secretary-general, appealed to the 100,000 persons who had gathered at a 1993 church rally in Munich to stop the spiral of violence in Germany. He urged participants to reach out to immigrants and to youth who were ready to resort to violence. Karl Lehmann, chairman of the Catholic German Bishops Conference, encouraged Germans to offer protection to foreign fellow citizens.[52] National sports organizations, counting millions of members, forged anti-right-wing alliances to reach young rightists in their leisure time hours.

An array of local and regional projects

Secular and religious initiatives were launched in all parts of Germany. Of the hundreds of projects that were designed to attract youth during after-school hours, a few typical ones should be noted. A Berlin-Brandenburg educational association issued a series of publications on right-wing extremism. The publications systematically analyzed the problems, the use of violence, and the causes of violence.[53] Local anti-fascist associations and democratic groups have sprouted in numerous parts of Germany. For instance, in the early 1990s representatives of twenty grassroots organizations and individuals, including many youth, formed an association in Maintal, a small city located between Frankfurt and Hanau in Land Hesse. The members have printed public posters calling for tolerance and human rights and have engaged in discussions with

cabinet ministers, shop representatives, students, academics, and police officers. They have organized anti-Nazi rock concerts and youth fairs. To cope
with the Nazi past, they have organized lectures and exhibits on the topic.
They forced a Republikaner to give up his city council post when they discovered that he had been an active Nazi during the Hitler period. They also
received permission from the city council, at the time dominated by an SPD-
Green coalition, to speak in the chamber on public and private discriminatory
practices against foreigners in Maintal. They received a modest yearly financial grant from the SPD-Green majority for their work. Once a CDU and a
rightist nationalist group won control of the city council, then all funds were
frozen.[54]

The story of one local history workshop in the town of Friedensdorf in
Land Brandenburg shows that limited progress can be made to reach, in this
instance, from twenty to thirty right-extremist youths. From 1991 on these
young people met with facilitators in the municipal-financed project. The
rightist youth were requested to look at the Nazi past, dig into the literature,
and interview historians, history teachers, and elders who were witnesses to
Nazi events. The project had no effect on the rabid rightists who remained
convinced that their cause was just. However, it had an effect on the more
moderate rightists who had doubts about their own cause.

More progress in the effort to look at the past was made in clubs where
democrats were also members. The staff organized trips to the German soldiers' cemetery in Halbe and talked about the general staff's role during World
War Two, the failed July 20, 1944 uprising against Hitler, and Stalin and Sta-
linism. At the meetings the staff sought to dispel the myths, stereotypes, and
biases held by the youthful members. However, the staff did not want the
discussions, devoid of indoctrination, to supplant materials covered in the
schools.[55]

In Berlin, a number of advertising, media, marketing, and architectural
firms launched an "Initiative of Understanding – Berlin Companies against
Violence from the Right." Member firms were asked to correct misleading
press reports abroad about the menace of the right, to cancel Christmas
bonuses and put the funds into youth projects, and to initiate socially sponsored projects. In 1991, young people in Berlin founded a working group
"Youth against Violence." Thirty to fifty students, apprentices, and employees sought through creative projects, training seminars, and support of school
projects to lessen the fear and isolation of those subject to rightist violence.

In October 1991, in Cologne 230 billboards carried huge advertisements
that said "Our first Cologne citizens were all foreigners. Many foreigners made
the city famous: the Romans who appeared over 2,000 years ago, the Italian
firm Farina, the foreign canal workers, the crews on the Rhine ships, the
Polish stonemasons, and the Turkish guest workers." The local democratic
parties voted for a city council resolution requesting the municipal authorities to protect foreigners and urging citizens to support actions promoting

democracy. Other cities embarked on similar campaigns to minimize the rightist threat.[56]

In May 1992 in the small town of Melsungen, in Land Hesse, a local "League against Hostility to Foreigners" organized a multicultural festival. The purpose was to portray the contributions made by different ethnic groups to German culture and to reduce the latent anti-foreigner sentiment among many Germans. According to the organizers the majority of Germans must no longer remain silent but must take the initiative to meet prejudices among local residents head-on. The 500 visitors to the festival could partake of the diverse culinary and cultural offerings. Italian children sang and danced, Turkish musicians played native songs, and a local school choir sang. Teachers at the local academic high school organized a course on prejudices and fears. The students mounted an exhibit, entitled "All human beings are foreigners." In the discussions, the students noted the contributions of foreigners to the economy.

Among the many imaginative grassroots efforts to combat prejudices and perhaps reduce them was a play staged in a pedestrian zone in the small town of Korback in Land Hesse. The purpose was to engage passersby who were asked to throw eggs and tomatoes at an actor portraying a foreigner. The reaction of the passersby ranged from shock and bewilderment to open aggression.[57]

Although the list of successful projects encouraged its sponsors, including an accord among numerous hotels not to rent rooms to NPD officials, in a number of eastern German towns the rightists in effect have dominated the cultural scene. There the few democratization projects have been ineffective. The mayors in these towns often denied that right-extremist violence was dominant. There have been exceptions: in the small hamlet of Altlandsberg in Brandenburg, the Indian-born mayor, Ravindra Gujjula, has told the local rightist youth, imbued with xenophobic views, that 7,000 foreign computer specialists, holding German green cards entitling them to a stay in the country, have created 33,000 new jobs for Germans within six months of their arrival in Germany. In 2006 in Berlin a public campaign was launched to encourage young migrants to apply for training in governmental offices, police, and fire services. In North Rhine-Westphalia an action plan was begun to encourage immigrants to become teachers.

As to German–Jewish relations, Federal President Johannes Rau and Chancellor Gerhard Schröder had a greater rapport with the Jewish community than some of the more conservative CDU/CSU leaders. In November 2000 the two SPD leaders spoke at a Berlin rally of 200,000 people commemorating the 1938 anti-Jewish *Kristallnacht*. The rally was preceded by a march from the central Berlin synagogue to the Brandenburg Gate. Speakers reminded the audience of the parallels between the Nazis' anti-Semitic policies and the Federal Republic era's neo-Nazi and skinhead attacks against

Jewish cemeteries and synagogues. They also mentioned death and bomb threats made to Jewish leaders.[58]

In the meantime, at the supranational level, more than 560 organizations from forty-six European states, including Germany, formed in 1992 an anti-racist network called "United for Intercultural Action," with headquarters in Amsterdam. The organizations pledged to promote the rights of refugees, minorities, and migrants and to bring an end to racism, fascism, nationalism, and discrimination. "United" scheduled numerous actions, such as conferences, campaigns, and seminars, for the member organizations.

In the European Union, non-governmental organizations formed in 1998 a "European Network against Racism." The Network has served as a forum for discussion and action. In 2007 the German government, which held the EU presidency for six months, pushed for an EU-wide criminalization of individuals denying the Holocaust. The German Minister of Justice Brigitte Zypries expressed hope that the 27 EU member states would make such a denial a criminal offense punishable by up to three years in prison. She also proposed the introduction of minimum sentences for individuals stirring up racial hatred, inciting violence, and using the Nazi swastika symbol. In addition, she called for greater cooperation among national police forces, such as making criminal records of individuals more easily available to police forces across European borders. The European Commissioner for Justice and Home Affairs, Franco Frattini, supported the German proposals, but the UK and Denmark opposed them as a restriction on freedom of speech. Typical of opposition sentiments, Daniel Hallan, a conservative European Parliament deputy from Great Britain, said that he saw no reason to impose a decision from Brussels on the national policy-makers. He contended that each nation should have the right to set its own procedures. After much discussion twenty states supported and seven states opposed the proposals.[59]

Schools and students

Since the early 1950s West German teachers have discussed the Hitler era, World War Two, and the Holocaust. In East Germany such subjects were covered within the context of a then dominant socialism. After 1990 eastern German teachers have covered the same topics as their western colleagues. The Länder have the responsibility as to what is taught in the classrooms, although a standing conference of Land ministers of education and cultural affairs coordinates policies at the national level. For instance, since 1960 the West German conference has issued guidelines on how the Holocaust is to be taught and what textbooks would be appropriate. The guidelines determine the topics to be covered for every grade and the teaching objectives to be achieved. Many high school students visit former Holocaust camps and memorial sites. Thereupon teachers schedule discussions as to the lessons to be learned from Germany's dark past, the ancestors' guilt, and the degree of responsibility that recent generations have for the past. Such discussions are designed to make the students aware of the values and institutions of a democratic society. Not all are interested.[60]

Public authorities also began a nationwide political education campaign in schools to combat xenophobic violence, improve social behavior, teach tolerance, and instill among students a sense of responsibility toward others. The authorities prepared and disseminated new anti-violence curriculum materials among the teachers, especially those in social studies, who were urged to discuss the themes of violence and tolerance in their classrooms.[61] Progressive educators felt that the schools had to make fundamental reforms in teaching techniques and content in order to stimulate youth who often are bored and prone to accept right-extremist views. They argued that the traditional emphasis on discipline, effort, and order had to be supplanted by new educational tools in classrooms with fewer students. The progressive educators viewed improved communication between students, parents, teachers, and administrators as an important tool to counter off-campus right-extremist propaganda aimed at students. The schools cannot place the blame for students' aggressive behavior only on the families, parents, and television viewing of such students. Rather, many schools and their bored or burned out teachers are to be blamed for the cold atmosphere, lack of stimulating instruction, and social neglect of students that often prevail. Yet even if school instruction was based on progressive pedagogical methods, it would be difficult to combat deep-seated xenophobic feelings found among many students. Such feelings are not always triggered by German youth attacking foreigners. At times, foreign youth have beaten up German right-wingers in public. Legislators and specialists have urged high schools to develop programs that would reduce the tension between foreign and German students. Some of the tension arises when the two groups compete for vocational training vacancies and for jobs. Uwe-Karsten Heye, chairman of the grassroots organization "Show Your Face!," held the three-tiered German school system (*Realschulen, Hauptschulen, Gymnasien*) partly responsible for the right-extremist scene. He contended that the system and more specifically the general and vocational high schools (*Realschulen* and *Hauptschulen*) were producing losers among the 10–15 percent of academically weak students who dropped out of these schools. Such students are receptive to the rightist scene.

Another source of tension arose at times in city schools when the number of foreign students in a classroom topped the 50 percent mark and the German students felt outnumbered. According to the specialists, teachers need to discuss openly shifts in the students' ethnic makeup and the importance of solidarity among all students. Those who are enrolled in the non-academic high schools often have feelings of worthlessness and of failure to achieve when they measure themselves against the high achievers in the academic-oriented *Gymnasien*. Teachers need to assist the "turned off" students in achieving realizable goals. Thereby such students might be less prone to turn to right-wing extremism.[62]

Progressive educators found one solution to racist and xenophobic views among students in the creation of project days or project weeks against violence. For instance, in 1993, in fourteen Land Brandenburg high schools, teams of eastern and western German specialists met with teachers and students to discuss the content of various special proposals that could be scheduled for a single day or a week. The projects, financed by the Land Ministry for Education, Youth, and Sports, turned out to be most successful. Participating students, some with disciplinary problems, and teachers gave a high score to the projects. The students discovered that learning can be fun at times and that such projects (one was entitled "We all live in one world") could be the harbingers of a new approach to education. One specialist warned, however, that many teachers were reluctant or uncertain of how to respond to rightist arguments voiced in class.[63]

Since 1995 the nationwide program "School without Racism – School with Courage" has made positive strides to reduce racism in schools. The prerequisite for a school's participation in the program, which originated in Belgium, is that 70 percent of the students, teachers, and staff must sign a statement pledging to fight against any form of discrimination. Such a program, for instance restoring tombstones in nearby Jewish cemeteries, must become a central project within the school. If the project is meritorious the school has a chance to win a prize.[64]

In 2001 the Berlin Senate funded DM 1.5 million for school and youth projects that would emphasize the creation of a democratic culture and for teachers to be trained in how to deal with rightist youth. In 2007, a criminal police unit initiated a nationwide contest for high school students to submit their best short films dealing with the dangers of right-wing extremism. The response and quality of the 200 submitted films was high. One documentary film, commissioned by the Thuringian *Verfassungsschutz*, dealt with the reasons why youth joined the right extremists and what their goals were. It was distributed throughout the Thuringian school system. Another Land *Verfassungsschutz* printed a highly praised cartoon book on the subject of xenophobia aimed at teenagers. Authorities also prepared and widely distributed to teachers anti-violence curricular materials to enhance classroom discussion with students. In addition the authorities supported leisure-time sport activities designed to channel youth's energies into a constructive path. As a result of public grants, a Federal Parents' Council organized a conference on violence that dealt with ways to reduce it.

Education specialists advised teachers to discuss at length the Nazi period, the Holocaust and its legacy. In dealing with the roots of xenophobia, they should emphasize the historic pattern of Germany's emigration and immigration, which led to assimilation and integration. The teachers should also point out that West Germany's post-World War Two "economic wonder" would not have been possible without the influx of Turkish and other guest workers. In addition, teachers should deal with the Basic Law's fundamental principles and allow maximum time for discussion among students on the topic of right-wing extremism. The teachers were encouraged to present their own views at the end of the discussion. If a student expressed anti-foreigner views in class, a teacher might discuss such views on a one-to-one basis with the student rather than tag such a student as a racist or neo-Nazi. Often youth have become involved at home or in the neighborhood in a stressful situation, in which they then act out their frustrations in hate against weaker individuals. If there is no teacher or social worker contact with such students, they might join a rightist gang and engage in violence.

As noted earlier, from the 1980s on many school age skinheads and hooligans turned to violence, especially at soccer games, to gain notoriety. At the time, authorities organized a few special school projects to reach them. But it was difficult to draw up a choice of projects that might be successful. This was evident especially when the social work community, although agreeing on the need to minimize violence and to schedule anti-aggressive training sessions, was split on the question of how to combat racism, xenophobia, and violence. One vocational school in Hesse had a simple answer. The teaching staff, students, and parents decided that students could no longer wear skinhead clothing, boots, and neo-Nazi symbols in the school.

Obviously the choice of school project has depended primarily on the teachers, specialists, administrators, and students. To give one example: in October 1992 in a Nuremberg *Gymnasium* several students suggested to their teacher, in the aftermath of the Rostock riots, that a day be organized in which all students would attend sessions devoted to the subjects of violence and xenophobia. To prepare for such a day, ten students met with two teachers twice a week. They agreed that on the special events day some students would present a play dealing with the question of how to train youth not to be violent. Other special events included poetry readings with regionally known authors and a discussion circle led by asylum seekers and social workers. Foreigners enrolled as vocational trainees in business firms chaired one circle, while still another discussed the topic of women and violence. One school room was set aside as a candlelit meditation center. An exhibition hall had photos and text on the subject of violence. The final event of the special events day was a two-hour assembly of all students. In the podium discussion students and representatives from the police, soccer fan clubs, and school administration took part. The reaction to the special day was generally positive among parents, teachers, and students. The local newspaper printed a lengthy article with photos. In a questionnaire subsequently distributed to 200 students, 85 percent viewed the day positively; the others felt additional themes also needed to be discussed. School authorities met with the student organizers to discuss possible pedagogic changes that could be made.[65]

In the small East German town of Beeskow near the Polish border a teacher took her students to an exhibition of neo-Nazi graffiti shown at the local town hall. They saw scrawlings of Aryan solidarity, *"Deutschland über alles,"* "Foreigners go home," and "Jews and Turks and other foreigners end up dead." In the classroom, the teacher opened a discussion on the graffiti's messages that drew the students' attention. According to them, there were not many ideologically committed rightist students in town. These rightist youth were often unemployed, had social problems, and were looking for friends.[66] Länder authorities also promoted exchange programs with youth in France, Poland, Israel, and other countries as a means of combating racism and xenophobia. But, according to some CDU politicians, schools can only play a limited role in influencing youth. The family remains the primary unit. As a consequence, in some cities evening courses for adults have been instituted on the theme of right-wing extremism.

In 2000, Wolfgang Thierse, then Bundestag president and the Amadeu Antonio Foundation honorary chairman, made a tour of east German high schools. In addressing students on the topic of youth and right-wing extremism, he deplored the fact that a majority of rightist violence incidents were not reported to the police because of the victims' fear of retribution.[67]

In February 2008 Berlin schools distributed a comic book called "The Search" designed to educate the pupils about Nazism, racist violence, and anti-Semitism. The Dutch cartoonist Eric Heuvel created the book that deals with the story of Esther, a fictional survivor of the Holocaust. The book was designed to complement work sheets in high school history classes and to reach especially the children who are least interested in schoolwork. If it made an impact in the first six months of distribution, then a nationwide distribution was planned.[68]

Youth and social workers

Despite the launching of imaginative school projects to reduce the students' violence against foreigners and other "enemies," especially in the former GDR, the severe shortage of social workers and other specialists in eastern Germany hampered attempts to wean rightists away from their destructive behavior. The purge of professional positions in eastern Germany in the 1990s did not help the tense social situation in which neo-Nazis and skinheads became increasingly bored and took to excessive drinking. To compound the problem, the rightist scene produced a schism among social workers. Conservative social workers felt that professionals should not make any concessions to rightist youth's demands unless the latter promised to make fundamental behavioral changes. These social workers, comparatively few in number, blamed the youth's violence on anti-authoritarian education and the lack of discipline, order, and Prussian virtues among youth, their parents, and society. The social workers pointed to the rightist youth's takeover of local youth clubs without the liberal social workers taking preventive counter-measures. When liberal social workers sought contacts with rightist youth the more conservative social workers would label their liberal colleagues in a derogatory manner as "national social workers."

In response, liberal social workers argued that to isolate young adolescent rightists, often as young as ten to fourteen years old, would only harden their behavior. At that age, the youth were still malleable to outside influences. Thus it was more important to show a genuine interest in the youngsters and not just their problems. They should be encouraged eventually to mingle with youth who were not rightists. In addition it was important to allow such youth to be among themselves in some of their free hours in rooms provided by the municipality, help the youth in conflict with their parents and in their search for a vocational training, and not impose on them a host of prohibitions, penalties, and regulations. Such negative measures would only lead to the rightist youth's provocative actions, willful destruction of property, and threats of violence. In some cases, social workers sought to contact the girlfriend or wife of a rightist male to warn him that a path of violence will only lead to tragedy. The social workers also steered the youth to imaginative programs, such as the organization of a bicycle tour or a parachute course for troubled youth.

In an unusual project in Milmersdorf, situated in a poor and conservative rural area of Brandenburg, the social worker Filippo Smaldino engaged fifty youths to rebuild a vacant timber framed house and make it a youth center. Smaldino, who had a good rapport with the local police, also organized a bus trip to Calcutta, India for which he received funding from German private foundations and regional sponsors. Twenty-one rightist youths fixed up an old decrepit bus and drove it to Calcutta. There they helped the poor slum inhabitants build a sidewalk in a muddy area. In a snowball effect, local German residents in Milmersdorf invited Calcutta families to their houses. In gratitude, Calcutta's mayor flew to Milmersdorf for a short visit. Despite Smaldino's successful efforts to win over some, but certainly not all, of the rightist youth, funds for his organization were cut so sharply in 2000 that he had to discharge temporarily seven out of eight staff members.[69]

Unfortunately these initial attempts to build a bridge to hardened right-wing youth failed to stem the violence that swept the country. The spiral of tension and the fanaticism of many neo-Nazis and skinheads led to the abrupt cancellation of numerous projects. The social and youth workers, therapists, and other professionals had become subject to massive pressure by public policy-makers whose hopes and desire for a violence-free society could not be met.[70] As noted earlier, the rightist violence was not only aimed at foreigners but also against leftists, punks, the homeless, and the gays. From the rightists' point of view, the police, who sweepingly considered all of them as neo-Nazis, were constantly harassing them. The rightists also complained that discos forbade their entering the premises if they wore bomber jackets. Thus the rightists viewed themselves as being in a daily war with their enemies, among them left anarchists.

Conservative and liberal social workers said that rightists who were or had been members of fanatic neo-Nazi organizations should not become housing project members because they would attempt to dominate and infuse the project with political propaganda and use force if necessary. The social workers' task has been daunting given, for instance, the rightist members' high use of alcohol. The social workers have known that they must not identify with the rightist goals and must make it clear that, despite their understanding for the rightist members' problems and difficulties, they do not share the views of the right-wing extremists, and will never tolerate the use of violence.[71] In Land Brandenburg, social workers started a model project in jails to wean away the rightist youth from their ideological views. In three years, 120 imprisoned youths were exposed to democratic perspectives. The experiment was deemed to be so successful that other Länder launched similar programs. Social workers have also worked with family members of rightist individuals to provide counseling and assistance. The parents are told that there are other families with similar problems. A hotline has been established to give family members a chance to come out of their isolation.

The exit strategy

In February 2001, Federal Minister of the Interior Otto Schily (SPD) recommended that the federal government begin a counseling and referral program to encourage right-wing extremists to change their political convictions and cut all ties to their former comrades. His program was to be a modified copy of the ongoing "Exit Germany" program that the Berlin-based private Center for Democratic Culture (*Zentrum Demokratische Kultur*) had sponsored since October 2000. The Center, which suggests local counter-strategies to right-wing extremism, received financial support from the Amadeus Antonio Foundation and from the *Stern* journal's campaign "Courage against Rightist Violence." According to the Center's director Bernd Wagner, his group, which has included a psychologist, a political scientist, and himself as a criminologist, would be more likely than government members to convince the rightist activists interested in the program to quit the movement. These rightists, who took the initiative and sought help from the Center, will not turn to government organizations for fear of judicial prosecution or for fear of bodily harm by the neo-Nazis still in the movement. The Center sees itself as not only a place to help rightists find housing and jobs, but as a place to reintegrate them into a democratic society. In its initial years the Center provided assistance primarily to neo-Nazis living in western Germany but thereafter sought ways to attract more eastern Germans into the program.[72] The specialists noted that the shorter the rightists had been in the movement, the quicker they were able to get out. However, for many rightists the thought of leaving their group and becoming social outcasts was a major obstacle in their exiting the scene. By 2006 the Center had helped 260 individuals to exit. However, for 2007 the federal government cut off all public funds, thereby making a continuation of the private program more problematic.

Minister Schily did not dispute the Center's strategy but said in a press interview that a government-sponsored national defector program would provide the extremists with protection from retribution by those still in the scene and new perspectives for the future. Potential defectors would be expected to provide information to prosecutors or to the *Verfassungsschutz*, abandon their rightist friends, and tell how they entered the rightist scene. In return they would be offered protection from retaliation by those staying in the movement, education or employment guidance, and housing support, as well as a witness protection program in which they would assume new identities. This would cost the government about DM 100,000 per person, but normally no cash would be given the individual. Under no circumstances should the exiting individuals be used as undercover informants for the government. Schily also announced that the program ought to be linked to a new witness amnesty measure that the Federal Ministry of Justice was drafting. He said "If someone has committed a punishable offense but helps with an investigation by, for example, leading the police to a weapons stash or providing a tip that prevents a bomb attack, the court should provide him a lesser sentence in return."[73] Schily and the Länder ministers of the interior set up an "Info-Telefon" that those thinking of exiting the rightist scene could use to contact the government team of specialists. Numerous parents of rightists also called the number to find out how they could wean their children away from the movement.

As one typical example of the program's procedural aspects, in Baden-Wuerttemberg the Stuttgart criminal office set up a counseling and intervention center on a one-year trial basis. The ten experts consisted of police psychologists, educators, and state security personnel. They knocked at the doors of 324 rightists, of whom 252 were ready to talk about themselves. Of the latter group, 84 were willing to leave the scene.[74] But, with few exceptions, those exiting would not receive any money; otherwise the temptation to enter the rightist scene for an eventual paid leave for exiting would be too great. In January 2001, the Lower Saxony government introduced a program to persuade right-wing sympathizers to rejoin the mainstream. Individuals who had been convicted of right-wing violent crimes were to receive counseling from a social worker while in prison.

On the national scene, after a six-month period, 700 individuals contacted government agents. Of these, 140, almost all men, were taken into the program. But the bulk of the 50,000 rightists, of whom nearly 10,000 were prone to violence, had no interest in abandoning the right-extremist milieu.[75] Even if they decided to leave the scene, whether their decision would last was uncertain. One right-extremist scene specialist and program critic asserted that only friends, and not a government bureaucrat, could help an individual exit the scene. Moreover, the money used to fund the exit program could be better used in projects dealing with racial prejudices.[76]

Public officials in several major German cities set up programs staffed by social workers to counsel neo-Nazis and skinheads who wanted to drop out of the right-wing milieu, but there were no major right-extremists among them. The life story of a leading neo-Nazi, Ingo Hasselbach, cited earlier, serves as one example of the difficulties of leaving the rightist scene. In 1993, before the government program began, he broke with the neo-Nazis for their role in the Mölln and Solingen firebombings. His resignation took some courage because neo-Nazis still in the movement did not forgive him for his decision, viewing it as high treason. Thereafter he lived with friends but had to change his domicile frequently to escape being murdered by his former colleagues. His mother received a bomb in the mail, which did not ignite when she opened the letter only because of a battery defect. The bomb threat was the turning point for Hasselbach. He went to the police, which sent him to the Federal Criminal Office. There for several hours he provided information about the neo-Nazi movement, some of which had not been available to the government agents. Soon they began to arrest neo-Nazi leaders whom Hasselbach had known. In revenge, some skinheads twice beat up Hasselbach's sister because her brother had also betrayed the names of skinheads to the government agents. On the building where Hasselbach had lived, someone painted the stark warnings "Ingo Hasselbach, We'll get you" and "Death to the traitor." In Berlin, leftist militants, who were angry at his earlier attacks on them and were skeptical of the sincerity of his conversion, also sought to physically attack him. The government invited Hasselbach to enter the country's witness protection program in exchange for further detailed information about neo-Nazi groups, but, not yet ready, he refused.

Instead, with the assistance of the filmmaker Winfried Bonengel, Hasselbach wrote a best-selling book, also translated into English, about his neo-Nazi past.[77] The book contained a mine of information about the rightist scene and provided valuable insight into his *Weltanschauung*. Yet, exaggeratedly, Hasselbach warned readers about the coming armed struggle of German rightists against the state.

As a former neo-Nazi leader, Hasselbach became an instant celebrity in some United States circles. He appeared on talk shows and received much publicity in the wake of a three-week cross-country luxury book tour organized by Random House, which had just published his book in English.[78] A Japanese television station paid DM 10,000 for an interview, which was not unprecedented for Hasselbach's television appearances. In 1996, *The New Yorker* printed a lengthy article written jointly by a young writer and Hasselbach. The article was accompanied by numerous photos, one showing a tough Hasselbach, with his blond hair and "pure steel eyes," looking firmly at the camera.[79] The filmmaker Bonengel and Hasselbach wrote the script of a movie called *Führer – Ex*, which depicted Hasselbach's life in fictional form. He appeared on a German television station with an Auschwitz survivor. He made a speech to audiences at a Jewish cultural center in Germany. Yet despite his leaving the rightist scene in 1993, a judge tried and convicted him in 1997 for having participated in 1992 in a firebombing of a leftist youth club and for having illegal weapons and trading in them. He received a mild eighteen-month jail sentence followed by parole. Eventually, Hasselbach, after his release, sought a safe haven and moved with his children to Sweden.[80]

Summation

Public and private responses to right-extremist violence have had a cyclical pattern. When the rightists use violence that leads to the deaths of or serious injuries to their victims then there is a momentary outcry among the politicians and the media about the right-wing menace. In response, to cite but one example, in August 2000 Chancellor Schröder praised the police and the judiciary for their rigorous action against such rightist violence, but also stated that there was a need to provide career opportunities for unemployed young people. However, the politicians' expressions of outrage soon abate once the violence ebbs.

In the meantime the government and private organizations have backed and financed thousands of imaginative and path-breaking projects, especially at the local level, that seek to wean youth away from a path of asocial behavior and rightist commitment. While these efforts have been quite successful, often they have not reached enough rightist youth who fail in schools, are unemployed, and lack family support at home. Thus the result of the numerous government-financed projects aimed at right-wing youth has not been a complete success. In many instances, there has been a shortage of qualified social workers or a lack of continuous financing. In addition, the hard core right extremists have remained violent and have not been persuaded to change course. As a consequence, relatively few extremists have taken advantage of the private and government exit programs, which provide support to rightists seeking to abandon their life of ideological commitment and violence. Regrettably few projects are directed toward adults who have supported right-extremist parties or who have applauded right-wing violence aimed at foreigners. Such adults have clung to a position that is antithetical to the democratic ethos.

The strategic purpose of the multifaceted efforts to reduce violence and provide neo-Nazi and skinhead youths with jobs and hope has been to strengthen the civil society in which a set of democratic values lie at the heart of the system and in which individuals help those who have become the victims of right-extremist violence. In such a society the police and the courts play a part in preserving the system, but the main thrust remains with citizens and foreigners alike who need to maintain a democratic culture. This difficult task is compounded by the fact that some of the right-extremist ideology comes from "the middle of society," the mainstream citizens, whose views, say on limiting immigration, are not that different from the views of the right-wing extremists.

Conclusion

Right-wing extremism

After Germany's crushing defeat in World War Two and the destruction of its cities, the Allies in 1945 divided the country into four zones and in 1949 into two states. Initially West and East Germany played only a modest role in world politics. But especially since unification of the two states in 1990, Germany has emerged as a key player on the international scene. This global role rests mainly on the country's political stability and economic power. The democratic political parties, whether large or small, have been the central players in policy-making. They have determined the direction the country has taken in domestic and foreign policies.

As detailed in this study, not all German political parties or citizens support the democratic system. However, as is true of most other European countries, the fragmented right-extremist forces have not been able to derail the country's political stability and its capacity for survival. Among these forces are the three right-extremist political parties (the Republikaner, which the government no longer considers right extremist; the DVU; and the NPD), neo-Nazi groups, skinheads, and New Right intellectuals. They have influenced especially those policies of Chancellor Kohl and successor CDU/CSU and SPD-led governments that have limited the rights of asylum seekers who want to settle in Germany. The three right-extremist parties, often at odds with one another, have maintained their separate existence. With few exceptions in the early FRG decades when other ultra-nationalist parties emerged, they have not been able to garner 5 percent of the minimum vote or three seats in the single-member constituencies, which is necessary to gain representation in the Bundestag.

The West German electoral architects agreed to this provision because the Weimar constitution had no equivalent requirement, thereby giving representation to numerous splinter parties. As a consequence, governing the Weimar state became much more difficult when compared to governing the FRG. During the Weimar era the Nazi party and the German National

People's Party (DNVP) had a membership of 100,000, which at times reached over 500,000, and numerous Reichstag seats. Moreover, nationalism and authoritarianism during Weimar had a great popular appeal, supported perhaps by 20–40 percent of the population. Prior to 1933, a high number of ordinary Germans as well as much of the civil service, the media, and the military did not back the democratic governments, especially during the Great Depression years. The worldwide economic depression in 1929 produced mass unemployment and the social welfare system breakdown that the German governments could not cope with.

One reason for the stability in the West German and all-German system since 1949 is that the rightist parties have not had the appeal that their predecessors had during the Weimar era. Moreover, from 1919 to 1933, numerous extremist parties gained representation in the Reichstag under a proportional representation electoral system, which was changed in the FRG era to prevent minor splinter parties from gaining legislative seats in the national parliament.

Thus the present rightist parties received just 1.4 percent of the vote in the federal elections held between 1986 and 2002. In the 2005 federal election, the NPD mustered only 1.6 percent of the total, a slight gain over 2002 when it received 0.4 percent. The party's not too hidden identification with the Nazi past most likely precludes it gaining a mass vote and sizable membership. This lack of success is also due to the frequent conflicts between the rival right-wing parties. However, in 2004 the NPD and DVU signed a "pact for Germany" in which they pledged not to form rival slates in future elections.

Although unsuccessful at the federal level the right-wing parties have been able to surmount the 5 percent electoral barrier in several Länder elections, which entitled them to some seats in Land legislatures. For instance, the DVU gained a remarkable 12.9 percent in the Saxony-Anhalt election of 1998 and emerged, as shown in polls, as the strongest of all parties among voters under 30 years of age.[1] The NPD amassed 9.2 percent in the Saxony election of 2004. When the rightist parties achieved such victories the reactions in Germany and abroad led to worry that a repetition of the Weimar Republic's downfall was in the offing. From 1919 to 1933, numerous centrist and extremist parties had gained representation in the Reichstag under a proportional representation system without the provision that a party needed to have at least 5 percent of the vote or gain at least three constituency seats. In the FRG era, the electoral barriers were not a hindrance to rightist parties gaining some Landtag seats.

Yet despite such electoral victories, the rightist parties were hardly able to profit from them. The Länder right-extremist *Fraktionen* were enmeshed in bitter infighting. They showed incompetence in their programmatic proposals, which weakened their case even further. In addition they could not break through the political barrier as the democratic parties' deputies shunned them repeatedly and did not support their unacceptable legislative proposals.

A challenge to democracy

There has always been in Germany, as in most other countries, a core of ideologues that prefer a right-wing authoritarian system.[2] As noted, from 1919 to 1933 numerous centrist and extremist parties gained representation in the Reichstag under a proportional representation system. However, in the FRG most German citizens who voted for one of the rightist parties in Länder elections were not ideologues but were protesting the establishment parties' failures to deal sufficiently with pressing political, economic, and social issues. Thus the rightists, paralleling the Left Party, have lashed out in recent years at cutbacks to the social welfare system, German military involvement in Afghanistan, and the evils of globalization. A substantial number of the German right-wing voters can be characterized as the losers in the relentless economic modernization process that is engulfing most states, made even worse by the severe economic recession battering the world since 2008. Many of these voters can be expected to support a right-wing party or movement, which is not committed to the basic democratic order.

As noted below, similar right-wing populist parties that feed on immediate issues of concern, such as a high level of immigration and cutbacks to the welfare state, have emerged across the European scene. Their leaders take advantage of the deep popular resentment created by domestic and foreign policy issues. As a result significant electoral shifts have taken place that produced new party configurations, especially conservative, in many European states. In Germany the continuing support for right-wing parties and the recent rapid rise of the democratic Left Party are two such indicators.

During the Federal Republic period from 1949 to the present, and especially since German unification in 1990, 80–93 percent of respondents in polls have supported the democratic system. This limited support for a right-extremist option stands in sharp contrast to some other European states, such as Austria, Italy, and East European countries, in which right-populist leaders, backed by many voters, have participated in governing the nation.[3]

As a warning against the spread of racism, racial discrimination, xenophobia, and all forms of discrimination, the Office of the United Nations Commissioner on Human Rights and the European Commission against Racism and Intolerance, an organ of the Council of Europe, have warned all member states to take more effective measures to combat the various forms of discrimination and the extremist movements, which pose a real threat to democratic values. In 2004, the German Institute for Human Rights requested the German government to take seriously the Council of Europe's reports and to adopt the EU guidelines for the protection of minorities, including an anti-discrimination law in employment.[4] The German government finally adopted this measure two years later.

Although German governments can count on the continuing popular backing for a democratic political culture in their country, they have been unable to win over the minority that opts for a rightist alternative. This minority, consisting primarily of young men, includes a sprinkling of Old Nazis and academics. Clustered in the three rightist parties and the intellectual New Right, it has had some influence on the Berlin policy-makers and on the mainstream public which have either agreed with them or yielded to them on the turbulent immigration issue and the less turbulent nationalism issue. According to three specialists, "The Right hopes to find more resonance with topics like curtailment of immigration, the rejuvenation of national interests and regionalism, and retreat from supranational alliances (such as the European Union and NATO). They slow down the dynamics of ongoing societal and transnational changes by demanding national-particularistic autonomy, economic autarky, ethnocultural, and political sovereignty."[5] However, unlike the rise of right-populist leaders in other European states, such as the late Jörg Haider in Austria, who have had a mass following, the colorless German rightist leaders have had relatively little support among the electorate.

Yet this study has also shown how a dangerous culture of pathological right-wing extremism has developed in Germany over the decades. It is not only clustered in the rightist parties but also in neo-Nazi cadre and skinhead groups, which emerge, grow, and wither frequently. As individuals with a low degree of self-worth, the youthful neo-Nazis and skinheads, living primarily in eastern Germany, have grown up in a perceived hostile environment. They are socially isolated and stigmatized and have difficulty finding employment. To compensate, they look for their role model to older middle-class citizens who share their attitudes and who blame the foreigners for their problems that are often caused by the ills of globalization. These youth will not look for support from their parents who have their own problems or from teachers who do not share their views.

Many of these fanatic neo-Nazis and skinheads do not hesitate to engage in violence against their proclaimed foes, whether they are foreigners, the handicapped, the homeless, Gypsies, or leftists. As a consequence, the rightists are often arrested and sentenced to years in jail. When they are freed, they consider themselves members of the rightist elite. Their political education comes from a plethora of rightist newspapers, books, internet computer sites, and musical offerings designed to educate and entertain them. This propaganda serves at the same time as a way to recruit high school and fraternity students and armed forces members. Although the success of such efforts is difficult to measure, there certainly has been no decline in recruitment as shown in the yearly *Verfassungsschutz* reports. One reason is that democratic youth organizations and political parties find it increasingly difficult to attract apolitical youth who are basically opposed to joining any organization but whose goal is to be consumer society members. In short, there is a latent threat to Germany's democratic system that will not fade unless the government deals more resolutely with pressing social and economic problems, especially in eastern Germany. Too many young Germans are unable to enroll in vocational training programs or find full-time jobs. Too many gravitate toward the neo-Nazi and skinhead groups. Too many have organized themselves into *Kameradschaften*, which dominate the danger-ous "National Liberated Zones" in small villages in eastern Germany. There the neo-Nazis set the tone for the cultural and at times the political life. Such a development will continue as long as eastern Germany remains an economically deprived region.

Immigration: source for controversy

Since 2000 the democratic political parties have asserted that Germany is truly a country of immigration in which a multicultural society thrives. This position was taken to reduce the bias against foreigners. Yet for decades the government failed to integrate foreigners into German society. Currently for-eigners are expected to take German language and civilization courses to ease their integration into the mainstream. However, such efforts have become less meaningful when some CDU and CSU deputies insisted in 2000 that Ger-many is shaped by a guiding culture (*Leitkultur*), a biased and elitist concept that leftists and moderate social democrats could not accept and that was eventually abandoned. Yet the concept of patriotism, espoused initially by rightists, has become more respectable among democrats in recent years. It was visible especially in the 2006 World Cup soccer games.

Restrictions on immigration may be eased in coming decades as the German population becomes older and the labor force shrinks. Perhaps the rightist anti-immigration and chauvinist position will become less persuasive to many citizens who vote for one of the establishment parties. Yet the terror-ism against foreigners is unlikely to ease as long as neo-Nazis and skinheads make them a primary target of opprobrium. Despite strong statements from the former Federal President Richard von Weizsäcker that right-wing violence against foreigners was unacceptable, the federal government has dragged its feet on this issue for too many years. It took resolute action only when it was worried about its image abroad, the possibility of declining foreign investments, and fewer tourists visiting the country.

Violence will also continue as long as the federal government, western German Länder, and municipalities fail to take the initiative to treat eastern Germans with respect rather than condescension. Too high a percentage of Germans, and not just the rightists, are still prejudiced, often without good reason, against foreigners, leftists, gays, the homeless, Gypsies, and the Jews. According to the Friedrich-Ebert Foundation, an SPD think tank, there is reason to worry about the future. In a study conducted in May–June, 2006, the authors, Oliver Decker and Elmar Brähler, on the staff of Leipzig Univer-sity's Institute for Clinical Psychology and Sociology, noted that xenophobic attitudes are widespread (25 percent and up) on some questions among the sample group of 5,000 Germans. Over 15 percent of those polled said that Germans are "naturally superior" to other people and that the country should have a strong leader. Twenty-six percent opted for a "single, strong party that represents the German community." About 37 percent agreed with the statement that foreigners only come to Germany to exploit the welfare state. Nearly 16 percent of western Germans and 6 percent of eastern Germans were anti-Semitic. In short, many in the political middle, who normally vote for the establishment parties, espouse views that are anti-democratic. According to the study's findings, "The term (right-wing extremism) suggests we are dealing with a marginal phenomenon. That's not at all the case." Right-wing extremism and the disadvantaged youth who support it are a political problem at the center of society. The survey's authors warned, "the fact that it has come to this touches the foundations of democratic society."[6] They also noted that well-off Germans were prejudiced against the country's marginal groups, such as the jobless and the socially disadvantaged. The authors concluded that most people supported a democratic system if it guaranteed their welfare, but in its absence turned swiftly to intolerance.[7]

Weimar and the Berlin Republic compared

There are several reasons why the current Berlin Republic (and its predecessor Bonn) is not like the Weimar Republic.[8] Weimar, at the outset in 1919, had to cope with the humiliation and resentment of the harsh Versailles Treaty imposed on Germany in 1923 with its catastrophic high inflation, in 1929 with the Great Depression and its mass unemployment, and in the 1920s and early 1930s with continuing political turmoil that saw frequent cabinet changes and fratricidal feuds between the social democratic and communist parties. Already in the 1920s the NSDAP received the support of segments of the powerful capitalist and bourgeois elite, the judiciary, the military, and intellectuals, but also of many desperate unemployed workers. The Weimar democratic system had little chance of survival and failed. In January 1933 Hitler rose to power as chancellor.

In making a comparison between the tumultuous Weimar era and the present FRG era, one can only hope that history will not repeat itself. The current Berlin Republic is politically stable but economically threatened. True, Germany faces many political, economic, and social problems paralleling those of other developed states. But the democratic system has a firm grounding and its future seems assured. No populist right-wing leader and no single right-wing party have surfaced to seriously challenge the current democratic government. In the postwar FRG era, unlike Weimar, there was more political stability and a commitment to democracy among the political, economic, and military elites. No right-extremist or populist leader has emerged in the decades since 1945 to match the popularity of Hitler, who already during the Weimar period had a substantial following. The FRG political leaders are deeply committed to upholding the democratic system and, at least in theory, guaranteeing a minimum of civil liberties to all.

Moreover, even though the FRG democratic leaders have not been able to solve the country's perennial unemployment problem within the framework of a global economy, the current deep recession does not yet match the Great Depression of the late 1920s and early 1930s. True, the current voters' disappointment with the existing major political parties indicates their failure to solve existing problems. But nevertheless most voters, despite some grumbling, remain committed to supporting the democratic system. Given the catastrophe of the Nazi past, it is most unlikely that they will support another Hitler, who is not even on the horizon.

However, despite the limited New Right intellectual influence on Germany's current domestic and foreign affairs, there is the chance that given unpredictable political or economic crises the New Right in the future might have a greater impact on the direction the country takes. The New Right's current strategy is to provide an intellectual content to the right-wing parties' platforms and to penetrate the German cultural scene. In a country that for some years seemed uncertain about its role in the world, New Right intellectuals have influenced those government policies, especially when the CDU/CSU governs, that limit foreigners' immigration and that emphasize the cultural artifacts of nationalism and patriotism. For the long run, the New Rightists opt for constitutional changes, such as a stronger federal president elected directly by the voters and the holding of national plebiscites. Some New Right ideologues quietly prefer a rightist authoritarian system whose leaders would not articulate the crass neo-Nazi slogans voiced by right-wing extremists and by the waning Old Right.

What have been the responses of the federal, Länder, and municipal governments to the rightist bloc? To stem its continuing strength, especially in eastern Germany where the tradition of a democratic culture and tolerance had little chance to develop after 1945, the governments, with the support of EU funds, have launched numerous grassroots civil democracy projects. Many of these projects, aimed at school-age youth, have been most imaginative. However, too often the promised funds are cut or teachers and social workers have difficulties reaching violent youth. The government's exit program to wean rightists away from their movement has had only a moderate success.

Thus, neo-Nazis and skinheads continue to commit violence against foreigners and other perceived foes and to deface Jewish memorial sites and gravestones. As a result, Charlotte Knobloch, Central Council of Jews in Germany president, warned in 2006: "Anyone who still talks in terms of unfortunate one-off incidents is failing to grasp a danger facing the whole of society. The aggression has become reminiscent of 1933."[9] She accused politicians and "the society," despite warnings, of deliberately neglecting the spiraling anti-Semitism and right-wing extremism. As a result of the violence, some foreigners have been reluctant to move to eastern Germany or have left the country altogether. Her controversial remarks, especially her reference to the Nazi takeover of 1933, had some effect, even though many observers disagreed with her statement that a parallel could be drawn between 1933 and the current situation. The SPD deputy Sebastian Edathy called for a "democracy summit," which would bring together political parties, religious communities, unions, and grassroots associations to develop a strategy to combat right-wing extremism. Petra Pau, a Left Party leader and Bundestag vice-president since 2006, proposed that the government introduce an independent watchdog to monitor right-wing extremism. Numerous politicians advanced other ideas, but many have not been implemented. Thus the "brown" danger and violence continues.

In recent years, the NPD has been the most active among the three rightist parties. Although the support that it received in several Länder elections was alarming to observers, who drew parallels to Nazi strength in Weimar elections, neither the NPD nor the other rightist parties ever received a single seat in the Bundestag from the 1960s to the present. Moreover, after 1969, once the recession ended, the NPD vote plummeted and the party lost all representation in the state parliaments and was nearly banned as a political party in 2001. However, in the meantime, German unification in 1990 produced a new surge of rightist sentiment among those youth who had problems at home and in school, and who had difficulties in getting vocational training or a job. The NPD especially gained support from these youth and from voters who were disappointed by the failure of mainstream parties to solve serious economic problems. These included a lack of sufficient public investments that resulted in a high degree of unemployment and cutbacks in the social welfare sphere. The failure of the mainstream parties to vote for enough public investments in the eastern German economy did not endear them to many marginalized eastern German voters. As a result, in 2005 for instance, the three rightist parties had 313 politicians who had won municipal council seats, a further indication that the rightist parties' efforts are concentrated at the local level.[10]

Should the three rightist parties coalesce into one party on the NSDAP model, the danger that they may succeed in gaining some seats in the Bundestag rises accordingly, especially if the 2008–2009 global recession continues on its destructive path. Although such a possibility exists, it is doubtful that most voters would cast their ballot for a right-extremist party given Hitler's disastrous foreign policies, World War Two, and the Holocaust. However, the violence against foreigners and other perceived enemies will continue because it is embedded in the structural changes in society. But it will not assume the utter ruthlessness of the totalitarian Nazi machine.

Links abroad

A survey of the German right-wing parties and groups must include the links that they have forged with their counterparts in foreign countries. These contacts are primarily individual ones and do not represent a threat to the German constitutional order. The German neo-Nazis have maintained ties with top foreign neo-Nazis, such as Ernst Zündel, a long-time resident in Canada, who has disseminated via the internet and the postal service a wide array of blatant neo-Nazi propaganda to Germany and other countries. The German neo-Nazis have also been assisted by Gary Lauck, the NSDAP/AO leader in the United States, who has illegally flooded Germany (and other European states) with neo-Nazi pamphlets and tracts, CDs, and paraphernalia. In addition, some German neo-Nazis also maintain links in the United States to the Ku Klux Klan, to Paul Weyrich and the Free Congress Foundation, as well as to the *Chronicles* journal of the Rockford Institute, which launched a cultural conservatism movement in the 1970s. The German rightists' links to a United States-based fundamentalist Christianity have not been shared by all rightists, some of whom accept paganism and reject a puritanical stance. The German neo-Nazis also maintain contacts with the Belgian Herbert Verbeke who heads the *Vrij Historisch Onderzoek* (Free Historical Research) organization. It publishes numerous tracts that are smuggled into Germany.

Officials of foreign right extremist parties have met publicly or privately with their German counterparts. One such encounter is at a yearly rally in Diksmuide (Belgium), organized by the Flemish nationalists, at which thousands of rightists participate. Many of them are members of the Austrian Freedom Party and the rival Alliance for the Future of Austria (once headed by Jörg Haider), Jean-Marie Le Pen's National Front in France, the British National Party, the Flemish Interest Party and Front National in Belgium, the Pim Fortuyn List in the Netherlands, the National Alliance and the Northern League in Italy, Christoph Blocher's Swiss People's Party, the Danish People's Party, the Norwegian Progress Party, and the National Action in Malta.[11] Their platforms call for sharp restrictions on immigration, a return to traditional values, an emphasis on nationalism, and a greater independence of their country from the European Union and other international organizations. Since the 1980s and early 1990s many of these rightist parties have become stronger, have gained parliamentary and cabinet seats, and have been responsible for shifts in their country's policies, such as stemming a large influx of foreigners coming legally or illegally into their country. As a consequence, these populist parties, often led by a charismatic leader, reap electoral support ranging upward from 10 percent of the voters. Many of the supporters are the "average folks," who normally would have cast their ballots for a democratic party.

Throughout Europe in the 2000s there is a trend toward the right, as expressed in chauvinism and nationalism, in the erection of barriers against an influx of immigrants, and in alleged threats to domestic security on the part of Islamic and other immigrant groups.[12] In the long run these moves toward the right could have disastrous consequences for the preservation of democratic systems, especially because some of the rightist themes have become those of the bourgeois middle class while other themes, such as the welfare system's preservation, also appeal to left and left-center parties in the political spectrum. European governments, to stop a potential rightist wave, will need to emphasize greater social equality, better education for the less talented pupils, and reduced unemployment. In eastern Europe especially, neo-Nazis and skinheads have committed numerous acts of violence, often concentrating their hate toward gays and Gypsies. The current violence does not appear to be a transitory phenomenon but seems embedded in the biases of the right extremists.

Despite their principled opposition to the European Union, the rightist leaders from Austria, Belgium, Bulgaria, and France, whose parties have representation in the EU Parliament, announced plans in January 2008 to form a pan-European party with a mission to "rescue the Western world" from Islam and other perceived threats, such as the disintegration of the family, Christian values, and European civilization. Organizers of the new "European Liberty Party" have pledged to seek the support of right-wing parties from at least three other countries. Thereby they would overcome the minimum of six parties and 20-seat threshold needed to form a party faction in the European Parliament. This was an attempt to revive the former right-wing European bloc known as ITS ("Identity, Tradition, Sovereignty"), headed by Mussolini's granddaughter Alessandra and Le Pen. It disbanded in November 2007 after the Greater Romania Party withdrew; leaving it without the 20 seats it needed. Whether the new European Liberty Party can gain the support of enough other European parties to form such a faction remains to be seen. The rightist leaders said that they would approach like-minded parties in Germany, Denmark, Cyprus, and the Netherlands, along with rightists in Croatia and Serbia, which are not EU members.[13] In Russia and Eastern Europe numerous ultra-nationalist parties and neo-Nazi and skinhead gangs have sprouted in the post-communist era. The gangs have been responsible for a dramatic rise in brutal violence against immigrants, Gypsies, and other disadvantaged groups. These rightist forces have made some impact on governmental policies.

German neo-Nazis can be expected to maintain valuable contacts with their brethren in Europe and other continents, especially in the Middle East. As early as the 1960s, leading West German neo-Nazis made connections to Arab movements, including the Palestinian Liberation Organization. In 1970 thirteen German paramilitary neo-Nazis were reported to have fought alongside the Palestine Liberation Organization against King Hussein's government in Jordan.[14] In 1997 the NPD youth organization declared its solidarity with Iraq and criticized the United States' economic imperialism.

The present and future

In Germany, a nationalist and patriotic spirit has emerged in recent years that, given the Nazi past, could not have arisen in the initial postwar period. This new spirit was initially fueled by the New Right and the neo-Nazis, and was seen as dangerous at the time. But when democratic youth appropriated the patriotic symbols and the flag as their own in the World Cup soccer matches of 2006 the problem disappeared. Patriotism has become respectable and a part of the nation's cultural fabric. What is more worrisome is a successful attempt by the rightist forces in some eastern German villages and towns to replace the democratic youth culture with their own culture. The rightist youth organize free-time activities, such as sports, and thereby become good-will ambassadors. Needless to say, they subtly propagandize the apolitical youth.[15]

What are the German governmental and private responses to the attraction that neo-Nazi and skinhead groups have for a segment of young men and women? As in other European countries, a minority of youth and other groups are racist, xenophobic, and anti-Semitic. They are the ones who participate in demonstrations against state policies and organize a yearly memorial march for the Nazi leader Rudolf Hess. A smaller minority of these bigoted youth has also been involved in acts of violence against their perceived enemies, especially in eastern Germany where structural unemployment ranges over 15 percent. There a marginalized male youth, backed by many older citizens, is rebelling against a society that favors the modernizers who constitute the upper two-thirds well-off population. The rightist youth often have uncaring parents, are poorly educated, underemployed or unemployed, and are neglected by the government. This divide produces a typical confrontation between traditionally conservative Old Politics youth and post-materialist New Politics adherents.[16] It means that the right extremists become strong wherever the establishment parties provide no answers to the fears of the average citizens when confronted with the relentless globalization process. Jobs become more uncertain, cities must cope with increasing social problems, and immigrants from eastern Europe and the Third World keep coming.

The responses of public and private policy-makers to the rightists have been multifaceted. The government has adopted a number of strategies to minimize the rightist threat. Undoubtedly, many local projects financed by governmental support have made an impact on the uncommitted youth. Unfortunately the projects have not had the same impact on the right radical fanatic youth who have rejected the democratic system and its civil society. This youth, clustered especially in eastern Germany, provocatively use Nazi-like symbols and are anti-Semitic, xenophobic, and violent. Government efforts to curb their activities and to reeducate them have largely failed.[17] Such failures should not result in abandoning efforts to reeducate rightist youth. On the contrary, it is crucial for democrats to provide support for engaged citizens in eastern German small towns and cities who are trying to create a democratic base in a rightist-dominated scene.

Despite the violence committed by the relatively few and the biases among many ordinary Germans there is hope that the latter will maintain their support for the country's democratic system and civil society. One poll in 2002, typical of others, estimates that 80 percent of respondents supported the system.[18] According to psychoanalytic studies, discussed in Chapter 2, the 20 percent of Germans who reject the system seek to deny and pass over the Nazi past. Rejection results in a deep-seated memory blockage, which in turn leads to a refusal to empathize with the fate of asylum seekers and refugees. The foreigners are depersonalized and made into abstractions. They are viewed as the weak, the sick, and the persecuted. Should the rightists empathize with the fate of refugees, which is not the case, it would signify an inner confrontation with the rightists' own past. Instead the memory blockage produces hard-heartedness and lack of sympathy for the victims, who are characterized as the miscreant foreigners. As Werner Bulbar notes, "one's own hatefulness is located in the stranger and one tries to destroy it there."[19]

The German courts and the police have played their part in curbing some of the violence but belatedly and only with prodding from human rights organizations. The courts have had to confront the issue of maintaining the civil rights of all citizens, which is a fundamental right in Germany and other democratic states. Thus the German courts have usually granted permission to rightist groups to hold political demonstrations, unless the municipal authorities can show that violence against the demonstrators will result. Civil rights for all citizens not only means freedom of assembly but also of speech. This is not the case with Holocaust deniers who have been tried and jailed for their public statements. Moreover, some rightists have lost their jobs because of their political beliefs, which is unfortunate in a society that should be able to tolerate dissenting and hateful views. According to Christian Roth, it is crucial for a democratic society to tolerate unorthodox rightist views. He argues, with justification, that these views should be challenged by societal groups and individual citizens rather than by ministers of the interior who have the power to disband rightist groups.[20] Many democratic youth are involved in this challenge as they seek to create a post-Auschwitz normality in which peace and social justice issues become paramount. As noted earlier, the writer Martin Walser did not touch on such issues in his controversial 1998 address in Frankfurt, when he was awarded the peace prize of the German Booksellers Association. He decried the continuing reminder of Auschwitz and called for a return to a state of normalcy. His arguments played into the hands of right-wing extremists who for decades have espoused a strong nationalist position.

Nevertheless, Walser's theme has had only a limited appeal. Numerous public demonstrations against rightists have taken place in which hundreds of thousands of citizens have shown their commitment to the democratic system. Polls have indicated that a substantial majority of Germans are not hostile to foreigners and Jews and that they do not condone violence against minority groups. They are committed to a democratic political culture and to a backing of supranational organizations. They oppose cutbacks to the welfare system and support integration of foreigners in their midst. Thus, despite the violence against foreigners and others generated by gangs of right-ist youth, especially in eastern German towns, and despite the DVU and NPD electoral successes in recent years in several Land elections, there is no reason why the democratic system, including its vibrant political culture, should not survive. Federal President von Weizsäcker noted in 1992, Germans "are faced with internal difficulties. However, we know that many other peoples have far greater problems. We have no reason and no right to be afraid. Germany today is not the Weimar Republic."[21]

One anti-fascist demonstrator in Berlin cogently summed up the situation: "We have to come to terms with our past and to remember that Nazism emerged when the public was silent and indifferent. In Germany, we have learnt this lesson well – you cannot keep quiet when Fascism is on the rise. If we don't speak out now, we may have another Hitler one day, and we will have only ourselves to blame."[22] In 2005, in a similar vein, Chancel-lor Schröder, speaking at ceremonies marking the sixtieth anniversary of the Buchenwald death camp liberation, said that "We will not allow lawless-ness and violence, anti-Semitism, racism and xenophobia to have a chance again ... The death of millions, the suffering of the survivors, the torment of the victims – this is the basis of our task to create a better future. We cannot change history, but this country can learn a lot from the deepest shame of our history."[23]

Notes

Introduction

1. Among the right-wing populist parties, none successful, are the League of Free Citizens, which Manfred Brunner founded in 1994 and which he dissolved in 2000. In the same year Ronald Schill, an ultra-conservative municipal judge founded the Schill Party in Hamburg. In December 2003 leaders of his party ousted him from his chairmanship position. Thereupon he founded a new party, Pro-DM-Schill, which opposed the introduction of the euro currency in Germany. It soon faded into obscurity. (See Frank Decker, "Von Schill zu Möllemann: Keine Chance für Rechtspopulisten?" *Forschungsjournal NSB* 16(4) (2003): 55, 60.) In 1996, a right-populist local party, Citizens Movement pro-Cologne (*Bürgerbewegung pro Köln*), was founded. It has maintained ties to neo-Nazis. In Bavaria, the Free Voters party holds some strength, but remains a regional party.
2. See, for earlier periods, Juan Linz, "Some Notes toward a Comparative Study of Fascism in Sociological-Historical Perspective," in *Fascism: a Reader's Guide*, ed. Walter Laqueur (Harmondsworth, England: Penguin, 1979).
3. Fritz René Allemann, *Bonn ist nicht Weimar* (Cologne: Kiepenheuer & Witsch, 1956).

1. The Setting

1. Richard Stöss, *Politics Against Democracy: Right-wing Extremism in West Germany* (New York and Oxford: Berg, 1991), 15–17; Bundesamt für Verfassungsschutz, "Right-wing Extremism in the Federal Republic of Germany – Situation Report – Updated Version/July 1998," internet edn; Wolfgang Kowalsky and Wolfgang Schroeder, "Einleitung: Rechtsextremismus – Begriff, Methode, Analyse," in *Rechtsextremismus: Einführung und Forschungsbilanz*, ed. Kowalsky and Schroeder (Opladen: Westdeutscher Verlag, 1994), 7–20.
2. Leonard Weinberg, "Introduction," in *Encounters with the Contemporary Radical Right*, ed. Peter H. Merkl and Leonard Weinberg (Boulder, CO: Westview Press, 1993), 5.
3. Seymour Lipset, *Political Man*, 2nd enlarged edn (Baltimore: Johns Hopkins University Press, 1981), p. 131; see also his "'Der Faschismus,' die Linke, die Rechte und die Mitte," *Kölner Zeitschrift für Soziologie und Sozialpsychologie* (1959): 401.
4. The Basic Law is the equivalent of a temporary constitution. In 1990 when the two Germanys were united, the Basic Law remained in effect, but with amendments.
5. Hans-Gerd Jaschke, *Rechtsextremismus und Fremdenfeindlichkeit: Begriffe, Positionen, Praxisfelder* (Opladen: Westdeutscher Verlag, 1994), 25–28.
6. See, e.g., Uwe Backes and Eckhard Jesse, *Politischer Extremismus in der Bundesrepublik Deutschland*. 3 vols (Cologne: Wirtschaft und Politik, 1989). See also Armin Pfahl-Traughber, *Rechtsextremismus: Eine kritische Bestandsaufnahme nach der Wiedervereinigung* (Bonn: Bouvier, 1993); Uwe Backes and Patrick Moreau, *Die extreme Rechte in Deutschland: Geschichte – Gegenwärtige Gefahren – Ursachen – Gegenmassnahmen* (Munich: Akademischer Verlag, 1993).

7. See Peter Dudek and Hans-Gerd Jaschke, *Entstehung und Entwicklung des Rechts-extremismus in der Bundesrepublik*, 2 vols (Opladen: Westdeutscher Verlag, 1984); Jaschke, *Rechtsextremismus und Fremdenfeindlichkeit*, 28–29, 144–148; Richard Stöss, *Die extreme Rechte in der Bundesrepublik* (Opladen: Westdeutscher Verlag, 1989) and *Rechtsextremismus im Wandel*. 2nd edn (Bonn: Friedrich-Ebert-Stiftung, 2007); Claus Leggewie, *Der Geist steht rechts* (Berlin: Rotbuch, 1987).

8. Theodor W. Adorno et al., *The Authoritarian Personality* (New York: Harper & Row, 1950).

9. Wilhelm Heitmeyer, *Rechtsextremistische Orientierungen bei Jugendlichen – Empirische Ergebnisse und Erklärungsmuster einer Untersuchung zur politischen Sozialisation* (Weinheim-München: Juventa, 1987); Wilhelm Heitmeyer et al., *Die Bielefelder Rechtsextremismus-Studie – Erste Langzeituntersuchung zur politischen Sozialisation männlicher Jugendlicher* (Weinheim-München: Juventa, 1992). See also Hannah Arendt, *The Origins of Totalitarianism* (New York: Harcourt, 1951).

10. Erich Fromm, *Escape from Freedom* (New York: Holt, Rinehart, & Winston, 1941) and *The Anatomy of Human Destructiveness* (New York: Holt, Rinehart & Winston, 1973); Adorno et al., *The Authoritarian Personality*.

11. See Deutscher Gewerkschaftsbund, "Bericht der DGB-Kommission 'Rechtsextremismus'" (Berlin: DGB, 2000), 17; Rudolf Leiprecht, Lena Inowlocki, Athanasios Markavism, and Jürgen Novak, "Racism in the New Germany: Examining the Causes, Looking for Answers," in *Racism in Europe: a Challenge for Youth Policy and Youth Work*, ed. Jan Laurens Hazekamp and Keith Popple (London: UCL Press, 1997), 108–109; Helmut Willems, S. Würtz, and R. Eckert, *Fremdenfeindliche Gewalt: Eine Analyse von Täterstrukturen und Eskalationsprozessen*. Research report (Bonn: Bundesministerium Familie und Jugend, 1993).

12. Cited by Leiprecht et al., "Racism in the New Germany," 109.

13. See ibid.

14. Deutscher Gewerkschaftsbund, "Bericht der DGB-Kommission 'Rechtsextremismus'" 17. See also Werner Bergmann and Rainer Erb, "Kaderparteien, Bewegung, Szene, kollektive Episode oder was?" in *Forschungsjournal Neue Soziale Bewegungen* 7(4) (1994): 26–34.

15. Quotation by Dale Tuttle, "The Assimilation of East Germany and the Rise of Identity-Based Violence Against Foreigners in the Unified German State," in *German Politics and Society* 31 (Spring 1994): 71. See Ted Gurr, *Why Men Rebel* (Princeton: Princeton University Press, 1970).

16. Herbert Kitschelt, *The Radical Right in Western Europe: a Comparative Analysis* (Ann Arbor: University of Michigan Press, 1995). See also Roger Karapin, "Radical-Right and Neo-Fascist Political Parties in Western Europe," *Comparative Politics* 30(2) (January 1998): 213–234.

17. Erwin K. Scheuch and Hans-Dieter Klingemann, "Theorie des Rechtsradikalismus in westlichen Industriegesellschaften," *Hamburger Jahrbuch für Wirtschafts- und Gesellschaftspolitik*, 12 (1967): 11–29.

18. Tuttle, "The Assimilation of East Germany," 63–83.

19. Edward E. Azar, *Protracted Social Conflict: Theory and Cases* (Hampshire, England: Gower, 1989).

20. See Pfahl-Traughber, *Rechtsextremismus*, 14–23.

21. Cas Mudde, "Right-Wing Extremism Analyzed," *European Journal of Political Research* 27 (1995): 203–224; Leonard Weinberg, "An Overview of Right-Wing Extremism in the Western World: a Study of Convergence, Linkage, and Identity,"

in *Nation and Race: the Developing Euro-American Racist Subculture*, ed. Jeffrey Kaplan and Tore Bjørgo (Boston: Northeastern University Press, 1998), 7.

22. For an anthropological perspective, see Verena Stolcke, "Talking Culture: New Boundaries, New Rhetorics of Exclusion in Europe," *Current Anthropology* 36(1) (February 1995): 1–24. See also Ralph Weiss, "Rechtsextremismus und vierte Gewalt," *Soziale Welt* 45(4) (1994): 480–504.

23. Werner Bohleber, "The Presence of the Past – Xenophobia and Rightwing Extremism in the Federal Republic of Germany: Psychoanalytic Reflections," *American Imago* 52(3) (1995): 332.

24. Ibid., 332–333.

25. Erwin K. Scheuch and Hans-Dieter Klingemann, "Theorie des Rechtsradikalismus in westlichen Industriegesellschaften"; Michael Minkenberg, "German Unification and the Continuity of Discontinuities: Cultural Change and the Far Right in East and West," *German Politics* 3(2) (August 1994): 169–192. See also Christoph Butterwegge, "Rechtsextremismus in Deutschland: Erscheinigungsformen – Entstehungsbedingungen – Gegenstrategien," *Zukunft* 1 (1994): 29–34; Klaus Wahl, Christiane Tramitz, and Jörg Blumtritt, *Fremdenfeindlichkeit: Auf den Spuren extremer Emotionen* (Opladen: Leske & Budrich, 2001).

26. Michi Ebata, "Right-Wing Extremism: In Search of a Definition," in *The Extreme Right: Freedom and Security at Risk*, ed. Aurel Braun and Stephen Scheinberg (Boulder, CO: Westview Press, 1997), 14.

27. Ibid.

28. See Adorno et al., *The Authoritarian Personality*. For relative deprivation theory, see Gurr, *Why Men Rebel*; Tuttle, "The Assimilation of East Germany," 71–72.

29. *Die Tageszeitung* (hereafter *taz*), November 24, 2006.

30. German Federal Statistics Office, *Facts on Immigration and Integration in Germany,* cited by German Embassy, Washington, DC, n.d.

31. Bundestag President Wolfgang Thierse citing 2002 poll in *taz*, December 12, 2003; 2004 poll in *taz*, December 3, 2004.

32. The naturalization process for foreigners also was shortened (Goethe Institute and Inter Nationes, *Foreigners in Germany – From Guest Workers to Fellow-Citizens* (Bonn, 11-2002)). See also Laura M. Murray, "Einwanderungsland Bundesrepublik Deutschland? Explaining the Evolving Positions of German Political Parties on Citizenship Policy," *German Politics and Society* 33 (Fall 1994): 23–56; René Del Fabbro, "Germany: a Victory of the Street," in *New Xenophobia in Europe*, ed. Bernd Baumgartl and Adrian Favell (London: Kluwer Law International, 1995), 132–147; Peter O'Brien, *Beyond the Swastika* (London: Routledge, 1996), 110–114.

33. Figures vary widely, but 200,000 is a widely accepted number. See *taz*, December 29, 2004; Jewish Telegraph Agency (JTA), April 19, 2007.

34. Angelika Timm, *Jewish Claims against East Germany: Moral Obligations and Pragmatic Policy* (Budapest: Central European University Press, 1997), see 15–64.

35. Rainer Erb, "Antisemitismus und Antizionismus," in *Fünfzig Jahre Israel: Vision und Wirklichkeit*, ed. Heiner Lichtenstein and Otto R. Romberg (Bonn: Bundeszentrale für politische Bildung, 1998), 228; see also 226–227.

36. Polls by Bielefeld and Tel Aviv Gallup Institutes, commissioned by and summarized in *Der Spiegel*, January 13 and 20, 1992.

37. Interview with Werner Bergmann in *taz*, June 15, 2002.

38. Forsa survey, commissioned by *Stern*, no. 48, 2003, cited by Susanne Urban, "Anti-Semitism in Germany Today: Its Roots and Tendencies," in *Jewish Political*

Studies Review 16(3–4) (Fall 2004), http://www.jcpa.org/phas/phas-urban-f04.htm (December 26, 2006).

39. 2006 survey cited in *Houston Chronicle*, November 10, 2006.

40. Forsa poll, commissioned by *Stern*, no. 48 (2003), cited by *taz*, November 20, 2003. See also Werner Bergmann and Rainer Erb, *Anti-Semitism in Germany: the Post-Nazi Epoch Since 1945* (New Brunswick, NJ: Transaction, 1997), 1–4, 6, 318; (trans. Belinda Cooper and Allison Brown, *Antisemitismus in der Bundesrepublik Deutschland: Ergebnisse der empirischen Forschung von 1946-1989* (Opladen: Leske & Budrich, 1991)); Marc Fisher, *After the Wall: Germany, the Germans and the Burdens of History* (New York: Simon & Schuster, 1995), 206–224; "Bitte kein Generalverdacht," *Freitag* 52, December 19, 2003; Wolfgang Benz, ed., *Antisemitismus in Deutschland: Zur Aktualität eines Vorurteils* (Munich: dtv, 1995). In Germany, a smaller segment of the population, fascinated by the cultural contributions that German Jews made to the country prior to the Hitler regime and atoning for the sins of their parents or grandparents, has espoused philo-Semitism.

41. Ursula Birsl, "Mädchen und Rechtsextremismus: Rechtsextremistische Orientierungen bei weiblichen und männlichen Jugendlichen," *Jugendpolitik* 3 (1993): 12–14.

42. According to a 2002 Bielefeld University study conducted by Wilhelm Heitmeyer, cited in *taz*, November 8, 2002.

43. *taz*, December 4, 2001.

44. See Birgit Meyer, "Mädchen und Rechtsextremismus: Männliche Dominanzkultur und weibliche Unterordnung," in *Rechtsradikale Gewalt im vereinigten Deutschland: Jugend im gesellschaftlichen Umbruch*, ed. Hans-Uwe Otto and Roland Merten (Opladen: Leske & Budrich, 1993), 214; Leiprecht et al., "Racism in the New Germany," 110–111.

45. Christel Hopf, Peter Rieker, Martina Sanden-Marcus, and Christiane Schmidt, *Familie und Rechtsextremismus: Familiale Sozialisation und rechtsextreme Orientierungen junger Männer* (Weinheim: Juventa, 1995), 158–163, 181–183.

46. Poll commissioned by the North-Rhine Westphalia Ministry for the Equality of Women and Men, cited in *taz*, August 3, 1995.

47. For an overview of women's role in the right-extremist movement, see Birgit Rommelspacher, "Das Geschlechterverhältnis im Rechtsextremismus," in *Rechtsextremismus in der Bundesrepublik Deutschland: Eine Bilanz*, ed. Wilfried Schubarth and Richard Stöss (Opladen: Leske & Budrich, 2001), 199–219.

48. Institut für Demoskopie Allensbach, *Demokratie-Verankerung in der Bundesrepublik Deutschland: Eine empirische Untersuchung zum 30jährigen Bestehen der Bundesrepublik* (Allensbach, 1979), 96.

49. 5 Millionen Deutsche: "Wir sollten wieder einen Führer haben...," *Die SINUS-Studie über rechtsextremistische Einstellungen bei den Deutschen* (Reinbek: Rowohlt, 1981), 8, 93; Thomas Schmid, "Right-Wing Radicalism in the Unified Germany," in *The Resurgence of Right-Wing Radicalism in Germany*, ed. Ulrich Wank (Atlantic Highlands, NJ: Humanities Press International, 1996), 73. (trans. James Knowlton. Original German edn: *Der neue alte Rechtsradikalismus* (Munich: Piper, 1993)). An EMNID survey of 1994 showed that about 5 percent or about 4 million Germans were convinced right-wing extremists and another 17 percent or about 13 to 14 million Germans held some rightist views (cited by Norbert Madloch, "Die Wählerwandlung der Rechten," *Wer redet da von Entwarnung: Texte und Analysen zum aktuellen Rechtsextremismus* [author's collective: edition ost, 1995], 15).

50. Survey by sociologists Alex Demirovic and Gerd Paul, Institute for Social Research, University of Frankfurt, cited in *dpa* 0240 news release, April 19, 1996.
51. Richard Stöss, *Rechtsextremismus im vereinten Deutschland* (Bonn: Friedrich-Ebert-Stiftung, 1999), 30.
52. Stöss, *Rechtsextremismus*, 29ff.; Stöss, *Politics Against Democracy*, 46–48.
53. Poll by Munich Institute polis, cited in *Die Zeit*, 52/2000.
54. 2003 poll by Wilhelm Heitmeyer of Bielefeld Institute, cited in the Bundestag by its president Wolfgang Thierse, in *taz*, December 12, 2003; Lower Saxony 2009 poll in *taz*, March 18, 2009.
55. Hans-Gerd Jaschke, "Sub-Cultural Aspects of Right-Wing Extremism," in *Political Culture in Germany*, ed. Dirk Berg-Schlosser and Ralf Rytlewski (New York: St. Martin's Press, 1993), 127.

2.   The German Right-Extremist Scene, 1945–1990

1. Abraham Ashkenasi, *Modern German Nationalism* (Cambridge, MA: Schenkman, 1976), 59.
2. Jeffrey Herf, *Divided Memory: the Nazi Past in the Two Germanys* (Cambridge, MA: Harvard University Press, 1997), 205; Richard Stöss, "Ideologie und Strategie des Rechtsextremismus," in *Rechtsextremismus in der Bundesrepublik Deutschland: Eine Bilanz*, ed. Wilfried Schubarth and Richard Stöss (Opladen: Leske & Budrich, 2001), 106–109.
3. Rand C. Lewis, *A Nazi Legacy: Right-Wing Extremism in Postwar Germany* (New York: Praeger, 1991), 38–41.
4. See Edmond Vermeil, *L'Allemagne contemporaine, sociale, politique et culturelle, 1890–1950* (Paris: Auteil, 1952–1953).
5. See Lee McGowan, *The Radical Right in Germany: 1870 to the Present* (London: Longman, 2002), 10–13.
6. Uwe Backes and Jesse Eckhard, *Politischer Extremismus in der Bundesrepublik Deutschland* (Cologne: Wirtschaft und Politik, 1989), 58.
7. See Ekkart Zimmermann and Thomas Saalfeld, "The Three Waves of West German Right-Wing Extremism," in *Encounters with the Contemporary Radical Right*, ed. Peter H. Merkl and Leonard Weinberg (Boulder: Westview Press, 1993), 50–74.
8. The BHE and another rightist party, the German Party (*Deutsche Partei*), merged to form the United German Party (*Gesamtdeutsche Partei*). In addition, a League of Expellees (*Bund der Vertriebenen*) was formed in 1958. See "Kurzer Überblick über die Geschichte des 'Bund der Vertriebenen' (BdV)," http://www.nadir.org/nadir/archiv/Antifaschismus/Themen/Revanchismus/nwh/bdv.html; *Junge Welt*, November 3, 2003.
9. Similarly, under Article 9 of the Basic Law, the government can ban associations that violate the penal code and oppose the constitutional order or the principles of international understanding.
10. For early studies, see J. D. Nagle, *The National Democratic Party: Right Radicalism in the Federal Republic* (Berkeley: University of California Press, 1969); Steven Warnecke, "The Future of Rightist Extremism in West Germany," *Comparative Politics* 2(4) (July 1970): 629–652.
11. McGowan, *The Radical Right in Germany*, 157.
12. Armin Pfahl-Traughber, *Rechtsextremismus: Eine kritische Bestandsaufnahme nach der Wiedervereinigung* (Bonn: Bouvier, 1993), 77–82.

13. Dieter Roth, "Die Republikaner," *Aus Politik und Zeitgeschichte* (supplement to *Das Parlament*) B37–38/90 (September 14, 1990): 45–46. See also Michael Stiller, *Die Republikaner: Franz Schönhuber und seine Rechtsradikale Partei* (Munich: Wilhelm Heyne, 1989), 106.

14. Dieter Roth and Hartmut Schäfer, "Der Erfolg der Rechten. Denkzettel für die etablierten Parteien oder braune Wiedergeburt?" in *Das Superwahljahr: Deutschland vor unkalkulierbaren Regierungsmehrheiten*, ed. Wilhelm Bürklin and Dieter Roth (Cologne: Bund, 1994), 123.

15. Hans-Joachim Veen, Norbert Lepszy, and Peter Mnich, *The Republikaner Party in Germany: Right-Wing Menace or Protest Catchall?* (Westport, CT: Praeger, 1993), 29–40. See also Hans-Gerd Jaschke, *Die "Republikaner": Profile einer Rechtsaussen-Partei* (Bonn: Dietz, 1994); Richard Stöss, *Die Republikaner – Woher sie kommen, was sie wollen, wer sie wählt, was zu tun ist* (Cologne: Bund, 1990); Claus Leggewie, *Die Republikaner: Phantombild der neuen Rechten* (Berlin: Rotbuch, 1989); Joachim Hofmann-Göttig, *Die neue Rechte: die Männerparteien* (Bonn: Demokratische Gemeinde, 1989).

16. *Frankfurter Rundschau*, June 20, 1989.

17. McGowan, *The Radical Right in Germany*, 161; Pfahl-Traughber, *Rechtsextremismus*, 56–67.

18. Richard Stöss, *Politics Against Democracy: Right-wing Extremism in West Germany* (New York and Oxford: Berg, 1991), 168; Heinrich Sippel, "Die Herausforderung unseres demokratischen Rechtsstaates durch Rechtsextremisten," in *Extremismus und Terrorismus* (BMI: Bonn, 1989), 44.

19. See Bernd Wagner, ed., *Handbuch Rechtsextremismus: Netzwerke, Parteien, Organisationen, Ideologiezentren, Medien* (Reinbek: Rowohlt, 1994), 26–27.

20. Marc Fisher, *After the Wall: Germany, the Germans and the Burdens of History* (New York: Simon & Schuster, 1995), 232–237.

21. Nicholas Fraser, *The Voice of Modern Hatred: Tracing the Rise of Neo-Fascism in Europe* (Woodstock, NY: The Overlook Press, 2001), 73–74, 87–88; Steffen Kailitz, "Aktuelle Entwicklungen im deutschen Rechtsextremismus" (Sankt Augustin: Konrad-Adenauer-Stiftung, November 2000), 33.

22. Cited by Stöss, *Politics Against Democracy*, 167.

23. Pfahl-Traughber, *Rechtsextremismus*, 83–86.

24. Wagner, ed., *Handbuch Rechtsextremismus*, 25.

25. Stöss, *Politics Against Democracy*, 178; Rudolf Müller, "Schule des Terrorismus: Die Wehrsportgruppe Hoffmann und andere militante Neonazis," in *Rechtsextremismus in der Bundesrepublik: Voraussetzungen, Zusammenhänge, Wirkungen*, ed. Wolfgang Betz (Frankfurt am Main: Fischer Taschenbuch Verlag, 1985), 238–255.

26. Christoph Butterwegge, *Rechtsextremismus, Rassismus und Gewalt: Erklärungsmodelle in der Diskussion* (Darmstadt: Primus, 1996), 37.

27. Stöss, *Politics Against Democracy*, 180–181.

28. *Der Spiegel*, 26 (1993).

29. *Germany Alert* (n.d., circa November 1998).

30. Heinrich Sippel, "Die Herausforderung unseres demokratischen Rechtsstaates durch Rechtsextremisten," 47.

31. Stefan Marks, "Skins und Hoods," in *Rechtsextremismus: Hintergründe, Meinungen, Gegenstrategien*, ed. Jusos in der SPD (Bonn, n.d.), 66–70; Landesamt für Verfassungsschutz Baden-Württemberg, *Skinheads* (Stuttgart, 1997), 3–11; Innenministerium Mecklenburg-Vorpommern, *Skinheads* (Schwerin, 1996), 8–14.

32. Tete Tetens, *The New Germany and the Old Nazis* (London: Secker & Warburg, 1961).
33. See Christoph Butterwege and Horst Iola, eds, *Rechtsextremismus im vereinigten Deutschland. Randerscheinigung oder Gefahr für die Demokratie?* (Bremen: Steintor, 1991) and Karl-Heinz Heinemann and Wilfried Schubarth, eds, *Der antifaschistische Staat entlässt seine Kinder: Jugend und Rechtsextremismus in Ostdeutschland* (Cologne: Pappy Rossa, 1992).
34. Survey by Central Institute for Youth Research, Leipzig, cited by Werner Bergmann, "Anti-Semitism and Xenophobia in the East German Länder," *German Politics* 3(2) (August 1994): 266. See also Michael Minkenberg, "German Unification and the Continuity of Discontinuities: Cultural Change and the Far Right in East and West," *German Politics* 3(2) (August 1994): 182.
35. Susann Backer, "New Perspectives on the Far Right in Germany," *German Politics* 4(2) (August 1995): 168.
36. Walter Süss, "Analysen und Berichte: Zur Wahrnehmung und Interpretation des Rechtsextremismus in der DDR durch das MfS," in *Staatssicherheit und Rechtsextremismus*, ed. Heinrich Sippel and Walter Süss (Bochum: Universitätsverlag Dr. N. Brockmeyer, 1994), 27–32.
37. *Frankfurter Rundschau*, February 24, 2001.
38. Other categories were the unemployed (14 percent), students (8 percent), and part-time workers (4 percent). Poll conducted by Loni Niederländer, cited by Benno Fischer, "DDR-Rechtsextremismus als Vorbote der Systemkrise," *Neue Gesellschaft-Frankfurter Hefte* 4 (April 1990): 335.
39. Cited by Bergmann, "Anti-Semitism and Xenophobia," 265.
40. Bernd Wagner, *Jugend-Gewalt-Szenen: Zu kriminologischen und historischen Aspekten in Ostdeutschland, Die achtziger und neunziger Jahre* (Berlin: dip, 1995), 37–74.
41. Presumably 1 percent did not respond. See Peter H. Merkl, "Are the Old Nazis Coming Back?" in *The Federal Republic of Germany at Forty-Five: Union without Unity*, ed. Peter H. Merkl (New York: New York University Press, 1995), 434–435; Wolfgang Brück, "Jugend als soziales Problem," in *Jugend und Jugendforschung in der DDR: Gesellschaftspolitische Situationen, Sozialisation und Mentalitätsentwicklung in den achtziger Jahren*, ed. Walter Friedrich and Hartmut Griese (Opladen: Leske & Budrich, 1991), 199.
42. Jan C. Behrends, Thomas Lindenberger, and Patrice G. Poutrous, *Fremde und Fremd-Sein in der DDR. Zu historischen Ursachen der Fremdenfeindlichkeit in Ostdeutschland* (Berlin: Metropol, 2003).
43. Wolfgang Kühnel, "Hitler's Grandchildren? The Reemergence of a Right-Wing Social Movement in Germany," in *Nation and Race: the Developing Euro-American Racist Subculture*, ed. Jeffrey Kaplan and Tore Bjørgo (Boston: Northeastern University Press, 1998), 152–153.
44. *New York Times*, February 2, 1994.
45. *New York Times*, May 15, 1991.
46. Walter Süss, "Analysen und Berichte," 18–24.
47. Merkl, "Are the Old Nazis Coming Back?," 434–435.
48. Bernd Holthusen and Michael Jänecke, *Rechtsextremismus in Berlin: Aktuelle Erscheinigungsformen, Ursachen, Gegenmassnahmen* (Marburg: Schüren, 1994), 36–37.
49. Süss, "Analysen und Berichte," 42. According to Süss, in 1984, in another poll, 50 percent of youth respondents still believed in the worldwide triumph of socialism; by May 1988 the percentage had shrunk to 10 percent (Süss, "Analysen und Berichte," 42–43).

50. Wagner, *Jugend-Gewalt-Szenen*, 46–47.
51. Ian J. Kagedan, "Contemporary Right-Wing Extremism in Germany," in *The Extreme Right: Freedom and Security at Risk*, ed. Aurel Braun and Stephen Scheinberg (Boulder, CO: Westview Press, 1997), 111–113.

3. Right-Extremist Parties

1. "'Republikanische Jugend': Schönhubers Teenietruppe," *Arbeitsgemeinschaft verfolgter Sozialdemokraten-Informationsdienst* 9(6) (June–July 1994): 9–11.
2. For an insiders' account of the party, see Michael Schomers, *Deutschland ganz rechts* (Cologne: Kiepenheuer & Witsch, 1990). Schomers, a Cologne television reporter, joined the Republikaner under an assumed name and observed it from within for seven months.
3. Armin Pfahl-Traughber, *Rechtsextremismus: Eine kritische Bestandsaufnahme nach der Wiedervereinigung* (Bonn: Bouvier, 1993), 43–46.
4. Hans-Joachim Veen, Norbert Lepszy, and Peter Mnich, *The Republikaner Party in Germany: Right-Wing Menace or Protest Catchall?* (Westport, CT: Praeger, 1993), 24–26.
5. *Frankfurter Rundschau*, October 14, 1994; *Der Spiegel*, December 26, 1994, 35–36.
6. Uwe Backes and Patrick Moreau, *Die extreme Rechte in Deutschland: Geschichte Gegenwärtige Gefahren – Ursachen – Gegenmassnahmen*. 2nd edn (Munich: Akademischer Verlag, 1994), 85.
7. *taz*, November 29, 2004.
8. *Der Spiegel*, December 26, 1994, 35; Veen et al., *The Republikaner Party in Germany*, 22; BMI, *Verfassungsschutzbericht 1996*, 119.
9. BMI, *Verfassungsschutzbericht 1996*, 119; BMI, *Verfassungsschutzbericht 2006*, 51.
10. Norbert Lepszy, "Die Republikaner: Ideologie – Programm – Organisation," *Aus Politik und Zeitgeschichte* (supplement to *Das Parlament*), B41–42, October 6, 1989: 3.
11. For an overview of right-wing parties, see Gerard Braunthal, *Parties and Politics in Modern Germany* (Boulder, CO: Westview Press, 1996), 103–109.
12. Jusos in der SPD, "Rechtsextremismus: Jusos gegen Republikaner," *Argumente, Juso-Informationsdienst* 5 (July 1994): 6; Norbert Lepszy and Hans-Joachim Veen, "Rechtsradikale in der parlamentarischen Praxis: Die Republikaner in kommunalen und Landesparlamenten sowie im Europaparlament," *Zeitschrift für Parlamentsfragen* 3 (1994): 209–214.
13. *taz*, September 2, 1998.
14. BMI, *Aktuelle Aspekte des Rechtsextremismus* (Bonn, 1994), 36–38. See also Norbert Lepszy, "'Die Republikaner' im Abwind," Konrad-Adenauer-Stiftung, No. 17, Aktuelle Fragen der Politik (Sankt Augustin, 1994).
15. Alexandra Cole, "The Republikaner: a Party at Odds With Itself," in *Germans Divided: the 1994 Bundestag Elections and the Evolution of the German Party System*, ed. Russell J. Dalton (Oxford: Berg, 1996), 136–137.
16. Hans-Joachim Veen, "Rechtsextremistische und Rechtspopulistische Parteien in Europa (EU) und im Europaparlament," in BMI, *Texte zur Inneren Sicherheit* (Bonn, 1997), 75.
17. BMI, *Aktuelle Aspekte des Rechtsextremismus*, 38–41.
18. *taz*, November 25, 1998.

19. Gillian More, "Undercover Surveillance of the Republikaner Party: Protecting a Militant Democracy or Discrediting a Political Rival?" *German Politics* 3(2) (August 1994): 284–292.

20. Backes and Moreau, *Die extreme Rechte in Deutschland*, 88–89; Juliane Wetzel, "Antisemitismus als Element rechtsextremer Ideologie und Propaganda," in *Antisemitismus in Deutschland: Zur Aktualität eines Vorurteils*, ed. Wolfgang Benz (Munich: Deutscher Taschenbuch Verlag, 1995), 115–117.

21. BMI, *Verfassungsschutzbericht 1993* (Berlin, hectographed), 80–81.

22. BMI, *Verfassungsschutzbericht 2006*, footnote 56, p. 84.

23. *Die Republikaner: Parteiprogramm 2002* (Berlin, 2002), 11.

24. The leaders made such demands in a map appended to the 1990 program draft, in internal discussion papers, and in leaflets. They also urged autonomy for Germans returning to Sudetenland and said that the 1955 Allied accord with Austria prohibiting that country's *Anschluss* (annexation) with Germany was unconstitutional (see *Die Zeit*, January 19, 1990; Kurt Lenk, "Grossdeutschland im Programm – Die 'Republikaner' nach Rosenheim," *Neue Gesellschaft-Frankfurter Hefte* 4 (April 1990): 327–331; Thomas Saalfeld, "The Politics of National-Populism: Ideology and Policies of the German Republikaner Partei," *German Politics* 2(2) (August 1993): 189.

25. *Die Republikaner: Parteiprogramm 1990*, 18; *1993*, 22.

26. Gerhard Paul et al., *Hitlers Schatten verblasst: Die Normalisierung des Rechtsextremismus* (Bonn: Dietz, 1990), 140–141.

27. Personal interview with Wolgang Hüttl, secretary-general, Bavarian Republikaner, Munich, December 10, 1990.

28. *New York Times*, March 8, 1993.

29. *Die Republikaner, Parteiprogramm 1993*, 48–58, 77–80. For commentary, see Klaus-Henning Rosen, "Hat der Wolf Kreide gefressen? Das neue Parteiprogramm der 'Republikaner'," *Vorgänge* 104 (April 1990): 22–31.

30. BMI, *Verfassungsschutzbericht 2003* (Berlin, 2004), 70.

31. Annette Linke, *Der Multimillionär Frey und die DVU: Daten, Fakten, Hintergründe* (Essen: Klartext Verlag, 1994), 38–39. See also Jürgen Elsässer, *Braunbuch DVU-eine deutsche Arbeiterpartei und ihre Freunde* (Hamburg: konkret texte 17, 1998).

32. Hans-Joachim Veen and Norbert Lepszy, "Republikaner und DVU in der parlamentarischen Praxis: Inkompetent, zerstritten und politikunfähig," *Aktuelle Aspekte des Rechtsextremismus* (Bonn: BMI, 1994), 42–43.

33. *Die Zeit*, no. 38, 1998.

34. Survey by Mannheim Forschungsgruppe Wahlen, cited by *Süddeutsche Zeitung*, April 28, 1998.

35. Viola Neu and Ulrich von Wilamowitz-Moellendorf, "Die DVU bei der Landtagswahl in Sachsen-Anhalt vom 26 April 1998," Konrad-Adenauer-Stiftung (Sankt Augustin, 1998), 1–8.

36. *taz*, October 15, 1998.

37. *taz*, September 11, 1999.

38. BMI, *Verfassungsschutzbericht 2003*, 76.

39. The new party consists of former SPD members, especially left-wing trade unionists, in western Germany and PDS members in eastern Germany.

40. See DVU, *Partei-Programm* (n.d. (c.1998)); *Deutsche National-Zeitung*, September 17, 1993.

41. Deputy Weidenbach, cited by Linke, *Der Multimillionär Frey und die DVU*, 62.

42. Backes and Moreau, *Die extreme Rechte in Deutschland*, 36–39. See also Vereinigung der Verfolgten des Naziregimes-Bund der Antifaschistinnen und Antifaschisten (VVN-BdA), Bremen, "Analyse der NPD," March 1999. For a survey of the NPD, see Toralf Staud, *Moderne Nazis. Die neuen Rechten und der Aufstieg der NPD* (Cologne: Kiepenheuer and Witsch, 2005).
43. *Die Tagesschau*, January 6, 2007.
44. Leonard Zeskind, "Fa & Antifa in the Fatherland," *The Nation*, October 5, 1998: 26–29.
45. *Die Zeit*, no. 41, 2002; BVS, *Verfassungsschutzbericht 2006*, 85–86.
46. *Blick nach Rechts*, no. 4, 1998.
47. *Süddeutsche Zeitung*, May 11, 1999. See also NPD, *Berichte*, June 25, 2001.
48. *Die Zeit*, September 10, 1998. Deckert eventually became chair of NPD's branch in Land Baden-Wuerttemberg, but national NPD officials removed him from office in 2005 for failing to abide by party decisions (*taz*, October 6, 2005).
49. *Der Spiegel*, October 23, 1995.
50. *Der Spiegel*, June 16, 1994.
51. Baden-Württemberg Landesamt für Verfassungsschutz, "Junge National Demokraten (JN): Jugendorganisation oder Sammelbecken für Neonazis?" (Stuttgart, 1997), 7–12.
52. *The Times* (London), March 12, 2005.
53. *Die Welt*, May 17, 2007; *Der Spiegel Online*, March 19, 2009.
54. Steffen Kailitz, "Aktuelle Entwicklungen im deutschen Rechtsextremismus," Konrad-Adenauer-Stiftung, No. 17 (Sankt Augustin, 2000), 13.
55. NPD, press release, November 5, 1999.
56. *Freitag*, November 12, 1999; *taz*, June 10, 2002. See also Omer Bartov, "The Wehrmacht Exhibition Controversy: the Politics of Evidence," in *Crimes of War: Guilt and Denial in the Twentieth Century*, ed. Omer Bartov, Atina Grossmann, and Mary Nolan (New York: The New Press, 2002), 41–60.
57. *Der Tagesspiegel*, September 20, 1998.
58. *Globe and Mail*, May 9, 2005. See also *Frankfurter Rundschau*, May 9, 2005.
59. *Frankfurter Rundschau*, June 4, 2007.
60. Cited by *Expatica*, February 26, 2005. See also *Die Zeit*, June 10, 1999.
61. Kailitz, "Aktuelle Entwicklungen," 13–14.
62. *New York Times*, August 27, 2000.
63. *taz*, July 24, 2001; *Freitag*, February 1, 2002.
64. Emnid poll, cited in *Die Welt*, August 8, 2000.
65. Klaudia Prevezanos, "Protecting Democracy: Germany Wants to Ban Far-Right Party," American Institute for Contemporary German Studies, At Issue Report (Washington, DC, December 2000), 3.
66. Ibid.
67. *Frankfurter Allgemeine Zeitung*, April 10, 2001.
68. *Süddeutsche Zeitung*, October 21, 2000; April 27, 2001.
69. German Information Center [hereafter GIC] (New York), *The Week in Germany*, October 11, 2002.
70. Ibid., March 23, 2003.
71. Interview with intelligence specialist Rolf Gössner in *Telepolis*, October 6, 2003. See also *taz*, February 1, 2002.
72. For details, see Gerard Braunthal, "The SPD, the Welfare State, and Agenda 2010," *German Politics and Society*, issue 69, 21(4) (Winter 2003): 1–29.
73. *Frankfurter Rundschau*, June 14, 2004.

224   *Notes*

74. Cited by *Expatica*, February 26, 2005.
75. *The Guardian*, February 11, 2005.
76. GIC, *The Week in Germany*, February 18, 2005.
77. *International Herald Tribune*, February 10, 2000. In February 2009 about 6,000 members of the NPD, neo-Nazi groups, *Kameradschaften*, skinheads, and anti-immigrant groups staged another mass demonstration in Dresden to commemorate the Allied bombing of the city. The marchers, constituting one of the largest neo-Nazi demonstrations in Germany, were outnumbered by democratic counter-demonstrators (United Press International, February 16, 2009).
78. *International Herald Tribune*, February 10, 2005.
79. *Der Spiegel*, October 6, 2006; *Atlantic Times*, October 2006.
80. Infratest-dimap survey, cited in *taz*, September 18, 2006. For list of villages, see *taz*, September 19, 2006.
81. *Washington Post, Der Spiegel*, September 18, 2006.
82. *Herald Sun* (Melbourne), September 18, 2006.
83. Interview with the political scientist Eckard Jesse in *taz*, October 30, 2004.
84. *Spiegel Online*, February 8, 2008; March 10, 2008.
85. *New York Times*, May 28, 2008.
86. *Los Angeles Times*, May 5, 2005.
87. Viola Neu, "DVU – NPD: Perspektiven und Entwicklungen," Konrad-Adenauer-Stiftung, Arbeitspapier 140/2004 (Sankt Augustin, 2004), 3.

4. Neo-Nazi Groups, Skinheads, and Violence

1. BMI, *Extremismus und Gewalt*, vol. 2 (Bonn, 1993), 19. For an overview, see Ingrid Skrypietz, "Militant Right-wing Extremism in Germany," *German Politics* 3(1) (April 1994): 133–139.
2. BMI, *Verfassungsschutzbericht 1997*, 70; BMI, *Verfassungsschutzbericht 2006*, 50–51; BMI, *Verfassungsschutzbericht 2007*, 52. In the 2007 and 2008 reports, the Republikaner is no longer listed as a right-wing organization because it has moderated its public stance.
3. James H. Anderson, "The Neo-Nazi Menace in Germany," *Conflict and Terrorism* 18(1) (January–March 1995): 39–46; *Deutsche Welle*, 27 December 2008; *Der Spiegel* Online, March 19, 2009.
4. Anderson, "The Neo-Nazi Menace in Germany," 41.
5. "Neo-Nazi Leader Christian Worch on Aims, Tactics," *Berlingske Tidende* (Copenhagen), August 5, 1993, reprinted in JPRS-TOT-94-024-L, June 15, 1994, 10; and Anderson, "The Neo-Nazi Menace in Germany," 42.
6. *New York Times*, September 28, 1992.
7. Uwe Backes and Patrick Moreau, *Die extreme Rechte in Deutschland: Geschichte – Gegenwärtige Gefahren – Ursachen – Gegenmassnahmen* (Munich: Akademischer Verlag, 1993), 135.
8. Ibid.
9. *taz*, April 26, 2002.
10. *Der Spiegel*, March 6, 1995.
11. Backes and Moreau, *Die extreme Rechte in Deutschland*, 136.
12. dpa news release, February 24, 1995.
13. National Socialist German Workers' Party/Foreign and Reconstruction Organization (AO: Auslands- und Aufbauorgaisation).

14. *Die Zeit*, January 13, 1995.
15. Backes and Moreau, *Die extreme Rechte in Deutschland*, 152–154.
16. Michael Schmidt, *Heute gehört uns die Strasse* ... *der Inside-Report aus der Neonazi-Szene* (Düsseldorf: Econ Verlag, 1993), 276.
17. Ibid., 277–278.
18. Backes and Moreau, *Die extreme Rechte in Deutschland*, 153.
19. *Frankfurter Allgemeine Zeitung*, August 22, 1995.
20. Backes and Moreau, *Die extreme Rechte in Deutschland*, 124–126.
21. Ingo Hasselbach and Tome Reiss, *Führer Ex: Memoirs of a Former Neo-Nazi* (New York: Random House, 1996), 94–95.
22. *New York Times*, February 2, 1994.
23. *taz*, February 12, 1998.
24. GIC, *The Week in Germany*, 18 November 1994; Arbeitsgemeinschaft verfolgter Sozialdemokraten, *AVS-Informationsdienst* 15(1) (January 1995): 9–10.
25. *taz*, June 1, 2007.
26. Bernd Siegler, "Der Apparat und die Rechten," in *Der Pakt: Die Rechten und der Staat*, ed. Bernd Siegler, Oliver Tolmein, and Charlotte Wiedemann (Göttingen: Verlag Die Werkstatt, 1993), 48–49.
27. *Der Spiegel*, January 12, 2001; *taz*, May 20, 2003.
28. BMI, *Verfassungsschutzbericht 2003*, 54–55; *taz*, March 18, 2009.
29. Ibid.
30. *taz*, March 22, 2003; *Süddeutsche Zeitung*, March 11, 2004.
31. *taz*, May 25, 2007.
32. *Süddeutsche Zeitung*, July 6, 1991.
33. *taz*, September 11, 2003; *Christian Science Monitor*, October 13, 2003.
34. *taz*, April 26, 2004; November 24, 2004; *Frankfurter Rundschau*, May 4, 2005.
35. Interview with Bernd Wagner, in *Die Zeit*, no. 27, July 1, 1999. For an overview, see Michael Kraske and Christian Werner, ... *und morgen das ganze Land: Neue Nazis, "befreite Zonen" und die tägliche Angst – ein Insiderbericht* (Freiburg: Heider, 2007).
36. Text "Schafft befreite Zonen" in *Stormfront*, n.d. See also *New York Times*, February 8, 1998; *Die Zeit*, no. 27, July 1, 1999; "Befreite Zonen," *Informationsdienst gegen Rechtsextremismus*, n.d.
37. *Die Zeit*, no. 27, July 1, 1999.
38. GIC, *The Week in Germany*, January 25, 2001.
39. BMI, *Extremismus und Gewalt*, vol. 2 (Bonn, 1993), 74.
40. BMI, *Verfassungsschutzbericht 2003*, 43.
41. *Rheinischer Merkur*, cited in GIC, *The German Tribune*, September 25, 1992.
42. *New York Times*, June 13, 1991.
43. *Der Spiegel*, 2/2001.
44. Thea Bauriedl, "Verstehen und doch nicht einverstanden sein: Zur Psychodynamik und Soziodynamik des Umgangs mit Rechtsradikalen in Deutschland," in *Rechtsextremismus bekämpfen: Aufklärung und Selbstvergewisserung*, ed Friedwart Maria Rudel (Essen: Klartext Verlag, 1995), 16–17; Zentrum Demokratische Kultur, "Eine aktuelle Einschätzung des rechtsextremistischen Potentials in Ostdeutschland," October 2000.
45. *Times* (London), November 13, 2004.
46. *New York Times*, February 28, 1999.
47. Associated Press news release, November 12, 2005.
48. *Expatica*, November 20, 2006.

49. Claus Leggewie, *Druck von Rechts: Wohin treibt die Bundesrepublik?* (Munich: Beck, 1993), 49–50.
50. *Die Zeit*, no. 41, 2002.
51. Joyce Marie Mushaben, "The Rise of Femi-Nazis? Female Participation in Right-Extremist Movements in Unified Germany," *German Politics* 5(2) (August 1996): 240, 243; Mushaben, "Rendering Right-Extremist Movements: Reflections on Betz and Minkenberg," *Politics* (CGGP Newsletter), no. 16 (Summer 2001): 10–13. In the United States, the ultra-conservative nationally syndicated radio host Rush Limbaugh has used the same term to denigrate the feminist movement.
52. GIC, *The Week in Germany*, December 10, 1993.
53. *taz*, March 29, 2001.
54. Kirsten Döhring, "Braune Schwestern im Aufwind?" *Der Rechte Rand*, April 30, 2005.
55. *New York Times*, September 28, 1992.
56. Hans-Joachim Maaz, "Gewalt, Rassismus und Rechtsextremismus in den östlichen Bundesländern," in *Rechtsradikale Gewalt im vereinigten Deutschland: Jugend im gesellschaftlichen Umbruch*, ed. Hans-Uwe Otto and Roland Merten (Opladen: Leske & Budrich), 178–181; Birgit Rommelspacher, "Männliche Gewalt und gesellschaftliche Dominanz," in Otto and Merten, *Rechtsradikale Gewalt*, 200–201.
57. *New York Times*, August 27, 2000; *taz*, October 13, 2000.
58. The Cologne Institute for Social Research and Social Policy conducted the study (GIC, *The Week in Review*, March 1, 1991).
59. Study by Christian Pfeiffer, Hanover criminologist (*Politik*, August 3, 2000).
60. See studies by Detlev Oesterreich, Gerda Lederer and colleagues, and Richard Stöss, cited by Werner Bergmann, "Anti-Semitism and Xenophobia in the East German Länder," *German Politics* 3(2) (August 1994): 267. See also Wolfgang Kühnel, "Gewalt durch Jugendliche im Osten Deutschlands," in *Rechtsradikale Gewalt*, ed. Otto and Merten, 237–246.
61. Professors Armin Falk, University of Bonn, and Josef Zweimüller, University of Zurich, conducted the study (Falk news release, August 26, 2005).
62. See Bernd Wagner, *Jugend-Gewalt-Szenen: Zu kriminologischen und historischen Aspekten in Ostdeutschland, Die achtziger und neunziger Jahre.* Berlin: dip, 1995.
63. See BMI, *Verfassungsschutzbericht*, various years.
64. Ibid.
65. Ibid.
66. BMI press release, March 30, 2007.
67. BMI, *Extremismus und Gewalt*, vol. 2 (Bonn, 1993), 20.
68. *The Local* (Stockholm), March 10, 2008; *Haaretz*, April 4, 2004; *Der Spiegel*, April 22, 2006.
69. *Frankfurter Rundschau* and *Tagesspiegel* survey, in http://www.f-r.de/fr/spezial/rechts/08.htm (September 27, 2000).
70. BMI, *Verfassungsschutzbericht 2006*, 44.
71. Surveys by Klaus Wahl, professor at the German Youth Institute, Munich, and Michael Kohlstruck, researcher, Technical University, Berlin, cited by *taz*, April 22, 2006.
72. *Die Zeit*, no. 29, July 17, 1992; "'Foreigners Out': Xenophobia and Right-wing Violence in Germany," *Helsinki Watch* (New York; Washington, DC, 1992), 17.
73. *Newsweek*, July 29, 1991.

74. Eva Kolinsky, "Multiculturalism in the Making? Non-Germans and Civil Society in the New Länder," *German Politics* 7(3) (December 1998): 209.
75. "'Foreigners Out,'" *Helsinki Watch*, 6; Roger Karapin, *Protest Politics in Germany: Movements on the Left and Right Since the 1960s* (University Park, PA: Pennsylvania State University Press, 2007), 191–218.
76. Ian J. Kagedan, "Contemporary Right-wing Extremism in Germany," in *The Extreme Right: Freedom and Security at Risk*, ed. Aurel Braun and Stephen Scheinberg (Boulder, CO: Westview Press, 1997), 113–114; Frank Tausch, "Hoyerswerda wird ausländerfrei," in *Un-Heil über Deutschland*, ed. Manfred Leier (Hamburg: Gruner & Jahr, 1993), 53–59.
77. Alan Watson, *The Germans: Who Are They Now?* 2nd rev. edn (Chicago: edition Q, 1995), 367.
78. Hasselbach and Reiss, *Führer Ex*, 302–303.
79. Walter Wüllenweber, "Der Feuerschein aus Rostock," in *Un-Heil über Deutschland*, ed. Leier, 21–31.
80. "'Foreigners Out,'" *Helsinki Watch*, 18–19.
81. Kagedan, "Contemporary Right-wing Extremism in Germany," 115.
82. "'Foreigners Out,'" *Helsinki Watch*, 20; *Die Zeit*, August 28, 1992.
83. *Die Zeit*, August 28, 1992; *New York Times*, March 4, 1993.
84. *New York Times*, December 12, 1992.
85. Yaron Svoray and Nick Taylor, *In Hitler's Shadow* (New York: Doubleday, 1994), 256.
86. *New York Times*, June 2, 1993.
87. *Berliner Zeitung*, November 2, 1993.
88. *Rhein-Neckar-Zeitung*, November 3, 1993.
89. Unidentified German newspaper, cited in the *New York Times*, November 2, 1993. See also GIC, *The Week in Germany*, November 5, 1993.
90. Nicholas Fraser, *The Voice of Modern Hatred: Tracing the Rise of Neo-Fascism in Europe* (Woodstock, NY: The Overlook Press, 2000), 55–61.
91. *New York Times*, February 8, 1998.
92. *Berliner Zeitung*, February 13, 1998.
93. Reuters dispatch, May 27, 1998; *Germany Alert*, May 28, 1998.
94. His name originally was Farid Guendoul.
95. *New York Times*, February 24, 1999; *Süddeutsche Zeitung*, September 24, 1999; March 2, 2001.
96. *Süddeutsche Zeitung*, March 2, 2001.
97. *taz*, December 12, 2000.
98. *taz*, December 21, 2004; *Der Spiegel*, March 8, 2005.
99. *Mut-gegen-rechte-Gewalt*, October 22, 2004.
100. *UK Telegraph*, April 30, 2006.
101. "Racism Warning Has German Hackles Raised," http://service.spiegel.de/cache/international/0,1518,416904,00.html (May 18, 2006).
102. *Frankfurter Rundschau*, October 9, 2000; November 23, 2000.
103. www.spiegel.de/international/germany/0,1518,503227,00.html (August 31, 2007); *taz*, December 21, 2008.
104. *Informationsdienst gegen Rechtsextremismus*, December 21, 2000.
105. *International Herald Tribune*, May 1, 2007.
106. GIC, *The Week in Germany*, January 21, 1994.
107. Bergmann, "Anti-Semitism and Xenophobia in the East German Länder," *German Politics* 3(2) (August, 1994): 273–274; *taz*, April 26, 2000.

108. Adolf Diamant, *Geschändete jüdische Friedhöfe in Deutschland 1945–1999* (Potsdam: Verlag für Berlin-Brandenburg, 2000).
109. *Süddeutsche Zeitung*, December 20, 1998; *taz*, September 25, 2000 and January 9, 2001.
110. *Süddeutsche Zeitung*, August 16, 1999.
111. *New York Times*, October 4, 2000; *taz*, January 30, 2001; July 27, 2001.
112. Werner Bergmann, "Antisemitismus in Deutschland," in *Rechtsextremismus in der Bundesrepublik Deutschland: Eine Bilanz*, ed. Wilfried Schubarth and Richard Stöss (Opladen: Leske & Budrich, 2001), 144.
113. *BBC News*, February 26, 2007.
114. *BBC News*, February 27, 2007.
115. *M & C News*, October 24, 2006; DW-World.de, *Deutsche Welle*, October 25, 2006.
116. DW-World.de, *Deutsche Welle*, October 25, 2006.
117. Rainer Erb, "Antisemitische Straftäter der Jahre 1993–1995," in *Jahrbuch für Antisemitismusforschung* 6, ed. Wolfgang Benz (Frankfurt: Campus Verlag, 1997), 169–171.
118. Thomas Heury, "Current Anti-Semitism in Eastern Germany," *Post-Holocaust and Anti-Semitism* 59 (August 1, 2007).
119. *taz*, October 9, 2000; December 8, 2000.
120. *Frankfurter Rundschau*, May 26, 2003.
121. Of the seventeen prohibited groups, the following ten have had the most visibility. They are listed according to whether they are prohibited at the federal or Land level, and the date of prohibition: the Nationalist Front (federal, November 1992); German Alternative (federal, December 1992); National Offensive (federal, December 1992); National Bloc (Bavaria, June 1993); Viking Youth (federal, November 1994); Free Workers Party (federal, February 1995); National List (Hamburg, February 1995); Direct Action/Central Germany (Brandenburg, May 1995); Comradeship Oberhavel (Brandenburg, August 1997); and Heide-Heim (Lower Saxony, February 1998). See Lee McGowan, *The Radical Right in Germany: 1870 to the Present* (London: Longman, 2002), 192, and Steffen Kailitz, "Aktuelle Entwicklungen im deutschen Rechtsextremismus," study no. 17, Konrad-Adenauer-Stiftung, Sankt Augustin, November 2000 (mimeographed), 33–34.
122. *Nürnberger Nachrichten*, September 1, 1992.
123. *New York Times*, January 1, 1993.
124. *New York Times*, September 26, 2004.
125. Landesamt für Verfassungsschutz Hamburg, "Gibt es eine Zusammenarbeit Deutscher Rechtsextremisten mit Islamisten und arabischen Nationalisten?" news release, January 17, 2001.
126. *taz*, September 19 and 22, 2008.
127. *Süddeutsche Zeitung*, March 4, 1998.

5.   Tools of Propaganda and Recruitment

1. For a survey of the right-wing media, see Thomas Pfeiffer, *Für Volk und Vaterland: Das Mediennetz der Rechten – Presse, Musik, Internet* (Berlin: Aufbau Taschenbuch Verlag, 2002).
2. Armin Pfahl-Traughber, "Der organisierte Rechtsextremismus in Deutschland nach 1945," in *Rechtsextremismus in der Bundesrepublik Deutschland: Eine Bilanz*, ed. Wilfried Schubarth and Richard Stöss (Opladen: Leske & Budrich, 2001), 75.

3. BMI, *Verfassungsschutzbericht 2005* (Berlin, 2006), 52. In 1999, 57 publications appeared with a total yearly circulation of 6.5 million (BMI, *Verfassungsschutzbericht 1999* (Berlin, 2000), 79).
4. Annette Linke, *Der Multimillionär Frey und die DVU: Daten, Fakten, Hintergründe* (Essen: Klartext Verlag, 1994), 73–74.
5. Armin Pfahl-Traughber, *Rechtsextremismus: Eine kritische Bestandsaufnahme nach der Wiedervereinigung* (Bonn: Bouvier, 1993), 125–126; *Blick nach rechts*, No. 15, July 24, 1996.
6. Linke, *Der Multimillionär Frey und die DVU*, 67–68.
7. *Junge Welt*, July 18, 1996.
8. For a survey of the more moderate journals that are part of the New Right scene, see Chapter 6.
9. Pfahl-Traughber, "Der organisierte Rechtsextremismus," 75.
10. Uwe Backes and Patrick Moreau, *Die extreme Rechte in Deutschland: Geschichte – Gegenwärtige Gefahren – Ursachen – Gegenmassnahmen.* 2nd edn (Munich: Akademischer Verlag, 1994), 229.
11. BMI, *Aktuelle Aspekte des Rechtsextremismus* (Bonn, 1994), 86.
12. *Junge Welt*, February 22, 2007.
13. BMI, *Verfassungsschutzbericht 2005*, 132.
14. The German publisher is not to be confused with Berg academic publisher in Oxford, England.
15. http://www.weltnetzladen.com/index.html (October 8, 2006).
16. Werner Filmer and Heribert Schwan, *Was von Hitler blieb: 50 Jahre nach der Machtergreifung* (Frankfurt am Main: Ullstein, 1983), 100–101.
17. Rand C. Lewis, *A Nazi Legacy: Right-Wing Extremism in Postwar Germany* (New York: Praeger, 1991), 41.
18. Rainer Erb, "Antisemitismus und Antizionismus," in *Fünfzig Jahre Israel: Vision und Wirklichkeit*, ed. Heiner Lichtenstein and Otto Romberg (Bonn: Bundeszentrale für politische Bildung, 1998), 229.
19. BMI, *Verfassungsschutzbericht 2005*, 109–110.
20. BMI, *Verfassungsschutzbericht 2006*, 105–106.
21. *Der Rechte Rand*, November/December 2004.
22. Alan Cornell, "The Depiction of Neo-Nazism in Police Shows on German Television," *German Politics and Society* 15(1) (Spring 1997): 22–45.
23. *New York Times*, December 15, 1993.
24. Angelika Nguyen, "Der Fall Ingo H.," *Freitag* 50 (December 6, 2002); *Jungle World*, March 3, 2004.
25. *Washington Post*, October 18, 2007.
26. For overviews see Burkhard Schröder, *Neonazis und Computernetze: Wie Rechtsradikale neue Kommunikationsformen nutzen* (Reinbek: Rowohlt, 1995); Bundesamt für Verfassungsschutz, *Rechtsextremistische Bestrebungen im Internet* (Cologne, 2000); Rainer Fromm and Barbara Kernbach, *Rechtsextremismus im Internet* (Munich: Olzog, 2001).
27. Cited in *Süddeutsche Zeitung*, November 16, 2000; *Mut gegen rechte Gewalt*, July 3, 2005.
28. *Blick nach rechts* 21(7) (1 April 2004): 5.
29. *taz*, August 30, 2000.
30. *Süddeutsche Zeitung*, February 7, 2001; *New York Times*, February 20, 2001; Klaus-Henning Rosen in *Blick nach rechts*, December 18, 2003.
31. International Middle East Media Center, news release, March 22, 2008.

32. *Süddeutsche Zeitung*, January 8, 2001; *Der Spiegel*, June 10, 2004.
33. *Süddeutsche Zeitung*, January 8, 2001.
34. *Süddeutsche Zeitung*, September 20, 2001.
35. Bundesministerium des Innern, *Verfassungsschutzbericht 1997* (hectographed, n.d.), 78–80.
36. Bundesministerium des Innern, *Verfassungsschutzbericht 1999* (Berlin, 2000), 84.
37. *New York Times*, August 9, 1999.
38. Reuters news agency, 6 December 2007; *Times Online* (London), December 7, 2007 www.technology.timesonline.co.uk/tol/news/tech_and _web/article3017069.ece.
39. Lewis, *A Nazi Legacy*, 84–85; Ian J. Kagedan, "Contemporary Right-Wing Extremism in Germany," in *The Extreme Right: Freedom and Security at Risk*, ed. Aurel Braun and Stephen Scheinberg (Boulder, CO: Westview Press, 1997), 122–134.
40. *New York Times*, November 10, 2001.
41. Wolfgang Benz, "KZ-Manager im Kinderzimmer: Rechtsextreme Computerspiele," in *Rechtsextremismus in Deutschland: Voraussetzungen, Zusammenhänge, Wirkungen*, ed. Wolfgang Betz. Rev. edn (Frankfurt am Main: Fischer Taschenbuch, 1994), 219.
42. Informations-, Dokumentations- und Aktionszentrum gegen Ausländerfeindlichkeit, für eine multikulturelle Zukunft, *Rechte Jugendliche und ihre Organisationsformen* (Düsseldorf: IDA, 1994), 90–91.
43. Nicholas Fraser, *The Voice of Modern Hatred: Tracing the Rise of Neo-Fascism in Europe* (Woodstock, NY: The Overlook Press, 2001), 85–86.
44. Benz, "KZ-Manager im Kinderzimmer," 221–227.
45. *Response* (Simon Wiesenthal Center) 21(2) (Summer 2000): 5.
46. *Süddeutsche Zeitung*, January 8, 2001; *Der Spiegel*, June 10, 2004.
47. According to the *New York Times* (December 2, 1992), the name "Oi" plays on the English name for the Nazi-era leisure-time organization "Strength through Joy." The first German LP of neo-Nazi rock was titled "Strength through Oi."
48. BMI, *Verfassungsschutzbericht 2007*, 101–103.
49. *US News & World Report*, January 23, 2006.
50. *The Independent*, August 17, 2005.
51. SPD, *AVS-Informationsdienst* 21(2) (3 December 2000): 19.
52. Innenministerium Mecklenburg-Vorpommern, *Skinheads* (Schwerin, 1996), 16–17; *New York Times*, December 2, 1992. For details see Renée Karthee, "Rock-Musik unterm Hakenkreuz," in *Un-Heil über Deutschland: Fremdenhass und Neofaschismus nach der Wiedervereinigung*, ed. Manfred Leier (Hamburg: Gruner & Jahr, 1993), 104–119. See also Dieter Baacke et al., *Rock von Rechts*. 2 vols (Bielefeld: Gesellschaft für Medienpädagogik und Kommunikationskultur, 1994, 1999); Michael Weiss, *White Noise – Rechts-Rock, Skinhead-Musik, Blood & Honour* (Hamburg: rat Verlag, 2000).
53. *Frankfurter Allgemeine Zeitung*, September 26, 1998; *Die Zeit*, January 31, 2002; BMI, *Verfassungsschutzbericht 2006*, 101.
54. Michael Weiss of the Antifaschistische Infoblatt, cited in *Frankfurter Rundschau*, August 7, 2000. See also Klaus Farin, "Rechts-Rock," in *Rechtsextremismus in Deutschland: Voraussetzungen, Zusammenhänge, Wirkungen*, ed. Betz, 142–144.
55. *Newsweek*, December 14, 1992.
56. *Newsweek*, December 14, 1992; *New York Times*, December 3, 1992.
57. *New York Times*, August 9, 2005.
58. *European Jewish Press*, October 30, 2006.
59. *New York Times*, February 8, 1994.

60. Ibid.
61. Wolfgang Kühnel, "Hitler's Grandchildren? The Reemergence of a Right-Wing Social Movement in Germany," in *Nation and Race: the Developing Euro-American Racist Subculture*, ed. Jeffrey Kaplan and Tore Bjørgo (Boston: Northeastern University Press, 1998), 168.
62. *Frankfurter Allgemeine Zeitung*, September 26, 1998.
63. SPD, *AVS-Informationsdienst* 20(5/6) (November–December 1999): 16.
64. *The Cowl* (Providence College, RI), March 17, 2005.
65. *Deutsche Welle*, September 15, 2004.
66. Claire Berlinski, "Rammstein's Rage," *JEWCY*, July 2, 2005.
67. BMI, *Verfassungsschutzbericht 2003*, 44.
68. Bernd Wagner, ed., *Handbuch Rechtsextremismus: Netzwerke, Parteien, Organisationen, Ideologiezentren, Medien* (Reinbek: Rowohlt, 1994), 182–183.

6. The New Right

1. For details, see Roger Woods, *Germany's New Right as Culture and Politics* (Basingstoke: Palgrave Macmillan, 2007); Günter Bartsch, *Revolution von Rechts? Ideologie und Organisation der Neuen Rechten* (Freiburg: Heiderbücherei, 1975); Diethelm Prowe, "National Identity and Racial Nationalism in the New Germany: Nazism versus the Contemporary Radical Right," *German Politics and Society* 15(1) (Spring 1997): 1–21; and Alice Brauner-Orthen, *Die Neue Rechte in Deutschland* (Leverkusen: Leske & Budrich, 2001). For a discussion of the New Right, see Jacob Heilbrunn, Robert Lieber, Hans-Georg Betz, and Peter Schneider, *Germany's New Right. Revival of Nationalism or Call for Normalcy?* (Washington, DC: Friedrich Ebert Foundation, 1997).
2. Michael Venner, *Nationale Identität: Die Neue Rechte und die Grauzone zwischen Konservatismus und Rechtsextremismus* (Cologne: Papyrossa, 1994), 15–17. On Nouvelle Droite, see Michael Minkenberg, "The New Right in France and Germany: Nouvelle Droite, Neue Rechte, and the New Right Radical Parties," in *The Revival of Right-Wing Extremism in the Nineties*, ed. Peter H. Merkl and Michael Minkenberg (London: Frank Cass, 1997), 71–79.
3. Volker Ullrich, "Das Weimar-Syndrom: Zur Geschichte und Aktualität der Parteienverdrossenheit in Deutschland," in *Extremismus der Mitte: Vom rechten Verständnis deutscher Nation*, ed. Hans-Martin Lohmann (Frankfurt am Main: Fischer Taschenbuch Verlag, 1994), 62–63.
4. See Clemens Heni, *Salonfähigkeit der Neuen Rechten: "Nationale Identität," Antisemitismus und Antiamerikanismus in der politischen Kultur der Bundesrepublik Deutschland 1970–2005: Henning Eichberg als Exempel* (Marburg: Tectum, 2007). In 1982 Eichberg immigrated to Denmark where he remained active politically, even seeking ties to Danish socialists.
5. Venner, *Nationale Identität*, 64–76.
6. Ibid., 50–58.
7. Jan Herman Brinks, "Germany's New Right," in *Nationalist Myths and Modern Media: Contested Identities in the Age of Globalization*, ed. Jan Herman Brinks, Stella Rock, and Edward Timms (London: Tauris, 2006), 128.
8. Jonathan Olsen, *Nature and Nationalism: Right-Wing Ecology and the Politics of Identity in Contemporary Germany* (Basingstoke: Macmillan, 1999), 130.

9. Hans-Gerd Jaschke, "Sub-Cultural Aspects of Right-Wing Extremism," in *Political Culture in Germany*, ed. Dirk Berg-Schlosser and Ralf Rytlewski (New York: St. Martin's Press, 1993), 130. See also Uwe Backes, "Gestalt und Bedeutung des intellektuellen Rechtsextremismus in Deutschland," *Aus Politik und Zeitgeschichte*, B 46/2001, 24–30.

10. Paul Hockenos, "Making Hate Safe Again in Europe," *The Nation*, September 19, 1994, 273.

11. For details, see Reinhard Opitz, *Faschismus und Neofaschismus* (Frankfurt: Verlag Marxistische Blätter, 1984), 351–370.

12. Armin Pfahl-Traughber, *"Konservative Revolution" und "Neue Rechte": Rechtsextremistische Intellektuelle gegen den demokratischen Verfassungsstaat* (Opladen: Leske & Budrich, 1998), 164–170.

13. Venner, *Nationale Identität*, 47–48.

14. Claus Leggewie, *Der Geist steht rechts: Ausflüge in die Denkfabriken der Wende* (Berlin: Rotbuch, 1987), 178–186.

15. Jay Julian Rosellini, *Literary Skinheads? Writing from the Right in Reunified Germany* (West Lafayette, IN: Purdue University Press, 2000), 36–41.

16. Ibid., 43–63.

17. Pfahl-Traughber, *"Konservative Revolution,"* 170–173.

18. Cited by Jacob Heilbrunn, "Germany's New Right," *Foreign Affairs* 75(6) (November–December 1996): 88. Several German specialists rebutted his article in Josef Joffe et al., "Mr. Heilbrunn's Planet: On Which the Germans Are Back," *Foreign Affairs* 76(2) (March–April 1997), 152–161.

19. Pfahl-Traughber, *"Konservative Revolution,"* 173–179.

20. Elliot Neaman, "A New Conservative Revolution? Neo-Nationalism, Collective Memory, and the New Right in Germany since Unification," in *Antisemitism and Xenophobia in Germany after Unification*, ed. Hermann Kurthen, Werner Bergmann, and Rainer Erb (New York: Oxford University Press, 1997), 194–195.

21. Annette Linke, *Der Multimillionär Frey und die DVU: Daten, Fakten, Hintergründe* (Essen: Klartext Verlag, 1994), 81–82.

22. Some specialists cite higher figures ranging from 35,000 copies (Wolfgang Gessenharter in *Kippt die Republik? Die Neue Rechte und ihre Unterstützung durch Politik und Medien* (Munich: Theodor Knaur, 1994), 195) to 100,000 copies (*MediumMagazin* 2/94). For an appraisal of the journal, see Helmut Kellershohn, *Das Plagiat: Der Völkische Nationalismus der "Jungen Freiheit"* (Duisburg: DISS-Verlag, 1994).

23. Hans Sarkowicz, "Publizistik in der Grau- und Braunzone," in *Rechtsextremismus in Deutschland: Vorraussetzungen, Zusammenhänge, Wirkungen*, ed. Wolfgang Betz (Frankfurt am Main: Fischer, 1994), 70.

24. Bundesamt für Verfassungsschutz, *Rechtsextremismus in der Bundesrepublik Deutschland: ein Lagebild*, 25–26.

25. Sarkowicz, "Publizistik in der Grau- und Braunzone," 69; *konkret* 1/95.

26. *Frankfurter Rundschau*, March 4, 1982.

27. Ibid.

28. Ibid.

29. Wolfgang Gessenharter, "Das Weltbild der 'Neuen Rechten,'" in *Rechtsextremismus in der Bundesrepublik Deutschland*, ed. Werner Billing, Andreas Barz, and Stephan Wienk-Borgert (Baden-Baden: Nomos, 1993), 70–71.

30. Armin Pfahl-Traughber, *Rechtsextremismus: Eine kritische Bestandsaufnahme nach der Wiedervereinigung* (Bonn: Bouvier, 1993), 106–109.

31. Other New Right journals, such as *Signal: the Patriotic Magazine*, *Sleipnir*, and *Staatsbriefe* (State Letters), have appeared less frequently than envisaged initially.

32. See Ernst Nolte, *The Three Faces of Fascism: Action Française, Italian Fascism, National Socialism* (London: Weidenfeld & Nicolson, 1965) and *Das Vergehen der Vergangenheit: Antwort an meine Kritiker im sogenannten Historikerstreit* (Berlin: Ullstein, 1987); Ernst Piper, ed., *"Historikerstreit": Die Dokumentation der Kontroverse um die Einzigartigkeit der nationalsozialistschen Judenvernichtung* (Munich: Piper, 1987); translated by James Knowlton and Truett Cates as *Forever in the Shadow of Hitler? Original Documents of the Historikerstreit, the Controversy concerning the Singularity of the Holocaust* (Atlantic Highlands, NJ: Humanities Press, 1993). See also Peter Wyden, *The Hitler Virus: the Insidious Legacy of Adolf Hitler* (New York: Arcade Publishers, 2001), 183–193.

33. Cited by Wyden, *The Hitler Virus*, 193.

34. For a *Frankfurter Allgemeine Zeitung* appraisal, see John Ely, "The *Frankfurter Allgemeine Zeitung* and Contemporary National-Conservatism," *German Politics and Society* 13(2) (Summer 1995): 81–121.

35. Rosellini, *Literary Skinheads?*, 35.

36. Cited by Heilbrunn, "Germany's New Right," 91. See also GIC, *The Week in Germany*, May 12, 1995.

37. Rosellini, *Literary Skinheads?*, 35–36.

38. *Junge Freiheit*, July 19, 1996.

39. *New York Times*, October 12, 1993.

40. Personal interview with CDU central office staff member, Bonn, August 10, 1989.

41. Gessenharter, "Das Weltbild der 'Neuen Rechten,'" 71–72.

42. *taz*, April 21, 2007.

43. *Frankfurter Rundschau*, July 7, 1989.

44. *Junge Welt*, November 3, 2003.

45. *New York Times*, November 5, 2003.

46. Jeffrey M. Peck, "You are making it difficult, Mr. Hohmann. Some very personal thoughts on anti-Semitism," American Institute for Contemporary German Studies (*AICGS Advisor*), November 26, 2003.

47. *New York Times*, April 1, 2000.

48. *taz*, September 10, 2001.

49. *New York Times*, January 14, 2008.

50. *Germany Alert*, June 27, 1998.

51. *Freitag*, November 24, 2000; *Süddeutsche Zeitung*, January 12, 2001.

52. Brinks, "Germany's New Right," 135.

53. *Deutsche Welle*, February 6, 2005; *Süddeutsche Zeitung*, February 8, 2005; *International Herald Tribune*, March 1, 2005.

54. *BBC News*, June 5, 2003; Heilbrunn, "Germany's New Right," 86–87.

55. Cited in Konrad H. Jarausch, Hinrich C. Seeba, and David P. Conradt, "The Presence of the Past: Culture, Opinion, and Identity in Germany," in *After Unity, Reconfiguring German Identities*, ed. Konrad H. Jarausch (Providence and Oxford: Berghahn Books, 1997), 44.

56. Ibid., 41, 44, 45.

57. *New York Times*, May 1, 1995.

58. Kurt Lenk, *Rechts, wo die Mitte ist: Studien zur Ideologie: Rechtsextremismus, Nationalsozialismus, Konservatismus* (Baden-Baden: Nomos, 1994), 380–383.

59. *New York Times*, December 29, 1998. For detailed analysis, see Caroline Pearce, *Contemporary Germany and the Nazi Legacy: Remembrance, Politics and the Dialectic of Normality* (Basingstoke: Palgrave Macmillan, 2008), 44–79.
60. Rosellini, *Literary Skinheads?*, 182.
61. Undated poll cited in the *Canadian Jewish News*, June 30, 2005.
62. The Balkan Action Council, December 10, 1998.
63. *New York Times*, November 29, 1998.
64. The Balkan Action Council, December 10, 1998.
65. *New York Times*, June 6, 2002; GIC, *The Week in Germany*, May 31, 2002.
66. *Die Zeit*, 20/2002; *Freitag*, May 17, 2002.
67. *Die Zeit*, 20/2002.
68. *New York Times*, March 20, 2001.
69. Ibid.
70. *taz*, March 22, 2001.
71. *New York Times*, November 23, 1997; January 10, 2001.
72. Ipos Institute of Mannheim poll, cited in GIC, *The Week in Germany*, November 30, 2001.
73. Daniel J. Goldenhagen, *Hitler's Willing Executioners: Ordinary Germans and the Holocaust* (New York: Alfred A. Knopf, 1996).
74. Cited in the *Charlotte Observer* (NC), July 1, 2006.
75. GIC, *The Week in Germany*, March 23, 2003.
76. Margarete Jäger, "Wie die Rechte Sprache prägt Steilvorlagen von Rechtsaussen," in *Rechte Netzwerke – eine Gefahr*, ed. Stephan Braun and Daniel Hörsch (Wiesbaden: Verlag für Sozialwissenschaften, 2004), 53; *Der Rechte Rand* 68 (January–February 2001).
77. *Süddeutsche Zeitung*, December 4, 2000; *Frankfurter Allgemeine Zeitung*, May 10, 2001; *New York Times*, November 20, 2000; May 13, 2001.
78. GIC, *The Week in Germany*, December 5, 2003.
79. Cited in *San Diego Union Tribune*, July 5, 2006.
80. Ibid.
81. Ibid.
82. See Pfahl-Traughber, *"Konservative Revolution" und "Neue Rechte,"* 228–230; Claus Leggewie, *Druck von rechts: Wohin treibt die Bundesrepublik?* (Munich: C. H. Beck, 1993). See also Heilbrunn et al., *Germany's New Right*; Gessenharter, *Kippt die Republik*, 126–128.
83. *Frankfurter Rundschau*, December 18, 1997.

7. Responses: Public and Private

1. Basic Law (*Grundgesetz*), Articles I (I); 2 (I); 3 (I) and (3).
2. UN International Convention on the Elimination of All Forms of Racial Discrimination, 1966, Article 5 (b); signed by the FRG on October 9, 1968, and ratified on December 17, 1973.
3. Document of the Copenhagen Meeting of the Conference on the Human Dimension of the CSCE (1990), paragraph 40.2.
4. Jewish Telegraph Agency, May 18, 1998.
5. Jane Kramer, "Neo-Nazis: a Chaos in the Head," *The New Yorker* (June 14, 1993), 69.
6. For a complete list and description of cases from 1990 to 2000 in which a death occurred, see *Der Tagesspiegel on Line*, September 14, 2000, http://195.170.124.152/

archiv/2000/09/13/ak-po-de-8.html. See also Rudolf Wassermann, "Die Heraus-forderung der Justiz durch Extremismus und Gewalt," BMI, *Extremismus und Gewalt*, Band III (Bonn, 1994), 105–124.

7. Dina Porat, Roni Stauber, and Raphael Vago, eds, *Anti-Semitism Worldwide 1995/6* (Tel Aviv: Tel Aviv University, 1996), 56–57.

8. Alan Watson, *Dangers from the Right?* (Chicago: edition Q, 1993), 34–35.

9. Klaus Breymann, "Gewalttaten rechtsorientierter Skinheads in Deutschland," in *Rechtsradikale Gewalt im vereinigten Deutschland: Jugend im gesellschaftlichen Umbruch*, ed. Hans-Uwe Otto and Roland Merten (Opladen: Leske & Budrich, 1993), 299–300.

10. GIC, *The Week in Germany*, January 12, 2001.

11. *Der Spiegel*, November 12, 1990.

12. Ingo Hasselbach and Winfried Bonengel, *Die Abrechnung: Ein Neonazi steigt aus* (Berlin: Aufbau, 1993), 113.

13. "'Foreigners Out,' Xenophobia and Right-Wing Violence in Germany" (New York: Helsinki Watch, October 1992), citing the government's response to a PDS parliamentary question, December 6, 1991, 34.

14. Peter Cullen, "Crime and Policing in Germany in the 1990s," in *Developments in German Politics 2*, ed. Gordon Smith, William E. Paterson, and Stephen Padgett (Durham, NC: Duke University Press, 1996), 289.

15. Cited by Rand C. Lewis, *A Nazi Legacy: Right-Wing Extremism in Postwar Germany* (New York: Praeger, 1991), 84.

16. Cullen, "Crime and Policing," 290; *Frankfurter Rundschau*, May 5, 1998.

17. Alan Watson, *The Germans: Who Are They Now?*, 2nd rev. edn (London: edition Q, 1995), 392–393.

18. Hans Oberländer, "Wie die Justiz mit Neonazis umgeht," in *Un-Heil über Deutsch-land: Fremdenhass und Neofaschismus nach der Wiedervereinigung*, ed. Manfred Leier (Hamburg: Gruner & Jahr, 1993), 180–182.

19. Martin Kreickenbaum, "German interior ministers end separation of police and intelligence services," *World Socialist Web Site*, http//www.wsws.org/articles/2004/jul2004/germ-j20.shtml.

20. *taz*, May 23, 2006.

21. *taz*, September 13, 2006.

22. GIC, *The Week in Germany*, September 30, 1994.

23. "'Foreigners Out,'" 34.

24. GIC, *The Week in Germany*, November 22, 1991; *New York Times*, November 30, 1991.

25. *New York Times*, October 10, 1991.

26. Watson, *The Germans: Who Are They Now?*, 390–396.

27. "'Foreigners Out,'" 34.

28. Irina Bohn, Dieter Kreft, Gerd Stüwe, and Georg Weigel, "Das Aktionsprogramm gegen Aggression und Gewalt," in *Rechtsradikale Gewalt im vereinigten Deutschland*, ed. Otto and Merten, 304.

29. Ian J. Kagedan, "Contemporary Right-Wing Extremism in Germany," in *The Extreme Right: Freedom and Security at Risk*, ed. Aurel Braun and Stephen Scheinberg (Boulder, CO: Westview Press, 1997), 122–123.

30. Ibid., 120–121.

31. Peter O'Brien, *Beyond the Swastika* (London: Routledge, 1996), 71. See also Brett Klopp, *German Multiculturalism: Immigration Integration and the Transformation of Citizenship* (Westport, CT: Praeger, 2002).

32. Hajo Funke, "Rechtsextemismus – Zeitgeist, Politik und Gewalt," in *Rechts-extremismus: Ideologie und Gewalt,* ed. Richard Faber, Hajo Funke, and Gerhard Schoenberner (Berlin: Gedenkstätte Haus der Wannsee Konferenz, 1995), 30–33.

33. *Süddeutsche Zeitung,* February 23, 2000.

34. *Süddeutsche Zeitung,* June 16, 2000.

35. *taz,* April 24, 1998.

36. Other organizations were the Information, Documentation and Action Center against Xenophobia and for a Multicultural Future; the Foundation for Democratic Youth; Action Courage; and the Network for Democracy and Courage.

37. *Süddeutsche Zeitung,* July 31, 2000.

38. *taz,* February 15, 2002.

39. *Süddeutsche Zeitung,* February 14, 2001.

40. *New York Times,* July 18, 2001.

41. *Frankfurter Allgemeine Zeitung Weekly,* February 4, 2005.

42. *Deutsche Welle,* DW-World.de, October 25, 2006, http://www.dw-world.de/dw/article/0.2144.2214527html.

43. AVS-Informationsdienst, Vol. 21, No. 1, February 2000.

44. *Deutsche Welle,* DW-World.de, October 25, 2006, http://www.dw-world.de/dw/article/0.2144.2214527html.

45. *Deutsche Welle,* DW-World.de, November 25, 2006, http://www.dw-world.de/dw/article/0.2144.2245946.00html.

46. *Deutsche Welle,* DW-World.de, October 17, 2006, http://www.dw-world.de/dw/article/0.2144.2206348.00html.

47. Wolfgang Kraushaar, "Radikalisierung der Mitte: Auf dem Weg zur Berliner Republik," in *Rechtsextremismus: Ideologie und Gewalt,* ed. Faber, Funke, and Schoenberner, 58–60.

48. Anja Weusthoff and Rainer Zeimentz, eds, *Aufsteh'n: Aktionen Gegen Rechts: Ein Handbuch.* 2nd rev. edn (Bonn: Vorwärts, 1994), 19–35.

49. *taz,* August 28, 1998; *Der Rechte Rand* 68 (January/February 2001): 7–8; 70 (May–June 2001): 5–6. See also Karl Weber, *Rechte Männer – eine sozialpsychologische Studie zu Rassismus, Neofaschismus und Gewerkschaften* (Hamburg: VSA-Verlag, 2001).

50. *taz,* August 4, 2000.

51. *New York Times,* December 4, 1992.

52. GIC, *The Week in Germany,* June 18, 1993.

53. For a description of projects, see Bernd Wagner, ed., *Handbuch Rechts-extremismus: Netzwerke, Parteien, Organisationen, Ideologiezentren, Medien* (Reinbek: Rowohlt, 1994), cited in Harald Wachowitz, "Ein Projekt mit rechten Jugendlichen," in *Wer redet davon Entwarnung? Texte und Analysen zum aktuellen Rechtsextremismus,* authors' collective (Berlin: edition ost, 1995), 145; Kurt Möller and Siegfried Schiele, eds, *Gewalt und Rechtsextremismus: Ideen und Projekte für soziale Arbeit und politische Bildung* (Schwalbach: Wochenschau-Verlag, 1996).

54. Klaus Seibert, "Bündnisarbeit in Maintal," in *Wer redet da von Entwarnung? Texte und Analysen zum aktuellen Rechtsextremismus,* authors' collective (Berlin: edition ost, 1995), 148-50.

55. Harald Wachowitz, "Ein Projekt mit rechten Jugendlichen," in *Wer redet da von Entwarnung?,* 146–147. For an overview of Land Brandenburg activities, see Julius H. Schoeps, Gideon Botsch, Christoph Kopke, and Lars Rensmann, eds, *Rechtsex-tremismus in Brandenburg: Handbuch für Analyse, Prävention und Intervention* (Berlin: Verlag für Berlin-Brandenburg, 2007).

56. Weusthoff and Zeimentz, eds, *Aufsteh'n,* 45–48, 98.

57. Ibid., 108–111.
58. *New York Times* and *taz*, November 10, 2000.
59. *Deutsche Welle*, DW-World.de, http://www.dw-world.de/dw/article/0.2144.2317 216.00.html; *taz*, April 21, 2007.
60. GIC, "Holocaust Education in Germany," May 13, 1998.
61. Kagedan, "Contemporary Right-Wing Extremism in Germany," 122–123.
62. Helmut Willems, Stefanie Würtz, and Roland Eckert, *Forschungsprojekt: Analyse fremdenfeindlicher Straftäter* (Bonn: BMI, 1994), 80–81.
63. Hilde Schramm, "Handeln in der Schule gegen Rechtsextremismus," in *Rechtsextremismus: Ideologie und Gewalt*, ed. Faber, Funke, and Schoenberner, 144–147.
64. *Frankfurter Rundschau*, March 3, 2001.
65. Hartmut Castner and Thilo Castner, "Rechtsextemistische Strömungen in der Schule und pädagogische Gegenmassnahmen," in *Rechtsradikale Gewalt im vereinigten Deutschland*, ed. Hans-Uwe Otto and Roland Merten (Opladen: Leske & Budrich, 1993), 389.
66. *New York Times*, April 18, 2003.
67. *taz*, March 3, 2000.
68. *New York Times*, February 4, 2008.
69. *Süddeutsche Zeitung*, March 2, 2000; April 1, 2000.
70. Franz Josef Krafeld, "Zur Praxis der pädagogischen Arbeit mit rechtsorientierten Jugendlichen," in *Rechtsextremismus in der Bundesrepublik Deutschland: Eine Bilanz*, ed. Wilfried Schubarth and Richard Stöss (Opladen: Leske & Budrich, 2001), 274–275, 278–279.
71. Reinhard Koch, "Deeskalation der Gewalt: Erfahrungen aus Projekten mit gewaltbereiten Jugendlichen in Sachsen-Anhalt," in *Rechtsradikale Gewalt im vereinigten Deutschland*, ed. Otto and Merten, 354.
72. *taz*, March 5, 2001; *Freitag*, no. 31, July 27, 2001.
73. GIC, *The Week in Germany*, January 12, 2001.
74. *Süddeutsche Zeitung*, February 19, 2001; February 22, 2001. See also "Neo-Nazi Dropout Tells her Story," *Spiegel Online*, May 28, 2008, http://www.spiegel.de/ international/germany/0,1518,druck-555870,00.html.
75. *taz*, September 11, 2001; *Die Zeit*, no. 20, 2001.
76. Burkhard Schröder, interviewed by *taz*, June 6, 2002.
77. For the updated and expanded book see Hasselbach and Bonengel, *Die Abrechnung: Ein Neonazi steigt aus*. See also "Einmal Nazi und zurück," *Tempo* (April 1996): 1–2, 53–54; Dirk Lehmann and Wolfgang Metzner, "Porträt des Berliner Neonazis Ingo Hesselbach," in *Un-Heil über Deutschland*, ed. Leier, 60–68.
78. See Ingo Hasselbach and Tom Reiss, *Führer Ex: Memoirs of a Former Neo-Nazi* (New York: Random House, 1996).
79. Tom Reiss, "Personal History: How Nazis are Made," *The New Yorker*, January 8, 1996.
80. For another account of an NPD member exiting the scene, see Christine Hewicker, *Die Aussteigerin: Autobiografie einer ehemaligen Rechtsextremistin* (Oldenburg: Igel, 2002).

Conclusion

1. Lars Riesman, "From High Hopes to On-Going Defeat: the New Extreme Right's Political Mobilization and its National Electoral Failure in Germany," *German Politics and Society* 78, 24(1) (Spring 2006): 71.
2. Estimates have ranged up to 5 percent. Peter H. Merkl contends that there is no more than a 2 percent core vote of real right-wing extremists in Germany

and the rest are temporary protest voters, in "German Responses to Extremist Challengers 1949–1994" (Working Paper 5.37, Center for German and European Studies, University of California, Berkeley, April 1996), 40.

3. Armin Pfahl-Traughber, *"Konservative Revolution" und "Neue Rechte": Rechtsextremistische Intellektuelle gegen den demokratischen Verfassungsstaat* (Opladen: Leske & Budrich, 1998), 225–227.

4. *taz*, June 9, 2004.

5. Hermann Kurthen, Werner Bergmann, and Rainer Erb, "Concluding Remarks: Questions for Further Research in Comparative Perspective," in *Antisemitism and Xenophobia in Germany after Unification* (New York: Oxford University Press, 1997), 259.

6. Survey commissioned by the SPD sponsored Friedrich-Ebert-Stiftung, cited in *taz*, November 9, 2006, and *Spiegel*, May 10, 2006. See also Oliver Decker et al., *Ein Blick in die Mitte: Zur Entstehung rechtsextremer und demokratischer Einstellungen* (Berlin: Friedrich-Ebert-Stiftung, 2008).

7. *Jewish Telegraph Agency Breaking News*, June 18, 2008; *Deutsche Welle*, DW-World.De, June 20, 2008. Another Bielefeld University study in 2006 showed that 61 percent of Germans polled thought that there were "too many foreigners living in Germany" (FinalCall.com. News, http://www.finalcall.com/artman/publish/article_2615.shtml, May 10, 2006). For an appraisal of the civil society, see Stephen Kalberg, "The FRG: a Burdened Democracy?" *German Politics and Society* 16 (Spring 1989): 33–40.

8. See Fritz René Allemann, *Bonn ist nicht Weimar* (Cologne: Kiepenheuer & Witsch, 1956).

9. *The Scotsman*, October 18, 2006.

10. *Los Angeles Times*, May 8, 2005.

11. For contrasting policies, see David Art, *The Politics of the Nazi Past in Germany and Austria* (Cambridge: Cambridge University Press, 2006).

12. *Christian Science Monitor*, May 15, 2002; *Die Zeit*, no. 41, 2002.

13. Associated Press release, January 25, 2008.

14. Rand C. Lewis, *A Nazi Legacy: Right-Wing Extremism in Postwar Germany* (New York: Praeger, 1991), 154–161.

15. Armin Pfahl-Traughber, *Rechtsextremismus: Eine kritische Bestandsaufnahme nach der Wiedervereinigung* (Bonn: Bouvier, 1993), 250; *Die Zeit*, no. 31, July 28, 2005.

16. Michael Minkenberg, *The New Right in Comparative Perspective: the USA and Germany* (Western Societies Program, Occasional Paper No. 32, Cornell University: Ithaca, NY, 1993), 2.

17. Peter H. Merkl, "Are the Old Nazis Coming Back?" in *The Federal Republic of Germany at Forty-Five: Union without Unity*, ed. Peter H. Merkl (New York: New York University Press, 1995), 468–473.

18. Bielefeld University Institute for Conflict and Violence Research poll, cited in *taz*, November 8, 2002.

19. See Werner Bohleber, "The Presence of the Past – Xenophobia and Rightwing Extremism in the Federal Republic of Germany: Psychoanalytic Reflections," *American Imago* 52(3) (1995): 333.

20. Christian Rath, "Bürgerrechte gelten auch für Rechtsradikale: Die Freiheit der Andersdenkenden ist kein linkes Privileg," in *Grundrechtereport 1999*, ed. Till Müller-Heidelberg et al. (Reinbeck: Rowohlt Taschenbuch Verlag, n.d.), 68–71.

21. GIC, *Federal Republic of Germany, Statements and Speeches*, November 8, 1992.

22. *Daily Times* (Lahore), May 14, 2005.

23. GIC, *The Week in Germany*, April 15, 2005.

Bibliography

Government documents

Baden-Württemberg Landesamt für Verfassungsschutz. "Junge Nationaldemokraten (JN): Jugendorganisation oder Sammelbecken für Neonazis?" Stuttgart, 1997.

Baden-Württemberg Landesamt für Verfassungsschutz. *Skinheads*. Stuttgart, 1997.

Bundesamt für Verfassungsschutz. *Rechtsextremistische Bestrebungen im Internet*. Cologne, 2000.

Bundesamt für Verfassungsschutz. "Right-wing Extremism in the Federal Republic of Germany – Situation Report – Updated Version/July 1998," internet edn.

Bundesministerium des Innern (BMI). *Aktuelle Fragen des Rechtsextremismus*. Bonn, 1994.

Bundesministerium des Innern (BMI). *Extremismus und Gewalt*, vols II, III. Bonn, 1993, 1994.

Bundesministerium des Innern (BMI). *Verfassungsschutzbericht*. Bonn, Berlin: various years.

Council of Europe and Berlin. "Local Democracy: a Civic Project," Barbara John, "Towards a tolerant and peaceful democratic European town with no racist, xenophobic and fundamentalist violence and discrimination." Strasbourg, 10 May 1995.

Der Bundesbeauftragte für die Unterlagen des Staatssicherheitsdienstes der ehemaligen Deutschen Demokratischen Republik, Reihe B, Nr. 2/1996. Walter Süss, "Analysen und Berichte: Zur Wahrnehmung und Interpretation des Rechtsextremismus in der DDR durch das MfS."

Der Bundeswahlleiter. "Bundesergebnis: Vorläufiges Ergebnis der Bundestagswahl 2005."

Goethe Institute and Inter Nationes. *Foreigners in Germany – from Guest Workers to Fellow-Citizens*. Bonn, November 2002.

Innenministerium Mecklenburg-Vorpommern. *Skinheads*. Schwerin, 1996.

Sippel, Heinrich. "Die Herausforderung unseres demokratischen Rechtsstaates durch Rechtsextremisten," in *Extremismus und Terrorismus*. BMI: Bonn, 1989, 43–62.

Stern, Susan. *Jews in Germany, 1995 and 1997*. Bonn: Inter-Nationes, Special Topic 6, 1997.

Veen, Hans-Joachim. "Rechtsextremistische und Rechtspopulistische Parteien in Europa (EU) und im Europaparlament," in *Texte zur Inneren Sicherheit*. Bonn: BMI 1997, 63–79.

Willems, Helmut, Stefanie Würtz, and Roland Eckert. *Forschungsprojekt: Analyse fremdenfeindlicher Straftäter*. Bonn: BMI, 1994.

Willems, Helmut, Stefanie Würtz, and Roland Eckert. *Fremdenfeindliche Gewalt: Eine Analyse von Täterstrukturen und Eskalationsprozessen. Research report*. Bonn: Bundesministerium Familie und Jugend, 1993.

Books and articles

Adorno, Theodor W., et al. *The Authoritarian Personality*. New York: Harper & Row, 1950.

Allemann, Fritz René. *Bonn ist nicht Weimar*. Cologne: Kiepenheuer & Witsch, 1956.

Anderson, James H. "The Neo-Nazi Menace in Germany," *Conflict and Terrorism* 18(1) (January–March 1995): 39–46.

Art, David. *The Politics of the Nazi Past in Germany and Austria*. Cambridge: Cambridge University Press, 2006.

Ashkenasi, Abraham. *Modern German Nationalism*. Cambridge, MA: Schenkman, 1976.

Azar, E. E. *Protracted Social Conflict: Theory and Cases*. Hampshire, England: Gower, 1989.

Baacke, D. et al. *Rock von Rechts*. 2 vols. Bielefeld: Gesellschaft für Medienpädagogik und Kommunikationskultur, 1994, 1999.

Backer, Susann. "New Perspectives on the Far Right in Germany," *German Politics* 4(2) (August 1995): 165–171.

Backes, Uwe. "Gestalt und Bedeutung des intellektuellen Rechtsextremismus in Deutschland," *Aus Politik und Zeitgeschichte* B 46 (2001): 24–30.

Backes, Uwe and Jesse Eckhard. *Politischer Extremismus in der Bundesrepublik Deutschland*. 3 vols. Cologne: Wirtschaft und Politik, 1989.

Backes, Uwe and Patrick Moreau. *Die extreme Rechte in Deutschland: Geschichte – Gegenwärtige Gefahren – Ursachen – Gegenmassnahmen*. 2nd edn. Munich: Akademischer Verlag, 1994.

Bartov, Omer. "The Wehrmacht Exhibition Controversy: the Politics of Evidence," in *Crimes of War: Guilt and Denial in the Twentieth Century*, ed. Omer Bartov, Atina Grossmann, and Mary Nolan. New York: The New Press, 2002, 41–60.

Bartsch, Günter. *Revolution von Rechts? Ideologie und Organisation der Neuen Rechten*. Freiburg: Heiderbücherei, 1975.

Bauriedl, Thea. "Verstehen und doch nicht einverstanden sein: Zur Psychodynamik und Soziodynamik des Umgangs mit Rechtsradikalen in Deutschland," in *Rechtsextremismus bekämpfen: Aufklärung und Selbstvergewisserung*, ed. Friedwart Maria Rudel. Essen: Klartext Verlag, 1995, 9–31.

Behrends, Jan C., Thomas Lindenberger, and Patrice G. Poutrous. *Fremde und Fremd-Sein in der DDR. Zu historischen Ursachen der Fremdenfeindlichkeit in Ostdeutschland*. Berlin: Metropol, 2003.

Benz, Wolfgang. "KZ-Manager im Kinderzimmer: Rechtsextreme Computerspiele," in *Rechtsextremismus in Deutschland: Voraussetzungen, Zusammenhänge, Wirkungen*, ed. Wolfgang Benz. Rev. edn. Frankfurt am Main: Fischer Taschenbuch, 1994, 219–227.

Benz, Wolfgang, ed. *Antisemitismus in Deutschland: Zur Aktualität eines Vorurteils*. Munich: Deutscher Taschenbuch Verlag, 1995.

Benz, Wolfgang, ed. *Rechtsextremismus in Deutschland: Voraussetzungen, Zusammenhänge, Wirkungen*. Frankfurt am Main: Fischer Taschenbuch, 1994.

Berg, Heinz Lynen von. "Rechtsexremismus in Ostdeutschland seit der Wende," in *Rechtsextremismus: Einführung und Forschungsbilanz*, ed. Wolfgang Kowalsky and Wolfgang Schroeder. Opladen: Westdeutscher Verlag, 1994, 103–126.

Bergmann, Werner. "Anti-Semitism and Xenophobia in the East German Länder." *German Politics* 3(2) (August 1994): 265–276.

Bergmann, Werner. "Antisemitismus in Deutschland," in *Rechtsextremismus in der Bundesrepublik Deutschland: Eine Bilanz*, ed. Wilfried Schubarth and Richard Stöss. Opladen: Leske & Budrich, 2001, 265–276.

Bergmann, Werner and Rainer Erb. *Anti-Semitism in Germany: the Post-Nazi Epoch Since 1945*. New Brunswick, NJ: Transaction, 1997. (Trans. Belinda Cooper and Allison Brown, *Antisemitismus in der Bundesrepublik Deutschland: Ergebnisse einer empirischen Forschung von 1946–1989* [Opladen: Leske & Budrich, 1991]).

Bergmann, Werner and Rainer Erb. "Kaderparteien, Bewegung, Szene, kollektive Episode oder was?" *Forschungsjournal Neue Soziale Bewegungen* 7(4) (1994): 26–34.

Billing, Werner, Andreas Barz, and Stephan Wienk-Borgert, eds. *Rechtsextremismus in der Bundesrepublik Deutschland.* Baden-Baden: Nomos, 1993.

Birsl, Ursula. "Mädchen und Rechtsextremismus: Rechtsextremistische Orientierungen bei weiblichen und männlichen Jugendlichen." *Jugendpolitik* 3 (1993): 12–14.

Bohleber, Werner. "The Presence of the Past – Xenophobia and Rightwing Extremism in the Federal Republic of Germany: Psychoanalytic Reflections." *American Imago* 52(3) (1995): 329–344.

Bohn, Irina, Dieter Kreft, Gerd Stüwe, and Georg Weigel, "Das Aktionsprogramm gegen Aggression und Gewalt," in *Rechtsradikale Gewalt im vereinigten Deutschland: Jugend im gesellschaftlichen Umbruch,* ed. Hans-Uwe Otto and Roland Merten. Opladen: Leske & Budrich, 1993, 301–309.

Braun, Aurel and Stephen Scheinberg, eds. *The Extreme Right: Freedom and Security at Risk.* Boulder, CO: Westview Press, 1997.

Braun, Stephan and Daniel Hörsch, eds. *Rechte Netzwerke – eine Gefahr.* Wiesbaden: Verlag für Sozialwissenschaften, 2004.

Brauner-Orthen, Alice. *Die Neue Rechte in Deutschland.* Leverkusen: Leske & Budrich, 2001.

Braunthal, Gerard. *The German Social Democrats Since 1969: a Party in Power and Opposition.* Boulder, CO: Westview Press, 1994.

Braunthal, Gerard. *Parties and Politics in Modern Germany.* Boulder, CO: Westview Press, 1996.

Braunthal, Gerard. "The SPD, the Welfare State, and Agenda 2010," *German Politics and Society,* issue 69, 21(4) (Winter 2003): 1–29.

Breymann, Klaus. "Gewalttaten rechtsorientierter Skinheads in Deutschland," in *Rechtsradikale Gewalt im vereinigten Deutschland: Jugend im gesellschaftlichen Umbruch,* ed. Hans-Uwe Otto and Roland Merten. Opladen: Leske & Budrich, 1993, 294–309.

Brinks, Jan Herman. "Germany's New Right," in *Nationalist Myths and Modern Media: Contested Identities in the Age of Globalization,* ed. Jan Herman Brinks, Stella Rock, and Edward Timms. London: Tauris, 2006, 125–138.

Bruck, Sabine van den and Renate Schmitz. "Monster, Mütter, Mitläuferinnen – 'Frauen und Rechtsextremismus' aus journalistischer Sicht," in *Frauen und Rechtsextremismus,* ed. Petra Wlecklik. Göttingen: Lamuv Verlag, 1995, 60–78.

Brück, Wolfgang. "Jugend als soziales Problem" in *Jugend und Jugendforschung in der DDR: Gesellschaftspolitische Situationen, Sozialisation und Mentalitätsentwicklung in den achtziger Jahren,* ed. Walter Friedrich and Hartmut Griese. Opladen: Leske & Budrich, 1991, 191–200.

Butterwegge, Christoph. "Rechtsextremismus in Deutschland: Erscheinigungsformen – Entstehungsbedingungen – Gegenstrategien," *Zukunft* 1 (1994): 29–34.

Butterwegge, Christoph. *Rechtsextremismus, Rassismus und Gewalt: Erklärungsmodelle in der Diskussion.* Darmstadt: Primus, 1996.

Butterwegge, Christoph and Horst Iola, eds. *Rechtsextremismus im vereinigten Deutschland. Randerscheinung oder Gefahr für die Demokratie?* Bremen: Steintor, 1991.

Castner, Hartmut and Thilo Castner. "Rechtsextemistische Strömungen in der Schule und pädagogische Gegenmassnahmen," in *Rechtsradikale Gewalt im vereinigten Deutschland: Jugend im gesellschaftlichen Umbruch,* ed. Hans-Uwe Otto and Roland Merten. Opladen: Leske & Budrich, 1993, 382–392.

Cole, Alexandra. "The Republikaner: a Party at Odds With Itself," in *Germans Divided: the 1994 Bundestag Elections and the Evolution of the German Party System,* ed. Russell J. Dalton. Oxford: Berg, 1996, 133–153.

Cornell, Alan. "The Depiction of Neo-Nazism in Police Shows on German Television," *German Politics and Society* 15(1) (Spring 1997): 22–45.

Cullen, Peter. "Crime and Policing in Germany in the 1990s," in *Developments in German Politics 2*, ed. Gordon Smith, William E. Paterson, and Stephen Padgett. Durham, NC: Duke University Press, 1996, 286–302.

Decker, Oliver et al. *Ein Blick in die Mitte: Zur Entstehung rechtsextremer und demokratischer Einstellungen*. Berlin: Friedrich-Ebert-Stiftung, 2008.

Del Fabbro, René. "Germany: a Victory of the Street," in *New Xenophobia in Europe*, ed. Bernd Baumgartl and Adrian Favell. London: Kluwer Law International, 1995, 132–147.

Deutscher Gewerkschaftsbund. *Bericht der DGB-Kommission "Rechtsextremismus."* Berlin: DGB, 2000.

Diamant, Adolf. *Geschändete jüdische Friedhofe in Deutschland 1945–1999*. Potsdam: Verlag für Berlin-Brandenburg, 2000.

Dornbusch, Christian and Jan Raabe. "RechtsRock: Das Modernisierungsmoment der extremen Rechten," in *Rechte Netzwerke – eine Gefahr*, ed. Stephan Braun and Daniel Hörsch. Wiesbaden: Verlag für Sozialwissenschaften, 2004, 123–131.

Dudek, Peter and Hans-Gerd Jaschke. *Entstehung und Entwicklung des Rechtsextremismus in der Bundesrepublik*. 2 vols. Opladen: Westdeutscher Verlag, 1984.

Eatwell, Roger. "Towards a New Model of the Rise of Right-Wing Extremism," *German Politics* 6(3) (December 1997): 166–184.

Ebata, Michi. "Right-Wing Extremism: In Search of a Definition," in *The Extreme Right: Freedom and Security at Risk*, ed. Aurel Braun and Stephen Scheinberg. Boulder, CO: Westview Press, 1997, 12–35.

Elsässer, Jürgen. *Braunbuch DVU - eine deutsche Arbeiterpartei und ihre Freunde*. Hamburg: konkret texte 17, 1998.

Ely, John. "The *Frankfurter Allgemeine Zeitung* and Contemporary National-Conservatism," *German Politics and Society* 13(2) (Summer 1995): 81–121.

Ely, John. "Republicans: Neo-Nazis or the Black-Brown Hazelnut? Recent Successes of the Radical Right in West Germany," *German Politics and Society* 18 (Fall 1989): 1–17.

Erb, Rainer. "Antisemitische Straftäter der Jahre 1993 bis 1995," in *Jahrbuch für Antisemitismusforschung 6*, ed. Wolfgang Benz. Frankfurt: Campus Verlag, 1997, 160–180.

Erb, Rainer. "Rechtsextremistische Gruppengewalt in den neuen Bundesländern," in *Rechtsextremismus in Deutschland: Voraussetzungen, Zusammenhänge, Wirkungen*, ed. Wolfgang Benz. Frankfurt am Main: Fischer Taschenbuch, 1994, 110–136.

Faber, Richard, Hajo Funke, and Gerhard Schoenberner, eds. *Rechtsextremismus: Ideologie und Gewalt*. Berlin: Gedenkstätte Haus der Wannsee Konferenz, 1995.

Fahr, Margitta-Sybille. "'Hinein ins neue Kampfjahr!' – Rechtsextreme Militanz und Terrorismus," *Bulletin* (Schriftenreihe des Zentrum Demokratische Kultur) 2 (1997): 7–11.

Farin, Klaus. "Rechts-Rock," in *Rechtsextremismus in Deutschland: Voraussetzungen, Zusammenhänge, Wirkungen*, ed. Wolfgang Betz. Frankfurt am Main: Fischer Taschenbuch, 1994, 137–153.

Farin, Klaus and Eberhard Seidel-Pielen. *Krieg in den Städten: Jugendgangs in Deutschland*. Berlin: Rotbuch, 1991.

Feit, Margret. *Die "Neue Rechte" in der Bundesrepublik: Organisation – Ideologie – Strategie*. Frankfurt: Campus, 1987.

Filmer, Werner and Heribert Schwan. *Was von Hitler blieb: 50 Jahre nach der Machtergreifung*. Frankfurt am Main: Ullstein, 1983.

Fischer, Benno. "DDR-Rechtsextremismus als Vorbote der Systemkrise," *Neue Gesellschaft-Frankfurter Hefte* 4 (April 1990): 332–338.

Fisher, Marc. *After the Wall: Germany, the Germans and the Burdens of History.* New York: Simon & Schuster, 1995.

Fraser, Nicholas. *The Voice of Modern Hatred: Tracing the Rise of Neo-Fascism in Europe.* Woodstock, NY: The Overlook Press, 2001.

Freie Universität Berlin, Otto-Stammer-Zentrum. "Rechtsextreme Einstellungen in der Region Berlin-Brandenburg," 11 August 2000.

Fromm, Erich. *The Anatomy of Human Destructiveness.* New York: Holt, Rinehart and Winston, 1973.

Fromm, Erich. *Escape from Freedom.* New York: Holt, Rinehart, and Winston, 1941.

Fromm, Rainer and Barbara Kernbach, *Rechtsextremismus im Internet.* Munich: Olzog, 2001.

5 Millionen Deutsche: "Wir sollten wieder einen Führer haben ..." Die SINUS-Studie über rechtsextremistische Einstellungen bei den Deutschen. Reinbek: Rowohlt, 1981.

Funke, Hajo. "Rechtsextemismus – Zeitgeist, Politik und Gewalt," in *Rechtsextremismus: Ideologie und Gewalt,* ed. Richard Faber, Hajo Funke, and Gerhard Schoenberner. Berlin: Gedenkstätte Haus der Wannsee Konferenz, 1995, 14–51.

Gessenharter, Wolfgang. "Das Weltbild der 'Neuen Rechten,'" in *Rechtsextremismus in der Bundesrepublik Deutschland,* ed. Werner Billing, Andreas Barz, and Stephan Wienk-Borgert. Baden-Baden: Nomos, 1993, 65–80.

Gessenharter, Wolfgang. *Kippt die Republik? Die Neue Rechte und ihre Unterstützung durch Politik und Medien.* Munich: Theodor Knaur, 1994.

Goldenhagen, Daniel J. *Hitler's Willing Executioners: Ordinary Germans and the Holocaust.* New York: Alfred A. Knopf, 1996.

Gurr, Ted R. *Why Men Rebel.* Princeton: Princeton University Press, 1970.

Hasselbach, Ingo and Winfried Bonengel. *Die Abrechnung: Ein Neonazi steigt aus.* Berlin: Aufbau, 2001.

Hasselbach, Ingo and Tom Reiss. *Führer Ex: Memoirs of a Former Neo-Nazi.* New York: Random House, 1996.

Heilbrunn, Jacob. "Germany's New Right," *Foreign Affairs* 75(6) (November–December 1996): 80–98.

Heilbrunn, Jacob, Robert Lieber, Hans-Georg Betz, and Peter Schneider. *Germany's New Right: Revival of Nationalism or Call for Normalcy?* Washington, DC: Friedrich Ebert Foundation, 1997.

Heinemann, Karl-Heinz and Wilfried Schubarth, eds. *Der antifaschistische Staat entlässt seine Kinder. Jugend und Rechtsextremismus in Ostdeutschland.* Cologne: PappyRossa, 1992.

Heitmeyer, Wilhelm. *Rechtsextremistische Orientierungen bei Jugendlichen – Empirische Ergebnisse und Erklärungsmuster einer Untersuchung zur politischen Sozialisation.* Weinheim-München: Juventa, 1987.

Heitmeyer, Wilhelm et al. *Die Bielefelder Rechtsextremismus-Studie – Erste Langzeituntersuchung zur politischen Sozialisation männlicher Jugendlicher.* Weinheim-München: Juventa, 1992.

Heni, Clemens. *Salonfähigkeit der Neuen Rechten: "Nationale Identität," Antisemitismus und Antiamerikanismus in der politischen Kultur der Bundesrepublik Deutschland 1970–2005: Henning Eichberg als Exempel.* Marburg: Tectum, 2007.

Herf, Jeffrey. *Divided Memory: the Nazi Past in the Two Germanys.* Cambridge, MA: Harvard University Press, 1997.

Heury, Thomas. "Current Anti-Semitism in East Germany." *Post-Holocaust and Anti-Semitism* 59 (1 August 2007).

Hewicker, Christine. *Die Aussteigerin: Autobiografie einer ehemaligen Rechtsextremistin.* Oldenburg: Igel, 2002.

Hockenos, Paul. "Making Hate Safe Again in Europe," *The Nation* (19 September 1994): 271–275.

Hofmann-Göttig, Joachim. *Die neue Rechte: die Männerparteien.* Bonn: Demokratische Gemeinde, 1989.

Holthusen, Bernd and Michael Jänecke. *Rechtsextremismus in Berlin: Aktuelle Erscheinungsformen, Ursachen, Gegenmassnahmen.* Marburg: Schüren, 1994.

Hopf, Christel, Peter Rieker, Martina Sanden-Marcus, and Christiane Schmidt. *Familie und Rechtsextremismus: Familiale Sozialisation und rechtsextreme Orientierungen junger Männer.* Weinheim: Juventa, 1995.

Informations-, Dokumentations- und Aktionszentrum gegen Ausländerfeindlichkeit, für eine multikulturelle Zukunft. *Rechte Jugendliche und ihre Organisationsformen: Begrifflichkeiten, Organisationen und rechte Szene. Ein Reader für MultiplikatorInnen in der Schule und Jugendarbeit.* Düsseldorf: IDA, 1994.

Institut für Demoskopie Allensbach. *Demokratie-Verankerung in der Bundesrepublik Deutschland: Eine empirische Untersuchung zum 30jährigen Bestehen der Bundesrepublik.* Allensbach, 1979.

Jäger, Margarete. "Wie die Rechte Sprache prägt Steilvorlagen von Rechtsaussen," in *Rechte Netzwerke – eine Gefahr*, ed. Stephan Braun and Daniel Hörsch. Wiesbaden: Verlag für Sozialwissenschaften, 2004, 45–56.

Jarausch, Konrad H., Hinrich C. Seeba, and David P. Conradt. "The Presence of the Past: Culture, Opinion, and Identity in Germany," in *After Unity: Reconfiguring German Identities*, ed. Konrad H. Jarausch. Providence and Oxford: Berghahn Books, 1997, 25–60.

Jaschke, Hans-Gerd. *Die "Republikaner": Profile einer Rechtsaussen-Partei.* Bonn: Dietz, 1994.

Jaschke, Hans-Gerd. *Rechtsextremismus und Fremdenfeindlichkeit: Begriffe, Positionen, Praxisfelder.* Opladen: Westdeutscher Verlag, 1994.

Jaschke, Hans-Gerd. "Sub-Cultural Aspects of Right-Wing Extremism," in *Political Culture in Germany*, ed. Dirk Berg-Schlosser and Ralf Rytlewski. New York: St. Martin's Press, 1993, 126–134.

Joffe, Josef et al. "Mr. Heilbrunn's Planet: On Which the Germans are Back," *Foreign Affairs* 76(2) (March–April 1997): 152–161.

Kagedan, Ian J. "Contemporary Right-Wing Extremism in Germany," in *The Extreme Right: Freedom and Security at Risk*, ed. Aurel Braun and Stephen Scheinberg. Boulder, CO: Westview Press, 1997, 107–137.

Kailitz, Steffen. "Aktuelle Entwicklungen im deutschen Rechtsextremismus," Konrad-Adenauer-Stiftung 17 (Sankt Augustin, 2000).

Kalberg, Stephen. "The FRG: a Burdened Democracy?" *German Politics and Society* 16 (Spring 1989): 33–40.

Kaplan, Jeffrey and Tore Bjørgo, eds. *Nation and Race: the Developing Euro-American Racist Subculture.* Boston: Northeastern University Press, 1998.

Karapin, Roger. *Protest Politics in Germany: Movements on the Left and Right since the 1960s.* University Park, PA: Pennsylvania State University Press, 2007.

Karapin, Roger. "Radical-Right and Neo-Fascist Political Parties in Western Europe," *Comparative Politics* 30(2) (January 1998): 213–234.

Karthee, Renée. "Rock-Musik unterm Hakenkreuz," in *Un-Heil über Deutschland: Fremdenhass und Neofaschismus nach der* Wiedervereinigung, ed. Manfred Leier. Hamburg: Gruner & Jahr, 1993, 104–119.

Kellershohn, Helmut. *Das Plagiat: Der Völkische Nationalismus der "Jungen Freiheit."* Duisburg: DISS-Verlag, 1994.

Kitschelt, Herbert. *The Radical Right in Western Europe: a Comparative Analysis.* Ann Arbor: University of Michigan Press, 1995.

Klopp, Brett. *German Multiculturalism: Immigrant Integration and the Transformation of Citizenship.* Westport, CT: Praeger, 2002.

Koch, Reinhard. "Deeskalation der Gewalt: Erfahrungen aus Projekten mit gewaltbereiten Jugendlichen in Sachsen-Anhalt," in *Rechtsradikale Gewalt im vereinigten Deutschland: Jugend im gesellschaftlichen Umbruch,* ed. Hans-Uwe Otto and Roland Merten. Opladen: Leske & Budrich, 1993, 350–355.

Kolinsky, Eva. "Multiculturalism in the Making? Non-Germans and Civil Society in the New Länder," *German Politics* 7(3) (December 1998): 192–214.

Kowalsky, Wolfgang and Wolfgang Schroeder. "Einleitung: Rechtsextremismus – Begriff, Methode, Analyse," in *Rechtsextremismus: Einführung und Forschungsbilanz,* ed. Wolfgang Kowalsky and Wolfgang Schroeder. Opladen: Westdeutscher Verlag, 1994, 7–22.

Krafeld, Franz Josef. "Zur Praxis der pädagogischen Arbeit mit rechtsorientierten Jugendlichen," in *Rechtsextremismus in der Bundesrepublik Deutschland: Eine Bilanz,* ed. Wilfried Schubarth and Richard Stöss. Opladen: Leske & Budrich, 2001, 271–291.

Kramer, Jane. "Neo-Nazis: a Chaos in the Head," *New Yorker* (14 June 1993): 52–70.

Kraske, Michael and Christian Werner. *... und morgen das ganze Land: Neue Nazis, "befreite Zonen" und die tägliche Angst – ein Insiderbericht.* Freiburg: Heider, 2007.

Kraushaar, Wolfgang. "Radikalisierung der Mitte: Auf dem Weg zur Berliner Republik," in *Rechtsextremismus: Ideologie und Gewalt,* ed. Richard Faber, Hajo Funke, and Gerhard Schoenberner. Berlin: Gedenkstätte Haus der Wannsee Konferenz, 1995, 52–69.

Kühnel, Wolfgang. "Gewalt durch Jugendliche im Osten Deutschlands," in *Rechtsradikale Gewalt im vereinigten Deutschland,* ed. Hans-Uwe Otto and Roland Merten. Opladen: Leske & Budrich, 1993, 237–246.

Kühnel, Wolfgang. "Hitler's Grandchildren? The Reemergence of a Right-Wing Social Movement in Germany," in *Nation and Race: the Developing Euro-American Racist Subculture,* ed. Jeffrey Kaplan and Tore Bjørgo. Boston: Northeastern University Press, 1998, 148–174.

Kurthen, Hermann, Werner Bergmann, and Rainer Erb. "Concluding Remarks: Questions for Further Research in Comparative Perspective," in *Antisemitism and Xenophobia in Germany after Unification.* New York: Oxford University Press, 1997, 257–262.

Leggewie, Claus. *Der Geist steht rechts: Ausflüge in die Denkfabriken der Wende Berlin.* Rotbuch, 1987.

Leggewie, Claus. *Die Republikaner: Phantombild der neuen Rechten.* Berlin: Rotbuch, 1989.

Leggewie, Claus. *Druck von rechts: Wohin treibt die Bundesrepublik?* Munich: C. H. Beck, 1993.

Lehmann, Dirk and Wolfgang Metzner. "Porträt des Berliner Neonazis Ingo Hesselbach," in *Un-Heil über Deutschland: Fremdenhass und Neofachismus nach der Wiedervereinigung,* ed. Manfred Leier. Hamburg: Gruner & Jahr, 1993, 60–68.

Leier, Manfred, ed. *Un-Heil über Deutschland: Fremdenhass und Neofaschismus nach der Wiedervereinigung.* Hamburg: Gruner & Jahr, 1993.

Leiprecht, Rudolf, Lena Inowlocki, Athanasios Markavism, and Jürgen Novak. "Racism in the New Germany: Examining the Causes, Looking for Answers," in *Racism in Europe: a Challenge for Youth Policy and Youth Work*, ed. Jan Laurens Hazekamp and Keith Popple. London: UCL Press, 1997, 91–121.

Lenk, Kurt. "Grossdeutschland im Programm – Die 'Republikaner' nach Rosenheim," *Neue Gesellschaft-Frankfurter Hefte* 4 (April 1990): 327–331.

Lenk, Kurt. *Rechts, wo die Mitte ist: Studien zur Ideologie: Rechtsextremismus, National-sozialismus, Konservatismus*. Baden-Baden: Nomos, 1994.

Lepszy, Norbert. "Die Republikaner: Ideologie – Programm – Organisation," *Aus Politik und Zeitgeschichte* (supplement to *Das Parlament*) B41–42 (6 October 1989).

Lepszy, Norbert. "'Die Republikaner' im Abwind," Konrad-Adenauer-Stiftung, No. 17, Aktuelle Fragen der Politik. Sankt Augustin, 1994.

Lepszy, Norbert and Hans-Joachim Veen. "Rechtsradikale in der parlamentarischen Praxis: Die Republikaner in kommunalen und Landesparlamenten sowie im Europa-parlament," *Zeitschrift für Parlamentsfragen* 3 (1994): 203–216.

Lewis, Rand C. *A Nazi Legacy: Right-Wing Extremism in Postwar Germany*. New York: Praeger, 1991.

Linke, Annette. *Der Multimillionär Frey und die DVU: Daten, Fakten, Hintergründe*. Essen: Klartext Verlag, 1994.

Lipset, Seymour M. "'Der Faschismus,' die Linke, die Rechte und die Mitte," *Kölner Zeitschrift für Soziologie und Sozialpsychologie* (1959): 401–444.

Lipset, Seymour M. *Political Man*. 2nd enlarged edn. Baltimore: Johns Hopkins University Press, 1981.

Maaz, Hans-Joachim. "Gewalt, Rassismus und Rechtsextremismus in den östlichen Bundesländern," in *Rechtsradikale Gewalt im vereinigten Deutschland: Jugend im gesellschaftlichen Umbruch*, ed. Hans-Uwe Otto and Roland Merten. Opladen: Leske & Budrich, 1993, 176–181.

Madloch, Norbert. "Die Wählerwandlung der Rechten," in *Wer redet da von Entwarnung: Texte und Analysen zum aktuellen Rechtsextremismus*. Author's collective: edition ost, 1995, 15–28.

Marks, Stefan. "Skins und Hoods," in *Rechtsextremismus: Hintergründe, Meinungen, Gegenstrategien*, ed. Jusos in der SPD. Bonn: n.d., 66–73.

McGowan, Lee. *The Radical Right in Germany: 1870 to the Present*. London: Longman, 2002.

Merkl, Peter H. "Are the Old Nazis Coming Back?" in *The Federal Republic of Germany at Forty-Five: Union without Unity*, ed. Merkl. New York: New York University Press, 1995, 427–484.

Merkl, Peter H. "German Responses to Extremist Challengers 1949–1994," Working Paper 5.37, Center for German and European Studies, University of California, Berkeley, April 1996.

Merkl, Peter H. and Leonard Weinberg, eds. *Encounters with the Contemporary Radical Right*. Boulder, CO: Westview Press, 1993.

Merkl, Peter H. and Leonard Weinberg, eds. *The Revival of Right-Wing Extremism in the Nineties*. London: Frank Cass, 1997.

Meuche-Mäker, Mainhard, ed. *Aufstieg und Fall des Ronald Barnabas Schill: Skizzen zur Schillschen Variante des bundesdeutschen Rechtspopulismus*. Hamburg: Rosa-Luxemburg-Bildungswerk, 2004.

Meyer, Birgit. "Mädchen und Rechtsextremismus: Männliche Dominanzkultur und weibliche Unterordnung," in *Rechtsradikale Gewalt im vereinigten Deutschland: Jugend im gesellschaftlichen Umbruch,* ed. Hans-Uwe Otto and Roland Merten. Opladen: Leske & Budrich, 1993, 211–218.

Minkenberg, Michael. "German Unification and the Continuity of Discontinuities: Cultural Change and the Far Right in East and West," *German Politics* 3(2) (August 1994): 169–192.

Minkenberg, Michael. *The New Right in Comparative Perspective: the USA and Germany,* Western Societies Program, Occasional Paper 32, Cornell University, 1993.

Minkenberg, Michael. "The New Right in France and Germany: *Nouvelle Droite, Neue Rechte,* and the New Radical Parties," in *The Revival of Right-Wing Extremism in the Nineties,* ed. Peter H. Merkl and Michael Minkenberg. London: Frank Cass, 1997, 65–90.

Minkenberg, Michael. "The Radical Right in Unified Germany: Dividing the Nation in the Name of the People," *Politik* (CGGP Newsletter) 16 (Summer 2001): 7–9.

More, Gillian. "Undercover Surveillance of the Republikaner Party: Protecting a Militant Democracy or Discrediting a Political Rival?" *German Politics* 3(2) (August 1994): 284–292.

Mudde, Cas. "Right-Wing Extremism Analyzed." *European Journal of Political Research* 27 (1995): 203–224.

Müller, Rudolf. "Schule des Terrorismus: Die Wehrsportgruppe Hoffmann und andere militante Neonazis," in *Rechtsextremismus in der Bundesrepublik: Voraussetzungen, Zusammenhänge, Wirkungen,* ed. Wolfgang Betz. Frankfurt am Main: Fischer Taschenbuch Verlag, 1985, 238–254.

Murray, Laura M. "Einwanderungsland Bundesrepublik Deutschland? Explaining the Evolving Positions of German Political Parties on Citizenship Policy," *German Politics and Society* 33 (Fall 1994): 23–56.

Mushaben, Joyce Marie. "Rendering Right Extremist Movements: Reflections on Betz and Minkenberg," *Politics* (CGGP Newsletter) 16 (Summer 2001): 10–13.

Mushaben, Joyce Marie. "The Rise of Femi-Nazis? Female Participation in Right-Extremist Movements in Unified Germany," *German Politics* 5(2) (August 1996): 240–261.

Nagle, John D. *The National Democratic Party: Right Radicalism in the Federal Republic.* Berkeley: University of California Press, 1969.

Neaman, Elliot. "A New Conservative Revolution? Neo-Nationalism, Collective Memory, and the New Right in Germany since Unification," in *Antisemitism and Xenophobia in Germany after Unification,* ed. Hermann Kurthen, Werner Bergmann, and Rainer Erb. New York: Oxford University Press, 1997, 190–208.

Neu, Viola. "DVU – NPD: Perspektiven und Entwicklungen," Konrad-Adenauer-Stiftung, Arbeitspapier 140/2004. Sankt Augustin, 2004.

Neugebauer, Gero. "Extremismus – Rechtsextremismus – Linksextremismus: Einige Anmerkungen zu Begriffen, Forschungskonzepten, Forschungsfragen und Forschungsergebnissen," in *Rechtsextremismus in der Bundesrepublik Deutschland: Eine Bilanz,* ed. Wilfried Schubarth and Richard Stöss. Opladen: Leske & Budrich, 2001, 13–37.

Nolte, Ernst. *Das Vergehen der Vergangenheit: Antwort an meine Kritiker im sogenannten Historikerstreit.* Berlin: Ullstein, 1987.

Nolte, Ernst. *The Three Faces of Fascism: Action Française, Italian Fascism, National Socialism.* London: Weidenfeld & Nicolson, 1965.

Oberländer, Hans. "Wie die Justiz mit Neonazis umgeht," in *Un-Heil über Deutschland: Fremdenhass und Neofaschismus nach der Wiedervereinigung,* ed. Manfred Leier. Hamburg: Gruner & Jahr, 1993, 174–182.

O'Brien, Peter. *Beyond the Swastika*. London: Routledge, 1996.

Olsen, Jonathan. *Nature and Nationalism: Right-Wing Ecology and the Politics of Identity in Contemporary Germany*. Basingstoke: Macmillan, 1999.

Opitz, Reinhard. *Faschismus und Neofaschismus*. Frankfurt: Verlag Marxistische Blätter, 1984.

Otto, Hans-Uwe and Roland Merten, ed. *Rechtsradikale Gewalt im vereinigten Deutschland: Jugend im gesellschaftlichen Umbruch*. Opladen: Leske & Budrich, 1993.

Paul, Gerhard et al. *Hitlers Schatten verblasst: Die Normalisierung des Rechtsextremismus*. Bonn: Dietz, 1990.

Pearce, Caroline. *Contemporary Germany and the Nazi Legacy: Remembrance, Politics and the Dialectic of Normality*. Basingstoke: Palgrave Macmillan, 2008.

Pfahl-Traughber, Armin. "Der organisierte Rechtsextremismus in Deutschland nach 1945," in *Rechtsextremismus in der Bundesrepublik Deutschland: Eine Bilanz*, ed. Wilfried Schubarth and Richard Stöss. Opladen: Leske & Budrich, 2001, 71–100.

Pfahl-Traughber, Armin. *"Konservative Revolution" und "Neue Rechte": Rechtsextremistische Intellektuelle gegen den demokratischen Verfassungsstaat*. Opladen: Leske & Budrich, 1998.

Pfahl-Traughber, Armin. *Rechtsextremismus: Eine kritische Bestandsaufnahme nach der Wiedervereinigung*. Bonn: Bouvier, 1993.

Pfeiffer, Thomas. *Für Volk und Vaterland: Das Mediennetz der Rechten – Presse, Musik, Internet*. Berlin: Aufbau Taschenbuch Verlag, 2002.

Porat, Dina, Roni Stauber, and Raphael Vago, eds. *Anti-Semitism Worldwide 1995/6*. Tel Aviv: Tel Aviv University, 1996.

Prevezanos, Klaudia. "Protecting Democracy: Germany Wants to Ban Far-Right Party," American Institute for Contemporary German Studies. At Issue Report. Washington, DC, December 2000.

Rath, Christian, "Bürgerrechte gelten auch für Rechtsradikale: Die Freiheit der Andersdenkenden ist kein linkes Privileg," in *Grundrechtereport 1999*, ed. Till Müller-Heidelberg et al. Reinbeck: Rowohlt Taschenbuch Verlag, 1999, 68–71.

Rensmann, Lars. "From High Hopes to On-Going Defeat: the New Extreme Right's Political Mobilization and its National Electoral Failure in Germany," *German Politics and Society* 78, 24(1) (Spring 2006): 67–92.

"'Republikanische Jugend': Schönhubers Teenietruppe," *Arbeitsgemeinschaft verfolgter Sozialdemokraten (AVS)-Informationsdienst* 9(6) (June–July 1994): 9–11.

Röhrich, Wilfried. *Die Demokratie der Westdeutschen: Geschichte und politisches Klima einer Republik*. Munich: C. H. Beck, 1988.

Rommelspacher, Birgit. "Männliche Gewalt und gesellschaftliche Dominanz," in *Rechtsradikale Gewalt im vereinigten Deutschland: Jugend im gesellschaftlichen Umbruch*, ed. Hans-Uwe Otto and Roland Merten. Opladen: Leske & Budrich, 1993, 200–210.

Rosellini, Jay Julian. *Literary Skinheads? Writing from the Right in Reunified Germany*. West Lafayette, IN: Purdue University Press, 2000.

Rosen, Klaus-Henning. "Hat der Wolf Kreide gefressen? Das neue Parteiprogramm der 'Republikaner'," *Vorgänge* 104 (April 1990): 22–31.

Roth, Dieter. "Die Republikaner," *Aus Politik und Zeitgeschichte* (supplement to *Das Parlament*), B37–38/90 (September 14, 1990).

Roth, Dieter and Hartmut Schäfer. "Der Erfolg der Rechten. Denkzettel für die etablierten Parteien oder braune Wiedergeburt?" in *Das Superwahljahr: Deutschland vor unkalkulierbaren Regierungsmehrheiten*, ed. Wilhelm Bürklin and Dieter Roth. Cologne: Bund, 1994, 111–131.

Saalfeld, Thomas. "The Politics of National-Populism: Ideology and Policies of the German Republikaner Partei," *German Politics* 2(2) (August 1993): 177–199.

Sarkowicz, Hans. "Publizistik in der Grau- und Braunzone," in *Rechtsextremismus in Deutschland: Voraussetzungen, Zusammenhänge, Wirkungen*, ed. Wolfgang Betz. Frankfurt am Main: Fischer, 1994.

Scheuch, Erwin K. and Hans-Dieter Klingemann. "Theorie des Rechtsradikalismus in westlichen Industriegesellschaften," *Hamburger Jahrbuch für Wirtschafts- und Gesellschaftspolitik*, 12 (1967): 11–29.

Schmid, Thomas. "Right-Wing Radicalism in the Unified Germany," in *The Resurgence of Right-Wing Radicalism in Germany*, ed. Ulrich Wank. Atlantic Highlands, NJ: Humanities Press International, 1996, 69–84. Trans. James Knowlton. Original German: *Der neue alte Rechtsradikalismus*. Munich: Piper, 1993.

Schmidt, Michael. *Heute gehört uns die Strasse . . . Der Inside-Report aus der Neonazi-Szene*. 2nd edn. Duesseldorf: Econ, 1993.

Schoeps, Julius H., Gideon Botsch, Christoph Kopke, and Lars Rensmann, eds. *Rechtsextremismus in Brandenburg: Handbuch für Analyse, Prävention und Intervention*. Berlin: Verlag für Berlin-Brandenburg, 2007.

Schomers, Michael. *Deutschland ganz rechts*. Cologne: Kiepenheuer & Witsch, 1990.

Schramm, Hilde. "Handeln in der Schule gegen Rechtsextremismus," in *Rechtsextremismus: Ideologie und Gewalt*, ed. Richard Faber, Hajo Funke, and Gerhard Schoenberner. Berlin: Gedenkstätte Haus der Wannsee Konferenz, 1995, 136–155.

Schröder, Burkhard. *Neonazis und Computernetze: Wie Rechtsradikale neue Kommunikationsformen nutzen*. Reinbek: Rowohlt Taschenbuch, 1995.

Schubarth, Wilfried and Walter Friedrich. "Einstellung ostdeutscher Jugendlicher zu Rechts- und Linksextremismus," *Freudenberg Stiftung* (May 1991).

Schubarth, Wilfried and Richard Stöss, eds. *Rechtsextremismus in der Bundesrepublik Deutschland: Eine Bilanz*. Opladen: Leske & Budrich, 2001.

Seibert, Klaus, "Bündnisarbeit in Maintal," in *Wer redet da von Entwarnung? Texte und Analysen zum aktuellen Rechtsextremismus*, authors' collective. Berlin: edition ost, 1995, 148–150.

Siegler, Bernd. "Der Apparat und die Rechten," in *Der Pakt: Die Rechten und der Staat*, ed. Bernd Siegler, Oliver Tolmein, and Charlotte Wiedemann. Göttingen: Verlag Die Werkstatt, 1993, 11–118.

Skrypietz, Ingrid. "Militant Right-Wing Extremism in Germany," *German Politics* 3(1) (April 1994): 133–139.

SPD Parteivorstand. "Die REP im Vorwahlkampf 1993." Bonn 1993. Hectographed.

Staab, Andreas. "Xenophobia, Ethnicity and National Identity in Eastern Germany," *German Politics* 7(2) (August 1998): 31–46.

Staud, Toralf. *Moderne Nazis. Die neuen Rechten und der Aufstieg der NPD*. Cologne: Kiepenheuer und Witsch, 2005.

Stiller, Michael. *Die Republikaner: Franz Schönhuber und seine Rechtsradikale Partei*. Munich: Wilhelm Heyne, 1989.

Stöss, Richard. *Die extreme Rechte in der Bundesrepublik*. Opladen: Westdeutscher Verlag, 1989. English edition: *Politics Against Democracy: Right-wing Extremism in West Germany*. New York and Oxford: Berg, 1991.

Stöss, Richard. *Die Republikaner – Woher sie kommen, was sie wollen, wer sie wählt, was zu tun ist*. Cologne: Bund, 1990.

Stöss, Richard. "Ideologie und Strategie des Rechtsextremismus," in *Rechtsextremismus in der Bundesrepublik Deutschland: Eine Bilanz*, ed. Wilfried Schubarth and Richard Stöss. Opladen: Leske & Budrich, 2001, 101–130.

Stöss, Richard. *Rechtsextremismus im vereinten Deutschland.* Bonn: Friedrich-Ebert-Stiftung, 1999.

Stöss, Richard. *Rechtsextremismus im Wandel.* 2nd edn. Bonn: Friedrich-Ebert-Stiftung, 2007.

Süss, Walter. "Analysen und Berichte: Zur Wahrnehmung und Interpretation des Rechtsextremismus in der DDR durch das MfS," Der Bundesbeauftragte für die Unterlagen des Staatssicherheitsdienstes der ehemaligen Deutschen Demokratischen Republik, Reihe B, No. 2 (1996).

Svoray, Yaron and Nick Taylor. *In Hitler's Shadow.* New York: Doubleday, 1994.

Tarrow, Sidney. *Power in Movement.* Cambridge: Cambridge University Press, 1995.

Tausch, Frank. "Hoyerswerda wird ausländerfrei," in *Un-Heil über Deutschland: Fremdenhass und Neofaschismus nach der Wiedervereinigung,* ed. Manfred Leier. Hamburg: Gruner & Jahr, 1993, 52–59.

Tetens, Tete. *The New Germany and the Old Nazis.* London: Secker & Warburg, 1961.

Timm, Angelika, *Jewish Claims against East Germany: Moral Obligations and Pragmatic Policy.* Budapest: Central European University Press, 1997.

Tolmein, Oliver. "Die Medien und die Rechten," in *Der Pakt: Die Rechten und der Staat,* ed. Bernd Siegler, Oliver Tolmein, and Charlotte Wiedemann. Göttingen: Verlag Die Werkstatt, 1993, 163–196.

Tuttle, Dale. "The Assimilation of East Germany and the Rise of Identity-Based Violence against Foreigners in the Unified German State," *German Politics and Society* 31 (Spring 1994): 63–83.

Urban, Susanne. "Anti-Semitism in Germany Today: Its Roots and Tendencies," *Jewish Political Studies Review* 16(3–4) (Fall 2004).

Veen, Hans-Joachim and Norbert Lepszy. "Republikaner und DVU in der parlamentarischen Praxis: Inkompetent, zerstritten und politikunfähig," in *Aktuelle Aspekte des Rechtsextremismus.* Bonn: BMI, 1994, 29–50.

Veen, Hans-Joachim, Norbert Lepszy, and Peter Mnich. *The Republikaner Party in Germany: Right-Wing Menace or Protest Catchall?* Westport, CT: Praeger, 1993.

Venner, Michael. *Nationale Identität: Die Neue Rechte und die Grauzone zwischen Konservatismus und Rechtsextremismus.* Cologne: Papyrossa, 1994.

Vermeil, Edmond. *L'Allemagne Contemporaine: Sociale, Politique et Culturelle, 1890–1950.* Paris: Aubier, 1952–1953.

Wachowitz, Harald. "Ein Projekt mit rechten Jugendlichen," in *Wer redet da von Entwarnung? Texte und Analysen zum aktuellen Rechtsextremismus,* authors' collective. Berlin: edition ost, 1995, 145–147.

Wagner, Bernd, ed. *Handbuch Rechtsextremismus: Netzwerke, Parteien, Organisationen, Ideologiezentren, Medien.* Reinbek: Rowohlt, 1994.

Wagner, Bernd. *Jugend-Gewalt-Szenen: Zu kriminologischen und historischen Aspekten in Ostdeutschland, Die achtziger und neunziger Jahre.* Berlin: dip, 1995.

Wahl, Klaus, Christiane Tramitz, and Jörg Blumtritt. *Fremdenfeindlichkeit: Auf den Spuren extremer Emotionen.* Opladen: Leske & Budrich, 2001.

Walendy, Udo. *Wahrheit für Deutschland – Die Schuldfrage des zweiten Weltkriegs.* Vlotho: Verlags für Volkstum und Zeitgeschichtsforschung, 1964.

Warnecke, Steven. "The Future of Rightist Extremism in West Germany," *Comparative Politics* 2(4) (July 1970): 629–652.

Watson, Alan. *Dangers from the Right?* Chicago: edition Q, 1993.

Watson, Alan. *The Germans: Who Are They Now?* 2nd rev. edn. London: edition Q, 1995.

Weber, Karl. *Rechte Männer – eine sozialpsychologische Studie zu Rassismus, Neofaschismus und Gewerkschaften.* Hamburg: VSA-Verlag, 2001.

Weinberg, Leonard. "An Overview of Right-Wing Extremism in the Western World: a Study of Convergence, Linkage, and Identity," in *Nation and Race: the Developing Euro-American Racist Subculture*, ed. Jeffrey Kaplan and Tore Bjørgo. Boston: Northeastern University Press, 1998, 3–33.

Weinberg, Leonard. "Introduction," in *Encounters with the Contemporary Radical Right*, ed. Peter H. Merkl and Weinberg. Boulder, CO: Westview Press, 1993, 1–15.

Weiss, Michael. *White Noise – Rechts-Rock, Skinhead-Musik, Blood & Honour*. Hamburg: rat Verlag, 2000.

Weiss, Ralph. "Rechtsextremismus und vierte Gewalt," *Soziale Welt*, 45(4) (1994): 480–504.

Wetzel, Juliane. "Antisemitismus als Element rechtsextremer Ideologie und Propaganda," in *Antisemitismus in Deutschland: Zur Aktualität eines Vorurteils*, ed. Wolfgang Benz. Munich: Deutscher Taschenbuch Verlag, 1995, 101–120.

Wippermann, Jost. "Die 'Junge Freiheit': Blockadebrecher der 'Neuen Rechten,'" in *Rechtsextremismus: Ideologie und Gewalt*, ed. Richard Faber, Hajo Funke, and Gerhard Schoenberner. Berlin: Gedenkstätte Haus der Wannsee Konferenz, 1995, 163–177.

Wlecklik, Petra, ed. *Frauen und Rechtsextremismus*. Göttingen: Lamuv Verlag, 1995.

Woods, Roger. *Germany's New Right as Culture and Politics*. Basingstoke: Palgrave Macmillan, 2007.

Wüllenweber, Walter. "Der Feuerschein aus Rostock," in *Un-Heil über Deutschland: Fremdenhass und Neofaschismus nach der Wiedervereinigung*, ed. Manfred Leier. Hamburg: Gruner & Jahr, 1993, 21–31.

Wyden, Peter. *The Hitler Virus: the Insidious Legacy of Adolf Hitler*. New York: Arcade Publishers, 2001.

Zeskind, Leonard. "Fa & Antifa in the Fatherland," *The Nation* (October 5, 1998): 26–29.

Zimmermann, Ekkart and Thomas Saalfeld. "The Three Waves of West German Right Wing Extremism," in *Encounters with the Contemporary Radical Right*, ed. Peter H. Merkl and Leonard Weinberg. Boulder, CO: Westview Press, 1993, 50–74.

Index

Achenbach, Ernst, 158
Action Front of National Socialists (ANS), 31
Action New Right, 139
Action Resistance, 138
Adenauer, Konrad, 23, 46
Adorno, Theodor, 6, 7, 11
Adriano, Alberto, 107
Africa Council, 109
Agenda 2010, 70, 87
Agrarian League, 19
Allied powers
  bombing raids, 49, 57
  critique of, 160
  on unification, 49, 140
Althans, Ewald, 29–30, 171
Altlandsberg (Brandenburg), 189
Amadeus Antonio Foundation, 182, 196
Amnesty International, 175
Angermünde (Brandenburg), 105
Anne Frank Center, 184–5
Anti-Defamation Forum, 182
anti-Semitism, 13–14, 110–14, 153, 161, 165
  in the DVU, 57
  in the FDP, 158
  in the GDR, 13
  in the NPD, 60, 62, 65
  in the Republikaner, 26
Apfel, Holger, 70, 71
Arendt, Hannah, 6
asylum seekers, 100, 101, 104
Augstein, Rudolf, 162
Auschwitz, 119, 120, 171
  see also Holocaust
authoritarian personality, 7
Austria, 110, 159, 203
  Freedom Party, 148, 157, 158
Autonomen (leftists), 64, 83, 88, 179
Autonomous Nationalists, 106
Azar, Edward E., 8

Backer, Susanne, 35–6
Backes, Uwe, 5

Basic Law (FRG), 104, 150, 159, 169
Bautzen, 107
Beckstein, Günther, 66, 157
Beeskow (Brandenburg), 194
Behrendt, Uwe, 33
Benoist, Alain de, 137, 148
Berdin, Norman, 88
Berg and Druffel publishers, 120
Berger, Almuth, 182
Berlin
  anti-right projects, 188, 192
  Brandenburg Gate, 171, 189
  Citizens Association, 155
  Holocaust Memorial, 63, 184
  House of Representatives, 179
  NPD in, 74
  rightist groups, 34, 83, 101, 111, 112
  rightist marches, 64–5
Berlin-Brandenburger-Zeitung der nationalen Erneuerung, 118
Bertelsmann Foundation, 125
Biedenkopf, Kurt, 160
Birkmann, Franziska, 33
Bismarck, Otto von, 22
Bitburg cemetery, 153
Blood and Honor, 91, 132
Bochum, 60
Bohleber, Werner, 10
Böhme, Herbert, 121
Bonengel, Winfried, 123, 198–9
Borchardt, Siegfried, 80
Bosbach, Wolfgang, 185
Botsch, Gideon, 73
Brähler, Elmar, 205
Brandenburg, 34, 70, 176, 181, 192, 196
Brandt, Willy, 30, 160
Bremen Land/city election 1987, 28
Brock, Robert, 57
Brumlik, Micha, 161
Bubis, Ignatz, 61, 111–12, 119, 123, 152, 153
  and Walser, 161–2
Bulbar, Werner, 212
Bundesrat, 68

Bundestag, deputies, 126
  1949 election, 23
Bundesverfassungsschutz, see Federal
  Office for the Protection of the
  Constitution
Bund Freiheit der Wissenschaft, 149
Busse, Friedhelm, 29, 80
Bütiker, Reinhard, 165
Butz, Arthur R., 28

Canada, neo-Nazi propaganda, 34, 120,
  124
Carl Friedrich von Siemens Foundation,
  142
Center for Democratic Culture, 196–7
Central Council of Jews in Germany, 26,
  72, 111, 125, 155–6, 183
  see also Ignatz Bubis; Heinz Galinski;
  Charlotte Knobloch; Paul Spiegel
Christian Conservative Germany Forum,
  155
Christian Democratic Union/Christian
  Social Union, as party, 21–2, 23
  links to New Right, 167–8
  on immigration, 12
Christian Social Union (CSU), 157
Christiansen, Lars, 103–4
Christopherson, Thies, 31
churches, 178, 185
  Catholic, 21, 181, 187
  Protestant, 21, 187
Citizens Movement pro-Cologne, 116,
  214 n.1
civil rights organizations, 178
Civitas program, 183
Clemens, Björn, 45
Cohn-Bendit, Daniel, 50, 109, 155
Cologne, 116, 188–9
concentration camps, 113, 157
  see also Holocaust
Conservatives, party, 19–20
Cottbus, 83, 176
Council of Europe, 128, 179
courts, Land, 61, 104, 107, 134,
  and public prosecutors, 172
  see also Federal Constitutional Court;
  judges
Criticón, 146–7, 148
cultural organizations, rightist, 121–2

Däubler-Gmelin, Herta, 129–30
David, Hellmut, 143
Decker, Oliver, 205
Deckert, Günter, 61, 163–2
Dehoust, Peter, 119–22
Deligöz, Ekin, 109
Deutsche Hochschullehrer-Zeitung, 119
Deutsche Kulturwerk Europäischen Geistes,
  121
Deutsche Monatshefte, 119, 143
Deutsche Soldaten-Zeitung, 117–18
Deutschland in Geschichte und Gegenwart,
  119
Deutschlandrat, 143
Deutschland Stiftung, 151
Die Welt, 144, 146
Diesner, Kay, 105
Diewerge, Wolfgang, 158
Doege, Gunnar, 107
Dorls, Fritz, 23
Dregger, Alfred, 152, 154
Dresden (Saxony), 60-1, 70, 71, 88, 101,
  115, 173
Dresden School, 122
Dudek, Peter, 6
Duke, David, 57
DVU, *see* German People's Union

East Germany, *see* German Democratic
  Republic
eastern Germany (post-unification),
  96–8
Ebata, Michi, 10
Economic Reconstruction Association
  (WAV), 23
Edathy, Sebastian, 185, 208
Egoldt, Herbert, 132
Ehrhardt, Arthur, 118–19
Eichberg, Henning, 138
Einblick, 118
electronic games, 128–30
  network, 122–8
Elite Guards (SS), 29
Entimon program, 183
Erfurt, 110, 111, 112
ethnopluralism, 141
Europa vorn, 146, 148
European Commission against Racism
  and Intolerance, 203
European Liberty Party, 210

European Monitoring Center against Racism and Xenophobia, 176
European Social Fund, 183
European Parliament
  elections (1989), 26, 28
  rightist parties in, 26, 210
European Union, 47, 56, 78, 140, 160, 190, 203, 209, 210
Evola, Julius, 138
exit strategy, 196–9

fanzines, 135–6
Faschos (GDR), 37, 38, 41
fascism, 5
Faust, Mathias, 57
Faye, Guillaume, 122
Federal Agency for Civic Education, 183, 185
Federal and Länder Ministries of the Interior, 30, 31, 32, 48, 67, 69, 80, 81, 83, 85, 91, 114, 117, 148, 170, 175, 176, 179, 181
Federal and Länder Offices for the Protection of the Constitution (*Bundesamt für Verfassungsschutz*), 5, 26, 28, 30, 32, 45, 48, 49, 67, 69, 104, 110, 125, 174, 177, 178, 192
Federal Border Guard (*Grenzschutz*), 101, 102, 174, 175, 176, 177
  renamed Federal Police, 173
Federal cabinet, on hate and violence, 180, 181
Federal Constitutional Court, 5, 24, 64, 66, 68, 69, 80, 87, 145, 169
Federal Criminal Office, 125, 173, 174, 198
  and criminal code, 176
Federal Inspection Office for Media, 132–3
Federal Ministry of Youth, Family, and Health, 121, 184
Federal prosecutor, 108, 176, 179
Federation of German Industry, 187
Filbinger, Hans Karl, 154
Ford, Henry, 155
foreign investments, 109, 114, 115
foreign right-wing parties, 209–10
foreigners
  attitude toward, 62, 97, 101, 178
  councils, 181

integration of, 181
number of, 11
  see also immigration
Foxman, Abraham, 132
France, *nouvelle droite*, 137–8
Frank, Anne, 113
Frankfurt/Main, 50
Frankfurter Allgemeine Zeitung
  and Martin Walser, 161–2
  political advertisements, 152–3
Franz Schönhuber Foundation, 145
Frattini, Franco, 190
Free Corps, 19
Free Democratic Party (FDP), 67, 157–9, 167–8
  German program, 158
Free German Workers' Party (FAP), 25, 30, 37, 79–81, 85, 103
Free Initiative Germany, 46
Freedom Party, *see* Austria
Freiberg, Konrad, 177
Freie Kameradschaften (Free Comradeship), 37, 67, 74, 80, 81, 86–9, 114, 205
French National Front, 27, 57
Frey, Gerhard
  as party leader, 27, 44, 48, 51–2, 161
  as publisher, 27, 117, 118
Friedensdorf (Brandenburg), 188
Friedman, Michel, 158
Friedrich-Ebert-Foundation, 205
Fritz Bauer Institute, 161
Fromm, Erich, 7
Fromm, Heinz, 68

gender issues, 14–15, 57
Gera (Thuringia), 108
German Alliance-United Right, 46
German Alternative, 37, 82–3, 91–2
German Conservatives party, 118
German Democratic Republic (GDR), 34–41
  foreigners in, 38
  social system, 79, 97
  Stasis, 39–40
German Empire era, 19
German Institute for Human Rights, 203
German League, 19
German League for Peace and Home, 149

German League for People and
Homeland, 44
German National Party, 115
German National People's Party (DNVP),
20, 202–3
German National Resistance, 92
German People's Union (DVU)
and elections, 52–8
legislators, 52
members and organization, 51
and New Right, 167–8
and NPD, 52
German People's Union-List D
(DVU-List D), 27–8
German Reich Party, 24
Germany
Basic Law, 5, 24
constitutional order, 24
in international affairs, 145
Leitkultur, 165–6
lost territories, 50, 62, 83, 84, 144
national pride in, 163–5
unification, 144, 164
Gerstenmaier, Eugen, 160
Gesicht Zeigen, 183, 185
Gestapo, 20, 29
globalization, 139, 211
Glotz, Peter, 122
Goethe Institutes, 115
Goldhagen, Daniel J., 165
Goppel, Thomas, 157, 164
Gorbitz (Saxony), 88
Grabert, Herbert, 119
Grabert, Wigbert, 119
Grabert publishing house, 120, 150
Graf, Steffi, 179
Gramsci, Antonio, 150
Great Depression, 20, 157, 202, 207
GRECE, 138, 150, 151
Greens, 67–8, 177
Gröber, Klaus, 157
Guben (Brandenburg), 106, 176
Gujjula, Ravindra, 189
Günzel, Reinhard, 155
Gurr, Ted, 8
Gypsies (Sinti, Roma), 10, 49, 56, 98,
102, 110, 181

Habermas, Jürgen, 151
Haider, Jörg, 45, 157, 158, 209

Hallan, Daniel, 190
Hamburg, 106, 175
Hamm-Brücher, Hildegard, 158
Hartz IV program, 70
Hasselbach, Ingo, 39–40, 83, 102, 123,
198–9
Hassemer, Winfried, 69
Havelland (Brandenburg), 107
Heer, Hannes, 63
Heidelberg Manifesto, 149
Heil, Hubertus, 73
Heinemann, Gustav, 30–1
Heitmeyer, Wilhelm, 6, 7, 11
Herder publishers, 142, 144
Herman, Eva, 124
Herzog, Roman, 111
Hess, Rudolf, 30, 62, 87, 122, 211
Heuvel, Eric, 194
Heye, Uwe-Karsten, 109, 185, 191
Hindenburg, Paul von, 20, 138
Historikerstreit, 151–2
Hitler, Adolf, 16, 20, 21, 22, 29, 30, 36,
67, 68, 72, 74, 79, 104, 113, 120,
121, 133, 137, 138, 143, 145, 151,
206–7
Hizbut, Tahrir, 115–16
Hockenos, Paul, 141
Hoffmann, Karl-Heinz, 32, 33
Hohenberg publishing house, 120–1
Hohenrain publishing house, 120
Hohmann, Martin, 155–6
Holocaust, 21, 26, 28, 30, 57, 72, 80,
82, 84, 110, 111, 112, 120, 121,
126, 148
denial, 171–2
German responsibility for, 151,
163
monument, 63, 161
survivors, 178
teaching about, 190–1
Homeland Loyal German Youth, 85
homeless persons, 107, 115
hostels, 101
Hoyerswerda (Saxony), 101, 178
Hübner, Frank, 83, 91–2

Im Brennpunkt, 142
immigration
influx, 26
laws on, 12, 16

immigration – *continued*
  opposition to, 130, 149–50, 168, 180, 204
  restrictions on, 178
Independent Social Democratic Party (USPD), 19
Irving, David, 28, 30, 57, 120
Islamista, 115–16
Israel, 35, 57, 72, 111, 112, 113, 114, 124, 169

Jaschke, Hans-Gerd, 6, 17, 141
Jesse, Eckhard, 5
Jews, 63, 80, 84, 87, 89, 114, 126
Jones, Bonsu, 100
journals, rightist, 117–18
judges, 114
  see also courts
Jung, Edgar Julius, 138
Junge Freiheit, 143, 145, 147–8, 165, 167
Jünger, Ernst, 138, 142, 144

Kahane, Anetta, 182
Kaltenbrunner, Gerd-Klaus, 142, 144
Kamara, Moctar, 109
Kameradschaften, see *Freie Kameradschaften*
Kanther, Manfred, 84
Kennedy, Duncan, 105
Kitschelt, Herbert, 8
Klingemann, Hans-Dieter, 8, 10
Klüter-Blättern, 121
Knobloch, Charlotte, 113, 166–7, 184, 207–8
Koch, Roland, 67, 156
Kohl, Helmut, 104, 105, 153, 154, 160, 163, 164, 178, 179, 201
Köhler, Gundorf, 32
Köhler, Horst, 72, 166, 184
Konrad Adenauer Prize, 143, 144, 151
Konservative Deutsche Zeitung, 118
Korback (Hesse), 189
Kramer, Jane, 172
Krebs, Pierre, 150–1
Kühnen, Michael, 29, 31, 82, 83, 85
Künast, Renate, 193
Kunze, Klaus, 145
Kupfer, Lothar, 102
Küssel, Gottfried, 85

Lafontaine, Oskar, 163–4
Land Youth League, 182
Lange, Amsgar, 147
Lauck, Gary Rex, 81, 171
League for Democracy and Tolerance, 183
League of Expellees and Dispossessed (BHE), 23
League of Free Citizens, 147
League of German Patriots, 66
League for a German People and Homeland, 46
leftists, 105, 106
Left Party, 177, 203
Left Party. PDS, 66, 72, 73, 74
Leggewie, Claus, 6
Lehmann, Karl, 187
Leitkultur (guiding culture), 165–6, 205
Le Pen, Jean-Marie, 27, 57, 138, 171
Leuchter, Fred, 61
Lewin, Schlomo, 33
Lipset, Seymour M., 5
Loritz, Alfred, 23
Lower Saxony, 23
Lübeck synagogue, 49, 112
Lummer, Heinrich, 155

Magdeburg, 109
Mahler, Horst, 68–9, 126, 139
Maintal (Hesse), 187–8
Mannichi, Alois, 110
Maron, Monika, 162
Marx, Peter, 71
Maschke, Günter, 160
Mecklenburg-West Pomerania, 66, 72–5, 106, 177
media, visual
  films, 122–4
  internet, 124–8
  television, 122
  videos, 121
Meier, Heinrich, 142
Melsungen (Hesse), 189
Merkel, Angela, 72, 110, 165, 166, 185
Mesovic, Bernd, 100
Meyer, Laurenz, 165
Michels, Robert, 145
Mietbauer, Frank, 107
Milbradt, Georg, 70, 72
Military Sport Group Hoffmann, 32

Milmersdorf (Brandenburg), 195
Ministry of the Interior, *see* Federal
    Ministry of the Interior
Ministry of State Security (Stasi, GDR),
    36
Minkenberg, Michael, 10
Moebus, Hendrik, 133
Moeller van den Bruck, Arthur, 138
Mohler, Armin, 142–3, 159
Möllemann, Jürgen, 158–9
Möller, Horst, 151
Mölln (Schleswig-Holstein), 103–4, 179
Mosley, Oswald, 118
Mozambique, 101, 107
Muegeln (Saxony), 109–10
multiculturalism, 30, 58, 68, 139, 141
Mulugeta, Ermyas, 108
Munich, 89
Müntefering, Franz, 157
music, mainstream, 179
    rightist, 130–5
Muslim Federation in Germany, 114
Mussgnug, Martin, 61

Nahrath, Wolfram, 84
Nation & Europa, 118–19, 122
National Activists, 31
National Alternative, 37, 83–4
National Bolsheviks, 139
National Democratic Party of Germany
    (NPD)
    ban on, 66–70
    and courts, 59, 62, 66
    creation of, 24
    and *Kameradschaften*, 58, 87
    and Länder elections, 24
    leaders, 61–2
    members, 25, 57–8
    and New Right, 167–8
    programs, 60
    three-column strategy, 62–6
    Women's Division, 57–8
    Young National Democrats, 29, 32, 58,
        61, 84, 128, 135
National Info-Telefone, 124
National Liberals, 19, 20
national liberated zones, 89–91, 109, 205
National List, 79–81
National Movement, 85
National Offensive, 85

national pride, 143, 163–5
national revolutionary movement, 138,
    139
National Socialism, 6, 9, 16, 20–1, 22,
    29, 146
National Socialist German Workers'
    Party (NSDAP), 20, 23, 29, 62, 67,
    116, 143, 157
    Overseas Organization, 81, 171
National-Zeitung/Deutsche Zeitung, 51
nationalism, 9, 141, 157, 164, 166
Nationalist Front, 37, 81, 121
NATO, 50, 60
Naumann, Werner, 158–9
Nehm, Kay, 108
neo-Nazis, groups, 28, 78–9, 102, 106,
    108
    paraphernalia, 119, 120
Neubauer, Harald, 44, 119
Neue Nachricht, 147
New Right, 137–68, 204, 207
Nietzsche, Friedrich, 138
No Exit (film), 123
Nolte, Ernst, 147, 151, 156
Noui, Omar Ben, 106

Oberhof (Thuringia), 105
Oettinger, Günther, 154
Old Right, 16, 137, 138, 139, 207
    see also New Right

Paeschke, Frieda, 33
Palestinians, 113, 114, 210
Pan-German League, 19
Pape, Martin, 25, 29, 79–80
Party of Democratic Socialism (PDS), 47,
    54, 70, 96
    see also Left Party; Left Party. PDS
Party of Work/German Socialists, 29
Passau (Bavaria), 51, 59, 110
Pastoers, Udo, 74
Patriotic Community of the New Front,
    31
patriotism, 164, 166, 205
Pau, Petra, 208
Peck, Jeffrey, 156
Peters, Michael, 103–4
Pfahl-Traughber, Armin, 117
Phoenix, 146
Pipkins, Robert, 105

Poland, 57, 60
police, 63–4, 84, 94, 99, 101–5, 108, 109, 114, 128, 131–2, 133, 134, 172, 173–7
Politische Hintergrundinformationen, 126
polls, *see* public opinion surveys
populism, *see* rightist populism
Potsdam (Brandenburg), 108, 112
Pöttering, Hans-Gert, 185
pride, *see* national pride
Primor, Avraham, 160
Prinzhorn, Thomas, 157
Profession: Neo-Nazi (film), 123
public opinion surveys, 11, 205
  on anti-Semitism, 13, 14
  on foreigners, 97, 100
  on GDR skinheads, 36–7
  on gender issues, 15, 95
  on German pride, 164–5
  on Hitler era, 161
  on Nazism, 16, 22, 35, 124
  on system support, 212–13
  reflecting rightist views, 16–17, 203

Räbiger, Sebastian, 85
racism, 8–9, 60, 62, 82, 115, 181
  organizations against, 182, 185, 190
Raiser, Konrad, 187
Rammstein, 134
Rau, Johannes, 164, 189
Reagan, Ronald, 153
recession, economic, 17, 203, 207, 208
Reemsta, Jan Philipp, 63
Regener, Michael, 134
Reich-Ranicki, Marcel, 162
Reichswehr, 19, 63
Republikaner, and DVU, 48
  in elections, 46–8
  founding of, 25–6
  Fraktionen, 46
  leaders, 44–5
  members, 45–6
  and New Right, 167–8
  organization, 26, 43–6
  programs, 26, 49–51
  voters, 27, 175
Richter, Christian, 107
Richter, Karl, 119, 122
Rieger, Jürgen, 81, 84
rightist populism, 5, 116, 203, 209

Ring Freiheitlicher Studenten, 145
Ringstorff, Harald, 73
Ritter, Gerhard, 22
Rockford Institute, 209
Rock-O-Rama, 132
Roeder, Manfred, 31, 59
Röhl, Klaus Rainer, 158
Röhm, Ernst, 29, 32
Romer, Otto Ernst, 119
Rose, Romani, 110
Rosellini, Jay Julian, 152
Rosenberger, Martina, 45
Rostock (Mecklenburg-West Pomerania) 64, 88, 101–3, 174, 179
Roth, Christian, 212
Roth, Claudia, 94
Rouhs, Manfred, 148–9
Rudolf, Germar, 171
Russian Liberal-Democratic Party, 57

SA, *see* Storm Troopers
Saarbrücken, 63
Sache des Volkes, 139
Sachsenhausen concentration camp, 112
Sander, Hans-Dietrich, 143
Saxony-Anhalt, 109, 177, 202
  Land initiative against rightists, 122
Schacht, Ulrich, 144, 145, 152
Schäuble, Wolfgang, 154, 156, 164
Scherer, Ellen-Doris, 61
Scheuch, Erwin, 8, 10
Schily, Otto, 67, 69, 112, 171, 182, 187, 196
Schindler's List (film), 122
Schirrmacher, Frank, 161, 162
Schlierer, Rolf, 44–5, 48, 50, 165
Schmalz-Jacobsen, Cornelia, 178
Schmitt, Carl, 45, 138, 143, 145, 167
Schnittcher, Gerd, 93
Schönbohm, Jörg, 94, 165
Schönborn, Meinolf, 81, 82
Schönhuber, Franz
  in European Parliament, 26–7, 47
  founder of Republikaner, 25–6
  party chairman, 44–5, 49, 154, 161
schools, and right extremism, 191–4
Schrenck-Notzing, Caspar von, 146
Schröder, Gerhard, 67, 71, 112, 165, 189
Schubert, Franck, 31
Schumacher, Kurt, 46

Schutzstaffel (SS), 29, 89, 93, 111
Schwammberger, Josef, 85
Schwerin, 73, 87, 112
Schwilk, Heimo, 144–5, 152
Seite, Berndt, 102–3
Seiters, Rudolf, 82, 174, 179
Siegerist, Joachim, 118
Siemens Foundation, 143
skinheads, and neo-Nazis, 34
   Blood and Honor, 91, 132
   in Europe, 34
   gangs, 33–4
   in GDR, 36–41
   Hammer Skins, 34, 91
   music, 130–5
   since unification, 91–6
   violence, 101–2, 114
   women, 94–6
Skinhead Saxonian Switzerland, 92
Social Democratic Party (SPD), 12, 47, 74
social workers, 194–6
Socialist Reich Party (SRP), 23–4
Socialist Unity Party of Germany
   (SED), 35
Society for Biological Anthropology,
   Eugenics, and Behavioral Research,
   84
Sohn, Gunnar, 147
Solingen (North Rhine-Westphalia), 104
Sonntag, Rainer, 92
Sontheimer, Michael, 123
Sorel, Georges, 138
Soviet Union, 151, 178
Spengler, Oswald, 138, 142
Spiegel, Paul, 89, 112, 113, 165
Spiegelman, Art, 122
SS, *see* Schutzstaffel
Staatsbriefe, 143
Stahl, Alexander von, 158, 179
Stahlhelm *Fraktion* (CDU/CSU), 154
Stahlhelm-Kampfbund für Europa, 115
Staud, Toralf, 74
Stawitz, Ingo, 52
Stein, Dieter, 147–8, 165
Stein, Shimon, 113
Steiner, Felix, 93
Stoiber, Edmund, 70, 89, 157
Stoph, Willi, 30
Storm Troopers (SA), 20, 29, 34, 73,
   78, 82

Stöss, Richard, 6, 16
Strasser, Gregor, 29, 78, 82
Strasser, Otto, 29, 78, 82
Strauss, Botho, 146
Strauss, Frans-Josef, 25, 142, 157
Struck, Peter, 73
Study Center Weikersheim, 154
Stuttgart Declaration, 74
Sudholt, Gert, 120, 121
Süss, Walter, 41
Süssmuth, Rita, 152, 154
Swierczek, Michael, 85
Syberberg, Hans Jürgen, 146

Tenner, Franziska, 123
Thadden, Adolf von, 23, 24, 119
Thielen, Friedrich, 24
Thierse, Wolfgang, 177, 194
Third Reich, 20, 21
Thor Steiner Company, 93
Thule Network, 90, 126–7
Thule Seminar, 150–1
Thuringia, 66, 176, 192
tourism, effect on, 73, 109, 114, 115
trade unions, 50, 57, 177, 178, 181, 185,
   186–7
Trittin, Jürgen, 165
Turks, 103–4, 107, 175

unemployment, 177, 183, 211
United Nations, 56, 170, 203
United States, 21, 34, 60, 87, 124, 125,
   126, 128, 139, 141, 161, 210
Usedom (Mecklenburg-West
   Pomerania), 73

Venner, Michael, 140
Verbeke, Herbert, 209
Verfassungsschutz, *see* Federal and Länder
   Offices for the Protection of the
   Constitution
Vergangenheitsbewältigung (coming to
   terms with the past), 159–60
Vietnamese, violence against, 101, 102,
   107
Viking Youth, 32, 84, 85
violence, neo-Nazi and skinhead, 31, 32,
   99, 110, 204, 205
   counter-measures, 178
Voigt, Udo, 61–2, 65, 69, 74, 122

Volksgemeinschaft, 141
Voss, Rainer, 172

Wagner, Bernd, 97–8, 103–4, 173, 196
Wagner, Herbert, 88
Waigel, Theo, 157
Waldheim, Kurt, 153
Walser, Martin, 33, 160–3, 212
Wegesin, Heiner, 86
Wehrmacht, 163
  exhibition, 63
Weimar Republic, 138, 139, 201–2,
  206–7
Weinberg, Leonard, 4
Weissmann, Karlheinz, 146, 152
Weizsäcker, Richard von, 154, 160, 163,
  175, 178, 205, 213
Welt am Sonntag, 144
Westerwelle, Guido, 67, 164
West Germany (Federal Republic of
  Germany), 21–34
Weyrich, Paul, 209
Wiese, Martin, 88–9

Winkler, Heinrich August, 151–2
Wolffsohn, Michael, 157, 162
women's rightist groups, 96
Worch, Christian, 79, 81, 87, 94
Working Circle of Conservative
  Christians, 156
World Cup soccer games (2006), 108,
  109, 165, 166
World War Two, responsibility for, 159
Wulff, Christian, 73
Wulff, Thomas, 87
Wurzen (Saxony), 90

xenophobia, 9–13, 38, 60, 97, 98, 103–4,
  115, 156, 179
Xenos program, 183

Zachert, Hans-Ludwig, 174
Zhirinovski, Vladimir, 57
Zion Church rock concert (GDR), 39
Zitelmann, Rainer, 145, 152, 158
Zündel, Ernst, 120, 124, 209
Zypries, Brigitte, 190

LN
460
.R3
B733
2009